D0078625

NUCLEAR WEAPONS AND NONPROLIFERATION

Selected Titles in ABC-CLIO's
CONTEMPORARY
WORLD ISSUES
Series

For a complete list of titles in this series, please visit
www.abc-clio.com.

Books in the Contemporary World Issues series address vital issues in today's society such as genetic engineering, pollution, and biodiversity. Written by professional writers, scholars, and nonacademic experts, these books are authoritative, clearly written, up-to-date, and objective. They provide a good starting point for research by high school and college students, scholars, and general readers as well as by legislators, businesspeople, activists, and others.

Each book, carefully organized and easy to use, contains an overview of the subject, a detailed chronology, biographical sketches, facts and data and / or documents and other primary-source material, a directory of organizations and agencies, annotated lists of print and nonprint resources, and an index.

Readers of books in the Contemporary World Issues series will find the information they need in order to have a better understanding of the social, political, environmental, and economic issues facing the world today.

NUCLEAR WEAPONS AND NONPROLIFERATION

A Reference Handbook

Second Edition

Sarah J. Diehl

James Clay Moltz

**CONTEMPORARY
WORLD ISSUES**

A B C C L I O

Santa Barbara, California
Denver, Colorado
Oxford, England

Library of Congress Cataloging-in-Publication Data

Diehl, Sarah J.
   Nuclear weapons and nonproliferation : a reference handbook / Sarah J. Diehl and James Clay Moltz. — 2nd ed.
       p. cm. — (Contemporary world issues)
   Includes bibliographical references and index.
   ISBN-13: 978-1-59884-071-1 (hard copy : alk. paper)
   ISBN-13: 978-1-59884-072-8 (ebook)
1. Nuclear weapons. 2. Nuclear nonproliferation. I. Moltz, James Clay. II. Title.

U264.D53 2008
355.8'25119--dc21

                                                                    2007017651

13 12 11 10 09 08   1 2 3 4 5 6 7 8 9 10

ABC-CLIO, Inc.
130 Cremona Drive, P.O. Box 1911
Santa Barbara, California 93116-1911

This book is also available on the World Wide Web as an ebook. Visit http://www.abc-clio.com for details.

This book is printed on acid-free paper ∞
Manufactured in the United States of America

Contents

Preface

As of 2007, nine countries possess approximately 27,000 nuclear weapons. The United States, Russia, China, the United Kingdom, France, India, Pakistan, Israel, and North Korea are known to have nuclear arsenals; a tenth country, South Africa, built and then dismantled six atomic bombs in the early 1990s. Other states, such as Iran, are suspected of pursuing clandestine weapon programs. However, approximately thirty nations with the technological capability to build nuclear weapons have not done so for various practical and political reasons, although their calculations may change if the international security environment shifts and more states test such weapons. Finally, nonstate groups, such as al Qaeda and Aum Shinrikyo have tried to acquire nuclear or radiological weapons. While states seek nuclear weapons for military deterrence and as status symbols, terrorists pursue them as the ultimate means of causing destruction, fear, and panic.

Although nuclear weapons have not been used in war since 1945, the large nuclear arsenals still held, particularly by the United States and Russia, continue to influence not only international relations but also human culture and psychology. The frightening power of nuclear weapons holds out the lure of ultimate security and status to national leaders, but the presence of nuclear weapons brings with it the risk of possible nuclear accidents, terrorism, war, and annihilation. This duality of nuclear weapons encompasses the deterrent role supporters believe they play, as well as the global threat they represent to those who seek their elimination. This book covers the development of nuclear weapons and the various efforts aimed at controlling and eliminating them.

Chapter 1 provides a history of the development and spread of nuclear weapons, ranging from the U.S. Manhattan Project to

North Korea's 2006 nuclear test and the ongoing International Atomic Energy Agency investigation of Iran's nuclear program. It describes the still-covert Israeli nuclear program, as well as the programs of countries (including Iran, North Korea, and Libya) supplied by the illicit network in nuclear technology masterminded by Pakistan's A. Q. Khan. The chapter also covers efforts to control nuclear weapons and the dissemination of nuclear-related technology. It highlights the dualistic nature of nuclear developments historically: Nuclear weapon states sought to aggrandize their power even while negotiating international initiatives to control nuclear technologies and preserve peace.

Chapter 2 discusses problems and controversies in the nuclear weapon and nonproliferation fields, raising a series of policy questions and providing viewpoints from a variety of perspectives. The desirability of eliminating nuclear weapons, for example, may depend on one's views of the value of nuclear weapons for deterrence or, alternatively, one's concern about the global environmental costs of nuclear weapon production or the chances of inadvertent nuclear war. Other issues addressed in the chapter include the desirable size of future nuclear arsenals (if they are going to exist), the threat of terrorist acquisition of nuclear weapons, and the issues surrounding a proposed ban on all nuclear tests. It also examines the effectiveness of the nuclear nonproliferation regime, the utility of sanctions, and the reasons why states don't always play by the rules.

Chapter 3 delves into policy issues concerning the U.S. nuclear complex, future U.S. nuclear weapon development, and Washington's evolving stance on international nonproliferation agreements. In December 2001, the United States concluded a Nuclear Posture Review that set the guidelines for the development and possible use of its nuclear arsenal. This chapter looks at the debates raised by that review and by recent U.S. programs and initiatives. In addition, it analyzes changes in U.S. policies toward nonproliferation treaties and questions of international verification under the Bush administration, including its emphasis on more flexible, voluntary approaches to combat nuclear proliferation.

Chapter 4 provides a chronological summary of the key events in the building of nuclear weapons, as well as in national and international efforts to halt their spread. It charts the competing nuclear weapon programs in several countries during World War II, the success of U.S. efforts, the role of espionage in the Soviet nuclear program in the 1940s, and the subsequent development of bomb programs in Britain, France, China, Israel, South Africa, India, Pakistan, and North Korea, some of them with knowing or unwitting foreign partners. The chronology includes the key nuclear tests, nuclear accidents, significant nonproliferation negotiations, treaty signings, and notable protest events.

Chapter 5 offers short biographies of the key players in worldwide nuclear proliferation and disarmament efforts. Interestingly, some of the very scientists who designed the weapons, once having seen their terrible force, became leaders of organizations advocating their abolition. Others remained strong supporters of a nuclear buildup and even urged the development of new, more powerful bombs and advanced missile defenses. Some, like the Soviet spy Klaus Fuchs and the Pakistani nuclear technology salesman A. Q. Khan, significantly spurred proliferation.

Chapter 6 includes facts and data on nuclear weapon technology, the growth of nuclear arsenals, and the international treaties aimed at halting further nuclear development and testing. It explains the differences between simple fission weapons and more powerful thermonuclear bombs, as well as the different materials (highly enriched uranium, plutonium, and tritium) used to produce them. The chapter also contains the texts of primary documents, such as a U.S. report on the damage from the first atomic bombs dropped on Hiroshima and Nagasaki, the Treaty on the Non-Proliferation of Nuclear Weapons, and recent United Nations resolutions.

Chapter 7 provides a selective list of national, regional, and international organizations and agencies that work on issues related to the spread of weapons of mass destruction, especially nuclear weapons. Some of these organizations oversee the implementation of particular treaties or other arrangements designed to control the spread of nuclear technology, prevent nuclear accidents, or limit nuclear testing. Others are nongovernmental organizations that provide information to the public about nuclear developments. The summaries describe the organizations' missions and provide contact information.

Chapter 8 offers a carefully selected list of print and nonprint resources for pursuing nuclear weapons and nonproliferation issues in greater depth. The information ranges from video documentaries on the U.S. Manhattan Project to histories of nuclear weapons efforts in various countries to Web sites with debates on current nonproliferation controversies. Chapter 8 also provides a guide for educators and others who are interested in finding published materials and multimedia products suitable for classroom and research purposes.

1

Background and History

The number of nuclear weapons in the world and the ability of national leaders to prevent their use have been critical measures of global security since 1945. Fortunately, the "enthusiasm" of states for acquiring nuclear weapons has risen and fallen over time. Early on, it appeared that any country that could acquire nuclear weapons would do so. But such varied influences as economic trade-offs, security guarantees from nuclear weapon states, and political factors caused many nuclear-capable states to give up nuclear weapon programs and others to not start them in the first place. Six of the nine states that currently possess nuclear weapons had already either acquired them or had gone a long way toward that goal by the time of the signing of the Non-Proliferation Treaty (NPT) in 1968. Since then, only four countries have deployed nuclear weapons and one, South Africa, dismantled its arsenal unilaterally by 1991.

But challenges to the NPT have increased in the era of globalization. Controlling information has become more difficult since the advent of fax machines, electronic mail, and the Internet. Similarly, the rise of non-state actors with an interest in acquiring nuclear know-how, materials, and weapons poses a threat not addressed by the state-targeted restrictions within the NPT. For example, the NPT regime only belatedly discovered A. Q. Khan's nuclear black market, which was centered in Pakistan but reached out to multiple production sites and trans-shipment points. At the same time, attitudes among the founders of the NPT regarding the acceptability of nuclear proliferation by democracies outside the regime or by important trading partners make it even more difficult to enforce NPT restrictions. In these respects, the NPT regime—which weathered the Cold War relatively successfully—now faces an unprecedented crisis of credibility in dealing with states like Iran, India, Pakistan, Israel, and North Korea and may be at risk of collapse.

Despite these problems, however, strong support still exists globally for new arms control treaties to reduce and reverse nuclear proliferation, if leadership can be found within the weapon states. Information received from studies completed after the U.S. invasion of Iraq in 2003 shows that safeguards and inspections can be effective, despite U.S. beliefs to the contrary in the run-up to the Iraq war. Moreover, new nonproliferation mechanisms—including the U.S.-led Proliferation Security Initiative and United Nations (UN) Security Council Resolution 1540—have been added to the nonproliferation toolbox since 2003 to help plug past loopholes in NPT and International Atomic Energy Agency (IAEA) controls for non-state actors. Finally, twenty-first-century technologies for verification and enforcement make cheating increasingly difficult, particularly as nongovernmental organizations now routinely obtain access to satellite data and other critical intelligence, via purchases from either commercial providers or member governments. Thus, there are grounds for believing strengthened international nonproliferation efforts—despite the new challenges of globalization—may be increasingly effective.

This chapter discusses the history of nuclear weapons and efforts to control proliferation. It highlights the tension inherent in the fact that efforts to both build and control nuclear weapons were initiated by the two superpowers during the Cold War. Since 2001, nuclear arsenals globally have declined substantially. But the increased fear of terrorism since the September 11 attacks has created new priorities in the United States and elsewhere that sometimes conflict with nonproliferation goals. Thus, as during the Cold War—when nuclear construction went hand in hand with efforts to halt proliferation—nonproliferation efforts in the twenty-first century are affected by other national objectives as states pursue new definitions of security.

Early Scientific Developments

The scientific concepts behind nuclear fission—the notion that atoms of certain elements can be split and thereby emit energy—

began to be developed in the first decade of the twentieth century from the work of British physicist Ernest Rutherford and others. Although Rutherford personally was skeptical that such energy could ever be controlled, some scientists were excited by the possibility that a limitless supply of nuclear energy might eventually be harnessed for peaceful purposes, including naval propulsion and the generation of electric power. At the same time, however, scientists recognized that nuclear power would possess a darker side: the potential to unleash unprecedented explosive power for military purposes. In 1903, British physicist Frederick Soddy discussed the potential of releasing vast amounts of energy drawing on forces within atoms. In a 1914 novel inspired by Soddy's work, entitled *The World Set Free*, science-fiction writer H. G. Wells described a future in which the civilized world benefits from an abundant supply of nuclear energy yet is laid to waste in a war in which nuclear weapons are used extensively. But the practical challenges of moving from the potential of nuclear energy to the realities of its production and use proved significant. Several obstacles faced scientists: identifying the right materials and chemical elements, developing technologies, allowing experimentation, and constructing equipment capable of harnessing the power of the reactions. None of these steps was trivial.

One central prerequisite to the practical development of nuclear fission—either for weapons or civilian uses—was the creation of a device capable of splitting the atom. Experimental physicists like Ernest Lawrence of the United States developed these concepts, leading to the construction of the first cyclotron at the University of California–Berkeley in the early 1930s. The cyclotron sent streams of protons (positively charged particles) crashing at high speeds into the nuclei of uranium atoms, with the aim of splitting off neutrons and thereby changing the physical properties of the original material. Hungarian Leo Szilard outlined the principle of a "chain reaction" in 1934, one of the essential processes required for a nuclear explosion. Building on this information, other scientists in Europe and the United States expanded knowledge about subatomic processes in a stream of scientific papers published during the 1930s, gradually filling in pieces of the puzzle. In Sweden in late December 1938, Austrian physicists Lise Meitner and her nephew Otto Frisch—both Jews who had been forced to leave laboratories in Nazi Germany—became the first to explain the mechanics of nuclear fission, drawing on experiments conducted by their colleague Otto Hahn back in Berlin. By this time, however, many nuclear physicists had begun to express fears about the implications of this work, given the rise of dictatorships in Nazi Germany, fascist Italy, and imperial Japan and the likelihood of war.

Military Uses of Nuclear Fission

In the late 1930s and during the first part of World War II, efforts to analyze the feasibility of nuclear weapons for military purposes took place in several countries, including the United Kingdom, Germany, Japan, France, the Soviet Union, and the United States. Several challenges remained. Scientists needed to manufacture an adequate quantity (critical mass) of fissionable material (either plutonium or highly enriched uranium) to create a self-sustaining chain reaction. This necessitated either irradiating uranium in a reactor and separating the small amounts of plutonium created (reprocessing) or culling rare uranium 235 isotopes from large amounts of natural uranium in a centrifuge or through other procedures (enrichment). Finally, scientists needed to learn how to configure an explosive device that could implode plutonium or force together small masses of uranium 235 to create nuclear fission, thereby giving off tremendous energy. The speed and intensity of the fission process would determine the kind of reaction and the yield: either a sudden powerful explosion or simply heat capable of driving a steam turbine for generating electricity or for propulsion. Several countries organized teams of physicists to discuss the relevant issues and to advise their governments regarding the likely availability of a usable weapon before the war's end.

Western intelligence sources believed the German nuclear weapon program under Nobel laureate Werner Heisenberg had made considerable progress by 1942. Although this information later proved false, the threat that Nazi Germany might beat the Allies to this terrible weapon induced first the United Kingdom and then the United States (in a far larger program) to pursue serious efforts to develop nuclear weapons. The two countries eventually combined their programs into the U.S.-led Manhattan Project. Although this work remained highly classified, it ultimately spanned numerous facilities across the United States at the University of Chicago, Hanford (Washington), Oak Ridge National

Laboratory (Tennessee), and Los Alamos National Laboratory (New Mexico) and included as key participants dozens of skilled foreign scientists and engineers who had fled Europe and fascism. Japan also pursued a serious (but underfunded) program during World War II, including the development of a cyclotron. But the results proved too little, too late, and the key facilities burned in the Allied bombing of Tokyo in April 1945 (Rhodes 1986, 612).

The U.S.-led effort was by far the largest and best funded, drawing on a nearly limitless budget and enjoying safe conditions without fear of enemy bombs. Under the scientific direction of a dynamic young physics professor named J. Robert Oppenheimer from the University of California–Berkeley and with the administrative supervision of Army Brigadier General Leslie Groves (in charge of personnel, construction, and organization), the U.S. team successfully overcame the many logistical, conceptual, and engineering obstacles and produced the first atomic bomb in the spring of 1945. They detonated this device in the predawn hours of 16 July 1945, at the so-called Trinity site in Alamogordo, New Mexico, creating a blinding flash and the largest man-made explosion in history. It sent a searing wave of heat and radiation from its epicenter, killing or contaminating everything for several miles. Before the blast, some of the scientists had feared that New Mexico itself might be completely vaporized. After the explosion, a purple cloud of radiation spread across the desert, killing exposed farm animals and wildlife that had not already perished after the initial detonation. Given the nearly $2 billion spent on the secret bomb program (a huge sum in 1945 dollars), those in charge felt pressure to use the bomb quickly, even if it ended up shortening the war by only a few weeks or months.

U.S. Use of Nuclear Weapons against Imperial Japan

Nazi Germany, the main wartime enemy that had threatened to dominate Europe and that had motivated most of the U.S. and European scientists to work on the weapon project, surrendered in May 1945. The remaining task for the United States and the Allies was to defeat the now isolated but still very dangerous and defiant Japanese empire, whose forces had killed hundreds of thousands of Allied forces in Asia and millions of Chinese, Filipinos, and other subjected people. In their brutal campaign through East Asia, Japanese forces had committed many atrocities against captured soldiers and civilians and had used biological and chemical weapons in China. However, more than a few scientists involved in the U.S. weapon program (particularly those who had fled Nazi oppression in Europe) expressed reservations about using nuclear weapons against Japan on humanitarian grounds. As an alternative, they suggested that a demonstration shot be scheduled to warn the Japanese and give them a chance to surrender first. But President Harry Truman faced a dilemma. The United States had only a small amount of fissile material available at the time. Officials feared that a test shot might fail to detonate and would reduce the availability of possibly needed weapons. Moreover, Japan had resisted surrender even in the face of extensive firebombing of its cities, which had destroyed much of Japanese industry and killed hundreds of thousands of its people. With large numbers of U.S. soldiers still fighting in the Pacific, President Truman decided to authorize the use of the two atomic weapons the United States had under construction—nicknamed Little Boy and Fat Man, because of their different shapes and designs—against Japanese cities. Little Boy was a gun-type bomb consisting of a core of two masses of highly enriched uranium set to collide into one another to cause a fission chain reaction. Fat Man—like the original Trinity test device—used a single plutonium core and an implosion mechanism to generate a fission chain reaction. Seeking cities with large industrial enterprises serving the Japanese military that had thus far avoided significant damage from conventional bombing, the United States dropped the Little Boy bomb on Hiroshima on August 6 and the Fat Man bomb on Nagasaki on August 9, obliterating much of the two cities (Takaki 1995). With these actions, the complex international politics of nuclear weapon production and nonproliferation efforts began in earnest.

Although analysts continue to debate how long imperial Japan could have continued the fight absent the U.S. use of atomic weapons (Hasegawa 2005), few doubt that the bomb shortened the war and thereby saved many thousands of U.S. lives. Given the massive civilian casualties from the ongoing firebombing of other cities, as well as the staggering Japanese military losses being suffered in the brutal island-to-island battles against U.S. forces in the Pacific, the shortening of the war undoubtedly saved Japanese lives as well. Yet other factors figured centrally in the eventual U.S. decision to use the atomic bomb, including fears in Washington about the Soviet Union's possible further advance in East Asia if the war continued another several months. Moscow had clear designs on Japanese territory, including numerous islands and parts of Japanese-controlled China and Korea. The Soviet Union's long-planned entrance into the Pacific theater of operations occurred the day after the Hiroshima bombing. Nevertheless, the bomb's devastating effects and the terrible radioactive sickness it inflicted on thousands of Japanese survivors in the targeted cities sent a chilling message to the world about the implications of such weapons and the necessity of preventing their future use. The U.S. demonstration of the power of the bomb also accelerated the ongoing nuclear weapon program in the Soviet Union, which benefited from an extensive network of informers within the United States—even spies within the bomb program itself (Rhodes 1986).

Early Efforts to Control Nuclear Weapons

Initial efforts to halt the spread of the atomic bomb quickly developed in the context of the newly formed United Nations. Soon after the Japanese surrender in mid-August 1945, Oppenheimer began to mobilize efforts to see that the program he had supervised did not lead to an international arms race and further death and destruction. In March 1946, under the rubric of the so-called Acheson-Lilienthal Commission established by President Truman, Oppenheimer's scientific committee issued a report calling for an international authority to govern all nuclear activities and to ensure, through a system of international inspections, that such programs remained oriented toward peaceful uses of nuclear energy. The report also called for the eventual elimination of nuclear weapons once the new international authority was in place and firmly established.

At the United Nations, U.S. representative Bernard Baruch delivered a speech in June 1946 that oulined a toughened version of the proposal and called for immediate penalties on any states that might violate its principles of peaceful use of atomic energy (Bunn 1992, 59–61). To Oppenheimer and others, however, it was clear that the Soviet Union would take exception to these discriminatory measures and reject the plan altogether. As expected, the Soviet Union countered that the United States should *first* eliminate its nuclear weapons as a prerequisite for any discussion of an international authority governing peaceful uses. Skeptics in the United States had only limited faith in Oppenheimer's original concept and expressed great wariness about Soviet intentions. As if to confirm these fears, Moscow eventually stiffened its opposition even further, arguing that its independence in the nuclear realm could not be limited. The Baruch Plan eventually died because of a failure to reach a workable compromise for starting the process of international control (Bundy 1988, 158–167; Rhodes 1986, 239–240).

Expanding the Nuclear Club and Weapon Arsenals

Behind these limited efforts at peacemaking, the United States, the Soviet Union, and the United Kingdom all accelerated their nuclear programs in the late 1940s. While the United States experimented with different sizes of weapons and tested them in the South Pacific, the Soviet Union rushed to complete a sprawling nuclear complex of laboratories, reprocessing facilities, and nuclear weapon test sites in an attempt to catch up to the U.S. program. Under the guidance of physicist Igor Kurchatov—who had access to an extensive Soviet intelligence network and large reserves of forced labor from prison camps—the Soviet bomb program succeeded in testing its first nuclear device in September 1949 at the Semipalatinsk site in Soviet Kazakhstan (Holloway 1994). The arms race now had two official members—and much sooner than most Americans had expected. Soon both countries had launched crash programs to develop a much more powerful three-stage (fission-fusion-fission) weapon, the so-called hydrogen (or thermonuclear) bomb. The working of a hydrogen bomb would begin with the ignition of a plutonium or uranium fission device (the primary assembly), which would fuse heavy hydrogen isotopes of deuterium and tritium gas enclosed in the assembly.

This fusion reaction would release energy and neutrons, causing additional fissions of the primary's material and the fusion of lithium and deuterium (in solid lithium deuteride) in a secondary assembly, releasing even more energy and neutrons. Finally, before the whole bomb blew itself apart, uranium in the secondary assembly would also fission, yielding much greater overall explosive power than a single fission bomb. Spurred by physicist Edward Teller, the United States developed the first such experimental device (a bus-sized apparatus called Mike) and exploded it at Eniwetok Atoll in the South Pacific on 1 November 1952, vaporizing the small island of Elugelab in a fireball 770 times more powerful than the Hiroshima blast. The size of the explosion shocked even the scientists who constructed the device (Rhodes 1995, 482–512; Gardner 1994, 8). Ironically, the "advantage" gained by the United States proved short-lived, as the Soviet Union tested a smaller but deliverable hydrogen bomb (developed by physicists Igor Kurchatov and Andrei Sakharov) at Semipalatinsk on 12 August 1953, proving that the arms race was now nearly even as to technology. Throughout the 1950s, the two countries tested hundreds of nuclear weapons of increasing power. These explosions took place on land, in the oceans, in the air, and in space. They created fallout that exposed millions of people to varying levels of radiation, particularly those living closest to the test sites in the South Pacific, Nevada, and Kazakhstan, as well as soldiers involved in post-explosion military exercises. In the continental United States, trace amounts of radioactivity appeared in foliage across the country and entered the human food chain. In October 1952, the United Kingdom joined the nuclear club by testing a plutonium fission bomb off the coast of Australia.

Renewed Efforts at Control under Eisenhower

In the early 1950s, Oppenheimer continued his behind-the-scenes efforts to put the nuclear genie back into the bottle, or at least to reduce the number of countries that might acquire the bomb. Fearful of the possible widespread proliferation of nuclear weapons, the Truman administration in its last year (1952) convened an expert committee under Oppenheimer to consider the implications of such an arms race. Their report expressed great pessimism and urged a candid explanation of the risks involved in the continuation of nuclear armament policies by various countries, including the United States. Incoming President Dwight Eisenhower was sympathetic to the concerns raised in the report and believed some positive steps must be taken. He proposed making a certain amount of U.S. and Soviet fissile material accessible under international controls to states that would agree to engage in exclusively peaceful uses. In December 1953, President Eisenhower announced before the UN a proposal calling for the removal of such material from U.S. and Soviet weapons stockpiles and for the expansion of peaceful nuclear cooperation internationally. An unspoken benefit of the concept for the United States was that the Soviet Union was believed to possess far less fissionable material, meaning that its weapon program could be expected to suffer more. Eisenhower's so-called Atoms for Peace proposal received widespread international support, particularly from states interested in nuclear assistance (Bundy 1988, 287–295). Yet the original arms control intentions mentioned by President Eisenhower were not realized, as the United States and Soviet Union simply replenished their weapon stocks by producing more and more fissile material.

In practical terms, Eisenhower's speech and the Atoms for Peace program expanded U.S. ties with many countries seeking access to peaceful nuclear technology. Over time, these trends supported the creation of the IAEA, which was established in Vienna in 1957. In most cases, the net result remained limited to the promotion of civilian nuclear power plants and locked recipient countries into dependence on controlled international supplies of fissile material, thus giving them few incentives to go to the great cost of developing the technology for their own nuclear fuel facilities. However, in a few cases (such as in India), nuclear cooperation resulted instead in furthering domestic nuclear weapon programs.

Development of Delivery Systems: Bombers, Missiles, and Submarines

A dilemma for U.S. and Soviet weapon producers during this period was the limited availability of delivery vehicles. Aircraft in the 1940s and 1950s lacked the necessary range to travel across the oceans without refueling, meaning that bombers either could not reach their targets or had to be based in friendly countries nearby. The establishment of the North Atlantic Treaty Organization (NATO) in 1949 created formal postwar links among the United States, Canada, and most Western European countries, as well as a framework of mutual security that required U.S. protection of these allies, including through nuclear means. In 1954, the United States also deployed the world's first nuclear-powered submarine, the USS *Nautilus*, gaining an unprecedented ability to cruise stealthily through the world's oceans without having to surface or refuel, as previous diesel-powered submarines did. Within six years, the U.S. Navy would deploy the first nuclear-powered submarine capable of launching nuclear-tipped ballistic missiles (the USS *George Washington*), providing a mobile delivery system that could be deployed close to Soviet shores. In addition, by 1955, the United States had begun to position nuclear weapons at military air bases in Western Europe for possible use against the Soviet Union. Moscow responded by creating the Warsaw Treaty Organization (or Warsaw Pact), which obligated the Soviet Union to come to the defense of communist states in Eastern Europe and gave it the right to deploy nuclear weapons on their territories for use against NATO forces in Western Europe. Lacking allies close to the United States, the Soviet Union also accelerated its development of intercontinental-range missiles.

In October 1957, the successful Soviet launch of the world's first long-range ballistic missile with a "peaceful" artificial satellite (*Sputnik I*) eliminated this vulnerability by giving Moscow the capability of delivering a nuclear weapon to the United States. Despite U.S. military advantages in other areas and the limitations of the liquid-fueled Soviet R-7 rocket as a weapon system, U.S. fears of vulnerability and the general U.S. lag in missile technology eventually became a political issue in the late 1950s. This so-called missile gap entered the 1960 U.S. presidential debate, and candidate John Kennedy claimed that the United States risked annihilation if it did not greatly increase its defense budget and rectify this shortcoming. By this time, the United States had only recently deployed its first intercontinental-range ballistic missile (the liquid-fueled Atlas D), after several test failures. Unknown to the U.S. public and belying the braggadocio of Soviet leader Nikita Khrushchev, surveillance flights by high-flying U-2 aircraft and reconnaissance satellites over the Soviet Union had already revealed that Moscow had built at most only a few dozen missiles

(Schwartz 1998, 232–238). Kennedy won the election and then felt obligated to pursue a buildup to protect his reputation and U.S. intelligence sources. The size of the U.S. nuclear stockpile reached 18,638 warheads by 1961, and 27,100 the following year (Rhodes 1995, 562). The United States also began formal adoption of the "triad" structure (land, sea, and air) for its nuclear delivery vehicles, eventually building a force with 1,000 land-based, solid-fueled Minuteman missiles, 656 solid-fueled Polaris missiles deployed on nuclear submarines, and some 500 nuclear-capable bombers (Bundy 1988, 352).

Other countries had also begun to develop independent nuclear weapon programs, including India, Israel, and China. France became the fourth state with an actual device when it tested its first nuclear weapon in February 1960 in the Sahara Desert. In 1958, Washington also began deploying nuclear-tipped cruise missiles on Taiwan and in South Korea for possible use against China, North Korea, and the Soviet Union.

The Cuban Missile Crisis and the Limited Test Ban Treaty

Public protests regarding the effects of atmospheric nuclear testing reached their peak in the late 1950s and early 1960s (Wittner 1997). Soviet support for certain left-leaning protest organizations in the West weakened some of this pressure, but the influence on the U.S. Congress and media could not be denied because of the medical data that supported the claims. A key turning point in the nuclear arms race between the United States and Soviet Union came in 1962, after U.S. spy planes detected Soviet efforts to station nuclear weapons on Cuba. Cuba's revolutionary leader, Fidel Castro, had recently turned the island from a U.S. protectorate into a socialist ally of Moscow. The Cuban Missile Crisis moved the two sides to the brink of nuclear war, as advisers to President Kennedy urged military action against this Soviet incursion into the Caribbean. Both countries hastily conducted nuclear tests in outer space during the crisis to show their resolve and to see if such blasts might be effective in stopping missiles from the other side, despite the risk that such launches might be misinterpreted as actual nuclear attacks. But it was Kennedy's measured policy of relying on U.S. naval superiority in the local waters around Cuba and a combined strategy of blockade and negotiation that eventually succeeded in settling the crisis. The Soviet Union agreed to withdraw its missiles in exchange for a secret U.S. pledge to remove nuclear-tipped missiles it had earlier placed in Turkey. The very real nuclear danger that the crisis exposed, however, led to the first serious efforts by the two sides to limit the arms race and improve their ability to manage future crises.

One of the first accomplishments stemming from the Cuban Missile Crisis was a response aimed at calming popular fears of nuclear conflagration and reducing the chances of inadvertent U.S.-Soviet nuclear war. The signing in June 1963 of the so-called Hot-Line Agreement established direct radio and telegraph links between the U.S. and Soviet capitals to facilitate more rapid and effective communications and prevent misunderstandings in case of any further nuclear crises. Later in the summer, the two superpowers took steps aimed at stabilizing the arms race and reducing environmental damage by banning atmospheric, sea-based, and space-based nuclear weapon tests (several of which took place *during* the Cuban Missile Crisis) in the Limited Test Ban Treaty of 1963, signed initially by the United States, the Soviet Union, and the United Kingdom (Bunn 1992, 32–48). All future tests would have to be conducted under less provocative and more controlled conditions below ground. The treaty was opened for signature and ratification by other countries in the fall of 1963 at the United Nations in New York.

The United States and the Soviet Union also continued to meet periodically on other nuclear issues, showing that despite fierce political differences the two sides recognized the importance of new efforts to reduce the nuclear danger.

During this period, a unique nonproliferation development occurred in Latin America: the creation of the first nuclear-weapon-free zone in a populated part of the world. After the Cuban Missile Crisis, Latin American states recognized the threat they faced if one of their territories again became a staging ground for foreign nuclear weapons or, indeed, if a country in the region developed its own bomb. Thus, after several years of negotiations, these states opened the Treaty for the Prohibition of Nuclear Weapons in Latin America and the Caribbean (also known as the Treaty of Tlatelolco) for signature in 1967. The treaty members pledged not to develop or accept nuclear weapons on their territories and agreed to restrict themselves only to peaceful uses of atomic energy, under a regionally based system of inspections. A set of protocols for those outside states then possessing nuclear weapons banned their use (or threat of use) against regional parties, as well as their stationing on territories that they may own in the region. The United States signed this protocol in 1968 and the Soviet Union in 1978. Although technical and political factors limited full implementation of the treaty until the 1990s, the agreement set an important precedent for later nuclear-weapon-free zones in the South Pacific (Treaty of Rarotonga, 1986), Africa (Pelindaba Treaty, signed in 1996, but not yet entered into force), Southeast Asia (Treaty of Bangkok, 1997), and Central Asia (Semipalatinsk Treaty, signed in 2006, but not yet entered into force).

Elsewhere, however, many states continued to pursue or consider acquiring nuclear weapons, including Australia, India, Israel, Norway, Sweden, Switzerland, and Yugoslavia, among others. India, for example, had acquired a 40-megawatt research reactor from Canada in 1955 without formal mechanisms to prevent the diversion of the fissile material it produced. India later acquired reprocessing technology that allowed it to begin separating plutonium from the spent fuel, thereby opening the door to a bomb program (Perkovich 1999). Elsewhere, the development of smaller-yield weapons by the existing nuclear weapon states also started a reconsideration of possibilities among developed countries in Europe that had previously given up bomb programs. Thus, the late 1960s did not seem promising for chances to halt further proliferation.

New Nuclear Powers and the Evolution of the Nuclear Non-Proliferation Treaty

After the test-ban treaty, however, the two superpowers began to push internationally for an agreement to prevent the spread of nuclear weapons to other countries. The 1964 test of a nuclear weapon by China—a country hostile to both the United States and the Soviet Union—catalyzed nonproliferation efforts already under way between the two superpowers as well as within the United Nations, of which communist China was not yet a member

(Lewis and Xue 1991). Similarly, Washington's inability to stop the Israeli nuclear weapon program became a sobering reminder that even U.S. friends and allies could not be counted on to restrain their nuclear capability. Under President Lyndon Johnson, the United States thought that it had reached a tacit agreement with Israel to supply Tel Aviv with conventional arms in return for a cessation of Israeli efforts to develop nuclear weapons. However, using a French-supplied reactor and reprocessing plant (at Dimona) and their own scientific know-how, the Israelis pushed forward with the design and acquisition of the key building blocks for a nuclear weapon by 1966. After the 1967 Arab-Israeli war, Israel completed its program and is believed to have deployed its first weapon by around 1968 (Cohen 1998, 278, 298). However, Israel publicly denied any nuclear weapon capability and pursued a deliberate policy of nuclear opacity, a strategy later followed by South Africa and, until 1998, by India and Pakistan. Indeed, suspicions about Israeli intentions during the early to mid-1960s helped animate U.S. interest in pursuing more formal international arrangements to prevent future nuclear weapon proliferation.

The negotiations at the United Nations on a formal treaty took several years, and the United States and Soviet Union played leading roles (Bunn 1992). Eventually, these efforts came to fruition in the signing of the 1968 Treaty on the Non-Proliferation of Nuclear Weapons (known as the Non-Proliferation Treaty, or NPT), which entered into force two years later. The NPT divided countries into two groups: the five states that had already tested nuclear weapons (the United States, the Soviet Union, Britain, France, and China), and the rest of the world that had not yet deployed these weapons. The basic concept underlying the NPT involved a bargain in which non–nuclear weapon states that agreed to give up their right to possess nuclear weapons would receive security guarantees against nuclear attack and access to peaceful nuclear technology for the production of energy, pharmaceuticals, and other civilian products. The nuclear weapon states agreed not to transfer nuclear weapons and related technology to non–nuclear weapon states and to transfer peaceful nuclear technology only under international safeguards. Significantly, they also pledged to work to reduce their arsenals and eventually dismantle them completely. Although France and China would remain nonsignatories to the NPT for two decades, the agreement for the first time provided a solid foundation for future nonproliferation efforts, enlisting an increasing number of states (including countries capable of producing nuclear weapons) in pledges to engage only in peaceful uses of nuclear energy.

The existence of the regime put new pressure on states that had long contemplated deploying nuclear weapons. Now, if they remained outside of the NPT, they would be treated as "suspect" by other countries in a way that they had avoided before the agreement. Signing up with the regime, however, meant a decision to forgo what many had previously sought to preserve as a back-burner option in case of the emergence of new threats to their security. The early success of the NPT regime could be measured by the number of states that had begun nuclear weapons programs, then stopped them and signed the NPT as non–nuclear weapon states in 1968: Norway, Sweden, Switzerland, and Yugoslavia.

The Early 1970s: Détente and the Beginnings of U.S.-Soviet Nuclear Arms Control

To redress its humiliation after the Cuban Missile Crisis, the Soviet Union had engaged in a major nuclear buildup. By the end of the 1960s, it had reached approximate parity with the United States in deployed strategic weapons (about 2,000 delivery vehicles for each country). Meanwhile, Washington faced increasing budgetary pressure from costs associated with the Vietnam War and sought to slow what it now saw as an "unwinnable" U.S.-Soviet arms race. Under President Richard Nixon, National Security Advisor Henry Kissinger masterminded a series of negotiations that led to the first arms control agreements and a brief period of détente in U.S.-Soviet relations. In 1972, the two sides reached agreement on offensive and defensive weapon limitations under the terms of the bilateral Strategic Arms Limitation Talks (SALT). The so-called SALT Interim Agreement for the first time put an aggregate ceiling on the total number of U.S. and Soviet nuclear launchers, although neither side had yet reached this ceiling. Under the companion Anti-Ballistic Missile (ABM) Treaty, the two sides banned nationwide missile defenses and allowed only limited site defenses. The aim of the ABM Treaty was to prevent a costly new arms race in defensive technologies while reducing incentives for either side to expand its offensive arsenal further as a counter to such defenses. The ABM Treaty allowed each side to construct two defensive sites, one for a major population center, a second for a missile complex (although a 1974 treaty amendment reduced this to one per side).

Unfortunately, behind the smiles and handshakes, both states were continuing to develop new weapons, albeit within the new restrictions. The United States had already begun to test a new type of offensive weapon with multiple, independently targetable reentry vehicles (MIRVs); the Soviet Union would soon follow suit, avoiding treaty limits on launchers by adding more warheads. Ironically, these systems would make it more likely that any future ABM system could be overwhelmed. Thus, the treaty may have dampened some pressures, but it failed to halt the arms race as originally intended.

Efforts to Halt Horizontal Proliferation to New Countries

Although many states welcomed the NPT and the beginnings of U.S.-Soviet arms control, a few countries shunned international nonproliferation efforts and continued on paths toward creating their own nuclear forces. Thus, just when it appeared that increases in the superpowers' nuclear arsenals (vertical proliferation) might be contained, the threat of another country developing its first nuclear weapon (horizontal proliferation) became a reality. In 1974, India shocked the world by testing a nuclear device, highlighting serious problems in prior Western efforts to share nuclear technology with developing countries. These events stimulated Pakistan to accelerate the acquisition of nuclear weapon technology at full speed.

Until 1974, the primary organization restricting international exports of nuclear technology was the NPT Exporters Committee (better known as the Zangger Committee, after its first chairman, Swiss official Claude Zangger). This group was a loose affiliation of nuclear supplier states that had developed a so-called trigger list of sensitive exports. It required that states receiving these technologies accept safeguards and periodic inspections of these technologies to ensure their peaceful use in accordance with the NPT.

But the treaty did not explicitly require that other national nuclear facilities be accessible to international inspection. India's test, as well as evidence that Canadian technology had been used to produce materials used in its secret weapon program, galvanized support for stronger mechanisms. In 1974, a new organization called the Nuclear Suppliers Group brought together states from both inside and outside the NPT (such as France) to strengthen export controls and safeguard requirements, which now included enrichment and reprocessing technologies. This requirement would help ensure that materials produced at facilities receiving international assistance, as well as other materials from unsafeguarded facilities, could not be made into weapons.

The Late 1970s and 1980s: From Arms Racing to Negotiated Reductions

Although the two superpowers continued to cooperate on nuclear nonproliferation to keep nuclear weapons from additional states, the détente era of the early 1970s dissolved over nuclear and other issues in the late 1970s. Soviet deployments of new, high-yield MIRVed missiles (known as SS-18s) and tests of antisatellite weapons in space led to U.S. accusations of Soviet intentions to undertake a disarming first strike. The Soviet Union's invasion of Afghanistan in 1979 and its deployment of mobile SS-20 missiles in Eastern Europe added to U.S. anxiety. These events pushed the United States into alliance with Pakistan to train and support Islamic rebels to fight against the Soviet occupation. However, this policy also led the United States to turn a blind eye toward Pakistan's increasing efforts to build a nuclear weapon by drawing on technology acquired from abroad, especially Europe.

The election of President Ronald Reagan in 1980 ushered in a period of intense U.S. nuclear saber rattling and an extended nuclear buildup. Public fears over the implications, however, combined with lingering effects from the 1979 Three Mile Island nuclear plant accident in Pennsylvania, led to the grassroots efforts in the United States (the so-called nuclear freeze movement) to halt U.S. and Soviet nuclear deployment at existing levels (Meyer 1990). The Reagan administration provided new funding to several controversial weapon systems, including the expensive B-1 bomber and the rail-based MX missile, while pushing forward with deployment of the intermediate-range Pershing II missile in Western Europe. In 1983, President Reagan also announced the Strategic Defense Initiative (SDI), a plan aimed at nullifying the Soviet advantage in nuclear explosive yield through the construction of a massive, multilayered missile defense system that would use thousands of space-based interceptors and dozens of high-tech lasers to shoot down thousands of Soviet MIRVed missiles in their boost phase (before they could deploy their multiple warheads). However, besides violating the ABM Treaty, the SDI system (dubbed "Star Wars" by critics) proved far too expensive, and the technology was inadequate to the task. With changing Soviet foreign and defense policies under Mikhail Gorbachev (1985–1991), a new era of arms control emerged in the late 1980s. First, the two sides signed the Intermediate-Range Nuclear Forces Treaty in 1987, banning a whole class of missiles—including the SS-20 and the Pershing II—with ranges from 500 to 5,500 kilometers. Then, Presidents George H. W. Bush and Gorbachev signed the Strategic Arms Reduction Treaty (START) in July 1991, providing for the first actual reductions (rather than ceilings) in long-range nuclear armaments, setting a limit of 6,000 warheads. After the Soviet breakup in December 1991, the United States pursued an agreement with the Soviet successor states to continue the START reduction process, signing the Lisbon Protocol in May 1992 with Belarus, Kazakhstan, Russia, and Ukraine. A START II agreement was negotiated in January 1993 between the United States and Russian President Boris Yeltsin, calling on the two sides to reduce their arsenals further to 3,000–3,500 warheads each. Unilateral declarations by the Bush and Gorbachev/Yeltsin administrations in 1991–1992 also removed tactical (short-range) nuclear weapons from U.S. and Russian surface ships, submarines, and aircraft.

Elsewhere, proliferation pressures flared in South America in the late 1970s and early 1980s, where military governments in Argentina and Brazil remained locked in a fierce bilateral rivalry, as well as a secret competition to become the first to achieve nuclear weapon status, drawing on technology provided by several Western suppliers. Both states refused to sign the NPT, thus heightening international concerns. Meanwhile, in Pakistan, evidence of a nuclear weapon program had become undeniable by the mid-1980s. Concerns in Congress about tacit U.S. support for such proliferation led to the passage of the 1985 Pressler Amendment (named for U.S. Senator Larry Pressler of South Dakota), which strengthened existing U.S. export control laws to require the president to provide certification each year that Pakistan did not possess a bomb and that U.S. assistance would reduce (not increase) the possibility of Pakistan acquiring one. Despite mounting evidence after 1985 of a Pakistani nuclear weapon program, however, the Reagan and Bush administrations continued to certify Pakistan's non–nuclear weapon status under the new law rather than lose the U.S. base of support for aiding anti-Soviet resistance forces in Afghanistan. Finally, after Gorbachev's decision to withdraw the Soviet military from Afghanistan in 1989, President Bush denied certification to Pakistan and terminated all U.S. aid.

New Threats to the Nonproliferation Regime: Iraq and North Korea

The 1990–1991 Gulf War had a major impact on international nonproliferation by exposing just how far a state could go toward building a bomb despite being a member of the NPT. Inspections only of declared nuclear facilities had proven inadequate in the case of Iraq. As a result of suspicions raised during the Gulf War and the passage of special UN resolutions aimed at eliminating Iraq's potential to manufacture weapons of mass destruction (WMD), the UN Special Commission on Iraq (UNSCOM) began a series of more thorough postwar inspections of Iraqi military and scientific research facilities aimed at certifying the full destruction of any WMD capabilities. Although the existence of an Iraqi chemical weapons program had been widely known before 1990, UNSCOM inspections revealed that Iraq had also developed biological weapons, and had nearly developed a nuclear weapon, despite having allowed required IAEA inspections of its declared nuclear facilities. Documents revealed that careful subterfuge and the creation of an extensive procurement network of dummy companies operating in Europe and the Middle East had allowed the Iraqi government to operate a large, secret nuclear weapon program in undeclared facilities inaccessible to the IAEA. These revelations led to tightening of export control mechanisms in many countries in Europe and to decisions under IAEA Director General Hans Blix to assert the IAEA's rights of special inspection in cases where it had reason to believe there might be important undeclared nuclear facilities in a country.

These new mechanisms were tested soon afterward in the case of North Korea. Pyongyang had signed the NPT under Soviet pressure in 1985 (as a condition of the intended sale of a nuclear power plant) but had delayed providing the IAEA with an official declaration of its nuclear facilities until 1992. IAEA inspectors soon discovered irregularities in North Korea's declarations regarding refueling activities at a 5-megawatt electric research reactor in Yongbyon. New sampling data provided evidence that two illegal refuelings had been conducted and that plutonium had been diverted for a secret weapon program. U.S. intelligence data gathered by spy satellites and provided to the IAEA also revealed the presence of two suspicious facilities believed to be undeclared spent fuel sites. After six inspections during 1992–1993, the IAEA took its report to the UN Security Council in early 1993 and demanded special inspections. North Korea responded by announcing that it would withdraw from the NPT, giving the required three months' notice. After heated negotiations with the IAEA and the United States, North Korea suspended its withdrawal (one day short of its effective date) but continued to block inspections at several sensitive facilities. Finally, after North Korea renewed its threat to withdraw from the NPT and in a tense environment where some U.S. observers had begun calling for preemptive attacks to prevent development of a North Korean bomb, former U.S. President Jimmy Carter went to Pyongyang and convinced President Kim Il Sung to agree to a deal. The draft agreement would require North Korea to shut down its existing proliferation-prone nuclear facilities in exchange for two proliferation-resistant light-water reactors and shipments of heavy fuel oil for energy production until the reactors could be completed. The two states codified this arrangement in the "Agreed Framework" of October 1994, after South Korea and Japan agreed to pay for the project by pledging some $4 billion in loans. The deal averted a crisis but raised questions about the NPT's ability to prevent proliferation within its own structures and processes when a country attempts to subvert treaty restrictions, refuses to comply with special inspections, or threatens to leave the treaty.

Successes in International Nonproliferation Efforts in the Early to Mid-1990s

Despite the problems in Iraq and North Korea, there were several positive developments in nuclear nonproliferation during the early 1990s. In 1991, South Africa, a longtime holdout from the NPT, declared that, as part of the move toward free elections and a black majority government, it would join the NPT as a non–nuclear weapon state. (South Africa would later reveal that it had built and then destroyed six nuclear weapons.) In 1992, two key nonsignatories—France and China—ratified the NPT as weapon states, thus pledging themselves to eventually eliminate their nuclear arsenals and, in China's case, adopt new export control obligations (which France had already adopted as part of its membership in the Nuclear Suppliers Group). As a result of a political rapprochement, longtime holdouts Argentina and Brazil agreed to become full members of the Treaty of Tlatelolco in 1994 (thereby renouncing nuclear weapons); Argentina also became an NPT member in 1995, and Brazil joined in 1998.

Perhaps more significant, during the early to mid-1990s there were successful efforts, particularly by Russia and the United States, to encourage three Soviet successor states that had inherited nuclear weapons on their territories (Belarus, Kazakhstan, and Ukraine) to return them to Russia and to join the NPT as non–nuclear weapon states, thereby renouncing future possession of nuclear weapons. Through the Nunn-Lugar Cooperative Threat Reduction Program (named for its two Senate sponsors), the United States pledged financial assistance and technology to aid in the process of dismantling weapons and to help secure the vast Soviet stockpile of weapon-usable nuclear materials. It also created innovative programs to employ former nuclear weapons scientists in civilian research efforts in cooperation with other Western countries.

Additional positive news for the cause of nuclear nonproliferation came as a result of the NPT Review and Extension Conference held in April–May 1995. This crucial twenty-fifth-anniversary gathering faced the decision of whether (and, if so, for how long) to extend the NPT's duration. Because of the perceived slow pace of U.S.-Russian arms reductions, the failures of the inspections regime in Iraq and North Korea, and questions about the long-term willingness of the five declared nuclear weapon states to dismantle their nuclear arsenals, serious doubts had been raised about the chances for the NPT's indefinite extension. The decision would require a consensus, involving the support of more than 170 non–nuclear weapon states. However, high-level lobbying by the United States and other key countries, such as South Africa and Canada, resulted in a compromise: indefinite extension in return for additional pledges by the nuclear weapon states to address issues of concern to the non–nuclear weapon states. One of these measures included the long-sought goal of early prog-ress toward negotiating a complete ban on further nuclear testing. A second pledge involved concerted efforts to complete a treaty banning further production of weapons-grade uranium and plu-tonium, thereby reducing the global availability of bomb-making materials. Although much work remained to be done, the results of the meeting cemented the presence of the treaty as an enduring factor in international nonproliferation policy.

In September 1996, after a controversial series of nuclear tests by France in the South Pacific, the weapon states moved to imple-ment part of their 1995 pledge by signing the Comprehensive Nuclear-Test-Ban Treaty. Although the agreement required the ratification of forty-four nuclear-capable states to enter into force, this treaty represented a serious effort to eliminate nuclear testing once and for all and a *moral* obligation on the part of the signato-ries (which included the United States, Russia, China, France, and the United Kingdom) not to test during the prolonged ratification process, which was still ongoing in 2007.

New Tensions in the Nonproliferation Regime: The Late 1990s to Early 2003

Despite this progress in nonproliferation efforts, the late 1990s witnessed the ramping up of nuclear tensions in South Asia, where India and Pakistan had remained outside the NPT but had refrained from testing weapons since the lone Indian explosion in 1974. With the election of Prime Minister Atal Behari Vajpayee and his Hindu Nationalist Party in 1997, India set itself on a course toward nuclear testing. Despite policy documents making Vajpa-yee's intentions clear, all the major powers expressed shock when he conducted multiple nuclear weapon tests in May 1998, bring-ing India's latent nuclear potential into public view and shifting India's policy from nuclear opacity to overt weaponization. India conducted six tests in a period of a few weeks. Pakistan hesitated, and then responded by testing its first nuclear device on 28 May 1998 and conducting five additional tests in a few days' time to match its rival. Although the United States and other countries sharply criticized these moves and placed economic and military sanctions on both countries, the weakness of the effort frustrated many of the non–nuclear weapon states (like Japan) that believed the international community should have enacted stronger mech-anisms in the face of such blatant proliferation.

The decision of the U.S. Senate to reject the recommenda-tion of the Clinton administration and defeat the Comprehensive Nuclear-Test-Ban Treaty in 1999—on the grounds that it could not be adequately verified and that future U.S. weapons testing might be required—delivered another serious setback to support-ers of nuclear nonproliferation. Internationally, many countries strongly condemned the U.S. Senate's action, stating that the net effect would be to encourage further testing by other states. Nev-ertheless, France, Britain, and Russia moved ahead to ratify the agreement.

George W. Bush took office in 2001, and his administration announced plans to conduct unilateral U.S. arms reductions, withdraw from the ABM Treaty, and construct national missile defenses. The administration acted on all of these pledges, despite the opposition of numerous foreign governments, including many within NATO. The Bush administration also used the terrorist attacks of September 11, 2001 to end remaining U.S. sanctions on India and Pakistan, stating its preference for a new policy of positive engagement. The move rewarded Pakistan, in particular, for offering its territory as a key staging area for U.S. forces fight-ing the Taliban in Afghanistan. In addition, U.S. policymakers voiced new fears about the possibility that terrorist groups (like Osama bin Laden's al Qaeda organization) might acquire access to weapons-grade nuclear materials and either build a nuclear device or, more likely, use conventional explosives to spread more easily obtainable radioactive waste using a so-called dirty bomb.

In the area of arms control, the Bush administration announced that as part of its new relationship with Russia it would enact unilateral cuts in the U.S. nuclear arsenal to 1,700–2,200 deployed strategic warheads (not counting those in reserve or on launchers undergoing repair). It also gave notice of its intended withdrawal from the ABM Treaty, effective in June 2002, to begin fulfilling its plan to build nationwide missile defenses. Russian President Vladimir Putin expressed his dissatisfaction with the U.S. withdrawal from the ABM Treaty, stating that amending the agreement would have been the preferable course of action. He also called for continued U.S.-Russian discussions toward a formal treaty to verify arms reductions and eliminate warheads on both sides.

The Bush administration announced in late 2001 in its Nuclear Posture Review that it would keep many of the nuclear weapons removed from its arsenal in a strategic reserve rather than destroying them. The administration also included in its 2003 budget request funds to make it easier for the United States to resume nuclear testing if such a decision were to be made in the future. Defense Department spokespersons defended these actions by saying that U.S. nuclear weapons needed to be ready to be redeployed, if conditions required it, and that new nuclear weapon designs (especially ground-penetrating, "bunker buster" versions) might be needed for the fight against rogue states and terrorists. But the moves brought considerable negative reactions from foreign governments that questioned U.S. commitments to disarmament and the test ban. China, in particular, indicated its frustration with new U.S. policies on reversible arms control and on missile defenses, which it considered threatening to its small nuclear arsenal.

U.S.-Russian negotiators agreed by the May 2002 summit in Moscow to allow the signing of an official pact pledging both sides to reach ceilings of 1,700–2,200 deployed strategic warheads by 2012. But this basic framework left unaddressed U.S.-Russian differences in the areas of reserve stockpiles and weapons elimination. Following the U.S. exit from the ABM Treaty, Russia withdrew from the START II agreement and has opted to keep its land-based MIRVed missiles, rather than build new, single-warhead missiles.

New collective approaches to proliferation challenges in the former Soviet Union resulted from the meeting of the leading industrialized countries, the Group of Eight (G-8), in Kananaskis, Canada, in June 2002. In response to the 9/11 attacks, attention now began to focus on the importance of securing fissile material at its source. With this in mind, the G-8 states pledged a total of $20 billion over the next ten years—half from the United States and the rest from the other G-8 countries (including Russia)—to heighten the security of nuclear and other WMD-related materials in the former Soviet Union and to continue the work of the U.S. Nunn-Lugar program. The new effort became known as the Global Partnership against the Spread of Weapons of Mass Destruction.

In the fall of 2002, the long-simmering nuclear crisis on the Korean Peninsula bubbled over once again with U.S. charges about Pyongyang's prior acquisition of uranium centrifuge technology from Pakistan in violation of the 1994 Agreed Framework. In the U.S. view, North Korea was now seeking to subvert the freeze on its plutonium program by developing a secret uranium enrichment effort to pursue a nuclear weapon. In a spiral of ill will and mistrust, the brinkmanship of the Kim Jong Il regime and the Bush administration led to the abandonment of diplomacy, the breakup of the Agreed Framework, and North Korea's withdrawal from the NPT. North Korea ordered all IAEA inspections and monitoring to end and restarted its plutonium-producing reactor in early 2003. Some critics charged that the Bush administration was too preoccupied with making its case for the invasion of Iraq and therefore had failed to focus enough attention on preventing a nuclear breakout in North Korea.

U.S. Secretary of State Colin Powell's speech to the UN General Assembly in January 2003 put together the administration's most convincing case for invading Iraq using controversial evidence suggesting that Iraq was pursuing nuclear weapons and other WMD. Despite the lack of a specific UN resolution in support of the war (most countries opposed intervention), the United States, the United Kingdom, and a token force of allied states invaded Iraq in March 2003. The Iraqi army failed to put up serious resistance, and the coalition forces quickly overwhelmed all organized opposition within a matter of weeks. In a foreshadowing of future events, however, the surprising presence of irregular forces and religiously inspired non-Iraqi fighters offered some of the fiercest opposition to U.S. and British forces. Subsequent events, studies, and revelations from Iraqis themselves would show that the administration's case regarding Iraq's WMD programs had been seriously flawed.

Post–Iraq Invasion Nonproliferation Efforts

Before the invasion of Iraq, new evidence appeared that Iran, a non–nuclear weapon state and member of the NPT, had been less than candid about its nuclear program. In August 2002, a group that opposed the Iranian government revealed that Iran had two, possibly weapons-related, facilities that had not been disclosed to the IAEA: a pilot facility to produce highly enriched uranium at Natanz, and a heavy-water facility at Arak. Later, in December 2002, the U.S.-based Institute for Science and International Security published satellite photos of the suspected site at Natanz, and a series of inspections by the IAEA confirmed that Iran had deliberately concealed several facilities that were active in its nuclear program. Iran subsequently denied the IAEA access to a facility in Tehran, setting up the beginning of a prolonged cat-and-mouse game regarding a possible nuclear weapon program. Most troubling, continuing IAEA inspections at other sites revealed traces of highly enriched uranium, although possibly not of Iranian origin. The IAEA determined that Iran had failed to disclose the full extent and purposes of all its various nuclear activities, as required. Although Iran temporarily halted its uranium enrichment activities pursuant to a deal with European nations, Tehran later announced that it would never give up its right to a complete nuclear fuel cycle and resumed enrichment activities.

Concerned about the possibility that Iran, other proliferant states, and terrorist groups may have acquired nuclear and other WMD-related technologies, the United States announced a cooperative program called the Proliferation Security Initiative (PSI) in May 2003. The PSI consisted of a voluntary group of states committed to using diplomatic, military, intelligence-related, and other measures to prevent shipments of WMD and associated technologies by land, air, and sea. The new program encouraged inspections of suspect cargoes. For ocean cargo, such efforts would be facilitated by boarding agreements with countries such as Liberia and Panama that register many commercial vessels. The organization quickly grew to more than fifteen core member states and more than sixty cooperating states. Major countries such as Russia, Japan, the United Kingdom, France, Germany, and Australia began coordinated naval exercises with the United States aimed at enforcing the PSI, thus providing an important new deterrent against possible transit of WMD technologies and delivery systems.

In December 2003, Libya, an NPT member but long considered a rogue state because of its secret WMD programs and record of past support for terrorism, announced that it would abandon its WMD efforts and associated delivery systems. This successful case of nonproliferation persuasion resulted from joint efforts by the United Kingdom and the United States and led to the complete inspection and full dismantlement of Libya's secret WMD facilities, as well as its acceptance of the IAEA's Additional Protocol. Inspectors discovered that Libya had procured advanced centrifuge technology and designs from Pakistan's Khan Laboratories, as well as blueprints for a nuclear weapon. Although some U.S. officials hinted that the war in Iraq had convinced Libya that it had to cease its WMD efforts, most evidence pointed to Libya's desire to end its wasteful spending on such materials and technologies and enjoy the benefits of trade and investment that had long been denied it by the international community. However, in the course of Libya's negotiations on the final dismantlement terms, considerable new information came out about the role of Pakistan, and particularly its chief nuclear scientist, A. Q. Khan, as an illicit supplier to Libya's nuclear program. These revelations put increasing pressure on the government of Pakistan to press charges against senior nuclear officials.

After the IAEA identified traces of highly enriched uranium on equipment found in Iran (now believed to be from Pakistan) and Libya disclosed its nuclear procurement activities involving Pakistani intermediaries and suppliers, the Pakistani government finally took action against its leading nuclear scientist in early 2004. After a series of interrogations, Khan admitted his role as a major illicit nuclear supplier with a worldwide network stretching into Southeast Asia, Europe, Africa, and the Middle East. Although he lost his government position and was put under house arrest, Khan's national reputation as the father of the Pakistani bomb allowed him to avoid jail. The U.S. and other intelligence networks had long known of Khan's activities, but Pakistan's public acknowledgment of Khan's activities was both a major accomplishment of the nonproliferation regime and a major blow to its credibility. Although Pakistan had remained outside the regime during the time of Khan's activities, the IAEA's failure to identify and halt his network—which was supplying technology to a number of NPT states, including Iran, North Korea, and Libya—presented a major embarrassment that undermined the regime's credibility and pointed to the importance of strengthening export control mechanisms internationally. The extent of Khan's proliferation network and the role of the Pakistani government and military in promoting (or at least turning a blind eye to) Khan's activities remain open questions. In May 2006, the government closed its investigation of Khan and refused to make him available for questioning by international inspectors.

But the IAEA found the value of its work partially redeemed by evidence coming out of postwar Iraq. Specifically, the release of the findings of the U.S. Iraq Survey Group in the so-called Duelfer Report in October 2004 confirmed the effectiveness of IAEA sanctions and the UN special inspections regime in Iraq (Duelfer 2004). The report stated that the U.S. investigators could find no evidence of Iraqi reconstitution of its nuclear program after 1991. The Duelfer Report directly contradicted and, in many respects, disproved the Bush administration's case for the war in Iraq. The IAEA and its U.S.-maligned Director General Mohamed ElBaradei reaped the rewards of their efforts in October 2005 when they jointly received the Nobel Peace Prize for their work to promote nuclear nonproliferation.

Stung by the Khan revelations and seeking international support for the PSI, the United States sought to work within the UN framework to strengthen formal nonproliferation mechanisms. Specifically, Washington's concerns about the threat posed by non-state actors in proliferation black markets led the U.S. government to propose a binding resolution of the Security Council to require states to enact legislation to make it illegal for non-state actors within their borders to possess WMD materials and technologies. Adopted in April 2004, UN Security Council Resolution 1540 also requires states to heighten security at state-controlled facilities with WMD materials and technologies and to report their progress to the United Nations. While compliance remains imperfect, the resolution has received widespread praise as a cooperative effort to increase nonproliferation compliance within existing international organizations. In addition, it has focused new global attention on the non-state actor and terrorist problems facing the nonproliferation regime.

As part of the new global understanding of post–September 11 proliferation challenges, international organizations, governments, and nongovernmental organizations have initiated parallel efforts to remove highly enriched uranium from the civilian fuel cycle. These have included the U.S.-funded Global Threat Reduction Initiative (GTRI), announced in May 2004, linking U.S., IAEA, and Russian efforts. Specifically, the GTRI seeks to reverse the process whereby both the United States and the Soviet Union had once provided research reactors and highly enriched uranium fuel to developing countries (for such purposes as producing medical isotopes). The initiative set up a schedule to retrieve nuclear fuel of U.S. and Soviet origin from more than 100 sites around the world or, where the reactors are still in operation, to replace the fuel cores with more proliferation-resistant low-enriched uranium. Also, in July 2006, the United States and Russia announced the Global Initiative to Combat Nuclear Terrorism, a new effort to set national standards for protecting and detecting nuclear weapons and materials and to facilitate international cooperation in technical means of combating nuclear terrorism. This initiative complements the UN International Convention for the Suppression of Acts of Nuclear Terrorism, which was opened for signature and signed by fifty countries in September 2005.

Attempts to Curb North Korea's Nuclear Program: 2003–2007

China has emerged as a more significant actor in Northeast Asian nonproliferation activities because of its concern about the implications of the worsening North Korean nuclear crisis. In spring 2003, it sponsored trilateral talks with North Korea and the United States that were aimed at resolving the dispute and returning Pyongyang to the NPT. Responding to U.S. demands for wider talks, Beijing successfully organized the so-called Six-Party Talks in August 2003, which brought together the three original parties plus neighbors South Korea, Russia, and Japan. After several fruitless rounds and in the face of increasing North Korean progress toward a nuclear weapon, the talks resulted in a seeming agreement on denuclearization in the fall of 2005. But North Korean–U.S. differences over recently tightened financial sanctions and the question of whether the deal included nuclear power assistance led to its rapid collapse. This series of events and mutual finger-pointing over fault finally culminated in North Korea's October 2006 test of a plutonium fission bomb with a half-kiloton yield. According to experts, North Korea's bomb fizzled. Nonetheless, North Korea became the tenth state to demonstrate a nuclear capability and the first nuclear state to have withdrawn from the NPT. The UN Security Council announced strong and unanimous sanctions against the North Korean regime in November, aimed specifically at military and WMD-related technologies and means of funding such programs. But early evidence suggested that incomplete implementation of cargo inspections, even by such U.S. allies as South Korea, would weaken their effectiveness. In late 2006, North Korea again agreed to return to the Six-Party Talks, under pressure from China. Finally, in February 2007, North Korea agreed to a deal in which it would shut down its nuclear facilities and allow the return of IAEA inspectors within sixty days in exchange for a phased package of financial, diplomatic, and energy-related incentives. Further steps were supposed to be negotiated, whose specific content and sequencing remained unclear as of April 2007. Notably, the February agreement left undecided the fate of North Korea's nuclear arsenal and fissile materials.

New Debates over Nuclear Arsenals

Among the major nuclear powers, divergent trends had become more pronounced. Within the United States, Congress began to reassert itself by canceling funding for the bunker buster bomb. The Bush administration announced deeper unilateral cuts in its reserve stockpile, but made no mention of plans to cut into the deployed force beyond existing treaties. The Russian Federation, by contrast, called for resuming talks aimed at further reductions in a follow-on agreement to the Moscow Treaty, which is scheduled to expire in 2012. Washington remained opposed to such talks, preferring to stick to unilateral measures. This debate highlighted differences of opinion as to whether nuclear weapons themselves or the intentions of states represented the most serious threat. The Bush administration sparred with other nuclear countries over whether international agreements should govern dismantlement or, according to the U.S. preference, such processes should be controlled only by national governments. In the United Kingdom, meanwhile, a major debate flared during 2006 over whether or not to continue deploying nuclear weapons at all, given the changes in the global security environment and the extremely high costs of building a new generation of nuclear submarines to carry them. In March 2007, however, the Parliament heeded Prime Minister Tony Blair's advice and approved a $40 billion nuclear modernization program. France maintained a flat trajectory in its nuclear arsenal, but had already begun plans for next-generation systems and showed few signs of further reductions. China's policy remained opaque, although experts noted no significant effort to engage in a nuclear arms race with other powers. One of the biggest question marks surrounded the intentions of smaller nuclear powers: Israel, India, Pakistan, and North Korea. These states remained outside NPT controls. Another growing concern was whether the emergence of new nuclear weapon states in particular regions might encourage long-standing NPT members to rethink their non-nuclear policies.

In 2006, the United States proposed a radical policy shift in offering to provide India nuclear technology in exchange for the latter's declaration of a range of civilian nuclear facilities that would henceforth be subject to IAEA inspections. The Bush administration argued that India's role as a democracy, the fact of its existing nuclear arsenal, and its responsible nonproliferation behavior merited a change in U.S. policy, despite India's non-membership in the NPT. Critics argued that the deal represented a dangerous undermining of the NPT regime and stemmed mainly from the coincidence of U.S. business interests and the administration's desire for continued Indian support in the war on terrorism. The deal placed no restrictions on India's future nuclear arsenal, although Congressional amendments required India to refrain from future nuclear testing. Ironically, it remained unclear as to whether India would accept such "meddling" in its nuclear policy, despite the possible benefits of U.S. acceptance of its nuclear program and its new willingness to provide civilian nuclear technology. As many expected, announcement of the deal led to broader international implications. Russia quickly announced an expansion of its nuclear cooperation with India, despite prior Nuclear Suppliers Group restrictions. China later moved ahead with a similar nuclear trade pact with longtime ally Pakistan, despite the latter's nonmembership in the NPT. Non–nuclear weapon states in the NPT complained that these actions weakened the treaty and the incentives of states within it to continue refraining from developing nuclear arsenals of their own. Critics also argued that adding subjective criteria to the determination of proliferation threats would weaken international solidarity for dealing with problem cases like Iran, where a settlement on shutting down Tehran's continuing uranium enrichment program remained elusive, despite trade and technological incentives offered by the European Union and the United States in June 2006. In April 2007, Iran's President Mahmoud Ahmadinejad claimed that Iran would soon be able to enrich uranium on an industrial scale, and would reconsider its membership in the NPT if Western countries continued to sanction Iran for pursuing a complete nuclear fuel cycle. Spurred by Iran's nuclear pursuit, Egypt, Jordan, and other Middle Eastern countries have announced plans to pursue their own nuclear energy programs.

One development provided more positive news regarding international nonproliferation efforts. The five states of former Soviet Central Asia—Kazakhstan, Kyrgyzstan, Tajikistan, Turkmenistan, and Uzbekistan—signed a treaty in September 2006 creating a nuclear-weapon-free zone in their region. The agreement prohibited nuclear weapons from being stationed in Central Asia and established a mechanism for enhanced cooperation in nuclear cleanup from Soviet-era nuclear testing and associated uranium milling and mining operations. This agreement considerably expanded the regions of the world now covered by nuclear-weapon-free zones and placed a new buffer in the middle of Asia helping to separate nuclear-armed India, Pakistan, Russia, and China.

Conclusion

Since 1945, the world has witnessed a dramatic proliferation of nuclear weapons. However, their absolute numbers have declined significantly since the end of the Cold War. But a range of problems still remain. Despite the end of the Cold War, the existing nuclear weapon states have thus far failed to dismantle their nuclear arsenals as required by the NPT. Within the treaty, several non–nuclear weapon states (including Brazil, Iran, and Japan) continue to assert their NPT right to develop technology to produce enriched nuclear fuel for power plants, even though this same technology can be used to create weapons-grade material for bombs. Finally, four nuclear weapon states (India, Pakistan, Israel, and North Korea) remain outside the regime and therefore pose a challenge to the NPT and its associated non-nuclear norms. Whether these states can be incorporated into the nonproliferation regime without weakening the consensus that holds the NPT and its associated export control system together remains to be seen.

In the context of the post-1945 period, much has also been accomplished to limit the spread of nuclear weapons. An overwhelming majority of countries, as well as many nongovernmental and international organizations, have committed themselves to the objective of nuclear disarmament. In the presence of new terrorist threats since 2001, many states have also undertaken new domestic, regional, and international measures to improve the security of nuclear weapon materials, strengthen export controls, and prevent possible diversions.

Looking ahead, greater transnational cooperation in solving regional security problems—which largely drive the "demand" for proliferation—is likely to be the most reliable route to future success in nonproliferation policies. Improving verification mechanisms to implement restrictive agreements will play a critical role too, particularly if states are going to make progress toward eventual nuclear elimination—if indeed that goal is achievable. Overall, a struggle is likely to continue for at least the next few decades between those who support a deterrent role for nuclear weapons and those who see nuclear weapons as heightening global tensions and placing the world's population at risk.

References

Bundy, McGeorge. 1988. *Danger and Survival: Choices about the Bomb in the First Fifty Years*. New York: Random House.

Bunn, George. 1992. *Arms Control by Committee: Managing Negotiations with the Russians*. Stanford, CA: Stanford University Press.

Cohen, Avner. 1998. *Israel and the Bomb*. New York: Columbia University Press.

Duelfer, Charles. 2004. *Comprehensive Report of the Special Advisor to the DCI on Iraq's Weapons of Mass Destruction*. Washington, DC: U.S. Government Printing Office. https://www.cia.gov/cia/reports/iraq_wmd_2004.

Gardner, Gary T. 1994. *Nuclear Nonproliferation: A Primer*. Boulder, CO: Lynne Rienner Publishers.

Hasegawa, Tsuyoshi. 2005. *Racing the Enemy: Stalin, Truman, and the Surrender of Japan*. Cambridge, MA: Harvard University Press.

Holloway, David. 1994. *Stalin and the Bomb*. New Haven, CT: Yale University Press.

Lewis, John W., and Litai, Xue. 1991. *China Builds the Bomb*. Stanford, CA: Stanford University Press.

Meyer, David S. 1990. *A Winter of Discontent: The Nuclear Freeze and American Politics*. New York: Praeger.

Perkovich, George. 1999. *India's Nuclear Bomb*. Berkeley, CA: University of California Press.

Rhodes, Richard. 1986. *The Making of the Atomic Bomb*. New York: Simon and Schuster.

Rhodes, Richard. 1995. *Dark Sun: The Making of the Hydrogen Bomb*. New York: Simon and Schuster.

Schwartz, Stephen I., ed. 1998. *Atomic Audit: The Costs and Consequences of U.S. Nuclear Weapons since 1940*. Washington, DC: Brookings Institution Press.

Takaki, Ronald. 1995. *Hiroshima: Why America Dropped the Atomic Bomb*. New York: Little, Brown.

Wittner, Lawrence S. 1997. *Resisting the Bomb: A History of the World Nuclear Disarmament Movement, 1954–1970*. Stanford, CA: Stanford University Press.

2

Problems, Controversies, and Solutions

The continued presence of large numbers of nuclear weapons in various states today raises several important questions, including how best to manage the threat of nuclear war, how to contain the risks of possible nuclear acquisition by additional states or by terrorists, and what tools to use to promote nuclear nonproliferation and work toward possible nuclear elimination. But there is little consensus on the answers.

To some officials and experts, the risk of nuclear weapons represents a cost worth paying if possessing these weapons can provide effective deterrence against potential enemies and thereby prevent war (Waltz, in Sagan and Waltz 2002). They believe no rival state will be so foolhardy as to attack a country with nuclear weapons and risk annihilation. This seemed to have been the thinking of North Korea's leadership when it tested its first nuclear weapon in October 2006.

Other world leaders and policy analysts, however, believe nuclear weapons are inherently risky, making war, accidental conflict, and environmental disasters more likely (Sagan, in Sagan and Waltz 2002). They also argue that nuclear weapons do not deter because they cannot realistically ever be used because of the damage they are likely to bring on their possessors in terms of retaliation. Thus, they believe nuclear weapons should be eliminated globally and countries should rely instead on cooperative security mechanisms (drawing on alliances and treaties) and conventional weapons. The views of many other officials and experts fall somewhere between those backing nuclear possession and those supporting nuclear elimination, and all have varying assessments about the feasibility of nuclear nonproliferation and disarmament efforts, the effectiveness of international treaties and organizations, and what constitutes an "acceptable" number of nuclear weapons for purposes of deterrence.

Given the fact that nuclear weapons have not been used in conflict since 1945, however, beliefs about their role in today's world and in security relations among states remain largely matters of faith. For example, no one knows for certain if nuclear weapons are required for military deterrence among great powers today. Other factors may be promoting peace among major states, such as shared commitments to democratic values or market economics and growing disinterest in seizing territory as a means of increasing national power and influence. Even so, many political leaders in the nuclear weapon states are very hesitant to give up their nuclear arsenals. Some leaders believe nuclear weapons are needed to protect against unpredictable future conflicts. Others see them as central to deterring rogue states and rising powers, which may themselves be seeking weapons of mass destruction. Still others may believe nuclear weapons are required to maintain great power status. Naturally, this increases incentives for other states to develop them. As George Perkovich (2006, 357) argues, "Demand for nuclear weapons . . . will not diminish if the states that already possess the weapons continue to flaunt them as emblems of national power." For the aforementioned reasons, some analysts fear that we are nearing the dissolution of the 1970 Non-Proliferation Treaty (NPT). Experts say that urgent collective action is needed to strengthen compliance, shore up challenged nonproliferation norms, and make more substantive progress toward the NPT's goal of total nuclear disarmament by all states.

This chapter surveys some key questions surrounding the role of nuclear weapons internationally and discusses a range of perspectives and possible solutions. It begins by examining the historical development, role, and problems associated with nuclear weapons from both strategic and practical viewpoints. It then examines how nuclear weapons relate to today's security challenges and how the presence of large quantities of nuclear material poses risks in regard to possible terrorist activities. Finally, it considers the international dilemma of trying to expand nuclear power generation while seeking simultaneously to prevent and reverse nuclear weapons proliferation. How these questions will be answered in the coming years will have a significant effect on global security, public health, and environmental safety. Cooperation among states and the peoples of the world will be necessary to address emerging proliferation threats, but increasingly divergent trends among the world's leading powers on how best to proceed pose a major challenge to the future success of these efforts.

Nuclear Weapons and Their Role during the Cold War

To place today's issues in context, it is useful to start by asking how nuclear weapons affected the Cold War. Although nuclear forces played a central role in the security policies of both the United States and the Soviet Union, the two sides managed to avoid nuclear conflict throughout the period from 1945 to 1991, despite several crises and frequent disputes. But the price tag of Cold War nuclear efforts was enormous. In the United States, the bill has been estimated at $5.5 trillion in a detailed study conducted by the Brookings Institution (Schwartz 1998). These costs included expenses for weapons development, deployment of delivery systems, and operational service, as well as subsequent costs for weapons dismantlement and environmental cleanup. The latter two activities are still ongoing in many former nuclear facilities across the United States and abroad. It is assumed that the Soviet Union spent somewhat less on its vast nuclear arsenal (given its widespread use of forced labor) but that its effort constituted a much greater proportion of the Soviet gross national product. Still, many argue that the price of these arsenals was worthwhile, for they believe nuclear weapons played a key role in preventing a major U.S.-Soviet war.

Indeed, experts as varied as historian John Lewis Gaddis, physicist Edward Teller, and political scientist Kenneth Waltz argue that nuclear weapons were at least *mainly* responsible for preventing direct superpower conflict during the Cold War. First, they point out how the horror of the bombing of Hiroshima and Nagasaki, as well as the ability of Washington and Moscow to threaten each other with total annihilation using nuclear weapons, created conditions of military deterrence. Second, they argue that once both sides possessed a minimum number of weapons that could be expected to survive a surprise first strike and be ready to fire back (weapons on airborne bombers, on submarines, or in hardened land-based silos), conditions of so-called mutually assured destruction could be said to prevail. In such circumstances, according to this argument, neither side dared risk attacking the other because of the unacceptably high cost even if it fired first, making any meaningful victory impossible. As analyst Thomas C. Schelling wrote during the height of the Cold War on the role of nuclear weapons, "Deterrence rests today on the threat of pain and extinction, not just on the threat of military defeat" (Schelling 1966, 23). Waltz (1981) makes the case that nuclear weapons made strategies for preventing war much cheaper and at the same time much more credible than earlier policies of deterrence with conventional forces. Facing the threat of possible annihilation, Waltz argues, U.S. and Soviet leaders became highly conservative about warfare rather than aggressive and opportunistic. From these perspectives, nuclear weapons played a *positive* and *stabilizing* role in the Cold War.

Looking at the same evidence, however, other experts, such as author Jonathan Schell, antinuclear activist Dr. Helen Caldicott, and physicist Hans Bethe, make the opposite case about the Cold War experience. First, they point out that Cold War relations were anything but stable. They note that the U.S.-Soviet arms race spun out of control, judging by the huge nuclear stockpiles numbering in the tens of thousands of weapons built by both sides—far in excess of what was needed for effective minimum deterrence. Second, they argue that nuclear weapons may have *exacerbated* tensions between the two sides, fomenting greater distrust and risking mutual annihilation in events like the Cuban Missile Crisis of 1962. Third, they highlight that the global consequences of stumbling into a nuclear war, unlike in a prenuclear age, became catastrophic and possibly deadly for all of humankind. As Schell observed about nuclear weapons and human civilization in his best-selling book, *The Fate of the Earth*, "We hold this entire terrestrial creation hostage to nuclear destruction, threatening to hurl it back into the inanimate darkness from which it came" (Schell 1982, 181). These critics conclude that only careful diplomacy—

and some level of luck—kept the world from stumbling inadvertently into a devastating World War III.

Finally, a third group of analysts makes the case that nuclear weapons neither prevented war between the superpowers nor exacerbated tensions during the Cold War. Instead, the weapons simply represented a peculiar military experiment carried out by both sides at great cost during the Cold War. Political scientist John Mueller argues that the terrible devastation caused by World War I and World War II was more than adequate to deter any World War III between the United States and Soviet Union—and it remains a powerful deterrent to great power warfare today. He concluded a provocative article on this subject by predicting that the nuclear arms race would eventually end from "atrophy" and "a dawning realization that, since preparations for major war are essentially irrelevant, they are profoundly foolish" (Mueller 1988, 79).

Although the U.S.-Soviet nuclear arms race did begin to wind down by the late 1980s and ended unexpectedly in 1991 with the internal breakup of the Soviet Union, thousands of nuclear weapons remain in the United States and Russia, hundreds in four countries (France, Britain, China, and Israel), several dozen each in India and Pakistan, and a handful in North Korea. Thus, despite Mueller's late–Cold War prediction, states do not seem to have accepted his lesson that building nuclear weapons and preparing for their possible use is "profoundly foolish." Notably, several states that either developed (South Africa) or once possessed nuclear weapons on their soil (Belarus, Kazakhstan, and Ukraine) have given them up voluntarily, setting an important precedent for future nonproliferation possibilities. However, even a small use of nuclear weapons would still constitute a "major war." Therefore, questions related to the role and effects of nuclear weapons remain highly relevant.

What Is the Role of Nuclear Weapons Today?

Although nine countries possessed nuclear weapons as of 2007, there has been little specific justification provided for many of these arsenals (beyond the very general concept of deterrence) since the end of the Cold War. In the years before 1991, Britain, France, and the United States regularly referred to the need to deter a Soviet attack as the rationale for the existence of their arsenals, whereas the Soviet Union and China regularly pointed to the U.S. threat and (during certain periods) to each other's weapons to justify their own arsenals. With the Cold War's demise, however, it is unclear what purpose nuclear weapons serve among countries that now frequently refer to one another as "partners" rather than "adversaries." In this context, critics argue that the U.S. and Russian maintenance of arsenals with several thousand nuclear weapons makes no sense. Supporters of these levels, however, point to the necessity of targeting existing military forces in possibly hostile countries (including those with nuclear weapons) and maintaining a hedge against the possible future deterioration of relations.

In the context of some of the smaller, regionally focused nuclear arsenals—as in India, Israel, Pakistan, and North Korea—deterrent concepts seem somewhat more credible, given the presence of realistic local military concerns. Israel points to the Arab countries surrounding it and a hostile Iran nearby, whereas India and Pakistan point at each other and, in India's case, at China as well. National pride and prestige seem to play considerable roles in the Indian and Pakistani cases, where cheering crowds greeted their nuclear tests in 1998. North Korea points to the rival government in Seoul and the presence of U.S. military forces in South Korea.

Nevertheless, even in cases of regional rivalries, it is not always clear what role nuclear weapons would play in foreseeable conflicts, which often hinge on internal ethnic, religious, and political issues or localized territorial disputes where nuclear weapons would be unusable. Significant changes in the world since 2001 also make some critics wonder about the continued relevance of nuclear deterrence against the threat many states worry about most: international terrorism. As Middle Eastern scholar Kaveh Afrasiabi asked in a 2007 *Asia Times* essay about the need for nuclear disarmaments, "Given the stateless nature of international terrorism, how is . . . nuclear deterrence supposed to operate against terrorists, and what possible scenario for such deterrence can be fathomed?"

But supporters of the nuclear arsenals argue that their role as an ultimate deterrent helps keep conflicts in check and, when they do break out, limited in scale because of a fear that they will escalate to the nuclear level. Indeed, some recent analysts have argued that the United States has achieved such an overwhelming superiority in operational readiness and technological capabilities that its arsenal puts it in a position of strategic superiority over other nuclear countries. Keir A. Lieber and Daryl G. Press (2006) make the case that the previous situation of mutually assured destruction between the United States and Russia has now shifted to conditions under which Washington could contemplate being able to conduct a successful first strike against its erstwhile enemy. They note that while both U.S. and Russian numbers have declined since the end of the Cold War, Russia's arsenal has "eroded" while U.S. forces "have become more lethal," mainly because of increased accuracy. China's forces, meanwhile, have failed to catch up and remain too tiny to pose much of a threat to the United States. Lieber and Press call this situation one of U.S. "nuclear primacy," harkening back to conditions at the dawn of the nuclear age.

While technically the United States may or may not have achieved such primacy, an argument can be made that political conditions—particularly the domestic and global taboo against nuclear use—make it impossible for the United States to achieve significant benefit from the situation. Moreover, history shows that states that other countries perceive as threatening will eventually face coalitions of adversaries or new technologies that put their advantages into question. Finally, there are those who would say—recalling early nuclear theorists—that numbers still don't matter and that no country would ever attack another country that might be able to fire back with at least one nuclear weapon, something certainly the United States cannot be sure of in regard to a host of possible future adversaries.

Are Nuclear Weapons Safe?

One issue that was frequently raised throughout the Cold War and remains salient today is nuclear safety. Even strong supporters of nuclear weapons want to be sure that they do not go off accidentally and that they are used only in the most carefully prescribed circumstances after exhaustive government deliberation. Fortunately, to date there have been no cases of an accidental launch of a nuclear weapon and no incidents of an accidental nuclear detonation. However, as more declassified information becomes available on the experience of past decades, there is considerable new data on a number of troubling accidents involving nuclear weapons.

Political scientist Scott Sagan (1993) has studied the past nuclear experience of the United States, which has arguably spent the most money and resources of any country to ensure the safety of its nuclear arsenal. Yet Sagan's work documents numerous dangerous incidents involving false nuclear alerts. In one case, a flock of birds set off a nuclear early warning radar; in another a computerized test tape of a nuclear attack was mistaken for several minutes as real. Confusing messages sent from personnel at far-off early warning sites have occasionally been misread as well. Still other incidents uncovered by Sagan include accidents involving B-52 aircraft near Thule Air Base, Greenland, and at Palomares, Spain, where nuclear weapons were mistakenly dropped and their conventional explosives ignited, dispersing dangerous radioactive material. Sagan argues that such evidence provides good reasons to oppose further nuclear proliferation and to try to reduce arsenals to an absolute minimum level, with a premium being put on safety.

Also supporting Sagan's arguments is the large body of evidence involving accidents aboard U.S., Russian, and other nuclear-powered ships and submarines, as well as those with nuclear weapons aboard. Although much of this information is still being declassified in various countries, there are dozens of confirmed cases of collisions with civilian vessels, hostile ships and submarines, and even friendly forces in the course of military exercises, and others in which nuclear weapons and/or nuclear reactors went to the sea bottom. In 1967, for example, a Soviet Golf II–class diesel submarine and the U.S. nuclear submarine *Scorpion* sank in accidents that killed all 179 Soviet and U.S. crew members and resulted in the loss of nuclear weapons aboard. A number of other such accidents occurred during the Cold War. To cite another example, two U.S. surface ships carrying nuclear weapons collided in a nighttime exercise in 1975, rupturing the fuel lines on the larger ship, spilling gasoline on the small one (the cruiser USS *Belknap*) and setting it on fire. Fortunately, the *Belknap*'s nuclear weapons did not explode during the two-hour blaze, but the risk was extremely high. In 1989, the Russian nuclear submarine *Komsomolets* suffered a serious fire and sank with forty-two crew members in the White Sea, taking three nuclear-tipped torpedoes to the ocean floor. These incidents highlight the security and environmental risks of broad proliferation of sea-based nuclear weapons, similar to the history of accidents with aircraft and ground-based systems. While military personnel certainly endeavor to handle nuclear weapons safely, technical problems, weather, and human error sometimes result in dangerous events, putting human lives and the environment at risk.

Finally, other authors, such as former U.S. missile officer Bruce Blair (1995), have discussed the related problem of inadequate command-and-control mechanisms in states with unstable or transitional political systems, as in South Asia and the Middle East. His work has highlighted the development of a dangerous automatic launch system by the Soviet Union, which might have been used in case of a first strike by the United States to ensure that a counterattack would be launched even if the top leadership in Moscow were killed, cut off, or disabled. To prevent the threat of an automatic nuclear war, Blair has urged all nuclear weapon states to de-alert their nuclear forces by separating warheads from missiles, thereby preventing inadvertent war through the possible malfunctioning of early warning networks, command mechanisms, and computers. To date, however, this has still not occurred.

In regard to the possible unauthorized use of nuclear weapons, it is important to note that nuclear weapons in the more advanced militaries (including those in the United States, Russia, France, and Britain) have so-called permissive action links (PALs) built into them. PALs require that operators provide a special launch code from their nation's capital to activate the warheads. Without the code, the weapons are unable to detonate themselves. Certain weapons also have additional safeguards against unauthorized use involving onboard environmental sensors that track altitude data and prevent the weapons from being detonated in situations for which they were not designed. Yet such technologies are not foolproof and could be overcome by sophisticated insiders, if not by hostile forces, given enough time. Moreover, countries like North Korea, Pakistan, India, and possibly Israel lack such devices, suggesting risks of nuclear command-and-control breakdowns in crisis situations, where unauthorized military or political leaders might be tempted to take matters into their own hands.

How Many Nuclear Weapons Are "Enough"?

Among those who accept the notion that the continued presence of nuclear weapons is inevitable now that they have been developed, debates over the number of nuclear weapons needed to deter another state from attacking vary greatly. During the Cold War, it was common practice for the United States and Soviet Union to match each other missile for missile, believing the enemy might interpret any sign of weakness as providing a window of opportunity to engage in coercion or outright attack.

By 1965, the United States, with more than 32,000 nuclear weapons, still had a significant lead over the Soviet Union. By 1985, however, the Soviet Union had caught up and then surpassed the United States with a total of 39,000 nuclear weapons. Ironically, in the political science and strategic literature, arguments about high numbers of weapons enhancing overall security—once a certain minimum level is reached and a state has a reliable second-strike capability—find little support. Cold War strategist Bernard Brodie wrote about the *irrelevance* of numbers, "Deterrence ... does not depend on superiority" (Brodie 1971, 274). Since the dawn of the nuclear age, many analysts have described deterrence as being possible with very few nuclear weapons. After all, they argue, what state would be willing to risk being hit in retaliation even by a single nuclear weapon?

However, state leaders have rarely followed this advice. The experience of the United States and Soviet Union during the Cold War showed how internal political forces tended to intensify pressures to build arms rather than reduce them. At the same time, however, Britain, France, Israel, and China generally managed to limit their arsenals to fewer than 500 weapons each. Among this group, Britain recently announced its plans to keep its arsenal under 200 weapons; yet, in March 2007, the British Parliament rejected going non-nuclear with a vote to replace its fleet of four nuclear-armed submarines. But the presence of the U.S. military alliance with Britain and France and its U.S. partnership with Israel have clearly played a role—along with cost and the perception of threats—in encouraging these three countries to keep fewer nuclear weapons than they might otherwise possess. In China, there was no such assurance, given its lack of a security guarantee from any other country after 1961 (when the Soviet Union broke ties with Beijing). Economic weakness may have been one restraining factor in the past. But China also appears to have embraced notions of minimal deterrence more fully than other states as a matter of policy and today still fields only some 200 strategic and tactical nuclear weapons, according to recent estimates. It remains to be seen if the continued expansion of the Chinese economy and its reaction to India's and Japan's military modernization programs will cause it to shift its past policies and undertake a significant nuclear buildup.

Certain Cold War nuclear dynamics seem to be repeating themselves in South Asia today. Immediately after their respective nuclear tests in May 1998, India and Pakistan both announced that they would not repeat the mistakes of the superpowers in building ever-larger nuclear arsenals. Since then, however, India has enunciated a nuclear triad doctrine that will require the development of additional nuclear weapons to be deployed on aircraft, submarines, and land-based missiles. Pakistan has stated it will try to match India's deployments. In practice, then, it seems that state leaders frequently believe an enemy will not find their possession of a few dozen nuclear weapons—however deployed—credible as a deterrent. Whether this is an accurate perception of the enemy's thinking or more of a psychological projection is, of course, debatable. But given the ability of nuclear states to produce more fissile material (plutonium and highly enriched uranium) and their desire to maintain the support of their nuclear scientists (who want to continue experimentation) and their militaries (each branch of which often wants its own nuclear force), pressures to develop larger and more dispersed arsenals can be very strong. These forces, in turn, make the process of reversing direction and engaging in arms reduction very difficult once the weapons are deployed.

In 2006, deployed *strategic* nuclear weapons (meant for use against enemy nuclear and military forces, industries, and population centers, as distinguished from short-range *tactical* nuclear weapons meant for use on the battlefield) among the world's nine nuclear powers consisted of about 9,000 warheads altogether. This estimate includes 5,236 strategic warheads for the United States; 3,500 for Russia; 348 for France, 192 for Britain; about 130 for China, fewer than 100 each for Israel, India, and Pakistan; and about 4 for North Korea (Norris and Kristensen 2006). But beyond these numbers, various countries (particularly the United States and Russia) also have several thousand additional strategic and tactical warheads in their *reserve* stockpiles, numbering approximately 18,000 weapons. Approximately 480 U.S. tactical nuclear weapons remain deployed in North Atlantic Treaty Organization (NATO) countries, representing the only weapons now stationed outside their country of origin.

Current plans under the Moscow Treaty call for the United States and Russia to reduce their strategic weapons to 1,700–2,200 deployed warheads, excluding those in the reserve stockpile and on delivery systems (including bombers, missiles, and submarines) undergoing repairs, thus putting the actual ceiling at around 2,500. These parallel reductions pledged by presidents George W. Bush and Vladimir Putin are to be achieved over a period of years and represent only a minor reduction from the levels of 3,000–3,500 warheads agreed to in the now-bypassed second Strategic Arms Reduction Treaty. However, it is likely that the two sides, either together or unilaterally, will seek to deploy fewer weapons after the Moscow Treaty's implementation date of 2012. The opposite is also possible, given the absence in the treaty of a requirement for warheads taken out of service to be dismantled (at U.S. insistence, given Washington's uncertainty about its future strategic plans).

Although these figures indicate progress toward deep reductions compared with Cold War numbers, some critics question whether these levels are low enough. A document issued by the Natural Resources Defense Council in 2001 reported on a detailed, independent study of the casualties that could be inflicted on Russia by one U.S. nuclear submarine carrying 192 nuclear weapons. The assessment estimated that 50 million Russians would be killed or injured, suggesting that a U.S. arsenal of fewer than 200 warheads alone could accomplish the U.S. goal of effective deterrence. Yet the report generated little public or congressional support for such dramatic reductions. Why should that be the case?

Given the uncertainty of exactly how many nuclear weapons are enough to deter, combined with the pressures within Congress and the U.S. military to uphold their responsibility to defend the country, U.S. leaders thus far have tended to err on the side of caution, meaning more than 1,500 deployed weapons. Such nuclear policies, however, seem to contradict statements by administration officials that the most serious threats to U.S. security are posed by states such as Iran and North Korea and terrorists groups that are believed to be "undeterrable" with nuclear weapons. Similarly, despite Russia's transition away from communist rule, its adoption of a more representative government, and its improved relations with both the United States and China over the past fifteen years, Moscow continues to base its security on the possession of large numbers of nuclear weapons. In fact, Russia is relying even more heavily on its nuclear forces than during the Cold War because of problems in maintaining large conventional forces and accompanying military personnel. Russian President Vladimir Putin has stated that terrorism represents the most serious security threat facing his country today. Yet Russia's continued possession of large numbers of nuclear weapons and dozens of sites with fissile material, ironically, only worsens that threat.

Given current, deeply ingrained beliefs about nuclear weapons and only limited interest in deep reductions within the United States and Russia, the challenge of moving to levels below 1,000 nuclear weapons in either country—let alone less than 100—will require the establishment of new national and possibly international security frameworks and understandings. In the absence of these conditions, there is likely to be only incremental progress toward nuclear reductions, as there has not been a fundamental shift in thinking regarding the acceptability of nuclear weapons. But this poses nonproliferation dilemmas, whether the weapon states admit it or not. As journalist and historian Selig Harrison writes, "Why should other countries forswear the nuclear option if the existing nuclear powers are upgrading their nuclear arsenals, talk openly of using them in future wars, and no longer even give lip service to the goal of phasing out nuclear armaments...?" (Harrison 2006, 1).

But several factors could change the calculations of the current weapon states. The first might be the accidental or intentional use of a nuclear weapon somewhere in the world. The shock of such an event, after more than sixty years without such horrendous damage, could provide the necessary spur to action among the world's population and governments. A second factor that may lead to greater nuclear cuts could be a decrease in the prestige or perceived utility of nuclear weapons. In the United States, for example, the increasing effectiveness of conventionally armed precision-guided munitions (particularly those using Global Positioning System signals) has made the U.S. military increasingly capable of substituting "smart" conventional weapons for previous nuclear weapon missions, such as destroying an adversary's military command-and-control centers. As other states acquire these types of weapons, nuclear arms may begin to appear as backward and increasingly abhorrent weapons and therefore less desirable. Other analysts, however, have speculated that advanced conventional weapons in the hands of some states may instead *increase* the desire of other states to develop nuclear weapons as an insurance policy against precision attacks. Finally, the possible seizure of a nuclear weapon or materials for a radiological dispersion device (RDD) could greatly accelerate states' efforts to reduce their stockpiles of weapons and fissile material. Given the seriousness of this threat, the factors involved are worth further investigation.

How Serious Is the Threat of Nuclear Terrorism?

Although many analysts have downplayed the possibility that a terrorist group could acquire and/or develop a nuclear weapon, there are good reasons to think this is not only a possible but also an attractive option for terrorists. An even more serious threat is terrorists acquiring radioactive source material for use in an RDD (or so-called dirty bomb), which could contaminate large areas of a major city and create locally significant health risks (Ferguson et al. 2004). Several specific factors migh spur terrorist interest in a nuclear device.

First, there is global fear of nuclear weapons and their devastating destructive capabilities, as well as of the suffering and death caused by the radiation they release. These factors may increase the allure of nuclear devices to terrorists. Second, although theft of a nuclear weapon might seem unlikely because of the extreme precautions exercised by most governments, the current existence of thousands of nuclear warheads of various sizes and yields in the United States, Russia, and seven other countries under varying conditions of protection makes the theft or diversion (such as by a paid insider) of one bomb a possibility that cannot be discounted. Third, even though constructing a complicated nuclear weapon of the compact size and enormous yield of the most sophisticated

U.S. and Russian bombs would be impossible for terrorists, development of a crude nuclear weapon from highly enriched uranium (HEU) would not be extremely difficult, even without a team of bomb physicists. Constructing an RDD would be relatively simple, although immediate casualties would likely be limited to the effects of the conventional explosive attached to it.

What materials are most worrisome? Current stockpiles of HEU in the world are abundant, representing some 1,900 metric tons of material (or enough for about 38,000 nuclear weapons) (Albright and Kramer 2004). The "good news" is that the vast majority of this material consists of HEU in military hands in the United States and Russia, meaning that it is generally under higher security than at civilian sites. However, stockpiles of this material continue to increase and move into the civilian fuel cycle as weapons are dismantled. Civilian HEU stocks consist of about 175 tons worldwide, including some 125 tons declared as excess to military uses. HEU is used as fuel in some 140 civilian nuclear reactors around the world. Fresh HEU fuel is highly reactive and can be made to explode simply by forcing two small spheres of the material into one another using a metal tube and a simple conventional explosive. A rogue state or terrorist would only need to divert about 50 kilograms of HEU to create a crude, gun-type device. The yield of this weapon could be enough to vaporize many city blocks. If detonated at ground level in a truck, it would spread clouds of radioactive particles for miles from the epicenter, contaminating and killing additional thousands of people. Because the security of Russian HEU has been a particular concern, the United States has spent an average of several hundred million dollars yearly since 1991 to help secure Russian fissile material through the Nunn-Lugar Cooperative Threat Reduction Program. Fortunately, conditions have improved, as has Russia's own capacity to fund protective measures. More recently, the Global Threat Reduction Initiative, a combined U.S., Russian, and International Atomic Energy Agency (IAEA) project, works to convert HEU reactors worldwide to low-enriched uranium and to repatriate fresh and spent fuel of U.S. and Russian origin to upgraded storage facilities.

A second material of concern is plutonium. There are an estimated 1,855 metric tons of plutonium in global civilian and military stockpiles (or enough for 225,000 weapons) (Albright and Kramer 2004). Unlike HEU, the bulk of available plutonium (some 1,600 metric tons) is at civilian facilities. Fortunately, most of this plutonium is not in separated (bomb ready) form, but instead is in radioactive spent fuel. Thus, it would need to be reprocessed (usually via arduous and toxic chemical methods). A smaller quantity of plutonium is contained in mixed-oxide (MOX) reactor fuel for use in light-water power reactors. It would be difficult for a terrorist group to seize either spent or MOX fuel and to separate out the plutonium for a bomb, but certainly not impossible. Perhaps the most vulnerable period is in the transit of these materials from reactors to reprocessing facilities, sometimes via ship. With plutonium, only about 8 kilograms of material would be needed to fabricate a bomb of the approximate yield of the Nagasaki weapon. But the engineering challenges of building a plutonium implosion device are considerably more complicated than building an HEU bomb, given the need for sophisticated triggering devices to create a symmetric implosion of the material.

As mentioned previously, a much easier and possibly more attractive option for terrorists might be to build a radiological weapon, or dirty bomb. An RDD involves the use of radioactive, but not weapons-grade, nuclear material, such as spent nuclear fuel, or even medical isotopes, packaged with a conventional explosive. A dirty bomb would not cause a nuclear explosion but could spread radioactive material across a wide area, contaminating a large city and spreading fear among its citizens. Besides the conventional blast's effects, hundreds of people could fall sick from radiation poisoning (if the material became airborne and was inhaled), and sections of the city affected by the radioactive dispersion would have to be decontaminated at very high cost, given the necessary precautions for handling radioactive debris. Unfortunately, radioactive material is available in significant quantities at thousands of sites worldwide under varying conditions of security, as well as in trace amounts in many widely available commercial products. Because of their radioactive properties, the materials of greatest concern are americium 241, californium 252, cesium 137, cobalt 60, iridium 192, plutonium 238, radium 226, and strontium 90 (Ferguson et al. 2004, 262). The risk that these materials could be diverted and used in an RDD has stimulated a number of government actions to mitigate chances of their seizure by terrorists and their transit across borders. IAEA, U.S. government, and other technical programs to increase safeguards at nuclear facilities, expand the number of states possessing portal-monitoring equipment (such as radiation detectors), improve port security, and provide training to border guards and other officials are working to reduce these threats. But such actions are still inadequate, given the large scale of the threat. Terrorist groups such as the Aum Shinryko cult in Japan and Osama bin Laden's al Qaeda network are known to have tried to acquire nuclear material for these purposes in the past.

Finally, besides explosive devices, terrorists might also use radioactive material to contaminate water or food supplies or harm an official or member of a target organization. Although the number of casualties would be much lower, public fears could be raised exponentially by such attacks, spreading chaos, disrupting communities, and harming local and national economies. Fortunately, gaining access to nuclear materials is more complicated for terrorists than acquiring or manufacturing chemical or biological agents, which have already been used in terrorist attacks (such as with anthrax after 9/11). But the use of radioactive polonium 210 to kill former Russian intelligence officer Alexander Litvinenko in London in late 2006 may be the first indicator of a wider effort to use such materials. Nonfissile materials such as polonium are also easier to obtain legally than substances that could be used for a bomb. Indeed, states with nuclear industries (or individuals within them) with some sympathies to the aims of terrorist groups or criminals might help them acquire radioactive substances for the purpose of contract killings or spreading fear. For these reasons, greater cooperation is needed among states possessing nuclear facilities of all types and local, national, and international law enforcement organizations. Efforts to move in this direction include the U.S.-led Proliferation Security Initiative, United Nations (UN) Security Council Resolution 1540, and the 2005 International Convention for the Suppression of Acts of Nuclear Terrorism.

Environmental and Health Effects of Nuclear Weapon Production

The large nuclear weapons complexes in the United States and Soviet Union were created at great speed and under the belief that attack from the other side could occur at any moment. Both had their roots in World War II facilities, but these sites expanded dramatically during the late 1940s and 1950s. Indeed, building nuclear weapons became one of the major postwar *economic* undertakings of both countries, requiring vast investments of money, energy, personnel, land, and material. (In 1956, for example, facilities under the U.S. Atomic Energy Commission consumed 12 percent of the total electricity produced in the United States [Schwartz 1998, 356].) But the priority in both countries—as well as in other countries that developed the bomb—was first and foremost national security; thus, environmental and health consequences took a distant second place in the ranking of priorities. As environmental expert Arjun Makhijani (2005, 20) writes, "It is a remarkable fact of nuclear weapons history and radiation risk that every nuclear-weapon state has first of all harmed its own people in the name of national security. For the most part, they have done so without informed consent."

As a result of this attitude, the handling of hazardous radioactive waste was often casual and poorly planned, leading to widespread contamination of significant areas of both countries. Materials were stored in leaky containers or simply dumped in landfills with no protection from the elements; radionuclides often migrated with rain down into the local water table. At the Hanford nuclear facility in eastern Washington State (where the United States produced much of the plutonium used in its early nuclear weapons), plant operators intentionally dumped more than 120 million gallons of liquid radioactive waste into the ground from 1946 to 1966 (Schwartz 1998, 361). Similarly, the long-term effects of handling radioactive and other hazardous materials were often not explained fully to workers at nuclear plants or residents in the surrounding areas, resulting in many health problems and higher rates of cancer. In the Soviet Union, prison camp laborers were sometimes forced to conduct hazardous activities (such as uranium mining) with no protection whatsoever; many died in a matter of months and were simply replaced by other prisoners.

The general populations in both countries and, indeed, much of the rest of the world received above-background doses of radioactivity as a result of fallout from widespread aboveground nuclear testing from 1945 through 1963. Ironically, the U.S. government secretly warned the Eastman Kodak Company of impending nuclear tests to avoid commercial lawsuits for damage to unexposed film thousands of miles away from the Nevada test site, but the general public received no such warnings regarding radiation that passed into their systems from airborne fallout or by ingesting milk or other animal products from livestock that had consumed plants contaminated with radioactivity. One study estimates that between 70,000 and 800,000 people will die prematurely from cancers caused by atmospheric nuclear testing before the signing of the Limited Test Ban Treaty in 1963, which required the United States and Soviet Union to halt above ground nuclear testing (Schwartz 1998, 395). It is clear that both governments knew about these problems, yet strict state secrecy, maintained in the name of national security, kept public opposition relatively limited until the late 1950s. After 1963, global antinuclear protests based on health concerns diminished, although many local communities near nuclear facilities continued to wrestle with leaks and other releases of radioactivity into their groundwater and surrounding airspace. The record in the Soviet Union was far worse in this regard given the greater lack of public information and opportunities for meaningful protest.

Even in the United States, however, ignorance remained a key reason for the lack of more public opposition and calls for oversight. Part of the reason for limited public knowledge was the failure of Congress to exercise adequate oversight of the nuclear infrastructure. During the 1950s, for example, it was considered unpatriotic to do so, and members who questioned the Atomic Energy Commission's nuclear policies risked criticism as communist sympathizers. In certain U.S. communities surrounding nuclear plants, moreover, the largesse expended by government agencies made citizens leery of opposing the activities at local plants, fearing that the shutdown of facilities would mean the loss of high-paying jobs. Even after two serious fires at the plutonium-processing facility at Rocky Flats, Colorado, in 1957 and 1969, workers remained relatively quiet, and the Atomic Energy Commission was able to keep information about the gravity of incidents from the general public (Ackland 1999). Thus, a situation of relative neglect of environmental and health concerns characterized most nuclear facilities even in the United States until the mid-1970s, when environmental legislation began to force the government to provide more information to the public.

The result is a legacy of improperly stored nuclear waste at many facilities that U.S. taxpayers are now paying to clean up.

At the Hanford facility, for example, efforts to halt leaks of liquid radioactive wastes from storage tanks and the remediation of buildings cost the government some $400 million annually, part of a multibillion-dollar national cleanup bill each year. In the former Soviet Union, remedial action has been much more limited because of the lack of financial resources, although some foreign assistance has been received from, for example, the United States, Norway, and Japan. Most surviving victims of U.S. radiation poisoning, ranging from Pacific Islanders affected by nuclear testing to ranchers living near the Nevada Test Site to workers who handled nuclear materials at Rocky Flats to orphans given doses of uranium in secret government tests during the 1950s, have only recently begun receiving compensation. Victims in the former Soviet Union are still waiting.

Why Haven't Nuclear Weapons Spread to More Countries?

During the 1950s, national leaders (together with many political scientists and strategists) assumed that whatever states could master nuclear power technology would also develop nuclear weapons in due course. In 1961, a secret report to President John Kennedy predicted that there would be as many as fifteen nuclear weapon states by 1975. But these predictions were not realized. Why is this so? Analysts provide differing assessments.

Among the so-called realist school, there was widespread belief during the Cold War that the main reason for nuclear restraint was the nuclear security guarantees provided by the United States and Soviet Union to their allies and friends. With the end of the Cold War, this argument still has resonance for many NATO countries as well as U.S. allies in Asia (such as Japan and South Korea).

A second perspective on this issue, however, argues that most states simply do not *want* to possess nuclear weapons, even though they could. These authors, such as Mitchell Reiss (1995), note that nuclear weapon possession comes with a great many diplomatic, financial, and environmental costs. It also exposes countries to possible military attack during the years it takes to make their first bomb and subsequently makes those countries more likely targets of other nuclear weapon states. In 2003, Libya decided to dismantle its nuclear weapon program largely, it appears, because of the financial and political trade-offs it faced for pursuing weapons of mass destruction compared with receiving foreign investment and developing its economy. South Africa seems to have made a similar decision.

Finally, a third perspective on this issue is that international treaties have helped slow or halt the development of nuclear weapons in many states. Regimes such as the NPT raise the costs of proliferation by making weapons technology much more difficult to obtain because of export controls and the challenges of trying to cheat on international inspections. For example, the results of U.S. intelligence studies conducted after the 2003 Iraq war showed that, to the surprise of many critics, the system of UN sanctions and on-site inspections had effectively ended Iraq's nuclear program after 1991. Other states are more concerned about their international reputations and the political impact of violating the international antinuclear taboo.

Although it is difficult to assert definitively which of the various schools of thought is correct, one observation can be made: Only 10 states—out of some 190 in the world today—have ever developed nuclear weapons (one, South Africa, no longer has such weapons). Thus, many countries with the scientific know-how to build nuclear weapons have chosen, for whatever reason, not to do so. Whether the number of nuclear weapon states will increase or decrease over time is difficult to predict. Beyond the countries already known to possess them, international suspicions have been raised about the long-term intentions of some countries, such as Iran, in regard to nuclear weapons. However, nuclear weapon programs generally require many years to develop the material, technology, and design information needed to deploy actual weapons. Normally, a plutonium bomb also needs to be tested because of the greater complexity of its design. This is usually a highly transparent event, as evidenced by the widespread detection of North Korea's very-low-yield (estimated at half a kiloton) plutonium bomb test in October 2006. For an HEU weapon, testing may not be required to ensure that a weapon design will work, but evidence of the large-scale uranium reprocessing facilities needed to create enough weapons-grade material is difficult to keep hidden. Still, deception is conceivable. But the status of a country's bomb program will generally remain ambiguous without a nuclear test. It is not clear, for example, whether South Africa (which gave up its nuclear weapons) or Israel (which is believed to have possessed nuclear weapons since the late 1960s) ever conducted a test. The absence of such an obvious event helped both countries maintain deniability of nuclear weapon capability for years. For a thermonuclear weapon, however, a test is normally required to verify that a particular design will work.

Another possible restraint on proliferation is the fact that all other countries today (with the exception of India, Pakistan, Israel, and North Korea) maintain legal obligations not to develop nuclear weapons as part of their membership in the NPT. If such states abide by the NPT, they have to provide at least three months' notice of any future intention to withdraw from the treaty. Critics, pointing to the covert weapon development activities of NPT members Iraq, North Korea, and Iran, argue that such agreements are made to be broken and that existing measures to verify the peaceful nature of civilian nuclear programs are inadequate to uncover secret weapon facilities. Following the first Gulf war, for example, inspectors with the UN Special Commission on Iraq discovered that Iraq had built nuclear facilities underground and sought to camouflage other facilities through a variety of means. The IAEA's failure to uncover Iran's Natanz facilities before satellite photographs publicly revealed its clandestine nuclear activities shows the continued ability of states to conceal underground facilities, at least in some circumstances. The fear of discovery seems to decrease among states that are already isolated from the international community and doubt the ability of the regime to improve their security.

Supporters of the NPT regime argue that the norm against nuclear development is still strong today among the vast majority of states. Although Japan has faced strong pressures recently— in the wake of North Korea's nuclear test—to move in the direction of a nuclear weapons program, concern about international political censure, trade and economic costs, and the disruption of Japan's military alliance with the United States all act as deterrents to any decision to withdraw from the NPT and develop nuclear weapons. Many other states, as long as international nonproliferation norms are maintained, continue to be affected by similar factors.

The Debate on the Comprehensive Nuclear-Test-Ban Treaty

Although the Limited Test Ban Treaty halted nuclear testing in the atmosphere, at sea, and in space by the early 1960s, the major nuclear powers continued nuclear testing underground until the mid-1990s. Hoping to slow proliferation and limit the development of new classes of nuclear weapons by those already possessing such bombs, in 1996 the key nuclear powers (including the United States and Russia) negotiated the Comprehensive Nuclear-Test-Ban Treaty (CTBT) in Geneva. The CTBT seeks to halt nuclear testing once and for all, banning underground testing and establishing a worldwide verification system that uses multiple-sensor technologies (including seismic monitors and hydro-acoustic stations) to detect any suspect explosions. The Vienna-based CTBT organization is supervising these activities. Stations around the world are already sending verification data, which is available to signatory countries. Russia, France, and Great Britain, among dozens of other states, have now signed and ratified the treaty. Other key signatories have not ratified it, however, including China, Iran, Israel, and the United States. Several other states with nuclear weapons (India, Pakistan, and North Korea) have failed even to sign the agreement. Taken together, forty-four nuclear-capable states are required to sign and ratify the agreement before it becomes legally binding. As of early 2007, only thirty-four had done so.

Supporters of the agreement argue that the CTBT will make it nearly impossible for any additional nuclear power to arise by preventing states from testing their prototype weapon designs. According to this logic, if states cannot test they will be impeded from developing nuclear weapons, particularly more sophisticated designs that are small and light enough for delivery on long-range missiles. In addition, supporters argue that existing nuclear states will be unable to develop new kinds of weapons without additional testing, thereby furthering progress toward the NPT's goal of eventual nuclear disarmament.

However, in 1999 the U.S. Senate voted to reject the CTBT on the grounds that it was not verifiable and that the United States might want to test in the future to ensure the reliability and safety of its nuclear arsenal as it ages. Specifically, some U.S. scientists and military leaders testified that the United States would probably be unable to detect very-low-yield nuclear tests. This deficiency might allow China and Russia to maintain and improve their arsenals and allow new states to conduct first tests while the United States continued to honor its no-test commitment. Supporters argued that challenge inspections permitted under the CTBT could be made against China and Russia; they also pointed out that new nuclear states would not be sophisticated enough to develop small nuclear weapons at the outset. But the dissenters won the day in what was an abbreviated debate led by Senate Republicans opposed to President Bill Clinton's foreign policy objectives. Ironically, the United States had already developed supercomputers to model nuclear tests and had shared this technology with Britain and France to help secure their ratifications. Given the importance of the CTBT to global nonproliferation and the marginal benefits of further testing, a committee appointed by President Clinton and headed by retired General John Shalikashvili concluded in a January 2001 report that ratifying the treaty would serve U.S. security interests.

In the latest U.S. debate about revisiting the treaty vote, however, the George W. Bush administration stated that it opposed the treaty. Its rationale was based less on verification problems than on the claim that the CTBT would limit future U.S. weapon options. Given the shift in U.S. attentions from the established nuclear powers to small nuclear programs in so-called rogue states and terrorist groups using underground facilities, the Bush administration wants to hold open the future option of testing small nuclear devices, including new, more reliable warhead designs and possible earth-penetrating weapons for counterproliferation and counterterrorist missions. Critics of keeping this option open argue that this sends the wrong signal to the world community regarding nuclear weapons and will encourage future testing by other states (such as India, Pakistan, and North Korea), as well as possible defections by states that have already ratified the treaty (such as Russia). The Bush administration also cites concerns about the age of the stockpile and the loss of technical skills in the U.S. nuclear laboratories needed for bomb making if testing is forever halted. The United States currently maintains a nuclear test moratorium, although it continues to conduct periodic subcritical tests of nuclear bomb components (i.e., explosions without a nuclear yield) allowed under the letter (if not the spirit) of the treaty. Thus, it appears that any further U.S. consideration of the CTBT will not occur until at least 2008. Given the continued unwillingness of other states—such as China, India, Pakistan, and North Korea—to ratify the treaty, its legal entry into force is effectively blocked, at least under existing rules. However, the monitoring system established under the treaty is functioning and successfully detected the seismic activity associated with North Korea's low-yield test in October 2006.

Civilian Nuclear Energy Promotion versus Nonproliferation Goals

Since the time of the U.S. Atoms for Peace program in the 1950s, an ongoing dilemma for nuclear nonproliferation efforts has been how to prevent states from developing nuclear weapons while allowing them to enjoy the benefits of civilian nuclear technology. President Dwight D. Eisenhower's Atoms for Peace program helped some 40 countries develop nuclear power and research programs, while receiving pledges from all that such materials and technologies would not be diverted to weapons uses. But the inadequacy of safeguards and the willingness of some countries to cheat on their obligations led to weapons proliferation in a few cases, such as with India. Similar principles, albeit with stricter safeguards requirements, ended up as one of the main principles of the NPT "bargain" in 1968: that all states willing to give up their right to nuclear weapons should be granted access to peaceful nuclear technology, particularly for power generation. Indeed, Article IV of the NPT makes this right explicit, stating, "Nothing in this Treaty shall be interpreted as affecting the inalienable right of all the Parties to the Treaty to develop research, production and use of nuclear energy for peaceful purposes without discrimination." The treaty therefore allows states in good standing to acquire the full nuclear fuel cycle—including nuclear enrichment and reprocessing facilities—as long as they accept safeguards and do not attempt to divert material or technology to a nuclear weapon program.

Unfortunately, by acquiring such technologies, non–nuclear weapon states can develop the capability to produce weapons-grade material, creating conditions of "virtual" nuclear weapon proliferation. Some analysts argue that Japan is in this position today, given its large stockpile of civilian plutonium (about 40 tons), which could be diverted to bomb-making purposes if Japan were to decide to withdraw from the treaty. Much of this material was reprocessed by companies in France and Belgium from Japanese spent reactor fuel and shipped back to Japan. But today Japan has its own reprocessing facilities and can conduct such work on its own. Iran is another country that has sought to achieve a full nuclear fuel cycle capability—the ability to create enriched nuclear fuel. It is still far behind Japan in terms of its ability to create weapons-grade material, and its stockpile of even low-enriched material is still tiny, but Iran's support for terrorist organizations in the Middle East and its president's continued threatening statements about Israel make many countries worried that Iran might act aggressively if it succeeded in building a bomb. The IAEA has noted on several occasions Iran's failure to provide full declarations of its nuclear facilities and access to suspected sites. For this reason, many NPT member states want Iran's nuclear program limited to having to purchase enriched reactor fuel from outside the country. Iran, however, has asserted its right to enrich uranium and develop a full nuclear fuel cycle to ensure its future energy independence. Iran's government has denied any weapons intentions, thus putting NPT members in a quandary. States like Russia want to continue to trade with Iran, as it is an NPT member and cannot be discriminated against according to Article IV of the treaty. The United States and other countries believe providing enrichment technology to Iran raises its capability to produce nuclear weapons. Most NPT states have agreed with the U.S. approach, which is why they—along with Russia—supported a set of political, economic, and military sanctions against Iran in 2006 over gaps in its NPT declarations and its insistence on building a full nuclear fuel cycle. However, the narrow focus of the sanctions allows Russia to continue its ongoing nuclear trade and fails to address activities not directly related to a possible nuclear weapon program. Within the NPT, Brazil is another state that has periodically asserted its right to enrich nuclear fuel, raising concerns among some NPT members regarding its intentions. Thus far, however, Brazil has avoided sanctions on its activities because of its willingness to cooperate with the IAEA.

How exactly are IAEA sanctions agreed upon and applied? According to the NPT, the IAEA can appeal to the UN Security Council to sanction states found in violation of their nuclear safeguards or other NPT agreements (such as diverting material or operating undeclared sites). The dilemma for NPT states is that the denial of technology even to states with blemishes on their safeguards records can weaken the consensus that underlies the treaty among non–nuclear weapon states. But the risk of such trade is that it can bring a potential proliferator closer to the capability of building nuclear weapons. Supplier states (like Russia) have insisted that Iran's rights outweigh the minor violations in its past declarations of its nuclear facilities. Of course, such nuclear trade provides significant cash to Russia's nuclear industry, providing an obvious conflict of interest.

Still, a question arises: Why not amend the NPT to remove the language from Article IV guaranteeing the right of all members to nuclear technology? Why not alter the language to exclude reprocessing and enrichment technologies, or guarantee access only to power-generation technology (which could, in some cases, be non-nuclear)? Negotiating a revision of the treaty to close this loophole, unfortunately, would be very complicated politically, as some countries are already well advanced and are deemed trustworthy. Their activities would have to be grandfathered in, while future capabilities would have to be denied. This sets up another double standard in an agreement that non–nuclear weapon states already believe to be fundamentally discriminatory, because it fails to specify when the nuclear weapon states must give up their nuclear arms. In all likelihood, opening up the NPT for amendment would lead to efforts by non–nuclear weapon states to close what they see as a loophole in Article VI (dealing with nuclear disarmament requirements) and assigning a time-bound framework for states to give up their nuclear weapons. Given the differing interests of states, such difficult negotiations might spell the death-knell of the NPT itself. For this reason, such a route to strengthening the treaty has been avoided thus far. Another option, which has been raised by a number of states and nongovernmental organizations alike, would be to open up an international nuclear "fuel bank" to provide low-enriched reactor fuel on demand to states in good standing with the NPT. Such an initiative would remove incentives for national nuclear fuel programs. Unfortunately, some of the critical states whose behavior the proposal is meant to influence (such as Iran) have opposed this effort as a means of limiting their nuclear independence, setting up a double standard, and violating their stated rights to a full fuel cycle under the NPT.

Another area where the NPT has been challenged in recent years is that of trade by NPT members with parties *outside* the treaty. However, Russia is not alone in acting in what it sees as its broader strategic and commercial interests in trading with countries such as India. After years of taking a hard line against nuclear trade with nonmembers of the NPT—as required by the treaty—the Bush administration changed U.S. policy to allow nuclear trade with India (provided certain conditions are met) in December 2006. The U.S. government stated that India's status as a democracy and its past good behavior in the area of nonproliferation merited such a shift, although some observers saw this move as motivated more by its desire for commercial gain from sales of nuclear technology and political support for its war on terrorism. Russia readily embraced the U.S. shift by expanding its nuclear trade with India. France and other nuclear suppliers welcomed the move as well, thus calling into question the exclusionary clauses of the NPT by making available previously denied nuclear technology. China responded by announcing a similar deal with non-NPT member Pakistan. Given the nuclear tests in both India and Pakistan in 1998, these moves may simply represent an effort to deal with nuclear reality in these countries, but the willingness of major NPT nuclear suppliers to go around the treaty puts its core nonproliferation values and mission in jeopardy. A related problem is the ability of new suppliers outside the NPT, such as Pakistan's A. Q. Khan, to subvert the NPT by trading in bomb-related technologies with NPT members (Corera 2006).

If the recent past is any indication, the NPT faces considerable future challenges. The 2005 NPT Review Conference ended without a consensus document among states on how well the treaty is being implemented and how to move forward to promote nonproliferation objectives in the future (Simpson and Nielsen 2005). Various fissures exist. One is a difference in interpretation between states that want near-term nuclear disarmament by the weapon states and those countries (including the United States) that want stricter controls against new proliferants. Another is a variance between those who want the inalienable right to a full fuel cycle and those who believe such capabilities put states too close to a nuclear weapon. The next NPT Review Conference will take place in 2010, although Preparatory Committee meetings to be held in 2008 and 2009 will likely give some indication of the prospects for success at that conference of members. One solution to avoid future disputes among the parties to the treaty might be to get all of the weapon states (NPT and non-NPT members) into discussions about how to move forward with actual nuclear disarmament (Harrison 2006).

Efforts to Eliminate Nuclear Weapons

Over time, state actors and various nongovernmental organizations have led periodic efforts aimed at complete nuclear disarmament. In the 1950s, leading activists and celebrities headed a strong movement to ban the bomb, focusing public attention on the health threats posed by extensive aboveground nuclear tests being conducted at the time. After the Limited Test Ban Treaty restricted nuclear testing by the United States, the Soviet Union, and Great Britain to underground explosions, the threat of airborne radiation dropped significantly. As a result, the popular movement for nuclear abolition waned.

During the 1960s, state efforts led to the negotiation and signing of the NPT in 1968, which entered into force in 1970. As part of their membership in the NPT, all non–nuclear weapon states pledged to refrain from acquiring and developing nuclear weapons; the five states that had already tested nuclear weapons by 1968 (the United States, Russia, China, France, and Great Britain) pledged to work toward ending the arms race and eventually eliminate their nuclear stockpiles. (France and China, however, refrained from entering the treaty until the 1990s.) The agreement encouraged many states that had once considered developing nuclear weapons (including Australia, Switzerland, and Sweden, among others) to give up past nuclear weapon programs and accept non–nuclear weapon status. Yet there was no enforcement mechanism for the disarmament pledge of the weapon states, except for the weight of world public opinion and the possible threat of dissatisfied member states to give three months' notice and withdraw from the treaty. Recent efforts to sanction North Korea for its nuclear weapons activities, for example, have resulted mainly in compromise gestures among critical trading states (such as China and South Korea), thus limiting the economic impact of the intended nonproliferation sanctions.

Besides the NPT, perhaps the most significant progress toward nuclear elimination during the Cold War was the development of several nuclear-weapon-free zones. These state-led regional efforts created entire continents or other areas where nuclear weapons could not be built, stationed, or tested. These efforts included the Antarctic Treaty (1961), the Outer Space Treaty (1967), the Treaty of Tlatelolco (1967, covering Latin America), and the Seabed Treaty (1971).

During the early 1970s, the détente era between the United States and the Soviet Union led to arms control agreements and the creation of several measures to increase nuclear safety as well as stability during crises. This progress kept protests against nuclear weapons to a minimum during the 1970s, although increasing environmental concerns in the United States led to significant localized efforts to ban nuclear activities at highly contaminated facilities like the Nevada Test Site and the plutonium-processing plant at Rocky Flats, Colorado.

In the 1980s, however, the renewed buildup of U.S. and Soviet nuclear forces stimulated the development of a much broader, popularly led nuclear freeze movement. This effort revived many of the themes of earlier test-ban protests but focused more attention on halting the U.S.-Soviet arms race than on eliminating nuclear weapons entirely. Many religious organizations supported this movement, which received considerable public attention and eventually influenced policymaking in the U.S. Congress. Elsewhere, the continuation of French nuclear testing in the South Pacific revived interest in banning the bomb. In 1985, shared opposition among the countries of this region created the Treaty of Rarotonga, a nuclear-weapon-free zone covering Australia, New Zealand, and a number of island countries, including the surrounding seas. Although the nuclear weapon states did not immediately recognize the zone, continued pressure helped limit nuclear testing and raised international awareness of this ongoing problem. The nuclear freeze movement eventually made some headway in congressional resolutions and restrictions on testing of the Strategic Defense Initiative to prevent a countervailing Soviet buildup. But changes in the Soviet Union under Mikhail Gorbachev began to reduce the need for such a movement, as the thaw in U.S.-Soviet relations that he engineered with President Reagan ushered in a new period of arms control. In the late 1980s, the two super-powers agreed to eliminate their intermediate-range nuclear weapons in Europe and began negotiating deep cuts in strategic nuclear arsenals. However, a fleeting chance to agree to a timeta-ble on total nuclear disarmament at the Reagan-Gorbachev sum-mit in Reykjavik collapsed because of U.S. insistence (and Soviet rejection) of its right to test space-based missile defenses.

After the breakup of the Soviet Union in December 1991, a new movement arose, aimed at complete nuclear elimination. The voluntary nuclear disarmament of South Africa, Belarus, Kazakhstan, and Ukraine gave added support to the concept that the spread of nuclear weapons was not an inevitable process and could indeed be reversed. States in Southeast Asia (Treaty of Bangkok, signed in 1995), Africa (Treaty of Pelindaba, signed in 1996), and Central Asia (Semipalatinsk Treaty, signed in 2006) cre-ated nuclear-weapon-free zone treaties, indicating the continued interest of many countries in establishing regional arrangements to eliminate nuclear weapons and to prevent outside states from introducing them into their areas. Members of the NPT agreed to extend the treaty indefinitely in 1995, obtaining a pledge from the nuclear weapon states that they would make enhanced efforts to reduce their nuclear arms and work toward disarmament.

Other calls for nuclear elimination came from the 1996 Can-berra Commission of international experts who drafted a final document spelling out how step-by-step progress by the nuclear weapon states could achieve eventual nuclear disarmament. Soon after, a group of retired U.S. and Russian military leaders, led by retired U.S. generals Andrew Goodpaster and Lee Butler, issued a letter calling for the phased elimination of nuclear weapons. But the South Asia nuclear tests in May 1998 and the failure of the CTBT to enter into force took the wind out of such popular move-ments. Similarly, the rise of new terrorist threats since 2001, the North Korean nuclear test, and Iran's apparent progress toward a full nuclear fuel cycle seem to have reduced the number of nuclear weapon states interested in pushing the issue forward on a prior-ity basis. Only in the United Kingdom did a serious debate on the possible phasing out of its nuclear arsenal take place in 2006, although largely because of the high cost of building a new generation of nuclear submarines to replace vessels that are nearing the end of their service lives. In late 2006, Prime Minister Tony Blair recommended a plan to go forward with the nuclear modernization program; and, in March 2007, Parliament overwhelmingly voted to rebuild Britain's fleet of four nuclear-armed submarines.

At present, there is no mainstream consensus in the United States about the desirability of near-term nuclear weapon elimination, and few within government circles or the congressional delegations of either the Republican or Democratic parties are pushing for such action. However, as noted previously, some senior retired officials from both parties have called for the United States to back nuclear elimination. Internationally, several states have called for greater progress toward nuclear disarmament and the need to move ahead with the CTBT and a ban on fissile material production worldwide. To date, however, there has been a lack of consensus to carry out such measures.

Efforts in the early twenty-first century to stimulate widespread popular activism for nuclear weapon elimination have not yet gained momentum. Among the populations of the major nuclear weapon states, the issue of nuclear elimination has failed to rank as a high-priority issue, compared to preventing terrorism, reducing crime and corruption, improving national economies, and other issues. Why is the nuclear issue not higher on people's agendas?

Beyond the impact of the terrorist attacks of 11 September 2001 and the war in Iraq in turning international attention elsewhere, there may be several reasons. First, unlike in the early 1960s, underground nuclear testing does not threaten human health. Second, unlike in the 1980s, a massive buildup of nuclear weapons is not taking place in the United States or in Russia. Instead, reductions are moving ahead. What proliferation is taking place—in countries like North Korea and possibly Iran—seems to some observers to merit the retention of nuclear weapons, given the extremist nature of these governments. Others argue that these regimes are not sensitive to deterrence, which reduces the need for nuclear weapons, but, from some vantage points, raises their importance for potential warfighting. The main group calling for nuclear elimination consists of non–nuclear weapon states in the NPT that believe the continued presence of nuclear weapons in some states in and of itself continues to promote proliferation in other countries.

Skeptics of the practicality of nuclear disarmament argue that further proliferation is inevitable, now that the technology has been developed. Indeed, authors like Kenneth Waltz have even argued that some horizontal nuclear proliferation to other countries may be a good thing if it induces caution on these possessor states (Waltz 1981). Once states acquire nuclear weapons, Waltz reasons, they will no longer be insecure and therefore will not need to attack enemies to ensure their security. Of course, this assumes that such states are by nature nonaggressive and their leaders rational. The spread of nuclear weapons to additional countries, moreover, may facilitate the access of nuclear materials to global terrorist organizations, which do not share the vulnerability of nuclear-armed states and therefore may use nuclear materials with abandon.

Despite the lack of serious efforts toward nuclear disarmament among current nuclear weapon states, many former officials and analysts continue to discuss and propose plans for sharp nuclear reductions or even complete nuclear elimination. In looking at first steps, former Johnson, Nixon, and Clinton administration official Morton H. Halperin suggests, "I would argue that it is impossible to come up with a scenario in which we would want to fire anything like 100 nuclear warheads. Therefore, a posture that gives us the capacity to fire up to 100 warheads…is a sufficient number of warheads to have in a posture where the missiles could be fired in hours or days [as opposed to hair trigger alert]" (Kimball 2002, 19). Halperin's plan calls for a "hedge" force of 900 warheads in a reserve stockpile, down from many thousands today. Other analysts suggest a different approach. Nuclear scientist Sidney D. Drell and former U.S. arms control negotiator James E. Goodby propose a plan of reductions that would move Russia and the United States to 500 warheads immediately (with a 500-warhead reserve) and then bring the number of operational weapons down to 250 weapons within a decade, with all tactical forces being eliminated (Drell and Goodby 2005). Notably, former secretaries of State George P. Shultz and Henry Kissinger, former Defense Secretary William Perry, and former Senator Sam Nunn go even farther. In a *Wall Street Journal* column they argue that "reliance on nuclear weapons for [deterrence] is becoming increasingly hazardous and decreasingly effective" (Shultz et al.

2007). For this reason, they suggest instead establishing the objective of "a world free of nuclear weapons and working energetically on the actions required to achieve that goal." Former Soviet leader Mikhail Gorbachev agrees, stating, "It is becoming clearer that nuclear weapons are no longer a means of achieving security" (Gorbachev 2007). He calls for a dialogue involving both the nuclear weapon states and the non–nuclear weapon states to develop a "common concept" for eliminating nuclear weapons.

At the policymaking level, however, critics of nuclear disarmament speak of the difficulty of ensuring that nuclear weapons and related technology could be completely destroyed in a manner that would be verifiable. They argue that one could never be sure that someone, somewhere, is not hiding a bomb in the basement that could be used to coerce other states. It is also impossible to eliminate knowledge of nuclear weapons, which means that the risk of a new bomb program would always exist. Supporters of nuclear abolition, however, make the case that verification by satellite and by airborne radiation detection has greatly improved over the years. They also add that states that attempt to cheat would face great risks of extraordinary international condemnation (and possible collective military action) if they were detected. Still, doubts about verification make state leaders nervous and have therefore prevented progress toward nuclear elimination. In addition, some states continue to believe nuclear arsenals grant them prestige that would vanish if they no longer possessed such powerful weapons. But such considerations may pale if terrorists manage to seize and use one of the weapons that states developed for deterrence against each other.

Final Considerations

Given the unwillingness of any of the existing nuclear weapon states to consider seriously nuclear disarmament in even the intermediate future and the threats posed by new nuclear states, questions about the longevity of the NPT and the international norm against nuclear proliferation have recently been raised by experts and former officials (Campbell, Einhorn, and Reiss 2004). Some are concerned that without greater leadership by major states to strengthen existing nonproliferation mechanisms and to increase verification mechanisms necessary to catch cheaters, much of the progress that has been achieved in nonproliferation will begin to unravel. Skeptics of treaties counter that devoted proliferators will always be able to avoid detection and therefore such agreements only hamstring honest states that comply with the rules. Treaty supporters counter that nonproliferation measures like the NPT have been helpful in raising the costs of proliferation, delaying access to technology, and thereby making it less likely for proliferation to occur.

These debates are likely to continue for several decades. The aim of this chapter has been to outline the main arguments of supporters and opponents regarding different policies and initiatives while offering some solutions for consideration by readers. Overall, a better-informed and more active population could help stimulate more responsible national nuclear policies, fuller discussion in the media, and greater attention by international organizations to these important issues.

References

Ackland, Len. 1999. *Making a Real Killing: Rocky Flats and the Nuclear West*. Albuquerque: University of New Mexico Press.

Afrasiabi, Kaveh L. 2007. "Iran and the Crisis of Disarmament." *Asia Times Online* (January 9). http://www.atimes.com/atimes/Middle _East/IA09Ak07.html.

Albright, David, and Kimberly Kramer. 2004. "Plutonium Watch: Tracking Plutonium Inventories." Institute for Science and Global Security (June). http://www.isis-online.org/global_stocks/plutonium _watch2004.html#table1.

Blair, Bruce. 1995. *Global Zero Alert for Nuclear Forces*. Washington, DC: Brookings Institution.

Brodie, Bernard. 1971. *Strategy in the Missile Age*. 1959. Reprint. Princeton, NJ: Princeton University Press.

Campbell, Kurt M., Robert J. Einhorn, and Mitchell B. Reiss, eds. 2004. *The Nuclear Tipping Point: Why States Reconsider Their Nuclear Choices*. Washington, DC: Brookings Institution.

Corera, Gordon. 2006. *Shopping for Bombs: Nuclear Proliferation, Global Insecurity, and the Rise and Fall of the A.Q. Khan Network*. New York: Oxford University Press.

Drell, Sidney D., and James E. Goodby. 2005. *What Are Nuclear Weapons For? Recommendations for Restructuring U.S. Strategic Nuclear Forces.* Washington, DC: Arms Control Association.

Ferguson, Charles D., William C. Potter, Amy Sands, Leonard S. Spector, and Fred L. Wehling. 2004. *The Four Faces of Nuclear Terrorism.* Monterey, CA: Center for Nonproliferation Studies, Monterey Institute of International Studies.

Gorbachev, Mikhail. 2007. "The Nuclear Threat." *Wall Street Journal,* January 31.

Harrison, Selig S. 2006. "The Forgotten Bargain: Nonproliferation and Nuclear Disarmament." *World Policy Journal* 23 (Fall), pages 1–13.

Kimball, Daryl G. 2002. "Parsing the Nuclear Posture Review." *Arms Control Today* 32 (March), pages 15–21.

Lieber, Keir A., and Daryl G. Press. 2006. "The End of MAD? The Nuclear Dimension of U.S. Primacy." *International Security* 30 (Spring), pages 7–44.

Makhijani, Arjun. 2005. "A Readiness to Harm: Health Effects of the Nuclear Weapons Complexes." *Arms Control Today* 35 (July/August), pages 16–20.

Mueller, John. 1988. "The Essential Irrelevance of Nuclear Weapons: Stability in the Postwar World." *International Security* 13 (Fall), pages 55–79.

Norris, Robert, and Hans Kristensen. 2006. "Global Nuclear Stockpiles, 1945–2006," *Bulletin of the Atomic Scientists* 36 (July/August), pages 64–66.

Perkovich, George. 2006. "The End of the Nonproliferation Regime?" *Current History* 105 (November), pages 355–362.

Reiss, Mitchell. 1995. *Bridled Ambition: Why Countries Constrain Their Nuclear Capabilities.* Washington, DC: Woodrow Wilson Center.

Sagan, Scott D. 1993. *The Limits of Safety: Organizations, Accidents, and Nuclear Weapons.* Princeton, NJ: Princeton University Press.

Sagan, Scott D., and Kenneth N. Waltz. 2002. *The Spread of Nuclear Weapons: A Debate Renewed.* 2nd ed. New York: W. W. Norton.

Schell, Jonathan. 1982. *The Fate of the Earth.* New York: Alfred A. Knopf.

Schelling, Thomas C. 1966. *Arms and Influence.* New Haven, CT: Yale University Press.

Schwartz, Stephen I., ed. 1998. *Atomic Audit: The Costs and Consequences of U.S. Nuclear Weapons since 1940.* Washington, DC: Brookings Institution Press.

Shultz, George P., William J. Perry, Henry A. Kissinger, and Sam Nunn. 2007. "A World Free of Nuclear Weapons." *Wall Street Journal*, January 4.

Simpson, John, and Jenny Nielsen. 2005. "The 2005 NPT Review Conference: Mission Impossible?" *Nonproliferation Review* 12 (July), pages 271–301.

Waltz, Kenneth N. 1981. "The Spread of Nuclear Weapons: More May Be Better." *Adelphi Papers* 171 (Autumn).

3

Special U.S. Issues

As the country with the world's largest economy, most advanced military, and most battle-ready nuclear arsenal, the United States is currently the most influential actor in global nuclear proliferation and nonproliferation affairs. While U.S. officials sometimes downplay the importance of this role, Washington's nuclear policies are scrutinized closely abroad and have a major impact on nuclear efforts elsewhere. One reason is the United States also has a great deal of political clout. What U.S. leaders say about proliferation threats and nonproliferation opportunities is listened to in the rest of the world. Another reason, however, is that some foreign countries and their militaries view the U.S. nuclear arsenal as a potential *threat* that must be deterred. Not all countries, of course, view U.S. nuclear weapons negatively. Indeed, countries allied with the United States have traditionally trusted U.S. nuclear weapons to be the ultimate guarantors of their own security, which has helped reduce proliferation pressures in these countries.

Historically, the United States has led or been a major partner in almost all international nonproliferation efforts, including the formation of the International Atomic Energy Agency (IAEA) in 1957, the signing of the Limited Test Ban Treaty in 1963, the implementation of the Non-Proliferation Treaty (NPT) in 1970, the signing of the 1972 Biological Weapons Convention, the formation of the Missile Technology Control Regime in 1987, the negotiation of the 1993 Chemical Weapons Convention, and the signing of the Comprehensive Nuclear-Test-Ban Treaty in 1996. Without the

United States, international nonproliferation mechanisms would be nowhere near as advanced as they are today.

This chapter seeks to explain the many facets of the current U.S. approach to nuclear weapons and nonproliferation. While the United States has done more than any other country to halt the spread of such weapons, it also continues to show the rest of the world how much it values its nuclear arsenal for purposes of defense and deterrence. This contradiction poses challenges to the effectiveness and credibility of U.S. nonproliferation efforts.

This chapter begins with a brief summary of the current status of the U.S. nuclear arsenal and U.S. policies toward nuclear weapons, including the question of deterrence. It then discusses contemporary U.S. nonproliferation efforts, examining both domestic and international aspects. Such topics as intelligence, verification, missile defenses, nuclear-weapon-free zones, and the role of public opinion are also covered.

Since 2001, policies followed during the George W. Bush administration have put less of an emphasis on formal international treaties. Instead, the administration has backed more flexible approaches such as the Proliferation Security Initiative and other voluntary mechanisms. It has also supported unprecedented nuclear cooperation agreements with countries like India, which remain outside the NPT. The question remains whether recent U.S. actions will enhance or undermine global nonproliferation regimes, as many other countries continue to prefer stronger and more comprehensive nonproliferation treaties, despite the required effort to negotiate and verify them.

For Americans, nonproliferation issues are not listed on national election ballots. But U.S. elected representatives are often required to take a stand on nuclear issues. Members of the U.S. Congress, for example, must vote on yearly budgets that pay for the U.S. nuclear infrastructure, including its production facilities, laboratories, and military bases. The U.S. Senate must also approve any formal treaty the president negotiates in the nonproliferation field. Finally, the president is the ultimate authority who would decide about the possible use of nuclear weapons in a time of war and who, with the help of top civilian and military leaders, sets U.S. policy regarding the size of the nuclear stockpile and the doctrine governing its use. Thus, it is important for all citizens, especially those of voting age, to understand these issues, form opinions, and support candidates who represent their particular views about what kind of nuclear policy they would prefer to see.

The Status of the U.S. Nuclear Weapons Complex

The U.S. nuclear infrastructure is a vast and geographically dispersed network of facilities. Although smaller than during the Cold War, it still includes several major production and design locations, a range of nuclear weapon storage sites, and about a dozen military bases in the United States and abroad where nuclear weapons are deployed in submarines, on bombers, and atop ballistic missiles.

The main U.S. nuclear weapon design facilities are the Los Alamos National Laboratory and Sandia National Laboratories, both in New Mexico, and the Lawrence Livermore National Laboratory in California. They employ 26,000 people and have a combined budget of nearly $6 billion. Other key facilities in the current nuclear complex include production facilities (such as the Y-12 Plant at Oak Ridge in Tennessee and the Savannah River Site in South Carolina) and weapons assembly and disassembly plants (such as Pantex in Texas, for nuclear components, and the Kansas City Plant for nonnuclear assemblies). Large U.S. nuclear weapons storage facilities include the Bangor nuclear submarine base in Washington State, the Kings Bay nuclear submarine base in Georgia, the Minot Air Force base in North Dakota, the Barksdale Air Force base in Louisiana, and the Kirtland Air Force base in New Mexico (Schwartz 1998).

The overall cost of operating the U.S. nuclear arsenal is approximately $40 billion per year (Norris, Kristensen, and Paine 2004). Much of the cost relates to expenses for the military personnel, scientists, and technologies required to keep the weapons safe, secure, and deliverable (if needed). A critical issue being discussed today within the U.S. nuclear complex is the future of the arsenal and its associated workforce, both of which are aging. Accordingly, there has been an extensive effort to assess the reliability of U.S. nuclear weapons. Known as the Stockpile Stewardship Program, its associated activities have spent an average of

$5 billion per year since the mid-1990s on maintaining the U.S. weapons stockpile—in fact, more than was spent each year during the Cold War. These costs are expected to increase dramatically if the United States moves forward with a controversial program known as the Reliable Replacement Warhead (RRW) program. The purpose behind the RRW program is threefold: (1) to increase the reliability of older-generation nuclear weapons, (2) to allow the United States to reduce its arsenal further by "modernizing" its remaining weapons, and (3) to provide work for a new generation of nuclear weapons complex employees, thus keeping the nuclear laboratories open.

Recent technical studies have shown that U.S. nuclear weapons are safe and reliable. What does deteriorate over time within these weapons, however, is their supply of tritium: the hydrogen isotope that "boosts" the power of thermonuclear weapons. Critics argue that some of the work to enhance the reliability of U.S. warheads is unnecessary, as there is no question that older weapons will detonate, albeit at a slightly lower yield (Norris, Kristensen, and Paine 2004). However, increased accuracy of the missiles makes the yield less important. Nevertheless, two programs are in the works to address the tritium issue. First, tritium is being made available during the process of dismantling some older weapons, providing a five-year tritium reserve as of 2007. Second, there is a new U.S. program to create more tritium by irradiating materials at the Watts Bar nuclear plant in Tennessee. This process is underway, and a processing plant will be built in South Carolina to separate and create new tritium for future weapons.

The goal of the proposed RRW program is to remove all old warheads from service and create a single, more modern warhead design that could be easily serviced and modified to the specific nuclear yield (or force) needed. Laboratory supporters argue that this will increase the arsenal's safety and reliability, while also training a new generation of nuclear workers. In March 2007, the Department of Energy announced that a contract for the first phase of the RRW program—design of a new submarine-based warhead—would be based at Lawrence Livermore National Laboratory (Koch 2007). But rival Los Alamos National Laboratories may still be in the running for other contracts, as Congress seems interested in trying to prevent the closure of either laboratory by dividing the work between them (Broad, Sanger, and Shanker 2007). Critics argue that the total program—estimated to cost at least $100 billion—is too expensive and militarily unnecessary, given the potency of the nuclear material in existing weapons. Questions also remain as to whether the final design will require further nuclear testing (or not) to prove its own reliability.

Questions that remain for the U.S. nuclear arsenal include the following: How long should the United States maintain multiple weapon-design facilities now that the Cold War is over? How should the United States deal with the declining availability of scientists and technicians who are capable of constructing nuclear weapons? What are the advantages (or possible disadvantages) of further consolidating U.S. nuclear weapons into fewer sites (including repatriating tactical nuclear weapons in Europe)? Should absolute nuclear yield or simply assurance of a nuclear detonation be the future measure of reliability for the U.S. arsenal? And might the United States use advanced, precision-guided conventional munitions to eventually replace nuclear arms?

U.S. Nuclear Weapons Policy

U.S. policies on nuclear weapons at any given time represent a number of competing influences. These include the preferences of the White House, the U.S. Defense Department, the Department of Energy (including the weapons laboratories), the State Department, the intelligence community, Congress, the expert community, and, to a lesser extent, the American public. During the 1960s, Secretary of Defense Robert McNamara established the U.S. policy of mutually assured destruction, meaning that the country should maintain the ability to ensure that it could fire a devastating second strike after any Soviet attack that would make a first strike unthinkable to Moscow. The policy eschewed the notion of U.S. (or Soviet) strategic superiority and instead adopted the underlying rationale of nuclear deterrence: deploying nuclear weapons to *prevent* their use by any other country against the United States. For this purpose, the United States maintained thousands of nuclear weapons during the Cold War on a ready-alert status for possible use against the Soviet Union or China.

Fortunately, after 1945, the United States never used any of these weapons. Today, the United States continues to possess more than 9,000 nuclear weapons of various sizes, although current plans will cut this number approximately in half by 2012.

More than 5,000 are long-range strategic weapons deployed in a ready-to-use status, although this number will drop to between 1,700 and 2,200 to meet the terms of the 2002 Moscow Treaty.

Outside the continental United States, several hundred U.S. tactical nuclear weapons are stationed at air bases in Belgium, Germany (two locations), Italy (two locations), the Netherlands, Turkey, and the United Kingdom (Woolf 2006). These weapons have been the subject of debate because of the perceived unlikelihood of a major war in Europe that would require nuclear weapons. There is also a lack of clarity as to which side (the United States or its North Atlantic Treaty Organization [NATO] allies) wants these weapons retained in Europe. During the Cold War, the argument was that these weapons were needed to protect Western Europe against a major Soviet land offensive, given Moscow's superiority in large battle tanks. Tactical nuclear weapons, it was believed, would stave off such an attack until larger numbers of U.S. troops could arrive on the continent. Since the overthrow of Eastern Europe's communist governments in 1989 and the breakup of the Soviet Union in 1991, the rationale for these U.S. tactical nuclear weapons seems to have disappeared—yet the weapons remain. Supporters argue that they help provide NATO with a deterrent capability against possible aggression by any state, including Russia or others, or non-state actors that might be tempted to use weapons of mass destruction (WMD). They also believe these weapons help keep U.S. allies in Europe from developing their own nuclear weapons. Opponents say these forces have no military utility, present a danger in case of terrorist attack on their storage facilities, and prevent an agreement with Russia to dismantle its even larger stockpile of tactical nuclear weapons, now estimated at around 6,000 warheads. Critics also argue that U.S. precision-guided conventional weapons now make these smaller nuclear forces redundant and unnecessary (Gormley 2006).

Despite the presence of thousands of nuclear weapons in the U.S. arsenal, the United States has pledged itself to eventual nuclear disarmament according to the NPT (specifically, Article VI). In addition, the U.S. government under both presidents Bill Clinton and George W. Bush has stated that nuclear nonproliferation is one of its top national security priorities. For these reasons, there are some inherent tensions in U.S. nuclear policies, which are similar to the policies of the other four states that are members of the NPT and yet still possess nuclear weapons (Russia, China, Britain, and France).

Official U.S. nuclear weapons policies are regularly enunciated by the U.S. government in nuclear posture reviews and in the official national security strategy. During the Clinton administration, the government issued a 1994 review that was intended as a means of reassessing the role of nuclear weapons after the end of the Cold War. However, internal feuds between reform-minded civilian officials and more conservative uniformed military personnel resulted in a compromise document that merely reasserted the need for nuclear weapons and the existing nuclear triad for deterrence (and possible use in conflict), albeit with lower numbers than before. Attempts by civilian officials to review the U.S. nuclear war plan—or the Single Integrated Operational Plan—were rebuffed, suggesting that, even in the United States, there are limits to civilian control over the military, at least in regard to the specifics of nuclear war planning (Nolan 1999). A civilian proposal to consider moving from a triad of nuclear forces (based on submarines, bombers, and missiles) to a smaller monad force (based only on submarines) also failed to move forward.

In 2001, the Bush administration undertook a much more ambitious review of U.S. nuclear forces and their role, although with a different focus and intention. The December 2001 Nuclear Posture Review announced a shift from the traditional triad to a new "triad" of defenses, offenses (both nuclear and conventional), and a reinvigorated defense research and development infrastructure (including for nuclear weapons). The document noted U.S. efforts to reduce reliance on nuclear weapons, although critics argued that the specifics of the report lowered the bar for nuclear use, setting off a stormy debate. Unlike past posture reviews, which named no specific adversaries that might be targeted with nuclear weapons besides Russia and China, the 2001 Nuclear Posture Review listed five other states (Iran, Iraq, Libya, North Korea, and Syria) even though—at the time—none of these states was believed to possess nuclear weapons. This shift in the announced U.S. targeting strategy broke with NPT principles stating that countries within the treaty that do not possess nuclear weapons should not be targeted by nuclear states (a so-called "negative" security guarantee) (Kimball 2002). Indeed, the 2001 Nuclear Posture Review reasserted a number of scenarios in which Washington might actually use such forces and stated, "These nuclear capabilities possess unique properties that give the United States options to hold at risk classes of targets important to achieve strategic and political objectives" (GlobalSecurity.org 2002). However, the document also recognized the increasing role of precision-guided conventional munitions in replacing nuclear weapons for some missions and the growing role of missile defenses in improving deterrence and making some forms of nuclear retaliation unnecessary (particularly when missile defenses are used against short- to medium-range missiles).

But the document disappointed those critics looking for some clearer U.S. commitment to eventual nuclear disarmament. Instead, the new policy noted that a "responsive nuclear sector" is "indispensable" for the United States. Part of the rationale for the revitalized infrastructure was the lower number of deployed nuclear weapons, compared with Cold War numbers, and the need to keep a "hedge" force and reconstitution capability in place should relations with existing adversaries or friends deteriorate and new nuclear deployments become necessary. The 2001 Nuclear Posture Review described nuclear weapons as having four fundamental missions: assurance (of friends and allies), dissuasion (of adversaries), deterrence (of attacks on U.S. and allied forces), and defeat (of the adversary, in case of war).

One of the early elements of the Bush administration's strategy was the planned development of nuclear bunker buster bombs for attacking deeply buried WMD targets in facilities operated by rogue states or terrorist groups. The administration argued that conventional weapons lacked the power to destroy such sites and called for research on low-yield nuclear options. Opponents of the plan cited the risk to the nonproliferation regime of U.S. development of new nuclear weapons, the lowering of the threshold to future nuclear use, and the unlikelihood that a low-yield weapon could do the job. Scientists who examined the problem indicated that high-yield nuclear weapons—which would release large amounts of radioactive fallout—would likely be needed and that new nuclear testing might also be necessary to prove the design. For these reasons, and because of concern over international political implications if the United States deployed such weapons, the U.S. Congress stopped the program by denying critical funding. Instead, funding was provided for a similar effort using powerful conventional weapons.

The most recent U.S. National Security Strategy—an overarching document required of the government every four years—outlines a number of specific roles and missions for nuclear weapons, while emphasizing the simultaneous importance of nuclear nonproliferation and, if necessary, counterproliferation to U.S. national interests (White House 2006). The document reemphasizes the Bush administration's policy to "act preemptively in exercising our inherent right of self-defense," although it notes U.S. preference for "nonmilitary actions." In addition, the 2006 policy statement outlines the need for *proactive counterproliferation efforts* to defend against and defeat WMD and missile threats before they are unleashed." Some of the specific means noted in the National Security Strategy include ballistic missile defense, the Proliferation Security Initiative (aimed at intercepting international shipments of WMD materials), and implementation of United Nations (UN) Security Council Resolution 1540 (aimed at enhancing domestic WMD protections worldwide and criminalizing WMD possession by non-state actors).

But the Bush administration's support for stricter nuclear controls has contained an important exception: states that are friendly to the United States. India, Israel, and Pakistan, key allies in the U.S. war on terrorism, have been exempted from pressure to disarm. In India's case, the administration has recently gone a step further to allow and encourage U.S. technical cooperation, at least in the nuclear power sector, despite the violation of the NPT that this action represents. Although long critical of past Russian sales of nuclear technology to India, the Bush administration signed new legislation in December 2006 allowing the same kind of cooperation the United States had once criticized. The U.S. government argued that it was only recognizing the reality of the Indian nuclear arsenal and pointed to India's strong nonproliferation record and its status as the world's largest democracy. It put the nuclear deal in the context of a new "strategic partnership" with India (Carter 2006). This shift in policy, however, goes directly against established principles under the NPT regime, which treat nuclear weapons and proliferation as the problem, not the politics of particular regimes. The NPT's universalist approach, critics of the deal argue, is crucial to rallying international opinion against all proliferators and states that attempt to remain outside the NPT. Philosophically, the new U.S. approach coincides with broader concepts such as "democratic peace theory," which posits that democracies are responsible actors and don't go to war with one another; therefore, they can be trusted with nuclear weapons (Perkovich 2006). From this perspective, the Bush administration has argued, there is no risk in tacitly accepting India's nuclear arsenal and allowing U.S. nuclear trade with this former pariah state to the NPT. Some analysts make the point in this regard that the negative impact of the deal on the nonproliferation regime has been overstated (Carter 2006). Members of Congress agreed overwhelmingly with this perspective in voting for the deal, although largely to promote stronger economic and military ties with India. Critics, however, argue that this double standard weakens the regime and incentives by nuclear-capable states within it to maintain their antiweapons pledges.

To make the nuclear deal more palatable within India, the Bush administration agreed that only selected "civilian" facilities would be subjected to IAEA safeguards. Thus, the agreement exempted a large number of designated "military" facilities, as in the NPT nuclear weapon states, from safeguards. This means India can continue to produce as much enriched material as it wants for weapons purposes from the non-safeguarded facilities. However, the United States will have to seek a waiver from the groups to go forward with any transfers of nuclear technology to India if it wants to do so without violating the group's guidelines, which require full-scope safeguards (and inspection rights) on all of a recipient country's nuclear facilities. While critics of the agreement have condemned its weakening of the NPT regime, many nuclear supplier countries have either supported the U.S.-Indian deal or at least failed to criticize it, likely because of their own desire to get a share of India's expanding nuclear energy market. Russia, for example, has announced plans to build four new nuclear reactors in India. But the contradiction between nonproliferation and other national interests makes the U.S.-Indian deal another example of a case in which broader policy concerns have trumped efforts to combat proliferation.

Treaties and Verification

As noted previously, a key shift under the Bush administration has been an effort to move away from formal treaties in the realm of international nonproliferation policy and instead to rely more on flexible, informal arrangements involving "coalitions of the willing" (or countries sharing U.S. perspectives on particular proliferation problems). This preference can be seen in the U.S. withdrawal from the Anti-Ballistic Missile (ABM) Treaty, its decision to quit talks on a strengthened inspection protocol for the Biological and Toxin Weapons Convention in 2001, its policy of refusing to consider ratifying the Comprehensive Nuclear-Test-Ban Treaty, and its decision to leave any weapons elimination requirements (and associated verification measures) out of the 2002 Moscow Treaty. These policies mark a sharp break with past U.S. practices.

This does not mean the Bush administration is opposed to international cooperation or multilateral nonproliferation efforts. However, its aim has been to streamline the process of agreement and to create action-oriented mechanisms that do not require cumbersome multinational bureaucracies, lengthy negotiations, and difficult decision-making structures where a small number of states can block productive and timely action. Some of the new organizations and measures supported by the Bush administration have included the Proliferation Security Initiative (to intercept WMD materials and technologies in transit), the Group of Eight–led Global Partnership Against the Spread of Weapons of Mass Destruction (to safeguard nuclear facilities and consolidate material), the Global Threat Reduction Initiative (to limit and secure highly enriched uranium worldwide), the Six-Party Talks (with North Korea), and UN Security Council Resolution 1540. Although some of these U.S.-led efforts have been criticized by traditional supporters of more formal international arrangements, on balance, these initiatives have helped plug a number of gaps in existing nonproliferation regimes. At the same time, weakened U.S. support for international treaties and verification mechanisms has made some countries skeptical of U.S. intentions regarding universalist (as opposed to selectively applied) nonproliferation objectives.

Since the 1990s, one of the main goals of the U.S. government in the field of international nonproliferation policy has been negotiating a fissile material cutoff treaty. This measure would halt production of plutonium and highly enriched uranium (HEU) as a means of preventing the further construction of nuclear weapons and reducing possible terrorist access to bomb-making material. A number of countries with smaller nuclear arsenals (such as India and China) have long opposed such a treaty, in part because most proposals would allow large, existing U.S. and Russian stockpiles of fissile material to be maintained, giving them a permanent nuclear advantage. One of the more complicated aspects of the treaty's negotiation has long been how the shutdown of production would be verified. In 2004, the Bush administration announced a major shift in U.S. policy by dropping all requirements for verification (Arms Control Association 2004). The rationale behind this change in approach was to avoid the long negotiation process necessary for such rules to be agreed upon, the costs of inspections in countries where there was no concern about proliferation, and the possibly complex politics of access to sites requiring inspection. Moreover, even without international measures, the United States could still provide a reasonable level of verification using its own national technical means (e.g., satellites, air sampling). Many foreign governments rejected these arguments as weakening international enforcement mechanisms and lessening means of putting *collective* pressure on states violating international agreements.

U.S. Missile Defenses and Efforts to Defend against Nuclear Attacks

Since the dawn of the nuclear age, in part because of its faith in the power of technology, the United States has been one of the leaders in pursuing missile defenses in the hope of constructing a shield against potential attacks. In 1962, the United States and the then Soviet Union tested nuclear-tipped ABM defenses in space. While these weapons proved capable of destroying incoming missiles, they also had highly damaging effects on satellites and on ground-based radars. One such test, Starfish Prime in July 1962, shorted out the power grid on the island of Oahu and permanently disabled at least six orbiting satellites, including U.S. communications and photo-reconnaissance spacecraft, as well as British and Soviet satellites. The electromagnetic pulse radiation from the blasts also made whole regions of space dangerous for human spaceflight. Thus, in 1963, the United States and the Soviet

Union ceased nuclear testing in space as part of the Limited Test Ban Treaty.

But the treaty did not make it illegal to deploy defenses using nuclear weapons. The United States moved forward with developing and deploying both nuclear-tipped antisatellite weapons on Johnston Island (an atoll located between the Hawaiian and the Marshall Islands) and a nuclear-tipped ABM system, as did the Soviet Union. Tests of their warheads, however, had to be conducted underground. One ABM-related test (called Cannikin) in November 1971 exploded a huge 5-megaton nuclear weapon under the island of Amchitka off the coast of Alaska (Kohlhoff 2002). The blast caused a major seismic tremor and considerable environmental damage to the island, stimulating antinuclear activists to form the Greenpeace organization. By the early 1970s, the United States decided to dismantle its antisatellite system, given the costs and its likely collateral damage to valuable space assets, such as reconnaissance and communications satellites. In 1975, however, the U.S. Air Force deployed 100 nuclear-tipped ABM interceptors at Grand Forks, North Dakota, in the so-called Safeguard system. The original goal of this project was to stop the few existing Chinese nuclear-tipped missiles as well as possible limited Soviet strikes. However, the massive numbers of Soviet nuclear weapons by the mid-1970s, the high costs of the system, and the likelihood that detonating nuclear weapons above Safeguard's radars would "blind" them with electromagnetic pulse radiation caused Congress to cancel the system just a few months after it achieved operational status, despite the U.S. expenditure of $12 billion (Schwartz 1998).

Although interest in missile defenses waned for the next several years, the rise of Soviet deployment of multiple warhead missiles (especially the large SS-18 missile) caused some U.S. political figures and military leaders to worry about a possible Soviet first strike against the United States. By the early 1980s, advances in computer technology and real-time space tracking and communications led some scientists and the Ronald Reagan administration to begin a major push in 1983 to develop missile defenses via the so-called Strategic Defense Initiative (SDI), popularly known as "Star Wars." The idea was to build a space-based missile shield that would intercept more than a thousand Soviet missiles in their boost phase and destroy them before they could deploy their multiple warheads. President Reagan pledged to share the system eventually with the Soviet Union and use it to work toward the total elimination of nuclear weapons. (Indeed, the president's strong commitment to test and deploy the SDI system prevented a deal for complete nuclear disarmament from being reached with the Soviet Union at the Reykjavik summit in 1986.) But the technological hurdles in terms of weapons, sensors, and space-launch capabilities, as well as the system's extremely high cost, prevented it from moving forward. Congressional Democratic leaders were also concerned about the implications of U.S. violation of the ABM Treaty, which might have resulted in a further buildup of Soviet offensive arms. In the end, changes in Soviet foreign policy under Mikhail Gorbachev rendered a Soviet attack much less likely, reducing the perceived need for the defensive system. The effort was finally scaled back under President George H. W. Bush and limited to a small continuing research program.

In the 1990s, missile defense supporters (primarily conservative Republican members of Congress and some scientists in the U.S. weapons laboratories) again began to push for renewed funding and deployment. First, in the wake of the 1990–1991 Gulf War, supporters lobbied successfully for further research on shorter-range theater missile defenses to protect U.S. allies and U.S. troops in the field. Second, in 1999, the Republican-led Congress approved legislation requiring the deployment of national missile defenses against the possible threat of a North Korean, Iraqi, or other rogue-state attack using ballistic missiles as soon as the technology was available. The goal was no longer the interception of more than a thousand Soviet missiles, as envisioned during the Reagan years, but only tens of missiles that a small, new nuclear power might launch. Although critics pointed out that such countries still lacked long-range missiles, supporters cited the possibility that they might buy foreign technology to speed up their programs, thus leaving the United States unprepared. However, in 2000, the Clinton administration decided that the technology to "hit a bullet with a bullet" had still not been proven and opted not to deploy such a system.

The George W. Bush administration came into office with a different philosophy in 2001. Bush's advisers believed the seriousness of the emerging missile threat merited immediate deployment of missile defenses in Alaska and California, whether or not the technology had been fully tested. They argued that the United States needed some defense and could learn as it went along, despite the higher financial costs of such an approach. After withdrawing from the ABM Treaty in 2002, the Bush administration moved forward to deploy a handful of interceptors in Alaska and California by the end of the president's first term in January 2005. These were supplemented by additional Aegis-system interceptors stationed on U.S. destroyers at sea. Although the Pentagon had declined to declare the missile defense system operational by spring 2007—because of inadequate testing—the administration and Congress continued to provide significant funding for the program to continue its development. Eventually, the administration's plan is to develop an integrated system of short-, medium-, and long-range defenses dispersed in forward locations on the territories of allies in Asia and Europe (including possibly Poland and the Czech Republic), at sea, in space, and in the United States. The cost of these deployments is still uncertain, and the technologies are still under development, particularly in regard to space-based systems.

Critics of missile defenses point to the ability of adversarial states to use so-called penetration aids dispersed by their missiles (such as metal chaff, balloon decoys, and small submunitions) to trick the defenses, as well as the possibility of using alternative delivery means, such as smuggling a weapon into the United States or delivering it via ship or small aircraft, thus avoiding the missile defense system. They argue that the calculus will always favor the attacking side, especially in terms of cost. Moreover, critics say that terrorists are particularly unlikely to use expensive and easily traceable ballistic missiles as their delivery system of choice. The Bush administration has argued that missile defenses—even ones that currently have limited operational value—provide some level of deterrence and encourage potential adversaries to give up their missile programs. To date, despite the initial U.S. missile defense deployment, North Korea and Iran have continued to develop their missile systems. Meanwhile, China's test of a kinetic-kill antisatellite weapon in January 2007 suggests that U.S. pursuit of robust missile defenses may have encouraged a reaction among foreign military space programs.

Overall, then, the prospect of making long-range offensive missiles obsolete through defenses seems remote. The best that is likely to be accomplished through existing missile defense efforts seems to be partial effectiveness against certain types of missile attack to supplement other forms of defense and diplomacy.

Of course, a more reliable route to improve chances for missile defense might be to achieve international agreements for further cuts in offensive weapons. But the level of trust necessary for such arms control agreements does not yet exist, and deep cuts are not being pursued seriously by leading world powers (Harrison 2006). Thus, the short-term conclusion is that missile defenses will go forward, but are unlikely to transform existing U.S. vulnerabilities to nuclear attack.

Intelligence, Nuclear Proliferation, and Counterproliferation

Experts agree that a critical component of any effective U.S. strategy to prevent nuclear proliferation is accurate and timely intelligence. Unfortunately, despite annual intelligence-gathering expenditures in the tens of billions of dollars, the United States has historically proven to have had a relatively poor record (Richelsen 2006). An exhaustive 1,000-page report issued in October 2004 by Charles Duelfer, the Central Intelligence Agency's (CIA) special advisor on Iraq's WMD, examined the WMD evidence used to justify the 2003 U.S. invasion. The study concluded that Saddam Hussein's government had no WMD on its territory before the invasion and had very little capability to reconstitute its pre-1991 capabilities because of the effectiveness of UN sanctions and inspections (Duelfer 2004). In other words, despite rallying the U.S. government, the American public, and the international community around the immediate threat posed by Iraq's WMD programs, the United States had gotten the facts wrong. Specifically, regarding nuclear enrichment and weapons research, the Duelfer Report found "no evidence to suggest concerted efforts to restart the program" in more than decade. The Iraqi biological weapons program had also remained largely moribund. Only in the chemical weapons area did Iraq appear to have some intention of reviving the program, although the report stated (based on extensive interviews with Iraqi scientists and officials) that the purpose of that effort was for future defense needs against Iran, not for use against the United States. Thus, the CIA's extensive search after the war to locate WMD in Iraq and to identify ongoing WMD programs had come up largely empty-handed.

To come to grips with the problem of U.S. intelligence gathering in the area of WMD technologies, the White House commissioned a special, bipartisan group of experts to examine U.S. intelligence collection practices. The commission's report, issued in March 2005, had a number of troubling conclusions. In a sharp critique of the quality of U.S. intelligence it stated, "Across the board, the Intelligence Community knows disturbingly little about the nuclear programs of many of the world's most dangerous actors" (Commission on the Intelligence Capabilities of the United States Regarding Weapons of Mass Destruction 2005). Strikingly, it commented, "In some cases, it knows less now than it did five or ten years ago." Overall, the commissioners (mainly former high-ranking government officials and members of Congress) described the intelligence community (including the CIA, the Defense Intelligence Agency, the National Security Agency, the National Reconnaissance Office, and other organizations) as "fragmented, loosely managed, and poorly coordinated." It called on the U.S. government to improve training of critical language and relevant area studies skills in organizations still populated heavily by Russian-language experts trained in Cold War techniques. It cited the lack of rigorous analysis of data collected as well, partly because of the absence of relevant knowledge about the diverse set of regionally based threats the United States now faces. In addition, the report noted the need to improve the use of technology for dealing with a new and "ever-changing" threat environment, rather than relying on old signals intelligence and photo-intelligence techniques that were better suited for dealing with the Soviet Union. The commissioners highlighted new computer-related technologies, WMD sampling mechanisms, and technical means of overcoming deception and denial strategies of adversaries trying to disguise or hide WMD facilities among areas requiring critical improvements. Some analysts argue, however, that reforms will not succeed unless senior U.S. officials stop "cherry-picking" intelligence data in a manner that emphasizes political criteria over factual accuracy (Pillar 2006).

Another reason for the increased importance of accurate and timely intelligence is the dispersed nature of the WMD threat in the twenty-first century, given the presence of new technologies for information distribution (such as fax machines, electronic mail, cell phones, and the Internet). New non-state actors, which are often harder to identify and track compared with nation-states, also play a more important role in the evolving threat environment than in the past. Nevertheless, state actors (such as Iran and North Korea) still remain objects of WMD concern and focus. Thus, various aspects of this increasingly complex problem require continued attention from the intelligence community. At the same time, evidence from the run-up to the 2003 Iraq war suggests that other U.S. political actors outside the executive branch (the White House and the government's official defense and intelligence agencies) need to ask more critical questions when assessing intelligence information provided to them. Many members of Congress and the U.S. media tended to support information coming out of the government uncritically, rather than analyzing it carefully. While this problem may continue, because of the inherent limits of using information in the political realm whose source and credibility remains (in some cases) classified, the experience of the Iraq War should provide a sobering reminder to U.S. policymakers of the importance of accuracy in matters of nonproliferation and, especially, military counterproliferation. Otherwise, the United States will find it difficult to lead other international efforts in the future.

U.S. Policy toward New Nuclear-Weapon-Free Zones

One area of U.S. nuclear policy that has frustrated many foreign observers, as well as some domestic supporters of nonproliferation efforts, relates to the U.S. policies toward nuclear-weapon-free zones. These regional treaties are typically agreements to adopt nonproliferation measures that are even stronger than those incorporated in the NPT. That treaty allowed foreign nuclear weapons to be stationed on a country's territory (in part because U.S. and Soviet nuclear weapons were already deployed in many client states in 1968) and permitted nuclear devices to be tested for peaceful purposes (originally to allow possible civil excavation using nuclear weapons, a practice that is now widely discredited on safety grounds). Today, states are giving up these rights in a number of areas of the world to improve regional security. Although the United States has pledged in various international nonproliferation meetings, including the 1995 NPT Review and Extension Conference, to support the formation of nuclear-weapon-free zones voluntarily arrived at by states in particular regions, in fact, under both the Clinton and current (at the time of publication) Bush administrations, Washington has placed its self-proclaimed rights to transit nuclear weapons internationally ahead of a number of zone treaties. The U.S. argument is that its nuclear forces are critical to the safety of allies and friends around the world and therefore it should be able to move weapons around the world's oceans and airspace when they are needed in particular regions. In practice, this mostly involves the transit of nuclear submarines armed with ballistic missiles, as U.S. nuclear-armed bombers and missiles are rarely (if ever) deployed abroad now, with the exception of the U.S. weapons in Europe. This policy and a restriction against use of nuclear weapons in (or from) nuclear-weapon-free zones has kept the United States (along with the other four NPT-recognized nuclear weapon states) from supporting the Bangkok Treaty in Southeast Asia. States in this treaty have given up the right to nuclear weapons and have pledged not to allow any foreign nuclear weapons to be stationed on their territories. They also retain rights under the treaty to deny foreign ships carrying nuclear weapons passage through their territorial waters. One such waterway within the Southeast Asian zone is the strategic Strait of Malacca, a key transit point for U.S. military vessels moving from the South China Sea to the Indian Ocean. Instead of welcoming this effort to prohibit nuclear weapons, Washington and other nuclear capitals continue to put their own nuclear rights above their non-proliferation goals.

The United States (joined by France and Britain) has also voiced its opposition to the 2006 Central Asian Nuclear-Weapon-Free Zone (the Semipalatinsk Treaty). This zone brings together the five former Soviet states of Central Asia, which together suffered tremendous environmental and human health damage from Soviet nuclear mining, milling, and especially testing before 1991. It represents an important new buffer zone without nuclear weapons in a region of the world populated by a number of nuclear-armed states: India, Pakistan, China, and Russia. Nevertheless, Washington has opposed the agreement because of an ambiguous clause in the treaty that recognizes the existence of prior security agreements that might be interpreted to allow Russia to reintroduce nuclear weapons into the zone in the future. States in the region, however, say the clause was put in mostly for political reasons and that Russia's redeployment of nuclear weapons is ruled out by current national policies of the Central Asian governments. A clause allowing each state in the region to determine whether to allow the transit of nuclear weapons through its territory is already part of the treaty at the insistence of the United States and other NPT weapon states. Thus, despite U.S. support for international non-proliferation objectives, Washington's policies are sometimes at odds with these goals.

U.S. Public Opinion and Nuclear Weapons

Public participation in nuclear decision making tends to be tied closely to fears of personal health and safety. When such conditions are not acute, members of Congress, executive branch officials (including the president), and military leaders tend to dominate nuclear policies with relatively little outside influence—except international events. Accordingly, U.S. public participation in nuclear weapons policy has declined significantly from its high points in the late 1950s and early 1960s, when atmospheric nuclear testing threatened human health, and during the early 1980s, when fear of the resumption of the U.S.-Soviet nuclear arms race motivated thousands of Americans and a number of U.S. cities to join the nuclear freeze movement. While there is public concern about North Korea's 2006 nuclear test and fear of future nuclear terrorist events, there does not seem to be any galvanizing issue to bring large numbers of people to try to influence government policy through the exercise of popular democracy. This could change in the future if there is a nuclear accident or perhaps if there are growing fears of nuclear proliferation.

Notably, current and many past U.S. nuclear policies appear to be at odds with beliefs of the average American voter. A survey conducted in March 2004 by a nonpartisan research organization at the University of Maryland—the Program on International Policy Attitudes (PIPA)—asked questions of a scientifically representative sampling of 1,311 Americans regarding their attitudes toward nuclear weapons (Kull 2004). The findings showed that the U.S. public is largely ignorant of actual U.S. government policies in the nuclear field and is significantly more interested in dis-armament than U.S. officials are. Regarding the Comprehensive Nuclear-Test-Ban Treaty, for example, 56 percent of respondents believed the United States had already become a member of the treaty, even though the Republican-controlled Senate rejected U.S. membership in 1999. A large majority (87 percent) believed the United States should be a member. In regard to possible nuclear use against threats posed by chemical or biological weapons, the PIPA survey found that 84 percent of respondents opposed using nuclear weapons for this purpose, preferring to rely (if necessary) on conventional arms. The question of the alert status of nuclear weapons exposed another divergence of views between the public and the U.S. government: Where current U.S. policy maintains large numbers of forces on hair-trigger alert in case of the need for a massive nuclear assault, 82 percent of respondents in the 2004 PIPA survey argued that the United States should work with other countries (such as Russia) to reduce the number of forces on a high-alert status. Finally, views on the number of nuclear weap-ons in the arsenal showed a major disconnect between official and public views. When respondents were asked how many nuclear weapons the United States needs for deterrence, the median response was 100, compared with the current actual stockpile of more than 9,000 weapons and a planned number of around 5,000.

A poll in March 2007 of 4,824 Americans found that nearly 80 percent of respondents either "strongly" or "somewhat" agreed with the idea that the international community—as opposed to the United States only—should decide what countries should be allowed to have nuclear weapons (UPI 2007). But 64 percent of respondents in the same poll also supported U.S. participation in efforts to limit foreign nuclear weapon capabilities.

Conclusion: U.S. Politics and Nonproliferation

The debate on how best to pursue U.S. nonproliferation objectives continues to revolve around a number of choices: unilateral ver-sus multilateral mechanisms, military hardware versus political cooperation, and informal arrangements versus formal treaties.

The Bush administration and more conservative politicians have generally sided with either unilateral or voluntary approaches, believing them to be more reliable, more flexible, and easier to implement. These approaches tend to place fewer restrictions on U.S. military actions, but they also leave similar options open to foreign militaries. For this reason, some Republicans and most Democrats have tended to opt for the second category of choices, believing multilateral treaties, principles of universality, and international enforcement will create greater long-term benefits to U.S. security. However, this debate is likely to continue—in some form—well into the future.

After the 2008 presidential election, the United States will again face a series of questions about the future direction of its nuclear complex. First, how will it define its nuclear security needs in relation to the NPT's requirement of eventual disarmament? Second, will the United States pursue active modernization of its nuclear arsenal (and renewed nuclear testing), or will it ratify the Comprehensive Nuclear-Test-Ban Treaty and move instead to downgrade and devalue nuclear weapons? Finally, will the United States seek new international treaties and endorse international verification mechanisms, or will it continue policies based on self-reliance and selectivity in its attitude toward international nonproliferation cooperation? The answers to these questions will likely go a long way toward defining the direction of U.S. nuclear and nonproliferation policies in the next U.S. presidential administration. To have a voice in nuclear decision making, citizens need to educate themselves on these issues and on the positions of their local and national candidates.

References

Arms Control Association. 2004. "The Bush Administration and the Fissile Material Cutoff Treaty: Reversing Course on Verification." Edited excerpts of roundtable discussion (September 2). http://www.armscontrol.org/events/FMCT_Excerpts.asp.

Broad, William J., David E. Sanger, and Thom Shanker. 2007. "U.S. Selecting Hybrid Design for Warheads." *New York Times*, January 7.

Carter, Ashton B. 2006. "America's New Strategic Partner?" *Foreign Affairs* 85 (July/August), pages 33–44.

Commission on the Intelligence Capabilities of the United States Regarding Weapons of Mass Destruction. 2005. *Report to the President* (March 31). http://www.wmd.gov/report/.

Duelfer, Charles. 2004. *Comprehensive Report of the Special Advisor to the DCI on Iraq's Weapons of Mass Destruction*. Washington, DC: U.S. Government Printing Office. https://www.cia.gov/cia/reports/iraq _wmd_2004.

GlobalSecurity.org. 2002. "Nuclear Posture Review [Excerpts]." Partial contents of U.S. Nuclear Posture Review of December 31, 2001 (posted January 8). http://www.globalsecurity.org/wmd/library/policy/dod /npr.htm.

Gormley, Dennis M. 2006. "Securing Nuclear Obsolescence." *Survival* 48 (Autumn), pages 127–148.

Harrison, Selig S. 2006. "The Forgotten Bargain: Nonproliferation and Nuclear Disarmament." *World Policy Journal* 23 (Fall), pages 1–13.

Kimball, Daryl G. 2002. "Parsing the Nuclear Posture Review." *Arms Control Today* 32 (March), pages 15–21.

Koch, Andrew. 2007. "Livermore Wins Warhead Design Contest." *Jane's Defense Weekly*. March 14.

Kohlhoff, Dean W. 2002. *Amchitka and the Bomb: Nuclear Testing in Alaska*. Seattle: University of Washington Press.

Kull, Steven. 2004. "Americans on WMD Proliferation." Program on International Policy Attitudes (PIPA), University of Maryland, April 15. http://www.pipa.org/OnlineReports/WMDProliferation/WMD _Prolif_Apr04/WMDProlif_Apr04_rpt.pdf.

Nolan, Janne E. 1999. *An Elusive Consensus: Nuclear Weapons and American Security after the Cold War*. Washington, DC: Brookings Institution Press.

Norris, Robert S., Hans M. Kristensen, and Christopher E. Paine. 2004. *Nuclear Insecurity: A Critique of the Bush Administration's Nuclear Weapons Policies*. Natural Resources Defense Council (September). http://www. nrdc.org/nuclear/insecurity/contents.asp.

Perkovich, George. 2006. "Democratic Bomb: Failed Strategy." *Policy Brief* 49 (November), pages 1–7.

Pillar, Paul R. 2006. "Intelligence, Policy, and the War in Iraq." *Foreign Affairs* 85 (March/April), pages 15–27.

Richelsen, Jeffrey T. 2006. *Spying on the Bomb: American Nuclear Intelligence from Nazi Germany to Iran and North Korea*. New York: W. W. Norton.

Schwartz, Stephen I., ed. 1998. *Atomic Audit: The Costs and Consequences of U.S. Nuclear Weapons since 1940.* Washington, DC: Brookings Institution Press.

UPI. 2007. "UPI Poll: Control of Nuclear Weapons." March 30.

The White House. 2006. The National Security Strategy of the United States of America. (March). http://www.whitehouse.gov/nsc/nss/2006/.

Woolf, Amy F. 2006. "Nonstrategic Nuclear Weapons." CRS Report for Congress (January 13). http://fpc.state.gov/documents/organization/61466.pdf.

4

Chronology

The development of nuclear weapons by ten countries since 1945—the United States, the Soviet Union, Britain, France, China, Israel, India, South Africa, Pakistan, and North Korea—constituted military, scientific, and political achievements. But these programs also involved tremendous domestic economic and environmental trade-offs. Internationally, nuclear weapons have radically changed how countries deal with each other and how the world's population thinks about the potentially deadly and terrifying power of technology. This chapter provides an overview of the history of nuclear weapons in a number of countries, as well as the parallel efforts to control and eliminate them.

1939   With the start of World War II in Europe, the U.S., British, and German governments separately begin to explore the possibility of building an atomic bomb. In the United States, Hungarian refugee and physicist Leo Szilard performs an experiment at Columbia University demonstrating the possibility of a chain reaction of atoms that could be used in a weapon.

Physicists in Germany and the Soviet Union inform their governments about a paper published in *Nature* magazine by physicists in France stating that uranium could be used in a chain reaction, releasing tremendous amounts of energy. The German War Office starts a government research program at the

1939
(*cont.*)
Kaiser Wilhelm Institute of Physics, bans uranium exports, and begins hoarding uranium from Czechoslovak mines under its control. In the Soviet Union, physicist Igor Kurchatov alerts his government and organizes the first Soviet study of nuclear fission.

In October, Alexander Sachs, a U.S. businessman, meets President Franklin D. Roosevelt and presents him with a letter drafted by Szilard and signed by Nobel Prize–winning physicist Albert Einstein warning of possible German acquisition of a nuclear fission bomb. Roosevelt decides to form the nine-member advisory Committee on Uranium, which recommends financial support for a thorough investigation of the possible uses of nuclear chain reactions.

1940
German refugee physicists Rudolf Peierls and Otto Frisch at the University of Birmingham in England calculate that fast-neutron fission of uranium 235 could create a nuclear explosion. Already at war with Nazi Germany, the British government sets up the secret Maud Committee to coordinate research on the possibility of building an atomic (nuclear fission) bomb. Separately, scientists at the University of California–Berkeley begin building a cyclotron to study chain reactions under the direction of Professor Ernest O. Lawrence. The Soviet government creates a uranium committee to develop methods of isotope separation and to achieve a controlled chain reaction. Soviet spies begin to collect information on uranium research in Germany, the United States, and the United Kingdom, including German refugee physicist Klaus Fuchs.

1941
Chemistry professor Glenn Seaborg and his colleagues at the University of California–Berkeley discover that neptunium emits electrons when irradiated, thereby forming a new element they call plutonium.

In July, the British Maud Committee concludes in a secret report that it would be possible to make a uranium bomb with the destructive force of 1,800 tons of TNT. Prime Minister Winston Churchill decides to pursue the atomic bomb and contacts the U.S. government.

As invading Nazi German forces sweep toward Moscow, President Roosevelt approves a U.S. atomic bomb program in October. Vannevar Bush, head of the National Defense Research Committee, calls a meeting of leading scientists, and funds are channeled to the top-secret so-called Manhattan Project. On December 7, Japanese planes bomb U.S. Navy ships in Pearl Harbor, Hawaii; the United States declares war on Japan. On December 11, Germany declares war on the United States.

1942   In March, Soviet leader Joseph Stalin passes atomic spy reports to prominent Soviet scientists and says that his country should pursue an atomic bomb. In June, German physicist Werner Heisenberg secretly informs the Nazi high command that the Third Reich lacks the resources to produce an atomic bomb during the war.

The U.S. government assigns responsibility for its bomb program to the Army Corps of Engineers and puts Brigadier General Leslie Groves in charge of the Manhattan Project. Groves appoints Berkeley physicist J. Robert Oppenheimer as scientific director. They select the remote Los Alamos Boys' School in New Mexico as the main site for the project and begin recruiting leading scientists, including many European refugees, from across the United States. In September, Groves acquires 59,000 acres in eastern Tennessee to use for factories to separate rare uranium 235 from naturally occurring uranium in sufficient quantities to make a bomb. The U.S. government builds a new town named Oak Ridge, in addition to huge gaseous diffusion plants for uranium enrichment.

At the University of Chicago on December 2, Italian émigré scientist Enrico Fermi and his colleagues produce the first controlled and sustained nuclear fission reaction in a jury-rigged laboratory built under the football stadium. Along with Szilard, Fermi designs the method of arranging graphite and uranium that makes the reaction possible; known as the "pile," it is a prototype reactor composed of 771,000 pounds of graphite,

1942
(*cont.*)
80,590 pounds of uranium oxide, and 12,400 pounds of uranium metal, costing $1 million to construct.

In Japan, the navy commits to developing nuclear power for propulsion and forms a committee to track atomic bomb research to determine if Japan should build such a weapon.

1943
Six Norwegians working with the British military succeed in disabling the heavy-water plant at Vemork. When the Germans resume operating the plant weeks later under tighter security, the United States drops 700 bombs on the plant, again setting back the German research program.

To acquire more uranium, the United States and Britain sign the Combined Development Trust to search out and acquire existing world supplies. Also, Britain sends a delegation of scientists, including Soviet spy Fuchs, to work in the U.S. bomb program. To pursue an alternative route to the bomb using plutonium, the U.S. government buys 500,000 acres in eastern Washington State and instructs the Hanford Engineering Works to build plutonium production reactors there.

The United States, Canada, and Great Britain sign the Quebec Agreement, providing for technical cooperation and pledging each side to refrain from using an atomic bomb without the consent of the other two.

A study by the Japanese Army Aeronautic Technology Research Institute declares that an atomic bomb is feasible. Prime Minister Hideki Tojo starts a major bomb-building effort at a Tokyo laboratory run by physicist Dr. Yoshio Nishina. However, the Japanese program cannot secure an adequate supply of uranium ore. The Japanese Navy also sponsors a parallel bomb development project at the University of Kyoto.

In the Soviet Union, physicist Igor Kurchatov directs the Soviet atomic bomb program at Laboratory No. 2 of the Academy of Sciences outside Moscow.

1944
In February, the Allies learn that Germany plans to relocate the damaged Norwegian heavy-water plant

to Germany, but Norwegian commandos working for the Allies blow up all of the heavy-water containers en route. In Japan, Nishina makes slow progress in his attempt to separate uranium isotopes.

In the fall, President Roosevelt rejects Danish physicist Niels Bohr's suggestion that he notify Stalin of the U.S. atomic bomb project.

1945   On April 12, President Roosevelt dies. Vice President Harry Truman succeeds him and for the first time learns about the Manhattan Project. On May 7, the war in Europe ends with the German surrender. Separate U.S. and Soviet teams in Germany seize atomic bomb materials (particularly uranium), relevant technology, and nuclear scientists from their respective occupation zones.

In the predawn hours of July 16, the world's first atomic bomb (nicknamed "the Gadget") is exploded by scientists working under Oppenheimer at the so-called Trinity test site near Alamogordo, New Mexico. The yield of the plutonium implosion device is equivalent to 18,600 tons of TNT. On July 21 at the Potsdam summit, President Truman receives General Groves's detailed report on the successful test; on July 24, he approves a draft plan to drop two bombs on possible target cities in Japan. On July 26, Truman gives the Japanese an ultimatum to surrender unconditionally to U.S. terms or face destruction from a "new weapon." The Japanese premier rejects the Potsdam ultimatum.

U.S. bombing raids on Tokyo effectively halt the Japanese atomic bomb program by destroying the main research facilities.

On August 6, a U.S. B-29 bomber drops an atomic bomb on the Japanese port city of Hiroshima, obliterating the city and killing an estimated 66,000 people. On August 9, the United States drops a second atomic bomb on the city of Nagasaki, killing some 39,000 people and injuring thousands more. The Soviet Union enters the Pacific war on August 9. On August 10, Japan surrenders, ending World War II.

1945
(*cont.*)
In August, the U.S. War Department, with President Truman's approval, releases a report by Princeton University physicist Henry Smyth detailing the bomb-building project. The Soviet Union receives a copy of the report, translates it, and distributes it to scientists working on the bomb project. Stalin orders an all-out effort to build an atomic bomb.

Soviet physicist Igor Kurchatov becomes scientific director of the bomb project under Lavrenti Beria, head of Stalin's secret police. In November, the Soviets begin construction of a plutonium production complex (Chelyabinsk-40) in the Urals.

India creates the Tata Institute of Fundamental Research to conduct nuclear research under physicist Homi Jehangir Bhabha's direction. France creates the Atomic Energy Commission to conduct military research.

1946
In January, the United Nations (UN) General Assembly establishes the Atomic Energy Commission (AEC) and calls for the elimination of nuclear weapons. In mid-1946, U.S. representative Bernard Baruch presents a report calling for control over global nuclear activities to the UN AEC. The Baruch Plan would eventually place all nuclear facilities worldwide under an international agency that would inspect and license nuclear activities. But the Soviet Union argues that all U.S. nuclear weapons must be destroyed *before* any international control system is established, which the United States rejects. No plan is adopted.

In April, Soviet scientist Yuli Khariton selects a remote site about 400 miles east of Moscow as the location for a secret nuclear weapons laboratory dubbed Arzamas-16. With prison labor, the Soviets build the first uranium graphite production reactor in the Urals (Chelyabinsk-40). In December, the Soviet Union achieves its first nuclear chain reaction at a laboratory in Moscow.

In July, the U.S. Congress adopts the Atomic Energy Act in an effort to maintain the U.S. monopoly over nuclear weapon activities and establishes its own Atomic Energy Commission to oversee nuclear activities. In October, the United States, the United Kingdom, and Canada form the Joint Development Agency to hinder foreign development of nuclear weapons by acquiring all of the uranium produced in the Congo, South Africa, and Australia.

Scientists at Los Alamos discuss the feasibility of building a thermonuclear (fission-fusion-fission) bomb as championed by physicist Edward Teller. Soviet scientists also begin to study such weapons.

In July, the United States tests a series of nuclear weapons at the Bikini Atoll in the Pacific Ocean in an exercise called Operation Crossroads. The United States forcibly relocates the inhabitants of Bikini Atoll to Rongerik, a smaller, less fertile atoll. On July 25, the United States detonates Shot Baker 90 feet below the water; the resulting plume drops a million tons of radioactive seawater, turning the pristine Bikini lagoon into a radioactive lake.

1947   In January, a six-member committee of the British cabinet secretly decides to proceed with the development of nuclear weapons. In May, the government asks British physicist and Los Alamos participant William G. Penney to head the bomb effort. In August, Britain's first nuclear reactor begins operating at Harwell.

In July, the National Security Act replaces the U.S. War Department with the Department of Defense and creates the U.S. Air Force, the National Security Council (NSC), and the Central Intelligence Agency (CIA).

In October, the U.S. Joint Chiefs of Staff estimate that 150 Nagasaki-type bombs would be sufficient to defend the United States and defeat the Soviet Union. The U.S. nuclear weapons stockpile now contains twenty to fifty weapons.

1948   Britain and Canada give up their veto on the U.S. use of nuclear weapons. In return for massive U.S. economic assistance, the United Kingdom ships two-thirds of its uranium ore to the United States and allows the United States to get all of the Belgian Congo's uranium ore for two years.

1948
(*cont.*)

In July, as more Soviet troops are being stationed in Eastern Europe, President Truman sends B-29 bombers to Europe to show that the United States will defend Western Europe with nuclear weapons if necessary. The NSC approves directive NSC-30, "Policy on Atomic Warfare," which authorizes the military to plan for the use of nuclear weapons in a war but reserves the decisions to use such weapons to the president.

From April 15 to May 15, the United States tests a series of nuclear weapons at Eniwetok Atoll in the Pacific under Operation Sandstone, demonstrating that small amounts of fissile material can be boosted to develop larger yields, thus allowing the United States to build more weapons with existing fissile material.

Newly independent India establishes its Atomic Energy Commission to begin work directly related to the exploitation of nuclear energy.

The Soviet government authorizes thermonuclear weapons research at the Physics Institute of the Soviet Academy of Sciences under Igor Tam, who recruits physicist Andrei Sakharov to work for him.

1949

With tensions in Europe rising over the Berlin Crisis, President Truman states that the atomic bomb should provide the central element in U.S. security policy. In April, Western nations form a military alliance, the North Atlantic Treaty Organization (NATO), to coordinate their defense against Soviet-bloc countries. The United States officially commits itself to the defense of Western Europe within NATO. Meanwhile, the Soviet Union begins to integrate the national armed forces of Eastern Europe.

In September, the Soviet Union tests its first atomic bomb at Semipalatinsk in Soviet Kazakhstan. The United States dubs the plutonium device—with a yield of 20–22 kilotons—Joe 1 after Stalin, although, at Beria's insistence, the bomb is an exact copy of the U.S. Fat Man device used at Nagasaki.

After the Soviet test, which is detected by U.S. spy planes conducting air sampling over China, the United States expands production of uranium and plutonium. AEC Commissioner Lewis Strauss urges President Truman to give highest priority to developing a thermonuclear (hydrogen) bomb.

On October 1, Mao Tse-tung, the communist leader of the newly formed People's Republic of China, calls the nuclear bomb a "paper tiger" that the United States uses to scare people. But the Chinese government, through physicist Qian Sanqianq, begins purchasing nuclear technology in Europe.

In Israel, the Weizmann Institute of Science is actively supporting nuclear research under the direction of Ernst David Bergmann. The institute's scientists collaborate with French nuclear scientists at the Saclay nuclear research facility.

1950   In February, the Soviet Union signs a treaty of alliance and mutual assistance with the People's Republic of China. The Soviet Union promises to defend China, if necessary, with nuclear weapons.

In June, the complex calculations for designing a U.S. hydrogen bomb are given to the first primitive electronic computer, the ENIAC, at the Aberdeen Proving Ground in Maryland.

In England, physicist Klaus Fuchs confesses that he has been passing nuclear secrets to the Soviet Union and is sentenced to fourteen years in prison. He provides evidence on other U.S. nuclear spies, including Julius and Ethel Rosenberg.

In April, the NSC issues NSC-68, which warns of the Soviet threat to world peace and calls for increased conventional and nuclear defenses. The U.S. atomic stockpile contains approximately 300 bombs, and the United States possesses 250 nuclear-capable aircraft.

On June 11, Truman authorizes sending eighty-nine sets of non-nuclear components to Britain for nuclear bombs to support the Strategic Air Command bomber units there. At this time, bomb designs call for the nuclear core of plutonium or uranium to be kept separate from the non-nuclear assembly, until the president authorizes them to be assembled into a complete bomb.

1951   While developing the hydrogen bomb, the United States accelerates its nuclear test program. It also establishes the U.S.-based Nevada Test Site (or Nevada Proving Ground) to economize on costs. More than 6,000 U.S. troops conduct maneuvers within 5–6 miles of the Nevada explosions, and many later develop health problems.

In the ongoing Korean War, Chinese troops sweep south to fight U.S. forces nearing their border. In April, the U.S. Joint Chiefs of Staff authorize nuclear retaliation against North Korean air bases in case of a major attack against UN forces in South Korea. President Truman approves the transfer of nine nuclear bomb cores to Guam. He also authorizes the use of nuclear weapons on Manchuria if large numbers of Chinese troops join in the fighting or if bombers are launched from Chinese bases.

In April, U.S. citizens Ethel and Julius Rosenberg are sentenced to death for passing U.S. nuclear secrets to the Soviet Union.

Mathematician Stanislaw Ulam and physicists Edward Teller and Richard Garwin develop a new design for a U.S. hydrogen bomb.

On September 24, the Soviet Union explodes Joe-2, a lighter and improved plutonium implosion bomb with a yield of 38–40 kilotons.

In Windscale (later renamed Sellafield), England, a second reactor starts producing plutonium for nuclear weapons.

1952   The UN replaces the failed AEC with the UN Disarmament Commission.

The United States can now mass produce nuclear weapons, and various fission cores are interchangeable among weapon assemblies. In January, the Joint Chiefs of Staff authorize the supreme allied commander in Europe, General Dwight Eisenhower, to begin planning for the use of nuclear weapons bombs by Navy and Air Force units to be stationed in Europe. Tactical nuclear weapons, capable of being delivered by planes, missiles, and artillery, soon begin to be allocated for the defense of Western Europe against a possible Soviet invasion.

In November, the United States detonates the first thermonuclear (hydrogen) bomb, the 10.4-megaton Mike device, in the Marshall Islands (which became UN Trust Territories administered by the United States after Japan's defeat), vaporizing the island of Elugelab. The weapon is 500 times more powerful than the bomb dropped on Nagasaki but is too heavy to be deliverable as a bomb. President-elect Eisenhower's staff drafts the New Look defense policy, emphasizing nuclear weapons and long-range bombers. The United States opens a new nuclear weapons laboratory at Livermore, California.

On October 3, the United Kingdom conducts its first nuclear test, a plutonium bomb with a yield of 25 kilotons, near Monte Bello Island off the coast of Australia. Because the British are worried about the effects of a ship-smuggled bomb, they explode the bomb inside the hull of a 1,450-ton frigate, creating a 1,000-foot-long crater.

1953   In the Soviet Union, First Secretary Nikita Khrushchev orders Stalin's internal security and nuclear tsar, Lavrenti Beria, removed from office and later executed. Vyacheslav Malyshev becomes head of the nuclear program, now code-named the Ministry of Medium Machine-Building.

Beginning in March, the United States tests a series of weapons at the Nevada Test Site. An estimated 18,000 military personnel participate in observer programs, tactical maneuvers, scientific studies, and other activities. In June, the United States shifts its nuclear arsenal from civilian to military custody. In the event of hostilities with the Soviet Union or China, NSC 162/2 states that the United States will consider nuclear weapons to be as available as other weapons.

After announcing its possession of a hydrogen bomb, the Soviet Union detonates the device at the Semipalatinsk site in Soviet Kazakhstan. The military evacuates tens of thousands of inhabitants from

1953
(*cont.*)

the surrounding area in a last-minute effort to protect them from radioactive fallout; some of those evacuated cannot return home for several months. Not a true thermonuclear (fission-fusion-fission) bomb, this device obtains nearly all its relatively modest 400-kiloton yield from fission, but it can be readily made into a deliverable weapon. In October, Britain conducts two atmospheric tests of fission bombs with yields of 8 and 10 kilotons at Emu Field in South Australia.

In December at the UN, President Eisenhower proposes his Atoms for Peace plan, which allows the dissemination of nuclear energy for peaceful purposes to all interested nations, but requires that they be willing to accept safeguards against military uses. He also calls for the creation of an international atomic energy organization.

1954

In January, the Indian Atomic Energy Commission sets up the Atomic Energy Establishment at Trombay and transfers all scientists working on nuclear power there. Also, the Department of Atomic Energy is created with Bhabha as its head, reporting directly to the prime minister.

The United States launches the world's first nuclear-powered submarine, the USS *Nautilus,* and deploys nuclear weapons at U.S. bases in Morocco and Britain.

On March 1, the 15-megaton hydrogen bomb Bravo detonated at Bikini Atoll causes the worst radiological disaster in U.S. history, as the bomb greatly exceeds its expected yield of 6 megatons. Although the weapon is tested from a stand, the lithium deuteride design allows the bomb to fit inside the bomb bay of a B-47 aircraft. Because of the U.S. failure to conduct pretest evacuations, the Marshall Islanders on four surrounding atolls are covered with the fallout plume, and a Japanese fishing boat and its twenty-three crewmen are heavily contaminated. In addition, many U.S. personnel are exposed to dangerously high radiation levels.

In June, after secret hearings, the U.S. AEC revokes Oppenheimer's security clearance over his past communist connections and alleged untrustworthiness.

The Soviet Union undertakes a military exercise after a nuclear detonation in September at a test site at Totskoe in the Urals. Civilians within 7 kilometers of ground zero are evacuated while 44,000 troops gather on a battlefield with various defenses, weapons, and animals at ranges of 5–8 kilometers from the epicenter. Although soldiers and the local population receive above-normal radioactive doses, a simulated battle is filmed in an attempt to develop regulations for future nuclear wars.

After the Chinese bombing of the Taiwanese-held islands of Quemoy and Matsu, the United States and Taiwan sign a security pact in December. President Eisenhower develops plans for the possible use of nuclear weapons against China. He secretly deploys nuclear weapons on the U.S.-held territories of Okinawa, Chichi Jima, and Iwo Jima and sends a nuclear-armed aircraft carrier to Taiwanese waters. He also sends nuclear bomb components to U.S. bases in Japan despite Japan's official non-nuclear policy.

1955   In January, Chairman Mao announces that China will obtain its own nuclear arsenal to counter U.S. weapons. The Chinese decision is influenced by growing U.S. involvement in Indochina and past nuclear threats against China during the Korean War and the Taiwan Strait Crisis. The Soviet Union increases cooperation with China and provides it with a cyclotron, a nuclear reactor, and fissile material for research. A smaller cooperative nuclear program is initiated by the Soviet Union with North Korea.

The U.S. nuclear arsenal stands at 2,422 weapons. In March, the United States begins stationing nuclear weapons in NATO countries, including West Germany, the presumed front line against a possible Soviet attack. A U.S. government agency concludes that the currently planned nuclear offensive against the Soviet Union would result in 77 million casualties in the Soviet bloc.

On May 14, the Warsaw Treaty of Friendship, Cooperation, and Mutual Assistance establishes the

1955
(*cont.*)

so-called Warsaw Pact, providing for a unified command of Eastern European armies with a headquarters in Moscow.

Despite talk of disarmament, the United States tests eighteen weapons and the Soviet Union tests six, including the world's first air-dropped hydrogen bomb. One Soviet test kills three civilians when its shock wave destroys a distant building.

1956

In July, a U.S. bomber crashes into a storage site containing three Mark 6 nuclear weapons in the United Kingdom. A fire damages the bombs but does not ignite their conventional explosives or their nuclear cores.

U.S., Soviet, and British atmospheric nuclear testing continues. In August, the Soviet Union agrees to provide aid to build Chinese nuclear industries and research facilities. Also, China starts a strategic missile program. Marshal Nie Rongzhen leads the organization that oversees both the nuclear and missile programs.

In November, after the Suez Crisis, French leaders hold a secret meeting with Israeli leaders in which they agree to provide Israel with a 24-megawatt (thermal) research reactor along with plutonium separation technology, possibly for a bomb program.

1957

In July, the UN officially establishes the International Atomic Energy Agency (IAEA); the new organization holds its first general conference in Vienna in October. This agency aims to help disseminate nuclear technology for peaceful purposes, promote nuclear safety, and administer a system of international nuclear safeguards to prevent the diversion of materials.

In April, the United States deploys nuclear weapons in Italy.

The United States conducts thirty-two nuclear tests, the Soviet Union conducts sixteen tests, and the United Kingdom conducts seven tests, including its first thermonuclear bomb off Malden Island in the Pacific.

At Mayak, a Soviet nuclear weapon facility, a breakdown in the cooling system of a tank holding more than 70,000 tons of radioactive sludge causes an explosion and releases a plume of radioactive fallout.

On October 4, the Soviet Union launches the world's first artificial satellite (*Sputnik*) aboard an R-7 missile, spreading fears in the West that Moscow now possesses long-range nuclear-armed missiles. The Soviet Union and China sign the New Defense Technical Accord, whereby the Soviet Union agrees to supply China with a prototype nuclear weapon, as well as missiles and related technical information.

Continued atmospheric nuclear testing prompts groups of scientists and citizens internationally to begin organized protests against the bomb. Tests are now spreading measurable amounts of radioactivity into plants and cows' milk across the globe. In August, the first demonstration of civil disobedience against nuclear weapon testing takes place at the Nevada Test Site when eleven protesters are arrested. In November, the Committee for a Sane Nuclear Policy is formed in New York to promote global nuclear disarmament.

In October, France and Israel sign a nuclear cooperation agreement. France agrees to help Israel design and build a nuclear facility in Dimona, which will include a plutonium-reprocessing plant that could be used to produce weapons-grade material.

1958   In January, Nobel Prize–winning scientist Linus Pauling and his wife, Eva Helen Pauling, present the UN secretary-general with a petition signed by 11,021 scientists worldwide that calls for an end to nuclear testing.

The United States moves to deploy nuclear-armed cruise missiles on Taiwan and in South Korea. In March, the German parliament approves deployment of U.S. nuclear weapons in West Germany. In August, the United States also deploys nuclear weapons in France.

Social turbulence in China, including the Great Leap Forward's heavy emphasis on popular participation in scientific and technical matters, interferes

1958
(*cont.*)
with China's nuclear research program. But China begins constructing the Northwest Nuclear Weapons Research and Design Academy (Ninth Academy).

Before announcing a nuclear testing moratorium at the end of the year, the United States tests a record seventy-seven nuclear devices. During Operation Hardtack I at the Pacific Proving Ground, the United States conducts a series of thirty-five tests to develop intercontinental ballistic missile (ICBM) and submarine-launched ballistic missile (SLBM) warheads and high-yield strategic bombs. The Operation Hardtack II series of thirty-seven tests at the Nevada Test Site introduces underground testing as a routine procedure to help reduce fallout. After holding five tests during the year, the United Kingdom stops conducting its own independent nuclear tests and joins forces with the United States. After Britain demonstrates that it can develop thermonuclear weapons, the United States allows collaboration with Britain on weapons development. All subsequent British nuclear weapons are based on U.S. designs.

The Geneva Conference of Experts agrees on the technical characteristics of a system to monitor nuclear tests in the atmosphere, underwater, and underground. The system would include land and shipborne control posts, overflights, and on-site inspections. Still the United States, Britain, and the Soviet Union can't agree on a test ban, and the Soviets conduct a new series of thirty-four tests.

The United States secretly stores four large thermonuclear bombs (each with a yield of 9–10 megatons) at Thule Air Base, Greenland, a territory of Denmark, for approximately ten months, violating Denmark's policy banning nuclear deployments within its borders.

1959
In February, the United States deploys nuclear weapons in Turkey, a member of NATO.

Because of a growing rift between Khrushchev and Mao regarding political, economic, and military policies, the Soviet Union tells China it will not supply a prototype bomb as promised.

In October, the United States deploys its first operational ICBM, the Atlas D. In September, France begins a program to develop ballistic missiles with a range of 3,500 kilometers for both land- and sea-based launches.

Through the Atoms for Peace program, the United States has now entered into nuclear cooperation agreements with forty countries.

In December, the Antarctic Treaty is signed by forty-two countries. The treaty obligates member states to use Antarctica only for peaceful purposes and prohibits all nuclear explosions, as well as the disposal of radioactive waste on the continent.

At the end of the year, President Eisenhower announces an end to the voluntary U.S. moratorium on nuclear testing but promises the United States will not resume testing without advance public notice.

1960
On February 13, France explodes its first nuclear weapon with a yield of 60–70 kilotons in the French-owned Algerian portion of the Sahara Desert and later tests two more. France's President Charles de Gaulle hails the first test as a great national achievement.

After the U.S. State Department issues a statement that Israel has a secret nuclear installation, Israeli Prime Minister David Ben-Gurion announces that Israel is building a 24-megawatt reactor "for peaceful purposes."

The Soviet Union refuses China's demand for more technical information concerning nuclear weapons and withdraws all of its advisers. China adopts an emergency plan to build an indigenous nuclear weapon. Construction of the gaseous diffusion plant at Lanzhou to produce weapons-grade uranium becomes a national crusade.

At a rally by a protest group from the Committee for a Sane Nuclear Policy in Madison Square Garden in New York City, 20,000 people gather to hear Eleanor Roosevelt, Norman Cousins, and other speakers call for an end to the arms race. Five thousand demonstrators then march after midnight to the UN in a symbolic call for change.

1960
(*cont.*)

In December, the U.S. Joint Strategic Target Planning Staff completes the Single Integrated Operational Plan 62; in the event of war, it calls for the launch of all U.S. strategic nuclear-delivery vehicles. It lists 2,021 strategic targets to be hit in the Soviet Union and China, killing an estimated 360–425 million people. The United States deploys nuclear weapons in the Netherlands and Greece.

1961

In January, an explosion at an experimental military reactor in Idaho kills three technicians. The same month, a B-52 carrying two 4-megaton bombs crashes in North Carolina. On one of the bombs, only a single switch prevents an explosion that would have been 1,800 times more powerful than that of the Hiroshima bomb.

In June, the Antarctic Treaty enters into force, making the southern polar region the world's first nuclear-weapon-free zone.

Just weeks after the construction of the Berlin Wall, *Life* magazine publishes its September issue devoted to how to survive radioactive fallout from a nuclear attack in which President John F. Kennedy states that the possibility of nuclear war is a fact of life. The group Physicians for Social Responsibility is founded to address growing public concerns about the health effects of nuclear testing.

On October 31, the Soviet Union explodes the largest nuclear weapon ever detonated over the Novaya Zemlya Island testing range in the Arctic Sea. Sakharov designs the 100-megaton Tsar Bomba on the orders of Khrushchev, who wants to make a political statement. Although the test's yield is reduced to 50 megatons for safety reasons, it proves that it is possible to build bombs of virtually unlimited power. Two weeks later, the United States begins its first underground nuclear test series at the Nevada Test Site, with approximately forty-four explosions.

On September 20, the United States and the Soviet Union sign the McCloy-Zorin Accords, setting out principles for negotiations toward complete disarmament. The accords call for the UN to supervise a disarmament process that would eventually eliminate all weapons of mass destruction (WMD), their delivery systems, and national armed forces in general. The UN General Assembly adopts the accords in December.

The U.S. stockpile of nuclear weapons deployed in East Asia reaches 1,600; about half are located at the Strategic Air Command (SAC) base on Okinawa, 600 in South Korea, 225 in Guam, 60 in the Philippines, and 12 on Taiwan.

Using the innovation of satellite-based, photo-reconnaissance technology, the United States obtains evidence that it has considerable superiority over the Soviet Union in numbers of nuclear weapons.

1962   The United States has an estimated 27,100 nuclear weapons, the Soviet Union 3,100, the United Kingdom 205, and France a few test bombs.

Beginning in July and running for a year, the United States conducts a series of nuclear tests for both military and nonmilitary uses at the Nevada Test Site. The largest test involves detonating a 104-kiloton device in a crater to investigate the potential of using thermonuclear devices for industrial excavation, such as canal and harbor construction. The test creates a crater 1,280 feet wide and 320 feet deep, but it is too contaminated to be accessible to human beings. Meanwhile, U.S. nuclear tests in space, launched from Johnston Island in the Pacific, disable several U.S. and foreign satellites.

Khrushchev decides that the Soviet Union should place intermediate-range, nuclear-armed missiles in Cuba to counter U.S. missiles in Turkey and to protect Cuba, newly communist from a U.S.-sponsored invasion. With Cuban President Fidel Castro's approval, the Soviet Union begins building secret ballistic missile installations there. In October, in what becomes known as the Cuban Missile Crisis, Kennedy confronts Soviet denials of this construction and calls for the immediate dismantlement of the sites, beginning two weeks of tense diplomacy. Ultimately, war is avoided when Khrushchev agrees to dismantle the missile installations in return for a public U.S. pledge not to invade

1962
(*cont.*)

Cuba and a secret U.S. agreement to remove its missiles from Turkey.

1963

On April 29, at the initiative of the president of Mexico, the presidents of Bolivia, Brazil, Chile, Ecuador, and Mexico announce that they are prepared to sign a multilateral agreement to make Latin America a nuclear-weapon-free zone. The Latin American nations begin negotiations to agree on language for a formal treaty.

The United States and Soviet Union sign the so-called Hot-Line Agreement on June 20 that establishes direct radio and telegraph links between the countries' leaders to prevent future crises and miscommunication. On August 5, the United States, the Soviet Union, and Britain sign the Limited Test Ban Treaty. The treaty allows only underground nuclear tests by the three countries beginning on October 10 and is of unlimited duration. The agreement is opened to signature by other states at the UN. France and China refuse to sign.

1964

In January, U.S. President Lyndon Johnson proposes a nuclear nonproliferation treaty before the Eighteen-Nation Disarmament Committee. The Soviet Union refuses to join the U.S. proposal because the United States has discussed forming a multilateral nuclear force with its NATO allies.

In July, the Organization of African Unity, convening its first summit in Cairo, formally calls for a treaty ensuring the denuclearization of Africa.

On October 16, China explodes its first atomic bomb at the Lop Nor test site; the uranium implosion device has a 22-kiloton yield. After the test, Premier Zhou Enlai calls for elimination of all nuclear weapons and pledges that China will not be the first to use nuclear weapons.

The United States conducts approximately thirty-nine underground nuclear tests, the Soviet Union nine, and Great Britain and France three apiece.

1965

In March, China adopts guidelines for full-scale pursuit of long-range missiles capable of carrying nuclear warheads. In May, China tests its first atomic bomb from an airplane.

1966   On January 17, a U.S. B-52 bomber carrying nuclear weapons has a midair accident and drops four nuclear weapons on Palomares, Spain. No nuclear explosions occur, but conventional explosives in two of the weapons scatter radioactive material over a populated area. The United States has to pay $182 million for recovery, cleanup, and compensation.

In July, France tests a nuclear weapon at the Mururoa Atoll in the Pacific Ocean. China launches a guided missile armed with a nuclear warhead at its test site in Xinjiang in October. U.S. and other intelligence agencies determine that Israel has now produced enough plutonium for a nuclear weapon at its Dimona facility. The Israeli government maintains that it will not be the first country to introduce nuclear weapons to the Middle East.

1967   The Outer Space Treaty is opened for signature at the UN in January. The treaty bans states from placing nuclear weapons (and other WMD) in orbit around the Earth or otherwise stationing them in outer space. It also limits the use of the moon and other celestial bodies exclusively to nonmilitary purposes.

At a regional meeting of Latin American countries in February, the first nuclear-weapon-free zone treaty covering a populated area is signed. The so-called Treaty of Tlatelolco pledges signatories to use nuclear materials and facilities exclusively for peaceful purposes and to prohibit testing, storing, and deploying nuclear weapons. The treaty establishes the Agency for the Prohibition of Nuclear Weapons in Latin America to monitor and ensure compliance with the treaty. However, numerous key states refuse to ratify the treaty, hampering its implementation.

China tests its first thermonuclear bomb in June with a 3.3-megaton yield at its Lop Nor test site. China needed only thirty-two months to move from its first atomic test to a thermonuclear weapon, the shortest period yet.

1967
(*cont.*)

In September, the United States announces that it will deploy a limited antiballistic missile system named Sentinel. The system is intended to counter a possible threat from China (believed to be immune from deterrence) and to add protection against the remote possibility of an accidental launch of an intercontinental missile by the Soviet Union.

The combined number of tactical and strategic nuclear weapons in the U.S. arsenal peaks at 32,500. The U.S. stockpile of nuclear weapons in territories in the Pacific Ocean also peaks at approximately 3,200 weapons. The Soviet Union has an estimated 8,850 nuclear weapons, the United Kingdom 270, France 36, and China 25.

1968

In January, a U.S. B-52 bomber crashes on the ice near Thule, Greenland. The conventional explosives surrounding all four nuclear weapons aboard detonate and scatter plutonium on the ice, requiring a costly cleanup operation, although adequate safety measures to protect the local workers are not taken. In March, a diesel-powered Soviet Golf II–class submarine (*K-129*) with three nuclear-tipped missiles aboard sinks off the coast of Oahu, Hawaii, killing its crew of eighty men. Two months later, the U.S. nuclear submarine *Scorpion* sinks with two nuclear torpedoes aboard in the Atlantic Ocean near the Azores, killing all ninety-nine crewmen. A few days later, a liquid-metal reactor aboard a Soviet nuclear submarine (*K-27*) releases radioactive steam, killing five sailors.

On June 12, the UN General Assembly approves the final text of the nuclear Non-Proliferation Treaty (NPT). On July 1, the United States, the United Kingdom, the Soviet Union, and fifty-nine other countries sign the NPT, which will become effective in 1970. China and France decline to sign. The five countries that have already tested nuclear weapons agree to eventual disarmament, and other signatories agree not to pursue such weapons in return for peaceful nuclear technology. The NPT requires that nuclear weapon states not transfer nuclear weapons or provide weapon-related assistance to non–nuclear weapon states and that non–nuclear weapon states conclude safeguards agreements with the IAEA.

On August 24, France tests its first hydrogen bomb from a balloon at the Fangataufa Atoll in the South Pacific, with a yield of 2.6 megatons. The blast blankets the atoll with radioactivity, rendering it off-limits to humans for six years.

Reportedly, Israeli Prime Minister Moshe Dayan approves nuclear weapons production of three to five bombs per year.

1969   In November, the first Strategic Arms Limitation Talks (SALT) begin between the United States and the Soviet Union in Helsinki, Finland. Differences between the two sides in the number of specific types of delivery systems lead to disagreements at the SALT meetings over what should be the focus of a future treaty.

The U.S. arsenal of strategic and tactical nuclear weapons declines—because old warheads are retired—to 28,200; the Soviet Union has 11,000, the United Kingdom 308, China 50, and France 36.

The Eighteen-Nation Disarmament Committee based in Geneva is enlarged and becomes known as the Conference of the Committee on Disarmament.

1970   The NPT enters into force with the U.S. and Soviet ratifications in March.

The IAEA, having been tasked under the NPT to establish nuclear controls at specific facilities, develops Document Information Circular 153, which becomes the basis for all bilateral safeguard agreements between the IAEA and the individual non–nuclear weapon states that are party to the NPT.

In August, the United States deploys the first missile with multiple, independently targetable reentry vehicles (MIRVs), the Minuteman III.

The United States conducts thirty-eight nuclear tests, the Soviet Union sixteen, France eight, and China

1970
(*cont.*)
one. The U.S. tests include a series in which radioactivity is deliberately vented out from underground for tracking purposes.

1971
Fifteen countries involved in nuclear technology exports form the NPT Exporters Committee (also known as the Zangger Committee for its chair, Swiss nuclear expert Claude Zangger). The committee seeks to establish consensus on the NPT clause requiring that nuclear equipment and material be under safeguards after export to a non–nuclear weapon state to ensure it is not diverted to a weapon program.

France's intermediate-range ballistic missile force, based in eighteen silos between Marseilles and Lyon, becomes operational in August. The missiles are armed with 120-kiloton MR-31 plutonium fission warheads.

China deploys the Dong Feng-4 missile, which can carry a 1-megaton warhead to a maximum range of 4,800 kilometers. Spurred on by China's nuclear tests, Indian Prime Minister Indira Gandhi secretly decides to proceed with the manufacture and test of a nuclear device.

The number of nuclear weapons in NATO Europe peaks at 7,300; Germany stores approximately half of them.

After Pakistan's defeat in the 1971 Indo-Pakistan War, Pakistan launches a clandestine nuclear weapon program.

1972
In January, France's first class of strategic missile submarines begins to patrol armed with MR-41 boosted fission warheads with a yield of approximately 500 kilotons.

On May 18, the Seabed Treaty enters into force. The treaty prohibits parties from placing nuclear weapons and any other WMD on the seabed and the ocean floor beyond a 12-mile coastal zone.

On May 26 in Moscow, U.S. President Richard Nixon and Soviet General Secretary Leonid Brezhnev sign two agreements to slow the arms race: the Anti-Ballistic Missile (ABM) Treaty and the SALT I Interim

Agreement. The ABM Treaty limits antimissile systems to two sites and bans nationwide missile defenses to reduce incentives for further arms racing. The Interim Agreement puts ceilings on the number of strategic land-based and sea-based launchers on each side, but it fails to ban MIRVs.

In October, Egypt and Syria launch a surprise attack on Israel, starting the Yom Kippur War. Temporarily unprepared to defend itself with conventional forces, Israel reportedly readies its nuclear-armed Jericho missiles for launch. After Israel counterattacks and corners the Egyptian Third Army, Soviet leader Brezhnev threatens to introduce Soviet troops to help the Egyptians. This prompts President Nixon to put the United States on worldwide nuclear alert. Both superpowers finally back down.

1973   Australia and New Zealand start proceedings in May at the International Court of Justice in The Hague, Netherlands, to prevent further French atmospheric nuclear tests in the South Pacific. The court states that France should avoid nuclear tests that cause radioactive fallout in the South Pacific. France conducts five atmospheric nuclear tests anyway.

On June 22, Nixon and Brezhnev sign an agreement on preventing nuclear war. The parties agree to work to avoid military conflicts and the outbreak of nuclear war between them and other countries, and to consult each other immediately if there is a risk of nuclear conflict.

1974   On May 18, India explodes a 12-kiloton plutonium bomb underground in the Rajasthan Desert near the town of Pokhran. The test, code-named Smiling Buddha, is motivated in part by India's concerns about nuclear-armed China and the two countries' border disputes. The Bhabha Atomic Research Center designed the nuclear device using plutonium created in a Canadian-supplied research reactor, which had U.S.-supplied heavy water as a moderator. As a nonmember of the NPT, India claims that it violated no

1974
(*cont.*)

international agreements. It says the test is a "peaceful nuclear experiment," not a bomb.

In July, the United States and Soviet Union revise the ABM Treaty to limit each side to only one ABM system, surrounding either the national capital or an ICBM base. The two sides also sign the Threshold Test Ban Treaty, which prohibits any underground nuclear weapon test having a yield exceeding 150 kilotons (or about 10 times the yield of the Hiroshima bomb). Under the agreement, the parties also agree to limit the number of tests to a minimum and to exchange technical data about underground nuclear tests.

In response to the Indian nuclear test, the Zangger Committee publishes two memoranda in August—together known as the Trigger List—specifying when IAEA safeguards should be required for exports of nuclear-related items to non–nuclear weapon states. The first memorandum covers nuclear materials that can significantly contribute to the manufacture of nuclear weapons, and the second covers equipment or material designed for processing, using, or producing fissile materials.

In November, U.S. President Gerald Ford and Soviet General Secretary Brezhnev sign the Vladivostok Accord, establishing a framework for a future SALT II agreement. The accord suggests a ceiling of 2,400 total strategic offensive delivery systems (ICBMs, SLBMs, and heavy bombers) for each side, a further subceiling of 1,320 MIRVed systems, a ban on constructing new land-based ICBM launchers, and limits on deploying new types of strategic offensive weapons.

South African Prime Minister John Vorster secretly approves a program to develop nuclear weapons as a deterrent. The initial plan is oriented toward peaceful nuclear explosions and constructing an underground nuclear test site.

1975

After India's explosion of a nuclear device, seven major nuclear supplier countries meet with the goal of considering restrictions on nuclear trade in addition to those in the NPT and Zangger Committee memoranda. This group, known as the Nuclear Suppliers Group (or the London Club), consists of representatives from the United States, the Soviet Union, Britain, France (not an NPT member), West Germany, Canada, and Japan (not an NPT member).

A single U.S. ABM deployment site with 100 interceptors and associated radars (the Safeguard system) is completed to protect ICBM silos at Grand Forks, North Dakota, at a cost of $12 billion. But Congress deactivates the site after only four months because of its high operating cost and the likelihood that its nuclear-tipped interceptors would "blind" the system's radars.

The first five-year NPT Review Conference is held in Geneva in May. The treaty now has ninety-one parties. The final document reaffirms strong support for the treaty, welcomes the various arms limitation agreements reached (particularly SALT I), but expresses concerns that the nuclear arms race has otherwise continued unabated. The United States has 28,100 nuclear weapons, the Soviet Union 23,500, the United Kingdom 350, France 188, China 185, and Israel approximately 20.

1976   The South African Atomic Energy Board secretly tests a full-scale model of a gun-type device using nonexplosive natural uranium.

1977   France's first thermonuclear warhead with a yield of 1 megaton enters service on a strategic missile nuclear submarine.

In July, the U.S. Jimmy Carter administration announces it has tested an enhanced radiation weapon (the so-called neutron bomb). The new weapon is a small hydrogen bomb with only one-tenth of the blast and heat (thus reducing damage to cities), but it produces high levels of radiation to kill troops and civilians. International public reaction is overwhelmingly negative.

In July, the Soviet Union informs the United States that one of its spy satellites has detected preparations for a nuclear test in the Kalahari Desert of South Africa.

1977 (*cont.*)	International pressure forces South Africa to cover the test shafts with concrete and abandon the site.

The Nuclear Suppliers Group adopts the Zangger Committee's Trigger List in September and expands it to include other nuclear-related technologies that should also be restricted, such as heavy-water production plants. The guidelines also introduce the term *sensitive facilities* (e.g., those undertaking plutonium reprocessing and uranium isotope separation) for which a transfer of technology should be handled particularly cautiously.

In December, a grassroots U.S. organization, Mobilization for Survival, holds its first national conference. This coalition of more than 280 affiliated groups aims to eliminate nuclear weapons, ban nuclear power, and reverse the arms race.

1978 The U.S. citizens' group Nuclear Weapons Facilities Task Force forms to support antinuclear organizing in communities near major nuclear weapon production sites.

In January, the Nuclear Suppliers Group transmits its new guidelines to the IAEA. They are published as IAEA Document Information Circular 254 and call on states to require IAEA safeguards to be applied to plants built in non–nuclear weapon states and to refrain from transfers of reprocessing and enrichment technology that could be useful in developing weapons.

President Carter signs the Nuclear Non-Proliferation Act in March to help ensure that U.S. materials will not be diverted to the production of nuclear weapons either directly or in third-party countries.

Under Prime Minister P. W. Botha, the South African government decides neither to acknowledge nor deny its nuclear capability. If threatened, however, the government will consider privately revealing its nuclear status to international powers such as the United States, possibly with a nuclear test, to compel international intervention on its behalf.

In June, the UN General Assembly, at the First Special Session on Disarmament in New York, provides a mandate to the newly reorganized Conference on Disarmament in Geneva to deal with nuclear arms control and general disarmament issues.

1979   On March 28, an accident in the cooling system occurs at the Three Mile Island Nuclear Plant near Harrisburg, Pennsylvania, releasing radiation into the atmosphere and requiring evacuation of the area. The accident boosts public support for a freeze on the production of nuclear weapons.

In June, Carter and Brezhnev sign the SALT II Treaty. It sets a ceiling of 2,400 strategic delivery systems and limits to 1,320 the number allowed to carry multiple warheads.

South Africa secretly produces its first usable nuclear weapon. It develops plans to produce seven nuclear weapons. On September 22, a U.S. surveillance satellite detects a brief, intense, double flash of light off the southern coast of Africa. U.S. officials surmise that the flash could have resulted from the test of a nuclear device with a yield of 2–4 kilotons. There is speculation that South Africa, Israel, or the two countries working together conducted a test; the South African government denies the accusations.

In November, a tape of a simulated missile attack mistakenly activates the U.S. early warning system. During the six minutes it takes to discover the attack is not authentic, fighters from Canadian and U.S. bases take off, and missile and submarine installations worldwide are placed on alert.

NATO ministers adopt a dual-track strategy in November to counter the Soviet deployment of highly accurate, multiple-warhead mobile SS-20 missiles that have a 5,000-kilometer range, permitting them to hit targets throughout Western Europe. One track calls for arms-control negotiations between the United States and Soviet Union to reduce all intermediate-range missiles; the other calls for deploying 464 single-warhead U.S. ground-launched cruise missiles and 108 Pershing II ballistic missiles in Western Europe, beginning in December 1983, in case talks should fail.

1980   After the Soviet Union's invasion of Afghanistan in December 1979, President Carter withdraws the SALT II Treaty from Senate consideration in January because of its expected defeat. Carter and Brezhnev both issue statements that their countries will comply with the treaty as long as the other side does.

The Convention on the Physical Protection of Nuclear Material is opened for signature in March. The convention calls for certain levels of physical protection (e.g., controlled access, surveillance by guards and electronic devices) during international transport of nuclear material and while in domestic use.

In June, a computer chip in the North American Aerospace Defense Command system fails, causing the system to mistakenly indicate a Soviet missile attack. About 100 U.S. B-52 bombers, along with other aircraft, are readied for takeoff before the error is detected. In September, an accident in a silo of a Titan II ICBM sends a reentry vehicle with a 9-megaton warhead 600 feet into the air, killing one person and injuring twenty-one others, although the warhead does not detonate.

The ten-year NPT Review Conference opens in August; the treaty now has 112 members. The participants fail to agree on a final declaration, largely because nuclear weapon states allegedly have not worked hard enough to fulfill their obligation to negotiate measures to halt the nuclear arms race.

1981   Incoming President Ronald Reagan orders several new nuclear weapon delivery systems (MX missiles, Trident submarines, and B-1 bombers) to overcome what he calls a "window of vulnerability" versus the Soviet Union.

In April, the U.S. nuclear submarine *George Washington*, carrying 160 nuclear warheads, collides with a Japanese freighter in the East China Sea while surfacing. The freighter sinks in fifteen minutes, killing two Japanese crew members.

On June 7, Israeli fighter planes bomb the Tammuz-1 (Osiraq) nuclear research reactor near Baghdad to prevent Iraq from developing nuclear weapons. The reactor, subject to IAEA safeguards, had not yet begun operating, but the Israeli attack reduces it to rubble.

1982   The World Health Organization estimates that a major nuclear war would kill 2 billion people—half of the Earth's population.

On June 12, almost 1 million people gather in New York City's Central Park to protest the nuclear arms race, making it probably the largest political demonstration in history. Subsequent resolutions calling for a freeze on further deployment of nuclear weapons win in eight statewide elections (California, Massachusetts, Michigan, Montana, New Jersey, North Dakota, Oregon, and Rhode Island) and several major city elections. The freeze proposal is endorsed by 150 national organizations, many major religious groups, and twenty-five of the largest U.S. trade unions. The referenda demonstrate a groundswell of disagreement with the Reagan administration's policy of increasing the U.S. nuclear arsenal and preparing to win and survive a nuclear war.

1983   On March 23, President Reagan calls for the development of a nationwide missile defense system drawing on proposed new technologies, including space-based interceptors, magnetic rail guns, and lasers. Officially known as the Strategic Defense Initiative (SDI), the press refers to the expensive military plan as "Star Wars."

After the success of various states' nuclear freeze referenda, the Democratic-controlled House of Representatives passes a nonbinding resolution in May advocating a nuclear freeze. A few weeks later, however, some supporters of the freeze legislation join those approving new funding for the MX missile.

Also in May, Roman Catholic bishops issue a pastoral letter, "The Challenge of Peace: God's Promise and Our Response," declaring support for an immediate U.S.-Soviet agreement to halt the arms race. More than 1 million copies of the letter are circulated, and it receives widespread press attention. The World Council of Churches adopts a resolution stating that the

1983
(*cont.*)
production, deployment, and use of nuclear weapons are crimes against humanity and must be condemned on ethical and theological grounds.

Under its dual-track strategy, NATO deploys U.S. ground-based nuclear cruise missiles in the United Kingdom and Pershing II nuclear missiles in Germany. In October, 3 million people across Europe demonstrate against these deployments in the largest political rally in European history.

The U.S. State Department determines that Pakistan—a key U.S. ally in the effort to back anti-Soviet Muslim fighters in Afghanistan—is developing nuclear weapons with help from China, including the design for a nuclear bomb.

1984
On March 21, the U.S. aircraft carrier *Kitty Hawk*, carrying several dozen nuclear weapons, collides with a Soviet Victor-class attack submarine carrying nuclear-armed torpedoes in the Sea of Japan. The Soviet submarine has to be towed to Vladivostok.

In April, the United States and China sign a nuclear trade agreement after the Chinese government agrees to join the IAEA and to accept IAEA inspections of any exported nuclear material and equipment.

1985
Pakistan secretly develops the capability to enrich uranium to weapons grade. The U.S. Congress enacts the Pressler Amendment stating that U.S. military sales and yearly aid to Pakistan will be cut off unless the U.S. president can certify that Pakistan does not possess a nuclear explosive device. The Reagan administration continues aid to Pakistan, despite concerns about its nuclear program, because it seeks Pakistan's help in ousting Soviet forces from Afghanistan.

At the fifteen-year NPT Review Conference, the 131 parties adopt a final declaration that pledges support for the treaty while calling for stronger nuclear disarmament measures. Under Soviet pressure, North Korea joins the NPT and agrees to open an indigenously constructed research reactor to IAEA inspections, once it completes a formal safeguards agreement.

The international organization Greenpeace sends a boat, *Rainbow Warrior,* to the South Pacific to protest French nuclear testing. While the boat is docked in Auckland, New Zealand, French secret service agents detonate a bomb on it, killing one person onboard and provoking international outrage.

On August 6, on the fortieth anniversary of the Hiroshima bombing, the Soviet Union declares a unilateral moratorium on nuclear testing after conducting ten tests in 1985. During this year, the United States conducts seventeen nuclear tests, France eight, and the United Kingdom one.

Also on August 6, members of the South Pacific Forum, including Australia and New Zealand, open the South Pacific Nuclear-Free Zone Treaty (the Treaty of Rarotonga) for signature. Each party agrees not to build nuclear weapons, not to allow stationing of the weapons of other states, and to seek to prevent nuclear testing and the dumping of radioactive materials in the zone and territorial seas. Article V allows each party to decide whether to allow ships and aircraft with nuclear fuel or materials within its territory.

South African President Botha decides that the nuclear weapon program will be limited to seven highly enriched uranium (HEU) fission devices. South Africa stops all work related to plutonium weapon development.

In November, Argentina and Brazil sign the Joint Declaration on Nuclear Policy, stating their commitment to develop nuclear energy exclusively for peaceful purposes and to undertake confidence-building measures, including eventual reciprocal visits to nuclear installations.

In December, a Nobel Prize is awarded to the organization International Physicians for the Prevention of Nuclear War.

1986   U.S. intelligence agencies report that Pakistan has the capability to produce HEU and to assemble nuclear weapons. In September, Pakistan conducts cold tests (i.e., instrumented detonations of simulated nuclear bombs) at Chagai. China aids Pakistan's nuclear

1986
(*cont.*)

efforts; the two countries sign an agreement on the peaceful uses of nuclear energy that includes the construction and operation of nuclear power reactors.

On April 26, an uncontrolled power surge at reactor No. 4 of the Chernobyl Nuclear Power Plant in Ukraine causes sudden overheating and an explosion that releases a highly radioactive cloud. The blast contaminates a large portion of the surrounding area and forces the emergency evacuation of workers and tens of thousands of people from nearby cities. Thirty-one staff and emergency personnel are killed trying to shut down the reactor. The Soviet government at first denies the accident, causing an international furor when airborne radiation is detected in many European capitals.

In October, a fire aboard a Soviet Yankee-class nuclear-powered ballistic missile submarine (SSBN) in the Atlantic threatens to cause a reactor explosion. The crew prevents a reactor incident, but four sailors die, and the submarine sinks along with sixteen nuclear weapons.

Also in October, the Israeli government arrests Mordechai Vanunu, a former mid-level nuclear technician at Israeli's Dimona nuclear facility, after he provides London's *Sunday Times* with information showing that Israel possesses approximately 150 nuclear weapons.

Soviet leader Mikhail Gorbachev calls for nuclear weapons to be eliminated by the year 2000. He proposes that the two superpowers first reduce their strategic arsenals by half; then remove all weapons from foreign countries, halt testing/development, and enlist other nuclear states; and finally, eliminate nuclear weapons altogether. In October, Reagan and Gorbachev almost reach an agreement to adopt a similar plan at the summit in Reykjavik, Iceland, but the U.S. commitment to pursue the SDI program scuttles the deal.

On December 11, the South Pacific Nuclear-Free Zone Treaty enters into force when the eighth member ratifies it.

1987   The Soviet Union ends an 18-month nuclear test moratorium in February but announces that it is willing to resume the moratorium if the United States will do the same.

In April, the Missile Technology Control Regime is established by seven industrialized countries: Canada, France, Italy, Japan, the United Kingdom, the United States, and West Germany. The Missile Technololgy Control Regime is designed to reduce the risk of nuclear proliferation via limits on the export of ballistic and cruise missile technologies for systems capable of delivering a 500-kilogram payload (roughly the size of an unsophisticated nuclear warhead) a distance of 300 kilometers.

In June, the New Zealand parliament bans any nuclear-powered ships and vessels carrying nuclear explosives from the country's ports. The government refuses to accept the U.S. practice of neither confirming nor denying the presence of nuclear weapons onboard its warships.

On September 15, U.S. Secretary of State George Shultz and Soviet Foreign Minister Eduard Shevardnadze sign an agreement to open nuclear risk reduction centers in each country's capital and to establish special bilateral communications links.

On December 8, Reagan and Gorbachev sign the Intermediate-Range Nuclear Forces (INF) Treaty, which requires the destruction of the countries' ground-launched ballistic and cruise missiles with ranges between 500 and 5,500 kilometers within three years of the treaty's entry into force. The INF Treaty contains stringent verification measures designed to ensure compliance with the ban, including on-site inspections and monitoring.

1988   In January, the United States creates the On-Site Inspection Agency to verify, on Soviet territory, Moscow's fulfillment of weapon elimination required under the INF Treaty and to fulfill its escort obligations for Soviet inspectors in the United States.

In April, the Danish parliament passes a resolution instructing the government to notify visiting war-

1988
(*cont.*)

ships that nuclear weapons are banned from Danish territory in peacetime.

In May, the United States and the Soviet Union sign the Agreement on the Notification of Missile Launches, which requires 24 hours' advance notice before the test launching of an ICBM or SLBM.

On June 1, the INF Treaty enters into force.

In August, the Soviet Union monitors an underground U.S. nuclear test, and in September, the United States monitors a Soviet test.

In September, Brazil adopts a constitution providing that all nuclear activities within its territory will be for peaceful purposes and must be approved by the National Congress.

In December, India and Pakistan sign an agreement prohibiting attacks on each other's nuclear installations and pledging to inform each other of their locations.

1989

In February, a U.S.-Soviet public organization linking antinuclear activists—the Nevada-Semipalatinsk Movement—is founded. In October, the final Soviet underground nuclear test occurs at the Semipalatinsk test range in Kazakhstan.

On April 7, the Soviet Union's Mike-class nuclear submarine *Komsomolets* sinks in deep water 300 miles off the coast of Norway after an uncontrollable fire, killing forty-two crew members. The submarine is carrying three nuclear-tipped torpedoes, which are not recovered.

In May, India successfully launches its Agni missile, which has a range of 2,500 kilometers and is capable of carrying small nuclear weapons.

In September, South Africa's newly elected president F. W. de Klerk, states in a secret meeting that to end South Africa's isolation from the international community, the country must dismantle both its political system of apartheid and its nuclear weapon program. The Y Plant stops producing HEU, and the nuclear test site in the Kalahari Desert is abandoned.

1990   Early in the year, South Africa secretly begins dismantling its nuclear weapon stockpile.

In June, U.S. President George H. W. Bush and
Soviet leader Gorbachev sign protocols to earlier treaties that provide for advance notification and on-site
inspections of tests above 35 kilotons. In September,
the United States finally ratifies the 1975 Threshold
Test Ban Treaty.

In August, under the leadership of Saddam Hussein, Iraq invades and occupies Kuwait. Iraq also engages
in a crash program to develop a nuclear weapon by
April 1991.

The twenty-year NPT Review Conference is held
with 140 members. Once again, the NPT parties strongly
disagree on whether the nuclear weapon states have
done enough to pursue their disarmament obligations.
On November 28, the presidents of long-time NPT holdouts Brazil and Argentina sign the Joint Declaration of
Common Nuclear Policy at Iguazú. Both countries
agree to use nuclear energy only for peaceful purposes,
to create a formal system of bilateral inspections, to give
up the right to conduct peaceful nuclear explosions, and
to adhere to a revised Treaty of Tlatelolco.

On September 27, the last Pershing II missiles
leave Germany, assisting the reunification of East and
West Germany in early October.

Having detected Pakistan's assembly of at least
one nuclear device, President Bush refuses to make
the certification required by the Pressler Amendment
and terminates military aid to Pakistan.

1991   In late February, U.S.-led coalition forces succeed in
ending the Iraqi occupation of Kuwait. The UN Security Council passes Resolution 687 in April, forcing
Iraq to consent to the destruction of its WMD facilities
and any ballistic missiles with a range greater than 150
kilometers. The IAEA and the newly formed UN Special Commission on Iraq (UNSCOM) begin inspecting
Iraq's undeclared weapon-related facilities. In September, IAEA inspectors discover a large number of

1991
(*cont.*)

documents related to Iraq's efforts to acquire nuclear weapons. Inspectors learn that Iraq had concealed its nuclear program by constructing buildings within buildings, designing weapon facilities to look like they had a peaceful purpose, hiding utility lines that would signal a nuclear facility, and placing facilities underground.

In his State of the Union address, President George Bush announces a shift in the SDI program to the more modest Global Protection against Limited Strikes program.

France's nuclear arsenal peaks at 538 weapons. At this time, the United States has an arsenal of 19,500 weapons; the Soviet Union has 35,000; the United Kingdom has 300; China has 434; Israel has approximately 100; and India and Pakistan have an unknown number.

On July 31, after almost ten years of negotiations, the United States and the Soviet Union sign the Strategic Arms Reduction Treaty (START). Both countries agree to reduce their nuclear arsenals to 1,600 strategic delivery vehicles and 6,000 deployed warheads, of which no more than 4,900 can be on ground-based ballistic missiles. Under START I, no more than 1,000 warheads are permitted on mobile missiles. The reductions are to occur within seven years. Both presidents also make additional unilateral pledges. Bush announces the withdrawal of all remaining ground-based tactical nuclear weapons and ship-based tactical nuclear weapons worldwide. Gorbachev commits to destroying tactical land-based ballistic missiles, artillery shells, and mines and to removing all tactical nuclear weapons from the Soviet Navy.

The United States eliminates its last ground-launched cruise and ballistic missiles covered by the INF Treaty, and the Soviet Union eliminates its last declared SS-20 missile. Pursuant to the INF Treaty, 2,692 missiles have been eliminated.

In July, South Africa joins the NPT as a non–nuclear weapon state and, in September, signs a full-scope safeguards agreement with the IAEA. Secretly, it finishes dismantling its existing nuclear weapons.

Also in July, the presidents of Argentina and Brazil sign the Agreement for the Exclusively Peaceful Uses of Nuclear Energy (also known as the Guadalajara Treaty). It prohibits the development, testing, and deployment of nuclear weapons. It calls for joint inspections of nuclear installations in the respective countries and sets up the Brazil-Argentine Agency for Accounting and Control of Nuclear Materials to administer the inspection arrangement in coordination with the IAEA.

In September, Pakistan Prime Minister Benazir Bhutto states that Pakistan could quickly produce a nuclear weapon in the event of a serious threat.

In October, the U.S. Congress passes the Nunn-Lugar legislation (named for its Senate cosponsors), which will provide $400 million to help dismantle Soviet WMD and delivery vehicles slated for destruction under the START I agreement, to heighten nuclear safety, and to prevent proliferation. On December 25, Russian Republic President Boris Yeltsin leads the presidents of the other fourteen republics in dissolving the Soviet Union. Gorbachev signs over control of the Soviet nuclear arsenal to Yeltsin. All the new republics, except Georgia, Latvia, Lithuania, and Estonia, agree to form a loose coalition known as the Commonwealth of Independent States (CIS). Russia, Belarus, Ukraine, and Kazakhstan have large numbers of the Soviet Union's strategic nuclear weapons on their soil, and tactical nuclear weapons are still distributed throughout former Soviet territory; the CIS leaders agree that all tactical nuclear weapons will be returned to Russia by July 1992.

On December 30, the CIS members sign the Minsk Agreement on Strategic Forces, which creates a joint CIS command over the former Soviet Union's nuclear arsenal. Russia, in consultation with Ukraine, Belarus, and Kazakhstan, will decide on the use of nuclear weapons.

1992   In April, French president François Mitterrand initiates a moratorium on nuclear testing. France finally decides to ratify the NPT as a nuclear weapon state and stops producing plutonium for military purposes.

South and North Korea sign the Joint Declaration for a Non-Nuclear Korean Peninsula. It bans both countries from testing, producing, acquiring, and deploying nuclear weapons and prohibits them from possessing facilities to produce weapons-grade fissionable material. After a long delay, North Korea signs a safeguards agreement with the IAEA. The U.S. Department of Defense announces its removal of all nuclear weapons from South Korea.

In May, North Korea reports to the IAEA that it has about 90 grams of plutonium subject to safeguards from a one-time reprocessing of defective fuel rods. However, chemical sampling from on-site IAEA inspections later in the year leads IAEA experts to conclude that North Korea has actually removed spent fuel on two or three other occasions since 1989, meaning that additional weapons-grade material could have been diverted to a bomb program. U.S. satellite photographs indicate a suspected reprocessing facility.

The United States, Germany, and other Western countries help establish two international science and technology centers, one in Russia and one in Ukraine, to provide former Soviet nuclear scientists and engineers with civilian research grants.

After the discovery of the advanced state of the Iraqi nuclear program, the IAEA's governing body approves new measures granting the IAEA the right to demand special inspections of undeclared nuclear facilities. Also, the Nuclear Suppliers Group agrees to tighten export controls on thousands of dual-use items and to require importing countries to accept full-scope safeguards of all their nuclear facilities. An IAEA inspection team, aided by UNSCOM inspectors, completes the destruction of key facilities and equipment at Al-Atheer, Iraq's main nuclear weapon design and development complex.

In March, longtime holdout China joins the NPT as a nuclear weapon state. However, two months later,

China conducts its largest nuclear test ever: a 1-megaton device.

Belarus, Kazakhstan, Russia, and Ukraine sign the Lisbon Protocol to START in May, thereby becoming legal inheritors of the Soviet Union's obligations under the treaty. All but Russia agree to join the NPT as non–nuclear weapon states as soon as possible. Within the year, the parliaments of Kazakhstan and Russia ratify START.

At their first summit in June, Presidents George Bush and Boris Yeltsin sign agreements to implement the U.S. Nunn-Lugar legislation approving unprecedented aid to the former Soviet Union for dismantling weapons and protecting fissile material. In the Russian city of Podolsk, a thief is caught at a train station after making off with 1.5 kilograms of HEU from a nuclear facility, confirming the proliferation threat posed by poorly guarded Russian nuclear sites.

The United States replaces its SAC with the U.S. Strategic Command, reducing its reliance on nuclear weapons. In July, as part of a general nonproliferation initiative, President Bush announces that the United States will no longer produce plutonium or HEU for nuclear explosives. In August, however, the United States launches its fourteenth Trident nuclear submarine equipped with twenty-four multiple-warhead missiles.

In June, Britain's defense minister announces that the British Navy will no longer routinely carry nuclear weapons on surface ships.

In October, Russian police arrest an engineer at the Luch nuclear material production plant near Moscow who is trying to sell 1.5 kilograms of HEU stolen from his employer.

1993   In January, Presidents Bush and Yeltsin sign START II. Once ratified, the treaty will require Russia and the United States to cut their deployed strategic nuclear arsenals to 3,000–3,500 warheads each. START II allows only single-warhead land-based ICBMs and only 1,700–1,750 SLBM warheads. Under START II, Russia will have to eliminate about forty submarines,

1993
(*cont.*)

1,500 ballistic missiles, and 7,000 warheads. The United States will have to eliminate several submarines, dozens of bombers, and hundreds of ground-based missiles. The treaty cannot go into effect before START I is ratified by the U.S. Congress and Russia's parliament.

In February, the Russian Ministry of Defense reports that all tactical nuclear weapons have been removed from naval surface vessels, submarines, and aircraft and put into storage. Russia also agrees to sell the United States 500 tons of weapons-grade HEU from dismantled nuclear weapons over a twenty-year period for approximately $12 billion.

Belarus ratifies START I and joins the NPT as a non–nuclear weapon state. By contrast, the Ukrainian Rada (parliament) adopts a new defense doctrine that designates as Ukrainian property the Soviet strategic nuclear weapons located on its territory. In October, the United States agrees to give Ukraine approximately $177 million to help eliminate its strategic nuclear arms. Ukraine conditionally ratifies START I—pending security guarantees and confirmation of $2.8 billion in foreign aid—but still refuses to join the NPT as a non–nuclear weapon state.

In February, UNSCOM announces that Iraq's nuclear weapon program has been destroyed but warns that long-term monitoring will be necessary to ensure that Iraq does not resume building WMD.

In March, North Korea refuses to allow a special IAEA inspection and gives notice that it will withdraw from the NPT in three months. After secret negotiations with the United States, Pyongyang suspends its withdrawal in June, pending further negotiations with Washington.

In a stunning public announcement, South African President de Klerk admits in March that South Africa had a nuclear weapon program from 1974 to 1990, during which time it constructed six nuclear bombs. But he declares that South Africa has eliminated these weapons. In September, the IAEA accepts South Africa's declarations that its weapons-related equipment and test shafts have been dismantled and destroyed.

In October, China conducts a nuclear test at its Lop Nor test site.

In November, the UN General Assembly approves a resolution calling on North Korea to cooperate with the IAEA in the full implementation of its safeguards agreement.

In December, U.S. Energy Secretary Hazel O'Leary holds the first of several so-called Openness Initiative press conferences to review recently declassified documents. Among other things, she discloses that the United States exploded 204 more nuclear devices than previously admitted publicly, and that the AEC conducted several hundred radiation experiments on unsuspecting U.S. citizens from the 1940s to the 1970s. Two new cases of HEU theft take place at Russian naval facilities; both thieves are caught.

As of December, the U.S. Department of Defense has pledged $789 million in weapon dismantlement and other nuclear-related assistance to the four former Soviet states with nuclear weapons. Russia promises to stop producing plutonium for nuclear weapons and to shut down the three reactors that produce weapons-grade plutonium. Kazakhstan joins the NPT as a non–nuclear weapon state, and the United States promises to give Kazakhstan more than $70 million in dismantlement and nuclear facility safety assistance.

1994   In January, U.S. President Bill Clinton, Russian President Yeltsin, and Ukrainian President Leonid Kravchuk sign the Trilateral Statement on the Non-Proliferation of Weapons of Mass Destruction and the Means of Their Delivery. It commits Ukraine to rid itself of nuclear weapons and transfer its warheads to Russia. In return, the United States and Russia agree to guarantee Ukraine's borders and to assist in its security as long as it joins the NPT as a non–nuclear weapon state. In February, the Ukrainian Rada ratifies START I without conditions, thus endorsing the Trilateral Statement.

In February, states at the Conference on Disarmament in Geneva begin negotiating a comprehensive nuclear-test-ban treaty.

1994
(*cont.*)

The United States and Russia sign the Moscow Declaration stating that both countries agree to detarget their strategic nuclear missiles away from one another by 30 May 1994.

In May, North Korea begins unloading spent fuel rods from its plutonium-producing reactor, and the IAEA announces that Pyongyang is no longer in compliance with IAEA safeguards. In June, former U.S. President Jimmy Carter goes to North Korea to try to break the impasse. On October 21, North Korea and the United States sign the so-called Agreed Framework that calls for North Korea to freeze and eventually dismantle its existing nuclear reactor program in return for two proliferation-resistant, light-water reactors to be supplied by 2003. No sensitive nuclear technology will be turned over, however, until North Korea opens all of its facilities to IAEA inspectors. The United States agrees to compensate North Korea for potential lost power from its own planned power reactors by supplying 50,000 tons of heavy fuel oil per year.

Small amounts of additional Soviet-origin, weapons-grade nuclear material are seized in Germany and Czechoslovakia, confirming that nuclear smuggling is a serious new threat.

On November 24, after months of negotiations, the United States airlifts 600 kilograms of at-risk weapons-grade uranium from the Ulba facility in Kazakhstan in a cooperative secret mission dubbed Operation Sapphire. The United States buys the uranium from Kazakhstan for an undisclosed amount of money (rumored in the tens of millions of dollars) plus technical assistance.

In November, Ukraine's Rada finally votes to ratify the NPT as a non–nuclear weapon state. In December, the presidents of the United States, Russia, Ukraine, Belarus, and Kazakhstan certify that START I has entered into force.

Argentina and Brazil ratify the Treaty of Tlatelolco, confirming their non–nuclear weapon pledges and accepting IAEA inspections of all nuclear activities.

1995   On January 25, a Norwegian-U.S. rocket designed to study the Northern Lights is launched from Norway's coast; the Russian military briefly mistakes this launch for a nuclear attack. A radar station notifies central early warning stations of a possible nuclear missile attack and alerts the highest levels of the Russian command, including President Yeltsin, about the possibility of launching a counterattack, but it is quickly called off.

On January 30, President Clinton decides to extend the U.S. moratorium on nuclear testing until a comprehensive test-ban treaty enters into force.

In April, before the NPT Review and Extension Conference marking the treaty's twenty-fifth anniversary, all five nuclear weapon states renew their pledges not to use nuclear weapons against non–nuclear weapon state that are parties to the NPT (unless attacked by such parties in concert with a weapon-possessing state) and to come to the aid of such parties if they are threatened with nuclear weapons. In May, NPT members decide (by consensus) that the treaty will be extended indefinitely and issue resolutions on principles and objectives for nuclear nonproliferation and complete nuclear disarmament. After the NPT is extended, however, China conducts two nuclear tests at the Lop Nor test site.

In June, newly elected French President Jacques Chirac decides to resume nuclear testing after a three-year moratorium to prove the efficacy of France's new TN-75 warhead and check the reliability of older French nuclear weapons. Despite worldwide protests, France conducts 20-, 30-, 40-, and 60-kiloton underground nuclear weapon tests at the Mururoa Atoll and detonates a 110-kiloton SLBM warhead at the Fangataufa Atoll. In July, about 150 French commandos storm and teargas a Greenpeace boat, the *Rainbow Warrior II*, after the ship enters the exclusion zone around the nuclear test site at Mururoa. The International Court of Justice rejects New Zealand's bid to stop further nuclear testing by France in the South Pacific. But President Chirac reduces France's nuclear posture by

1995
(*cont.*)

dismantling its two ground-to-ground nuclear missile systems, capping a five-year, 15 percent reduction of its nuclear arsenal.

The Nobel Peace Prize is awarded to the Pugwash Conferences on Science and World Affairs and its president, Joseph Rotblat, for their efforts to eliminate nuclear weapons.

On December 15, ten countries (Brunei, Indonesia, Cambodia, Laos, Malaysia, Myanmar, the Philippines, Singapore, Thailand, and Vietnam) sign the Southeast Asian Nuclear-Weapon-Free Zone Treaty. Each party agrees not to develop, acquire, station, transport, or test nuclear weapons and not to dump any radioactive material or wastes into the sea or atmosphere. Each party retains the right to refuse transport of nuclear weapons through its territorial waters, a clause opposed by some of the nuclear weapon states.

In March, the United States, South Korea, and Japan sign an agreement formally establishing the Korean Peninsula Energy Development Organization (KEDO), based in New York, to organize construction of two light-water power reactors in North Korea. Other countries (including Australia, Canada, New Zealand, the European Union, Singapore, Malaysia, the Philippines, Italy, Finland, Greece, the Netherlands, and Indonesia) join or contribute funding. In September, a group of U.S. Department of Energy technicians starts operations at Yongbyon to safeguard the spent fuel storage pond, including packing the 8,000 nuclear spent fuel rods into watertight canisters. Also, the IAEA sends a team of inspectors to North Korea to monitor its compliance with the NPT and the Agreed Framework.

1996

In January, the U.S. Senate ratifies START II by an overwhelming majority. But the Russian Duma still has not ratified it.

North Korea bars IAEA inspectors from measuring the plutonium levels in the 8,000 nuclear spent fuel rods being moved into storage at the Yongbyon facility. In October, the UN General Assembly passes a resolution urging North Korea to comply fully with the IAEA nuclear safeguards agreement.

In January, France detonates a 120-kiloton device at Fangataufa Atoll in the South Pacific. French authorities admit a release of radioactive iodine 131. Facing massive international protests, French President Chirac declares that France has achieved its goal to guarantee its nuclear deterrent and announces a testing moratorium. In March, France signs the protocols to the South Pacific Nuclear-Free Zone Treaty, together with the United States and the United Kingdom, and closes its national nuclear test site in the region.

In April, forty-three African states sign the African Nuclear-Weapon-Free Zone Treaty (or the Pelindaba Treaty). The treaty pledges members will not develop, manufacture, acquire, possess, control, station, or test any nuclear explosive device. It also prohibits research on nuclear weapons and the dumping of radioactive wastes within the zone. The treaty will become effective after it is ratified by twenty-eight African states. Egypt says it will not ratify the treaty until Israel joins the NPT.

In July, China conducts its forty-fifth nuclear weapons test at the Lop Nor test site, and then announces a testing moratorium.

Also in July, the International Court of Justice issues an advisory opinion, responding to the UN General Assembly's request for a ruling on the legality of nuclear weapons. The court holds that the threat or use of nuclear weapons, with their potential to destroy all civilization and the ecosystem of the planet, would generally be unlawful under the UN Charter's humanitarian rules for armed conflicts. But it accepts possible use in cases of extreme self-defense. Following the opinion, the UN General Assembly adopts a resolution that calls on all states to begin multilateral negotiations on a convention to ban nuclear weapons.

On September 24, the Comprehensive Nuclear-Test-Ban Treaty (CTBT) is opened for signature; 71 states sign, including all five nuclear weapon states.

1996
(*cont.*)

Under the CTBT, each party agrees not to carry out any further nuclear tests in any environment. The treaty creates the CTBT Organization to oversee the implementation of the treaty and verification of compliance. For the treaty to enter into force, all forty-four states with existing nuclear infrastructures must ratify it.

Ukraine and Belarus transfer their last Soviet-era nuclear weapons to Russia for destruction.

In September, the United State receives shipments of spent nuclear fuel from research reactors in Chile, Colombia, France, Sweden, and Switzerland under its program to reduce the use of HEU internationally in civilian reactors. The Department of Energy promotes conversion of civilian reactors from HEU to low-enriched uranium fuel, which is harder to convert to weapons-grade material.

In December, former commander in chief of the U.S. Strategic Air Command, General Lee Butler, and the former supreme allied commander in Europe, General Andrew Goodpaster, release a joint statement emphasizing the diminished role of nuclear weapons and calling on all nuclear weapon states to work toward the elimination of these weapons. Later, sixty-one other retired generals and admirals from seventeen countries release a similar statement.

1997

In January, the United States adds to its nuclear arsenal a modified B61 thermonuclear bomb with yield options from roughly 10 kilotons to 340 kilotons and a limited earth-penetrating capability.

In March, the European Parliament calls on its members to support negotiation of an anti–nuclear weapon convention. At the UN on April 7, the Lawyers' Committee on Nuclear Policy releases the Model Nuclear Weapons Convention. Drafted by an international group of lawyers, scientists, and disarmament experts, the convention sets out procedures to dismantle and destroy all nuclear weapons in a series of graduated steps, to safeguard weapon materials, and to ensure compliance with the requirement to abolish nuclear weapons. Abolition 2000, an international network of more than 700 organizations, aims for the convention to be adopted by 2000.

The IAEA's board of governors approves more intrusive verification measures in May, known as the 93+2 program. States can voluntarily agree to the new measures by adding to their existing safeguards agreements through the so-called Additional Protocol. The IAEA will gain greater access to information about all aspects of a state's nuclear fuel cycle facilities and use state-of-the-art technologies to trace nuclear activities through environmental sampling and remotely operated surveillance and monitoring systems.

In July and September, the United States conducts its first subcritical nuclear experiments in an underground tunnel at the Nevada Test Site, in which chemical explosives generate high pressure on nuclear weapon materials without causing a nuclear explosion. Critics argue that the U.S. experiments violate the spirit if not the letter of the CTBT.

In August, the British Department of Health reports that it has found plutonium in children's teeth throughout the United Kingdom. It concludes that the cause of the plutonium is radioactive discharges from the Sellafield plutonium-reprocessing plant.

In September, Russian Security Council Secretary-General Aleksandr Lebed claims that 100 suitcase-sized nuclear weapons, meant to be used by Soviet commandos in time of war, are now missing in Russia. Other officials deny the claim.

France's new socialist prime minister, Lionel Jospin, confirms that France intends to maintain its nuclear weapon capability as a deterrence measure. However, the French government continues to decrease spending on nuclear weapons, and the French nuclear arsenal falls to 450.

The United States deploys the last of eighteen Trident nuclear submarines capable of carrying 192 nuclear warheads on twenty-four missiles.

In February, presidents from five Central Asian countries (Kazakhstan, Kyrgyzstan, Tajikistan, Turkmenistan, and Uzbekistan) call for a nuclear-weapon-free zone in their region. The United States and Russia

1997
(*cont.*)
agree to extend the date for completing START II nuclear weapons reductions from 1 January 2003 to 31 December 2007, given delays in ratification of the treaty in both countries, as well as economic difficulties in Russia that will slow its compliance.

Scientists at the U.S. National Cancer Institute estimate that bomb tests conducted in Nevada during the 1950s eventually may cause 10,000–75,000 extra thyroid cancers.

Over strong Russian objections, NATO members sign protocols in December making Poland, Hungary, and the Czech Republic full members of NATO and thus eligible for protection under the U.S. extended nuclear deterrent.

1998
As of January, the U.S. government, under the Radiation Exposure and Compensation Act of 1990, has paid U.S. citizens approximately $225 million.

In February, the European Parliament adopts a resolution calling on the United States and all governments to refrain from carrying out subcritical tests of nuclear weapons. Despite this plea, the United States conducts three more subcritical tests, and Russia conducts five such tests at its Novaya Zemlya test range.

In February, the UN and Iraq sign a memorandum of understanding stating that Iraq will cooperate fully with UNSCOM and the IAEA and provide unrestricted access to WMD-related sites. In August, however, Iraq decides to stop cooperating until the UN Security Council ends sanctions on Iraq.

In March, the United Kingdom completes its Strategic Defense Review and plans a major reduction in its nuclear arsenal. It removes all its air-delivered WE177 bombs from service and begins to dismantle them. Its only remaining nuclear delivery system, the Trident submarine, is also scaled back; the number of submarines on patrol is reduced to one, and the number of warheads per submarine is reduced to forty-eight. The United Kingdom also announces that its total nuclear arsenal will be unilaterally reduced to fewer than 200 operationally available warheads.

In April, Britain and France become the first nuclear weapon states to ratify the CTBT, banning all nuclear weapon tests.

In May, India's newly elected government shocks the world by conducting a series of nuclear weapon tests. Indian officials state that on May 11 India conducted three tests: a fission device with a yield of about 12 kilotons, a thermonuclear device with a yield of about 43 kilotons, and a subkiloton device. On May 13, India detonates two more nuclear weapons. Indian Prime Minister Atal Behari Vajpayee identifies China and Pakistan as the security reasons compelling the tests. Pakistan responds by conducting five nuclear weapon tests on May 28 in the Chagai Hills with an announced yield of 40–45 kilotons and an estimated yield of 6–13 kilotons. Two days later, it conducts one smaller test. (Using seismic and other monitoring information, U.S. experts conclude that both countries greatly inflated the yields and perhaps the numbers of tests, and the second stage of India's thermonuclear test most likely failed.) In response to these tests, the United States imposes strict economic sanctions on India and Pakistan.

In June, the UN Security Council condemns the Indian and Pakistani nuclear tests and urges the countries to become members of the NPT as non–nuclear weapon states. The so-called New Agenda Coalition (Brazil, Egypt, Ireland, Mexico, New Zealand, Slovenia, South Africa, and Sweden) issues a document calling for a nuclear-weapon-free world and outlining immediate steps that the nuclear weapon states can take to comply with their obligations under the NPT to pursue disarmament.

In August, North Korea tests a three-stage intermediate-range ballistic missile (Taep'o-dong-1); it flies for 1,380 kilometers over Japanese territory before landing in the Pacific Ocean after the third stage fails. In response to the missile launch and allegations that a nuclear facility is being constructed at Kumchang-ri, the United States and Japan suspend promised nuclear power assistance to North Korea.

1998
(*cont.*)

In December, thirty-nine environmental and peace organizations led by the Natural Resources Defense Council achieve a settlement in a ten-year National Environmental Policy Act lawsuit involving the Department of Energy's (DOE) $6 billion-per-year program managing radioactive waste and cleanup of environmental contamination caused by U.S. nuclear weapon production. Under the settlement, the DOE will create a publicly accessible database providing details about contaminated sites.

Russia's defense minister declares operational ten Topol-M ICBMs with a range of 10,500 kilometers. The Topol-M carries a single warhead, although it is capable of carrying three nuclear warheads and can be deployed in silos and mobile launchers. Russia plans for forty Topol-M missiles to be built by the end of 2000 at a cost of $30 million apiece.

1999

In January, international terrorist Osama bin Laden tells reporters that acquiring nuclear weapons for the defense of Muslims is a religious duty, as Muslims would then be able to destroy the United States as a superpower.

In February, India and Pakistan sign a memorandum of understanding to try to reduce the risks of accidental and unauthorized use of nuclear weapons in their countries. The two countries agree to notify each other immediately in the event of any accidental, unauthorized, or unexplained incident that could create a fallout risk or an outbreak of nuclear war. Later, Pakistan-backed militants cross into the Indian-controlled area of Kargil in the Kashmir region of the Himalaya Mountains and spark weeks of fighting, including air strikes, raising fears of a nuclear confrontation.

In April, NATO issues its new Strategic Concept, including air-delivered nuclear weapons and a small number of the United Kingdom's Trident warheads. Several hundred U.S. B61 bombs, officially unacknowledged, still remain at ten air bases in seven European countries (Belgium, Germany, Greece, Italy, the Netherlands, Turkey, and the United Kingdom).

In March, Los Alamos National Laboratory fires a Taiwanese-born computer scientist (Wen Ho Lee) for allegedly stealing information related to the W-88 nuclear warhead. In April, the DOE suspends all scientific work on computers containing sensitive nuclear weapon–related information at three national weapons laboratories: Los Alamos, Sandia, and Lawrence Livermore. The DOE works to increase security in response to suspicions of Chinese nuclear espionage.

In August, India's National Security Advisory Board issues a draft report on an Indian nuclear doctrine calling for a nuclear arsenal deployed on a triad of air-, land-, and sea-based launchers.

The *Bulletin of the Atomic Scientist* publishes an article on a secret DOE report revealing that Israel, which has refused to sign the NPT, has enough weapons-grade plutonium to build at least 250 nuclear weapons. Israel acquires the first of three Dolphin-class submarines from Germany as a possible nuclear delivery system (using cruise missiles).

On October 18, the Republican-controlled U.S. Senate votes to reject the CTBT, citing questions about its verifiability. The U.S. rejection leads to widespread international criticism.

For programs associated with the Nunn-Lugar legislation from 1991 to 1999, the United States has spent a total of $2.7 billion. As of December, these programs have helped deactivate 4,854 former Soviet nuclear warheads, destroyed 373 long-range ballistic missiles, eliminated 354 missile silos, sealed 191 nuclear test tunnels, and cut up twelve nuclear submarines capable of carrying 160 strategic missiles.

In April, India test fires a nuclear-capable, intermediate-range ballistic missile, the Agni-2, from a rail platform. Pakistan responds by testing a medium-range missile, the Ghauri, and a short-range ballistic missile, the Shaheen-1. In August, China tests the DF-31 ballistic missile, which has a range of 8,000 kilometers. These are land-based, road-mobile missiles with launch preparation times of less than fifteen minutes. The United States conducts several tests of systems designed to intercept and destroy attacking

1999
(*cont.*)

nuclear missiles. The United States also conducts three subcritical nuclear weapon tests.

In December, the UN Security Council establishes a new inspection regime for Iraq—the UN Monitoring, Verification, and Inspection Committee (UNMOVIC)—as a follow-on to UNSCOM. Iraq has refused to allow UNSCOM inspectors into the country since December 1998 and has also dismantled UNSCOM automated video-monitoring systems at known and suspected WMD facilities.

2000

In March, soon after the election of new Russian President Vladimir Putin, the Russian Duma ratifies both the CTBT and the seven-year-old START II, opening the way for talks to begin on further weapon reductions under a proposed START III.

The DOE announces that cleaning up environmental contamination from the U.S. nuclear weapon program will cost $168–$212 billion. Some of the worst sites include the Hanford facility in Washington, the Savannah River plant in South Carolina, Rocky Flats in Colorado, and the National Engineering and Environmental Laboratory in Idaho. At Hanford, about 54 million gallons of liquid radioactive waste are left over from Cold War bomb making, of which 1 million gallons has leaked into the soil. The U.S. National Academy of Science reports that many nuclear weapon sites will pose risks to humans and the environment for tens or even hundreds of thousands of years.

The final document of the May 2000 NPT Review Conference includes a pledge brokered by the eight-country New Agenda Coalition for "an unequivocal undertaking by the nuclear-weapon states to accomplish the total elimination of their nuclear arsenals," and a commitment by all members to stop nuclear testing. The NPT now has 187 members. Only Cuba, India, Israel, and Pakistan remain outside the treaty.

Former Los Alamos scientist Lee pleads guilty to a single charge of mishandling nuclear secrets; but the government drops 59 other charges, citing lack of evidence. The DOE announces that the world's most powerful laser, which is being built at Lawrence Livermore National Laboratory, will be delayed six years until 2008 and will cost at least $2.2 billion, double the original estimate. The laser project, known as the National Ignition Facility (NIF), will have 192 laser beams focusing energy on a single target, allowing nuclear scientists to simulate a thermonuclear explosion. It is a key component of the U.S. Stockpile Stewardship Program, which is designed to maintain nuclear warheads by using high-powered computers and the NIF laser to gauge weapon performance.

In October, Russia conducts two underground subcritical weapon tests at the Novaya Zemlya test site. In December, *Arms Control Today* estimates that since 1990, when START I went into effect, the United States has reduced its deployed strategic nuclear warheads from 10,563 to 7,519 and Russia has reduced its forces from 10,271 to 6,464.

2001   In January, former chairman of the Joint Chiefs of Staff John Shalikashvili releases his government-mandated CTBT study, which concludes that the United States must ratify the CTBT if there is to be an effective effort to halt the spread of nuclear weapons.

India test fires its Agni-2 intermediate-range missile, which has a range of 1,375 miles and can carry a nuclear payload of up to 1 ton. The Pakistan Navy announces that it may put nuclear missiles on its submarines; India has announced similar intentions.

At Britain's Faslane naval complex, 500 people protest the launching of the country's fourth Trident missile submarine, the HMS *Vengeance*.

In March, the CIA creates the Weapons Intelligence, Nonproliferation, and Arms Control Center to bring together about 500 analysts, scientists, and support personnel to focus on nonproliferation and arms control issues. A newly declassified internal CIA study reveals that every major intelligence assessment from 1974 to 1986 substantially overestimated the Soviet Union's plans to modernize and expand its strategic nuclear arsenal.

2001
(*cont.*)

Russian military officials report that, because of a fire at a ground relay station, they have lost control of four military satellites crucial to their network that provides early warning of a nuclear attack.

The eighty countries that have ratified the CTBT (including France, Russia, and the United Kingdom but not China, India, Israel, North Korea, Pakistan, and the United States) continue working on the organization that will verify treaty compliance. The International Monitoring System Committee has a 2001 budget of $83 million and a staff of more than 200. More than 100 stations currently relay data by satellite and cable to the CTBT Organization headquarters in Vienna.

In June, a detailed report released by the Natural Resources Defense Council shows that the nuclear weapons on a single U.S. Ohio-class nuclear submarine (of which the United States has eighteen) could kill or injure 50 million Russians, or more than one-third of the population.

On September 11, jets hijacked by terrorists fly into the Twin Towers of the World Trade Center in New York and into the Pentagon outside Washington. A fourth hijacked jet fails to reach its target and crashes in Pennsylvania. The prime suspect is Osama bin Laden's al Qaeda network based in Afghanistan. Because of its need for assistance in the war on terrorism being carried out in Afghanistan, the United States drops its 1998 nonproliferation sanctions on Pakistan and India, resuming normal trading relations and the possibility for economic assistance. Documents obtained by the U.S. military confirm that Osama bin Laden has sought to acquire nuclear weapons.

On September 13, the Conference on Disarmament concludes its annual session in Geneva without any nuclear disarmament accomplishments. Representatives from many of the countries express disappointment that the conference has failed to do any useful work in the past several years.

In December, President George W. Bush provides formal notice to Russia that the United States will withdraw from the 1972 ABM Treaty in six months.

2002   In January, the U.S. Defense Department provides an overview on the U.S. Nuclear Posture Review (NPR) that had been submitted to Congress on 31 December 2001. The NPR shows a shift in U.S. focus from deterring its former rival Russia to stopping the development of WMD by terrorists groups and states of concern. Controversial sections of the NPR call for the United States to design and perhaps build new nuclear weapons, particularly offensive weapons to be used against reinforced, underground targets, and to consider renewed testing of nuclear weapons.

President Bush proclaims in his State of the Union address that the United States will not allow states in the "axis of evil"—North Korea, Iran, and Iraq—to acquire WMD. In March, the United States refuses to certify that North Korea is complying with its commitments under the 1994 Agreed Framework.

In May, Russian President Putin and President Bush sign the Strategic Offensive Reduction Treaty (SORT, or Moscow Treaty). Each country agrees to reduce the number of its deployed strategic warheads to 1,700–2,200 by 2012.

In June, U.S. withdrawal from the ABM Treaty takes effect, allowing it to build a nationwide anti-ballistic missile defense system. In response, Russia renounces the START II agreement and says it will maintain its multi warhead ICBMs that had been scheduled for deactivation.

In September, North Korean and Japanese leaders release the Pyongyang Declaration in which Korean leader Kim Jong Il reiterates North Korea's intent to abide by all international restrictions on its nuclear program and to maintain a moratorium on its ballistic missile testing through 2003. However, in October, the United States charges North Korea with secretly acquiring uranium enrichment technology from Pakistan. After Pyongyang fails to deny the charge, the United States refuses to hold further talks with North Korea until it completely dismantles its nuclear program. KEDO halts monthly shipments of heavy fuel oil to North Korea in December. In response, North Korea

2002
(cont.)

disables IAEA monitoring equipment at its nuclear facilities and insists that all IAEA inspectors leave the country.

Informants and satellite images reveal that Iran has also been pursuing two paths that could lead to nuclear weapons in violation of its obligation as a member of the NPT. In August, the National Council of Resistance of Iran, a group opposed to Iran's government, announces that Iran has two potentially weapon-related facilities it had never declared to the IAEA: a pilot-scale facility to enrich uranium at Natanz and a heavy-water facility at Arak. Iran claims it is developing a nuclear power plant. Despite the concern of Western countries, Russia declares that it is increasing civilian nuclear cooperation with Iran.

In October, Congress approves a Bush administration–backed resolution authorizing the use of force against Iraq, if needed, to stop its feared nuclear and other WMD programs. In November, the UN Security Council adopts Resolution 1441, sponsored by the United States and Britain, which states that Iraq must dismantle any WMD programs or face serious consequences. Iraq accepts the UN resolution, and UNMOVIC inspectors return to Iraq to search for WMD for the first time in nearly four years.

Cuba becomes the 188th party to the NPT and ratifies the Latin America Nuclear-Weapon-Free Zone treaty, which goes into effect as all Latin American states have now ratified it.

Citing terrorist concerns, the U.S. government deploys Special Forces teams around the country to detect possible nuclear and radiological weapons, and the U.S. Postal Service procures potassium iodide pills to protect its 750,000 employees in case of a nuclear or radiological attack. In November, President Bush establishes the Department of Homeland Security to combine 170,000 employees from twenty-two different agencies to help protect the United States from terrorist attacks.

After spending fourteen years and $4.5 billion on studies, the DOE recommends, and the Bush administration agrees, that Yucca Mountain, about 90 miles from Las Vegas, be used to bury thousands of tons of highly radioactive waste created by nuclear weapon facilities and power plants. The projected cost of the storage facility is $40 billion. Nevada officials and environmental groups challenge the safety of the plan.

In June, the leaders of the Group of Eight countries introduce a new initiative, the Global Partnership Against the Spread of Weapons and Materials of Mass Destruction, to help prevent terrorists from stealing or buying weapons-usable nuclear material from facilities in Russia or another former Soviet state. The United States pledges $10 billion over ten years, and the other countries combined pledge another $10 billion. In August, the United States, with the aid of Russian and Yugoslav authorities, transports more than 5,000 fuel rods containing enough HEU to make two nuclear bombs from the Vinca Institute in Belgrade, Yugoslavia, to Russia where it will be down-blended for use in a commercial nuclear power reactor.

2003   As recommended by the 2001 Nuclear Posture Review and requested by the Bush administration, the U.S. Congress votes to repeal the ban (in the 1993 Spratt-Furse Amendment) on research into low-yield nuclear weapons (with a yield of less than 5 kilotons). But Congress requires a future vote before producing such weapons. The Los Alamos National Laboratory produces the first plutonium weapon pit built in the United States in fourteen years, part of a $1.5 billion modernization program to create several new pits for weapons each year.

The U.S. Senate and Russian Duma ratify the 2002 Moscow Treaty. A joint U.S.-Russian effort removes 17 kilograms of Russian-origin HEU from a Soviet-era research facility in Bulgaria and returns it to Russia to be down-blended and used in civilian nuclear plants.

UNMOVIC Executive Chairman Hans Blix and IAEA Director General Mohamed ElBaradei state that although Iraq has not been entirely forthcoming, ongoing IAEA and UNMOVIC inspections have found

2003
(*cont.*)

no convincing evidence that Iraq has been pursuing nuclear, chemical, or biological weapons. Nevertheless, President Bush and U.S. Secretary of State Colin Powell argue that Iraq is trying to build WMD and must be disarmed by force. On March 19, the United States, supported by Great Britain, begins air strikes and cruise missile attacks against Iraq, followed by a major ground offensive. On May 1, President Bush declares victory over Iraqi forces and says U.S. troops are searching for WMD.

In January, North Korea announces that it will withdraw from the NPT, effective immediately. The IAEA Board refers the North Korean crisis to the UN Security Council. North Korea says it will reprocess the 8,000 spent fuel rods at the Yongbyon Nuclear Complex, which experts say could yield enough plutonium for five to six nuclear weapons. North Korea also starts operating its 5-megawatt electric (MWe) reactor at Yongbyon, which can produce enough plutonium for an additional bomb per year, and plans to resume construction of a larger plutonium-producing reactor. China agrees to host three-party talks with North Korea and the United States in April in hopes of resolving the crisis. North Korea states that it already possesses nuclear weapons, but will abandon its nuclear program if provided with security guarantees, the removal of sanctions, and both economic and energy assistance. The United States rejects the deal and demands that North Korea first dismantle its nuclear program.

In February, the IAEA conducts inspections in Iran, during which Iranian officials admit that they are building two uranium enrichment plants at Natanz and a heavy-water production facility at Arak.

In June, Iran denies IAEA inspectors access to the Kalaye Electric Company in Tehran to take environmental samples. The IAEA subsequently issues three reports concluding that for the past two decades Iran has breached its IAEA safeguards agreement. Specifically, Iran violated NPT rules by secretly importing 3,960 pounds of uranium from China, acquiring undeclared foreign technology, and attempting to develop undeclared uranium centrifuge and laser enrichment programs.

In May, President Bush proposes the Proliferation Security Initiative, a new cooperative international effort to stop shipments of WMD-related materials and technology by land, sea, and air. The Proliferation Security Initiative is an informal arrangement among an initial eleven countries (Australia, France, Germany, Italy, Japan, the Netherlands, Poland, Portugal, Spain, the United Kingdom, and the United States), although by year's end fifty other states agree to cooperate with its WMD interdiction efforts.

In mid-summer, the North Koreans allow South Korea, Japan, and Russia to join new Six-Party Talks on the nuclear crisis. These states convene for the first time in August, but make no progress.

In October, David Kay, the director of the U.S. government's Iraq Survey Group, testifies to Congress that no WMD have yet been located, and there is no evidence that Iraq took steps after 1998 to produce fissile material for a nuclear weapon. He concludes that thirteen years of UN sanctions and inspections effectively ended the nuclear effort.

In October, Iran signs an Agreed Statement with Germany, Britain, and France declaring that it does not intend to build nuclear weapons and will cooperate more fully with the IAEA in exchange for the Europeans' confirmation of Iran's right to peaceful nuclear energy and provision of greater access to modern technologies and goods. Iran signs, but fails to ratify, the IAEA's Additional Protocol, although it submits to further IAEA inspections, temporarily suspending enrichment-related activities at Natanz and providing additional information.

In the fall, U.S. and British intelligence officials seize thousands of centrifuge parts for enriching uranium in transit from Malaysia to Tripoli; the equipment provides evidence that Libya, a member of the NPT, is pursuing a clandestine nuclear weapon program. On December 19, after this seizure, Libyan leader Colonel

2003
(*cont.*)
Muammar Gadhafi announces that Libya will disclose and dismantle all its WMD programs and immediately allow IAEA inspectors to search nuclear sites in Libya, in exchange for the lifting of international sanctions, improved trade and security relations, and other economic incentives. Gadhafi agrees to abide by the NPT, which Libya ratified in 1975. IAEA inspectors find that Libya's nuclear weapon program is fairly rudimentary, despite purchases of centrifuge components from Pakistan's Khan network.

The U.S. DOE releases a report on radiological dispersal devices, commonly called "dirty bombs," and recommends improved security measures. Meanwhile, in the former Soviet republic of Georgia, police find cesium 137 and strontium 90, materials that could be used in a dirty bomb, in a taxi cab en route to Turkey. Thai police arrest a man in Bangkok who is trying to sell cesium 137, and Russian authorities arrest the deputy director of Atomflot, the agency responsible for storing Russian naval reactor fuel, on charges that he was plotting to smuggle nuclear materials to a buyer in the Baltic region. At the Group of Eight summit, the leaders issue an action plan on securing sources of radioactive materials that could be used by terrorists in dirty bombs.

In November, the United States convinces the other KEDO board members (the European Union, Japan, and South Korea) to stop building two light-water nuclear power reactors promised to North Korea under the 1994 Agreed Framework.

2004
In January, Pakistani authorities admit that the founder of Pakistan's nuclear program (A. Q. Khan) had provided unauthorized assistance to Iran's nuclear program. Khan then publicly confesses to having run an international nuclear black market from the late 1980s that encompassed companies and contacts in several countries, including Germany, Malaysia, Japan, South Africa, and the United Arab Emirates. After Khan's televised confession, Pakistan's President General Pervez Musharraf strips Khan of his cabinet position, but grants him a full pardon.

The findings of U.S. inspectors call into question the U.S. rationale for invading Iraq. In an extensive report dated September 30, the Iraq Survey Group (headed by chief U.S. weapons inspector Charles Duelfer) concludes that the 1991 Gulf War and subsequent UN sanctions and inspections effectively destroyed Iraq's nuclear weapon program and inventory of missiles over 150 kilometers in range. The British government's Butler Report similarly faults British intelligence for mistaken claims about Iraq's WMD programs.

In Libya, IAEA teams continue inspecting, monitoring, and dismantling efforts. Libya agrees to sign the IAEA's Additional Protocol and ratifies the CTBT. Russia, the United States, and the IAEA send 16 kilograms of HEU fuel from Libya's Tajura Nuclear Research Center to Russia to be down-blended into low-enriched uranium (LEU) fuel.

In April, the UN Security Council adopts Resolution 1540, which requires states to implement measures to prevent terrorist organizations and other non-state actors from acquiring or developing nuclear, chemical, or biological weapons.

The United States announces a new international cooperative effort in May known as the Global Threat Reduction Initiative (GTRI), designed to identify and secure HEU and spent reactor fuel worldwide. In a related effort, the United States and Russia also agree to retrieve Russian-origin fresh and spent HEU from research reactors around the world. The United States will fund the recovery efforts while Russia will supply experts and equipment. In September, ninety states endorse the GTRI; more than $400 million is committed to prevent global traffic in nuclear and radiological materials. By the fall, Russia's atomic energy agency has recovered about 1,980 pounds of enriched uranium from Libya and sites in Eastern Europe.

Throughout the year, IAEA inspectors visit nuclear facilities in Iran and request additional information. In June, the IAEA Board finds that Iran, although somewhat cooperative, still has not answered questions about the origin and use of its advanced P-2

2004
(*cont.*)

centrifuges, its laser enrichment tests, and sources of LEU and HEU trace materials found at various locations in Iran. Furthermore, the Board notes that Iran has not stopped all enrichment and reprocessing activities.

Six-Party Talks on halting North Korea's nuclear program are held in February and June, but reach no solution.

On November 15, Iran concludes the Paris Accord with France, Germany, and the United Kingdom (the EU-3), in which Iran pledges again to temporarily suspend a specific list of enrichment and reprocessing activities and permit IAEA verification. In return, the EU-3 promises to give Iran access to certain nuclear and other technologies and to promote its membership in the World Trade Organization.

2005

The Stockholm International Peace Research Institute reports that eight countries still actively deploy a total of 13,470 nuclear weapons, while holding another 14,000 weapons in reserve stockpiles.

In March, the chairman of the U.S. Joint Chiefs of Staff releases a draft "Doctrine for Joint Nuclear Operations," which states that nuclear weapons may be used to preempt the use of chemical and biological weapon programs by non–nuclear state or terrorist groups. More than 470 physicists sign a petition opposing the draft policy as it allows the United States to use nuclear weapons against non–nuclear weapon states. In October, Congress decides to cancel a controversial nuclear bunker buster program.

In a major policy shift, the Bush administration decides to initiate civilian nuclear cooperation with India, an overt nuclear weapon state that has never joined the NPT. The U.S. Nuclear Non-Proliferation Act, U.S. export regulations, and Nuclear Supplier Group guidelines currently prevent the United States from providing nuclear aid to a non-NPT nuclear weapon state; these regulations must be changed before U.S. nuclear trade with India can begin. But France also agrees to new nuclear cooperation with India.

North Korea says it has finished extracting 8,000 additional spent fuel rods from its 5-MWe Yongbyon reactor to use to make plutonium for nuclear weapons and is resuming construction of 50- and 200-MWe reactors. In July the Six-Party Talks resume.

Iran reaches an agreement with Russia to return spent fuel from the Russian-built Bushehr reactor, and to continue suspending its HEU program while it negotiates with the EU-3 and submits to further IAEA inspections. But in May, the Iranian Guard Council mandates continued nuclear development. Intelligence reports indicate that Iran received technical information and practical assistance from North Korean scientists and technicians on how to build civilian and military nuclear programs.

In May, the seventh NPT Review Conference ends without a joint statement after three weeks of debate among the 153 states participating.

In August, Iran removes the IAEA seals at the Isfahan Uranium Conversion Facility to resume uranium conversion activities. On September 24, the IAEA announces that Iran has breached its agreement to comply with its safeguards obligations.

According to an expert panel that monitors UN Security Council sanctions on al Qaeda and the Taliban, these groups still seek nuclear and radiological weapons. On September 15, fifty countries sign the UN International Convention for the Suppression of Acts of Nuclear Terrorism. This treaty outlaws the possession, use, or threat of use of radioactive material by any person who intends to cause physical injury, property damage, or blackmail. Later, the IAEA reports that in 2004, there were 121 known cases of illicit trafficking of radiological and nuclear materials, a substantial increase from earlier years.

On September 19, the members of the Six-Party Talks seem to reach a breakthrough agreement in which North Korea commits to abandoning its nuclear programs and returning to the NPT and IAEA safeguards in return for a U.S. pledge that it has no intention to attack North Korea and the provision of energy, trade, and economic benefits by other states. However,

2005
(*cont.*)
almost immediately the parties disagree over whether the pledged assistance involves light-water reactors, which North Korea now openly demands. The United States rejects this condition.

In October, the IAEA and its head, Mohamed ElBaradei, are awarded the Nobel Peace Prize.

2006
In February, the IAEA adopts a resolution calling on Iran to suspend enrichment-related activities, ratify and implement the Additional Protocol, and provide more information regarding its nuclear program. But Iranian officials demand instead that the IAEA remove all remaining seals and surveillance equipment at its nuclear facilities used to enrich uranium. In March, the UN Security Council demands that Iran end uranium enrichment within 30 days, but it sets forth no penalties or sanctions for noncompliance. Iranian President Mahmoud Ahmadinejad announces that his country has a full-fledged uranium enrichment capability after a report that the Natanz plant has successfully created a small stock of LEU.

In March, President Bush and Indian Prime Minister Manmohan Singh formally sign an agreement to cooperate on nuclear energy development and technology.

After the signing, Russia transfers fuel for two nuclear reactors to India in spite of a U.S. request to delay the transfer until after the Nuclear Suppliers Group alters its guidelines to permit it.

The May issue of the *Bulletin of the Atomic Scientists* reveals that China has approximately 200 nuclear warheads, about half the 400 warheads previously estimated. The authors estimate that China actively deploys only some 130 nuclear warheads for delivery by land-based missiles, sea-based missiles, and bombers. The previously larger estimates had assumed that China had developed more tactical nuclear weapons, but the authors found no evidence for this.

In late spring, the IAEA discovers new HEU contamination on vacuum pumps from the former Physics

Research Center at Lavizan-Shian, which the Iranians razed in 2004 before the IAEA could inspect it. In June, the five permanent members of the UN Security Council plus Germany offer Iran a more generous package of incentives for forgoing its uranium enrichment program, including help in constructing additional light-water reactors, a promise to lift U.S. sanctions, and an agreement to back Iran for membership in the World Trade Organization. Iran allows a deadline for its response to pass, saying it is still studying the proposal.

In June, the United States and Russia agree to extend the Comprehensive Threat Reduction programs for seven years, and in July, they announce the Global Initiative to Combat Nuclear Terrorism, a new effort to identify nuclear terrorists, track and secure weapons-grade materials, and coordinate responses against terrorists. Also, the U.S. Customs and Border Protection and the National Nuclear Security Administration sign agreements with several countries to implement the Megaports and Container Security Initiatives, which involve help in installing radiation detectors and identifying suspicious cargoes.

As part of the U.S.-funded GTRI, a multinational team transfers 139 pounds of spent HEU research reactor fuel from Uzbekistan to Russia. U.S. nonproliferation assistance programs in the former Soviet Union now total $9 billion since 1992. The funds have helped deactivate 6,828 former Soviet nuclear warheads, destroyed 485 ICBM silos, eliminated 155 long-range bombers, and cut up 29 ballistic missile nuclear submarines.

In Britain, a parliamentary debate starts over whether the country should move toward nuclear disarmament or undertake the great expense of replacing its aging Trident submarines. In December, Prime Minister Tony Blair announces his plan to maintain a force of slightly less than 200 nuclear weapons with a new fleet of submarines. The French defense minister states that it is modernizing its nuclear arsenal and

2006
(*cont.*)

maintains the right to use nuclear weapons against biological or chemical weapons facilities, even in a non–nuclear weapon state.

On July 4, North Korea conducts its first long-range missile test since 1998, a Taep'o-dong-2 possibly capable of reaching Alaska. North Korea also launches six short-range missiles. But the Taep'o-dong-2 fails after less than a minute of flight. On July 15, the UN Security Council imposes limited sanctions on North Korea for its missile tests and demands that it suspend its ballistic missile program.

On July 31, the UN Security Council, through Resolution 1696, calls on Iran to comply with its IAEA obligations and to suspend all enrichment-related and reprocessing activities within a month or face possible economic and diplomatic sanctions. Iran refuses to comply.

In August, the U.S. National Nuclear Security Agency, under the umbrella of the 2004 Global Threat Reduction Initiative, transfers 45 kilograms of HEU that could be used for a nuclear bomb from a research reactor in Poland to Russia.

On September 8, Kazakhstan, Kyrgyzstan, Tajikistan, Turkmenistan, and Uzbekistan sign the Central Asian Nuclear-Weapon-Free Zone, thus agreeing never to acquire nuclear weapons nor permit them within their borders. The United States, Britain, and France object to the Central Asian Nuclear-Weapon-Free Zone's provision barring transport of nuclear weapons through the region and an ambiguous provision that might allow Russia to redeploy nuclear weapons into certain states according to a joint security agreement signed in 1992.

On October 9, North Korea conducts an underground nuclear weapon test. International monitoring experts determine that the plutonium-fueled bomb probably fizzled, as it had a yield of less than half a kiloton. On October 14, the UN Security Council adopts Resolution 1718 demanding that North Korea not conduct further nuclear tests, return to the NPT, and abandon its nuclear weapon program. In December, the Six-Party Talks resume but North Korea refuses to talk about giving up its nuclear weapons until the United States lifts restrictions on its financial dealings abroad.

Iran begins using a second cascade of centrifuges to expand its capacity to enrich uranium. On December 23, the UN Security Council adopts Resolution 1737, which calls on Iran to suspend all proliferation-sensitive nuclear activities, including those related to uranium enrichment, plutonium reprocessing, and the development of possible delivery systems for nuclear weapons. The UN mandates that all states refrain from transferring any equipment, technology, or financial assistance to Iran that could contribute to such capabilities. The resolution urges a negotiated, diplomatic solution to bringing Iran into compliance with its IAEA obligations.

On December 19, President Bush signs legislation authorizing the United States to proceed with civilian nuclear assistance to India.

2007   In January, the U.S. secretary of Energy fires the head of the National Security Agency, Linton Brooks, because of continuing security lapses at nuclear weapons facilities. In February, North Korea agrees at the Six-Party Talks to begin closing its nuclear facilities and to allow IAEA inspections in exchange for fuel, food, and other aid. Also, the United States and Japan will discuss normalizing relations with North Korea and lifting trade and financial sanctions. The agreement gives North Korea sixty days to take steps toward halting its nuclear program but leaves to later negotiations the issues of whether and how Pyongyang will dispose of its nuclear weapons and fissile material. In March, the U.S. Department of Energy announces that the Nuclear Weapons Council has selected the Lawrence Livermore National Laboratory to develop the first new nuclear warhead under the Reliable Replacement Warhead program. In Britain, the Parliament ends

2007
(*cont.*)

a debate over whether to go non-nuclear by approving an approximately $40 billion program to replace the country's fleet of four nuclear-armed submarines.

On March 24, the UN Security Council unanimously approves Resolution 1747 authorizing additional sanctions against Iran because of its continued uranium enrichment activities. The resolution bans the export of all weapons to Iran, asks countries to restrict loans and financial aid to Iran, and freezes the assets of institutions and officials with links to Iran's missile and nuclear programs. In April, in defiance of the UN sanctions, Iranian President Ahmadinejad claims that his country can now enrich uranium on an industrial scale.

Sources

Arms Control Today: http://www.armscontrol.org/act.

Bulletin of the Atomic Scientists: http://www.bullatomscithebulletin.org/index.htm.

Chang, Gordon G. 2006. *Nuclear Showdown, North Korea Takes on the World*. New York: Random House.

Cirincione, Joseph, Jon Wolfstahl, and Miriam Rajkumar. 2005. *Deadly Arsenals: Nuclear, Biological, and Chemical Threats*. 2nd ed. Washington, DC: Carnegie Endowment for International Peace.

Congressional Research Service Reports: http://fpc.state.gov/c4763.htm.

Corera, Gordon. 2006. *Shopping for Bombs*. New York: Oxford University Press.

Federation of American Scientists: http://www.fas.org.

Gardner, Gary T. 1994. *Nuclear Nonproliferation: A Primer*. Boulder, CO: Lynne Rienner Publishers.

Holloway, David. 1994. *Stalin and the Bomb*. New Haven, CT: Yale University Press.

International Atomic Energy Agency: http://www.iaea.org.

Lewis, John W., and Xue, Litai. 1991. *China Builds the Bomb*. Stanford, CA: Stanford University Press.

Monterey Institute of International Studies, Center for Nonproliferation Studies: http://cns.miis.edu.

Natural Resources Defense Council: http://www.nrdc.org/nuclear.

Nuclear Age Peace Foundation, "The Nuclear Files": http://www.nuclearfiles.org/index.html.

Nuclear Threat Initiative: http://www.nti.org.

Perkovich, George. 1999. *India's Nuclear Bomb*. Berkeley: University of California Press.

Preston, Diana. 2005. *Before the Fallout: From Marie Curie to Hiroshima*. New York: Berkeley Books.

Rhodes, Richard. 1986. *The Making of the Atomic Bomb*. New York: Simon and Schuster.

Rhodes, Richard. 1995. *Dark Sun: The Making of the Hydrogen Bomb*. New York: Simon and Schuster.

Richelson, Jeffrey T. 2006. *Spying on the Bomb*. New York: W. W. Norton.

Schwartz, Stephen I., ed. 1998. *Atomic Audit: The Costs and Consequences of U.S. Nuclear Weapons since 1940*. Washington, DC: Brookings Institution Press.

Welsome, Eileen. 1999. *The Plutonium Files*. New York: Dial Press.

5

Biographical Sketches

The nuclear weapons story cannot be told without understanding the motivations and actions of a number of influential scientists, policymakers, spies, and concerned citizens in the United States and other countries who have been involved in either building or attempting to ban the bomb. This chapter profiles these individuals and provides essential biographical information on their lives and work. In some cases, scientists involved in bomb making later played a major role in efforts to limit or reverse nuclear proliferation.

Hans Bethe (1906–2005)

Born in Strasbourg (then in Germany) on 2 July 1906, Hans Bethe demonstrated an early genius in math. In 1928, he received his Ph.D. in physics from the University of Munich. Bethe did postdoctoral work at Cambridge and at Enrico Fermi's laboratory in Rome. In 1933, the German government forced him to leave his teaching post at the University of Tubingen because his mother was Jewish. He fled first to Great Britain, where he worked with physicist Rudolf Peierls. In 1935, Bethe moved to the United States, where he joined the Cornell University faculty. Bethe wrote a series of groundbreaking papers exploring how stars produce energy as well as important texts on the relatively new field of nuclear physics. When World War II broke out, Bethe helped the war effort by developing radar at the Massachusetts Institute of

171

Technology. In 1943, spurred by fears that Nazi Germany was building a nuclear weapon, he accepted J. Robert Oppenheimer's request to move to Los Alamos and head the theoretical division. His group mathematically assessed the explosive properties and design specifications of the proposed bombs.

But Bethe was disturbed by the devastation of Hiroshima and Nagasaki in 1945. After the war, he returned to Cornell, became an adviser to the U.S. government, and organized atomic scientists to urge controls on nuclear technology. In December 1945, he founded the Federation of Atomic Scientists (later the Federation of American Scientists) with other Manhattan Project personnel to advocate for international control of nuclear energy. Bethe also argued against the United States pursuing a crash program to develop a hydrogen bomb. Despite his stance, when President Harry Truman approved the hydrogen bomb program, Bethe returned to Los Alamos to once again head the theoretical division. He claimed that he hoped to demonstrate that a hydrogen bomb wouldn't work and to serve as a voice for disarmament at the weapons lab.

While maintaining his post at Cornell, Bethe became a member of the President's Science Advisory Committee in 1956. In that capacity, he urged the negotiation of a treaty banning almost all nuclear weapon tests and chaired a committee that designed an international verification system (not adopted at the time) composed of seismic stations. Bethe later worked to defeat a Pentagon proposal to put nuclear-armed antinuclear missile rockets around several major U.S. cities, arguing that such systems could be defeated easily. In 1983, Bethe opposed President Ronald Reagan's Strategic Defense Initiative, explaining its numerous flaws and noting possible countermeasures, such as low-tech decoys.

Bethe won the 1967 Nobel Prize in Physics for his studies on how stars shine. He won several other scientific honors, including the Max Planck Medal, the Eddington Medal of the Royal Astronomical Society, and the Enrico Fermi Award. He wrote numerous articles and books on astrophysics, nuclear physics, and nuclear weapons programs.

Source

Garwin, Richard L., and Frank von Hippel. 2005. "In Memoriam: Hans Bethe (1906–2005)." *Arms Control Today* 35 (April), http://www.armscontrol.org/act/2005_04/Bethe.asp.

Schweber, Silvan S. 2000. *In the Shadow of the Bomb*. Princeton, NJ: Princeton University Press.

Homi Jehangir Bhabha
(1909–1966)

Born to a wealthy and politically connected family in Bombay, Homi Bhabha entered Cambridge University in England at age 16. At Cambridge, he took degrees in mechanical engineering and mathematics and then earned a Ph.D. in theoretical physics. He worked at the Cavendish Laboratories in Cambridge, primarily on cosmic rays (radiation from outer space), and toured Europe, meeting many leading physicists, including Niels Bohr and Enrico Fermi.

When World War II started in 1939, Bhabha returned to India to become a professor of theoretical physics at the Indian Institute of Science at Bangalore. To pursue his interests in cosmic rays and nuclear physics, Bhabha—with funding from a family trust—established the Tata Institute of Fundamental Research in 1944. Bhabha became the first director of the institute and began promoting nuclear energy as a path to Indian industrial development.

The Indian government set up the Atomic Energy Commission in 1948, with Bhabha as its chair, and broke ground for the Atomic Energy Establishment at Trombay (renamed the Bhabha Atomic Research Center in 1966). In 1954, Bhabha became head of India's newly formed Department of Atomic Energy, answering directly to the prime minister. In 1955, Canada supplied India with a heavy-water research reactor that produced plutonium. Bhabha designed the nuclear power program to maximize the production of plutonium that could be used for weapons fuel, although India officially opposed nuclear weapons.

After China exploded an atomic bomb in October 1964, Bhabha tried to convince the Indian government to change its position and pursue nuclear weapons. The compromise he reached with the prime minister permitted Bhabha to accelerate India's nuclear power program and to work on peaceful nuclear explosions for possible industrial projects, such as building harbors and digging water reservoirs. In early 1965, Bhabha unsuccessfully sought to acquire a U.S. nuclear explosive device (or the designs for one) to speed up India's peaceful nuclear explosion program. He believed India needed to demonstrate a dramatic nuclear achievement to offset the prestige China gained by testing a nuclear device.

Although Bhabha died in an airplane crash in January 1966, eight years before India detonated its first nuclear device, the infrastructure and training programs he had put into place provided the necessary building blocks for India's bomb. He is now widely viewed as the "father" of the Indian nuclear weapon program.

Source

Perkovich, George. 2001. *India's Nuclear Bomb: The Impact on Global Proliferation*. Berkeley: University of California Press.

Hans Blix (1928–)

Hans Blix was born in 1928 in Uppsala, Sweden. He attended the University of Uppsala, Columbia University, and Cambridge University where he earned a Ph.D. In 1959, he also earned a doctorate in law at Stockholm University and became a professor there. From 1963 to 1976, Blix worked at the Swedish Ministry of Foreign Affairs and served as its legal adviser on international law. In 1976, he became under-secretary of state in charge of international development cooperation, and in 1978, he was appointed Sweden's minister for Foreign Affairs. While at the Ministry for Foreign Affairs, Blix was a member of Sweden's delegations to the United Nations (UN) General Assembly and the Conference on Disarmament.

In 1981, Blix became director general of the International Atomic Energy Agency (IAEA), a post he held until 1997. During his tenure, the extent of Iraq's clandestine nuclear weapons program became apparent during the UN Special Commission on Iraq (UNSCOM) inspections after the 1991 Gulf War. In 2000, when UNSCOM was replaced by the UN Monitoring, Verification and Inspection Commission (UNMOVIC), the UN secretary general appointed Blix to head the new organization and oversee renewed inspections of Iraq's weapons of mass destruction (WMD) programs. Before the March 2003 invasion of Iraq, Blix oversaw 700 inspections of 500 different sites in Iraq. He reported to the UN Security Council that UNMOVIC found no WMD and argued that UNMOVIC should be allowed to continue inspections rather than withdraw before a U.S. invasion. Inspections after the U.S.-led invasion vindicated Blix and UNMOVIC; Blix publicly criticized the United States and Britain for exaggerating prewar intelligence on Iraq's WMD program.

In 2003, the Swedish government established the independent WMD Commission and appointed Blix chair. Under Blix's direction, the thirteen international nonproliferation experts produced a major 2006 report, *Weapons of Terror: Freeing the World of Nuclear, Biological and Chemical Arms*. The report reviewed the current state of WMD threats and responses and proposed sixty steps for reducing associated dangers.

Sources

Blix, Hans. 2006. "Repairing the Nonproliferation Regime." http://www.armscontrol.org/events/20060125_transcript_blix.asp.

Blix, Hans. 2005. *Disarming Iraq*. London: Bloomsbury Publishing.

Niels Bohr (1885–1962)

Born in Copenhagen to a wealthy Jewish family, Niels Bohr completed his doctorate in physics at the University of Copenhagen in 1911, where he then became a professor. Bohr published his theory of atomic structure in 1913. He proposed the existence of a series of discrete electron orbits around the nucleus, and that electrons could move from high energy states to low by emitting photons. For his work on quantum physics, Bohr received the Nobel Prize in Physics in 1922.

Bohr founded the Institute for Theoretical Physics in Copenhagen, which would become the center of nuclear physics in Europe until the outbreak of World War II. In 1939, Bohr toured the United States for four months and discussed the new discovery by scientists working in Germany that uranium 235 would allow for a fission chain reaction. Because of the rarity of the 235 isotope of uranium (0.7% in nature), however, Bohr dismissed the idea of a fission weapon on the grounds that it would be too costly and difficult to make.

Germany occupied Denmark in April 1940, and Bohr found his freedom curtailed because of his Jewish ancestry and anti-Nazi views. In September 1941, Bohr had a controversial meeting in Copenhagen with Werner Heisenberg, his former student and now head of the German nuclear program. Although after the war Heisenberg claimed that his former teacher had misunderstood his intentions, Bohr came away from the meeting convinced that Nazi Germany intended to actively pursue an atomic bomb. This belief spurred Bohr to aid the U.S. bomb program.

In September 1943, warned that he was soon to be deported to Germany, Bohr made a daring escape to Sweden with help from the Danish resistance. A few weeks later, Bohr was flown to London in the bomb bay of a British Mosquito fighter bomber. Bohr became a consultant to the British bomb program and in December 1943 joined a delegation of British scientists on a trip to Los Alamos National Laboratory to review the U.S. bomb project. He sat on a committee that designed the implosion initiator for a plutonium bomb. However, his role was mainly advisory.

To avoid a nuclear arms race, Bohr believed the United States, Britain, and the Soviet Union should establish international controls on the use of atomic energy before the United States built and used a nuclear bomb. Bohr had his friend, U.S. Supreme Court Justice Felix Frankfurter, forward his arguments against secrecy and for openness on scientific issues to President Franklin D. Roosevelt, who in turn said he would be interested in British Prime Minister Winston Churchill's views. In 1944, Bohr met with both leaders, but both men expressed concern that the Soviet Union not be given any information about the bomb. In September 1944, Roosevelt and Churchill dismissed Bohr's idea for international control of nuclear energy. In June 1950, Bohr wrote an open letter to the UN, calling for the free exchange of scientists and ideas in order to control nuclear weapons. Bohr helped establish the European Council for Nuclear Research and worked to keep it a civilian scientific organization, untouched by the military. Bohr wrote more than 100 scientific publications and won the first Atoms for Peace Award in 1957.

Sources

French, A. P., and P. J. Kennedy, eds. 1985. *Niels Bohr: A Centenary Volume*. Cambridge, MA: Harvard University Press.

Pais, Abraham. 1994. *Niels Bohr's Times: In Physics, Philosophy, and Polity*. New York: Oxford University Press.

Rhodes, Richard. 1995. *The Making of the Atomic Bomb*. New York: Simon and Schuster.

Helen Broinowski Caldicott (1938–)

A native of Australia, Helen Caldicott graduated from the University of Adelaide Medical School in 1961 and became a pediatrician. In 1971, she led protests against France's atmospheric nuclear bomb tests in the South Pacific. As a doctor and the mother of three young children, she appeared on Australian radio and TV programs to explain the medical dangers of the tests' radioactive fallout, which tainted drinking water and food. Her appearances galvanized a popular movement to stop the tests and eventually influenced France to restrict itself to underground nuclear testing. Caldicott also challenged the Australian government's plan to sell uranium—the raw fuel for nuclear technology—on the world market. By speaking to uranium miners about the harmful health effects of radiation, she helped convince the Australian Council of Trade Unions to adopt a ban on mining, transporting, and selling uranium from 1975 to 1982.

In 1977, Caldicott moved to the United States and became an associate professor of pediatrics at Harvard Medical School. Concerned about the spread of nuclear weapons and power reactors, she revived the moribund group Physicians for Social Responsibility (PSR) in 1978. Coincidentally, PSR's first advertisement appeared the same day as the worst nuclear accident in U.S. history at the Three Mile Island reactor in Pennsylvania; more than 500 physicians joined the group immediately, and hundreds more joined for several weeks thereafter.

In 1980, Caldicott resigned from Harvard to work full-time against nuclear dangers. She traveled the world lecturing and inspiring the formation of groups similar to PSR. Caldicott cofounded the Women's Party for Survival (later renamed the Women's Action for Nuclear Disarmament) and the International Physicians for the Prevention of Nuclear War, which won the Nobel Peace Prize in 1985. During the Reagan administration, Caldicott led PSR-sponsored symposia across the United

States on the nuclear threat. In 1982, PSR produced an Academy Award–nominated documentary, *Eight Minutes to Midnight*, based on these presentations.

Caldicott resigned as president of PSR in 1983. In 1987, she returned to Australia, where she narrowly lost election to parliament. She returned to the United States in 1995 and has continued lecturing and writing on nuclear and environmental issues. Caldicott has written several books and has received numerous awards for her nuclear disarmament and peace work.

Source
Caldicott, Helen. 1996. *A Desperate Passion*. New York: W. W. Norton.

Mohamed ElBaradei (1942–)

Born in Egypt in 1942, Mohamed ElBaradei attained a bachelor's degree in law in 1962 at the University of Cairo. He began his diplomatic career in 1964, serving in the Permanent Missions of Egypt in the UN in New York and Geneva; his responsibilities included political, legal, and arms control issues. ElBaradei earned a doctorate in international law at New York University of Law in 1974 and later served as a special assistant to Egypt's foreign minister and as a professor of international law at New York University. ElBaradei joined the IAEA Secretariat in 1984, taking on several high-level policy positions, including as IAEA's legal adviser and later assistant director general for external relations.

ElBaradei became director general of the IAEA in 1997. He has presided over an expansion of the agency's original mission of tracking countries' nuclear activities into investigations and negotiations with countries that have been secretly developing nuclear weapon programs and defying their IAEA obligations. During ElBaradei's tenure, the IAEA has been confronted with North Korea's withdrawal from the Non-Proliferation Treaty and its declaration of a nuclear weapons capability, Iran's disclosure of a covert nuclear program, the revelations about A. Q. Khan's extensive nuclear black market, and the debate over whether Iraq had nuclear weapons in 2003. Before the U.S.-led invasion of Iraq in March 2003, ElBaradei argued that ongoing IAEA inspections had found no evidence that Iraq had or was trying to build nuclear weapons. The positions of ElBaradei and the IAEA on Iraq was vindicated after the U.S. invasion, as the Iraq Survey Group found no evidence that Iraq had a nuclear weapon program.

ElBaradei and the IAEA received the 2005 Nobel Peace Prize for their efforts to prevent nuclear weapons proliferation. When accepting the prize, ElBaradei urged the United States and other nuclear powers to reduce their weapons stockpiles sharply and to redirect their spending to funding international efforts to eliminate poverty, armed conflict, and insecurities that prompt some countries to pursue nuclear weapons. In 2005, ElBaradei was appointed to a third term as director general.

Sources

"Dr. Mohamed ElBaradei: Director General." IAEA Web site. http://www.iaea.org/ABOUT/DGC/dgbio.html.

Pomper, Miles A. 2005. "ElBaradei, IAEA Win Nobel Peace Prize." *Arms Control Today* 35 (November), http://www.armscontrol.org/act/2005_11/NOV-Nobel.asp.

Klaus Fuchs (1911–1988)

Born and raised in Germany, Klaus Fuchs became an active member of the Communist Party in 1932 while studying physics and mathematics at the University of Kiel. When Hitler's Gestapo began rounding up communists in 1933, the 21-year-old Fuchs fled to England. He received a Ph.D. in physics from Bristol University in 1937 and moved to Edinburgh to work with Max Born, one of the pioneers in quantum physics.

In May 1940, the British deported Fuchs to Canada for being an enemy alien. After spending seven months in a primitive army camp there, Born won Fuchs's release, and he returned to Born's lab. Soon thereafter, in May 1941, Rudolf Peierls, another German refugee, requisitioned Fuchs to aid British atomic bomb research in Birmingham. When he learned the nature of the work, Fuchs decided to inform the Soviet Union, establishing contact through another member of the Communist Party. Fuchs believed the Soviet Union, as a British ally fighting Hitler's Nazis, had a right to know about the atomic bomb research. He passed to his secret contact all the reports he prepared for Peierls on issues related to bomb fuel and design.

Fuchs became a British citizen because of his bomb work, and in 1943 joined a group of British scientists sent to Los Alamos, New Mexico, to help design the plutonium-type U.S. bomb. Regarded as an excellent scientist and a genial colleague, Fuchs made significant contributions to the U.S. program, all the while regularly passing classified information to a Communist Party contact, Harry Gold. Fuchs provided the Soviets with a full description of the U.S. plutonium implosion device, the results of the first bomb test at the Trinity site, and an explanation of how the United States designed and assembled the Fat Man bomb dropped on Nagasaki.

After World War II ended, Fuchs remained at Los Alamos until June 1946 to aid Edward Teller's effort to design a hydrogen (thermonuclear) bomb. Before he left, Fuchs filed jointly for a patent related to the super bomb's ignition and reviewed every document in the archives on thermonuclear weapon design. He returned to England to work on a British atomic bomb at the Harwell Atomic Research Facility, where he became the head of the theoretical division and continued his espionage through 1949.

In 1949, the U.S. Federal Bureau of Investigation (FBI) began a full-scale investigation into Soviet espionage. When finally confronted by the FBI, Fuchs confessed. In March 1950, an English court convicted him of passing military secrets to a foreign country and sentenced him to fourteen years in prison. After serving nine years in Wakefield Prison, Fuchs was deported to East Germany. He became director of the Institute for Nuclear Research in Rossdorf, and died in 1988.

Sources

Conant, Jennet. 2005. *109 East Palace: Robert Oppenheimer and the Secret City of Los Alamos*. New York: Simon and Schuster.

Rhodes, Richard. 1995. *Dark Sun: The Making of the Hydrogen Bomb*. New York: Simon and Schuster.

Leslie Groves (1896–1970)

Leslie Groves, the son of an Army chaplain, grew up on military bases across the United States. After two stints at civilian colleges, Groves entered West Point, where he graduated fourth in his class in 1918. He then joined the Army Corps of Engineers, where he served briefly in France at the end of World War I, completed his training in the United States, and then served in several U.S. and foreign posts. Eventually, he was assigned to the Corps' headquarters in Washington, DC. Groves rose quickly through the ranks, eventually joining the Army's General Staff in 1940. In 1941, he became assistant chief of the Quartermaster Corps' Construction Division and was responsible for Army building projects in the run-up to World War II, including the construction of the Pentagon in Arlington, Virginia.

After his success in managing the Pentagon project, Groves sought overseas combat duty. Instead, he was promoted to brigadier general and, in September 1942, formally took charge of the Manhattan Project. Groves administered what became a $2 billion secret budget and a staff that grew to more than 125,000. A burly, gruff man, he governed by intimidation. Groves coordinated an effort that involved some of the largest U.S. companies including Du Pont and Monsanto, the world's most famous scientists, and several U.S. university laboratories, as well as key military personnel. Groves instituted the practice of having civilian contractors manage large government projects, which is still used in many U.S. nuclear weapon facilities today. Despite his efforts to keep the Manhattan Project secret, spies such as Klaus Fuchs at Los Alamos kept the Soviet Union informed of technical developments.

After the war, Groves oversaw the Manhattan Project's transfer to the civilian Atomic Energy Commission (AEC). In 1946, he sat on a committee appointed by President Truman charged with developing a plan for international control of nuclear technology. This effort culminated in the Acheson-Lilienthal Report. Groves retired from the military as a major general in 1948, and he worked for Sperry Rand, a military equipment manufacturer, until 1961. In 1962, he published his memoirs *Now it Can Be Told: The Story of the Manhattan Project*.

Sources

Norris, Robert. 2003. *Racing for the Bomb: General Leslie R. Groves, the Manhattan Project's Indispensable Man*. South Royalton, VT: Steerforth Press.

Rhodes, Richard. 1995. *The Making of the Atomic Bomb*. New York: Simon and Schuster.

Werner Heisenberg
(1901–1976)

Born into an intellectual family, Werner Heisenberg excelled in school and was very active in the New Boy Scouts, which instilled him with a strong sense of German patriotism. He entered the University of Munich in 1920, excelled in theoretical physics, received his doctorate in 1923, performed postdoctoral research with Niels Bohr at Copenhagen in 1924, and became a professor at the University of Leipzig in 1927.

Heisenberg developed his famous uncertainty principle in March 1927. He hypothesized that the position and momentum of a subatomic particle cannot be known simultaneously. This work—which now forms the basis of quantum mechanics—resulted in Heisenberg's receipt of the 1932 Nobel Prize in Physics.

As Adolph Hitler rose to power in the late 1930s, many Jewish physicists left Germany because of persecution. Heisenberg, although he was not Jewish, was attacked in a *Schutzstaffel* (SS) newspaper for studying "Jewish physics," interrogated several times by the gestapo, and denied a professorship at the University of Munich. Heinrich Himmler, the commander of the SS, finally intervened to stop the attacks, and drafted Heisenberg into the German bomb project as head of the theoretical division of the German nuclear program in 1939. Heisenberg produced several technical reports on the usefulness of atomic energy and the feasibility of producing a bomb, but he mistakenly rejected the use of carbon as a neutron moderator, focusing instead on heavy water, which slowed the bomb program significantly. Heisenberg also miscalculated that it would take tons of uranium 235 to build a bomb.

In September 1941, Heisenberg traveled to German-occupied Copenhagen to meet with his mentor Niels Bohr. He later claimed that he planned to inform Bohr, and by proxy the Allies, that he understood how to induce nuclear fission, but that he wanted instead to create a physicists' pact to slow weapons research. Bohr was unconvinced. In June 1942, Heisenberg informed Albert Speer, the new armaments minister of the Third Reich, that Germany could not build a bomb without a massive expenditure that the war-torn economy could ill afford. Speer decided to invest in the V-2 rocket project instead, and German nuclear research never developed a reactor that could produce weapons-grade material. After the fall of Nazi Germany, Heisenberg and other prominent German scientists were captured by the Allies in Operation Alsos and interned in England through December 1945.

Whether Heisenberg helped or hindered the German atomic bomb program remains a subject of debate. Thomas Powers, in his book *Heisenberg's War*, claims that Heisenberg deliberately slowed the German program. Others make the case that Heisenberg simply miscalculated and therefore argued against the feasibility of a German bomb program for technical (rather than moral) reasons.

After the war, Heisenberg directed the Max Planck Institute for Physics and Astrophysics from 1946 to 1976. He supported the peaceful use of nuclear energy and was the scientific policy director for the European Center for Nuclear Research. In 1957, Heisenberg, along with eighteen other German physicists, signed a public declaration (the Gottingen Declaration) urging that Germany renounce the future possession of atomic weapons of any kind and declaring that the signatories would not take part in producing, testing, or designing nuclear weapons. He also opposed placing U.S. tactical nuclear weapons in West Germany. Throughout his later life, Heisenberg wrote books and essays on the intersection of physics and philosophy and the role of science.

Sources

"Werner Heisenberg (1901–1976)." American Institute of Physics Web site, http://www.aip.org/history/exhibits/heisenberg/p01.htm.

Heisenberg, Jochen. "Who Was Werner Heisenberg?" http://werner-heisenberg.unh.edu.

Powers, Thomas. 2000. *Heisenberg's War: The Secret History of the German Bomb*. Reprint ed. New York: Da Capo Press.

Abdul Qadeer Khan (1936–)

A. Q. Khan was born in Bhopal, India, and migrated with his family to Pakistan during the 1947 partition. Khan received a Ph.D. in metallurgy in Germany. Between 1972 and 1975, Khan worked in the Netherlands for Urenco, the British-Dutch–West German uranium-enrichment group. While there he gained access to sensitive data concerning the Urenco gas-centrifuge enrichment plant. In mid-1975, Dutch authorities banned Khan from enrichment-related work because they suspected he was sending classified technology to Pakistan. Khan returned to Pakistan in 1976, where he used his personal knowledge of gas-centrifuge equipment and international industrial suppliers to develop Pakistan's nuclear weapon program.

Khan led the uranium-enrichment program and worked on weapon designs at the Engineering Research Laboratories (later renamed A. Q. Khan Research Laboratories) at Kahuta near Islamabad. Khan built a gas-centrifuge uranium-enrichment plant at Kahuta based on designs he had obtained illegally from Urenco and equipment purchased secretly from Europe, Canada, and the United States. In 1976, Dutch authorities charged Khan with trying to steal secret designs from a former Urenco colleague. In 1983, a Dutch court sentenced Khan in absentia to four years in prison for trying to steal enrichment secrets. Khan never served his prison sentence, and the court's ruling was later overturned on procedural grounds. Khan apparently obtained a complete installation for improving weapons-grade uranium from a West German company and actively recruited Western-trained scientists to work at Kahuta.

Until Pakistan's nuclear tests in May 1998, Khan helped maintain Pakistan's policy of deliberate ambiguity about its nuclear weapons capability. He claimed that the Kahuta reactor provided fuel for a power reactor being built with Chinese assistance in the mid-1990s, not for weapons. After Pakistan's five nuclear tests in May 1998, Khan stated that India's earlier tests had compelled his country to prove its nuclear capability and that Pakistan's bomb would help guarantee peace.

In January 2004, Khan publicly confessed that from the late 1980s on he had provided Iran, North Korea, and Libya with the technologies, designs, engineering, and advice to build nuclear weapons. While advising the Pakistani government and heading Khan Laboratories, he had run a secret network that encompassed companies and contacts in several countries to sell nuclear technologies and know-how to many states and possibly to terrorist groups, such as al Qaeda. Khan was apparently motivated by a pro-Islamic, anti-Western personal ideology and by financial gain. Following his confession, Pakistan's President, General Pervez Musharraf stripped Khan of his cabinet position, but pardoned him based on his scientific contributions to the country. The Pakistani government refuses to allow other nations or the IAEA to interrogate him, despite many unanswered questions about his nuclear proliferation network, including whether it was supported by the government.

Source
Corera, Gordon. 2006. *Shopping for Bombs: Nuclear Proliferation, Global Insecurity, and the Rise and Fall of the A.Q. Khan Network.* New York: Oxford University Press.

Igor Kurchatov (1903–1960)

Born in the southern Urals, Igor Kurchatov graduated in three years from Crimea State University with a physics degree. He then went to the Polytechnical Institute in Petrograd (later Leningrad, now St. Petersburg) to study shipbuilding and to work at the Pavlovsk Observatory. There he wrote his first scientific paper on the radioactivity of snow. In 1925, he joined the Physical-Technical Institute and established his reputation as a physicist, researching a phenomenon called ferroelectricity (the spontaneous electric polarization in crystals).

In 1932, Kurchatov became the head of a Leningrad research team investigating the new field of nuclear physics. During the 1930s, Kurchatov actively participated in the international community of nuclear physicists, publishing many articles outside the Soviet Union. In the spring of 1937, Kurchatov began working on the Radium Institute's cyclotron (a device that accelerates charged particles using magnets and electrical fields), eventually taking charge of it. By the late 1930s, he was named to a government commission on nuclear research. After the Germans invaded the Soviet Union in July 1941, Kurchatov left Leningrad to help the war effort, working with a group that developed a means of protecting ships from magnetic mines (which earned him the Stalin Prize). In 1943, when the Soviet government realized that Western scientists were working on an atomic bomb, the State Defense Committee named Kurchatov as the leader of a secret nuclear research program and elected him to the Soviet Academy of Sciences. Kurchatov concluded that a plutonium bomb was the most promising approach and asked Soviet agents abroad to investigate specific questions related to that technology. By 1944, Kurchatov had about 100 researchers, engineers, and technicians working on the bomb project.

After the United States bombed Hiroshima on 6 August 1945, Stalin met with Kurchatov and ordered him to accelerate his work, no matter the cost. While secret police chief Lavrenti Beria retained overall responsibility for the atomic project, Kurchatov became scientific director of the directorate set up to build the bomb. He became known as an exceptional leader, able to coordinate political officials, managers, and scientists skillfully.

Kurchatov succeeded in testing the first Soviet atomic bomb (dubbed Joe-1 in the West and modeled on the first U.S. plutonium-type bomb) on 29 August 1949. For his efforts, Stalin named Kurchatov a Hero of Socialist Labor and awarded him a large financial bonus, a car, a country home, and other rare benefits in the Soviet Union.

Throughout the late 1940s and early 1950s, Kurchatov oversaw the development of new bomb designs. In 1951, his team tested a new plutonium bomb that was about half the weight and twice the yield of Joe-1. Again, Stalin awarded him the country's highest honor: Hero of Socialist Labor. Now in a race with the United States to produce a much more powerful fusion (thermonuclear) bomb, in August 1953 Kurchatov tested the first hydrogen bomb capable of being weaponized; it yielded a 400-kiloton force. After a November 1955 test of a 1.6-megaton bomb at Semipalatinsk that inadvertently killed three people, Kurchatov withdrew from weapon testing and turned his attention to the peaceful uses of nuclear energy. Greatly upset by the damage caused by the 1955 thermonuclear bomb test, he began to lobby internally against future nuclear testing.

Kurchatov's success brought him immense prestige in the Soviet Union. He was allowed to travel to England and visit physicists and laboratories. But he later suffered two strokes and, in late 1957, was forced to take the blame for the explosion of a waste storage tank at a plutonium production plant that exposed tens of thousands of people to high levels of radiation and rendered the area uninhabitable. Kurchatov died in February 1960 and was given a special burial in the Kremlin Wall. In 1991, the Institute of Atomic Energy in Moscow was renamed the Kurchatov Institute in his honor.

Sources

Holloway, David. 1994. *Stalin and the Bomb: The Soviet Union and Atomic Energy, 1939–1956.* New Haven, CT: Yale University Press.

Khariton, Yuli, and Yuri Smirnov. 1993. "The Khariton Version." *Bulletin of the Atomic Scientists* 49 (May), pages 20–31.

Ernest Lawrence (1901–1958)

Born in rural South Dakota to Lutheran schoolteachers, Ernest Lawrence was always fascinated by science. He entered St. Olaf College at 16, although he quickly transferred to the University of Minnesota. He completed a Ph.D. in physics at Yale University in 1924, writing his dissertation on the photoelectric effect—the emission of electrons from matter when struck by light. In 1928, after further research and teaching at Yale, Lawrence joined the faculty of the University of California–Berkeley, where he began building a device that would accelerate particles to extremely high velocities: the cyclotron. To finance the much larger machines that he envisioned, Lawrence obtained funds from a combination of private, state, federal, and industrial donors. At his burgeoning Radiation Laboratory at Berkeley, Lawrence gathered an interdisciplinary team of scientists and eventually built a cyclotron with a 5,000-ton, 15-foot-long magnet that required its own building. Lawrence won the 1939 Nobel Prize in Physics for inventing the cyclotron and for the results achieved with it, particularly the creation of artificial radioactive elements. In 1940–1941, scientists in his laboratory discovered that irradiated uranium decayed into a new element, plutonium, which was fissionable and could be used to generate nuclear energy.

In 1941, Lawrence (along with his Berkeley colleague, physicist Robert Oppenheimer) joined the Manhattan Project to apply his cyclotron technology to enriching uranium, calling the result a "calutron" in honor of his home university. During the war, the Radiation Laboratory became a military facility with security guards and checkpoints, and Lawrence served as an adviser for the secret government facility at Oak Ridge, Tennessee, where industrial-scale calutrons produced enriched uranium for the bomb used on Hiroshima. Lawrence, as a scientific adviser to the 1945 U.S. Interim Committee, suggested that the United States should demonstrate the atomic bomb before a delegation of Japanese officials rather than use it on a city.

After the war, Lawrence continued to advise the U.S. government on nuclear matters and promote the Berkeley Radiation Laboratory as part of the nuclear weapons complex. Lawrence initially opposed the transfer of atomic energy matters to the civilian AEC, but he withdrew from the debate when other scientists argued that the military should not control the direction of scientific research.

Lawrence consistently argued that the United States should maintain a large stockpile of nuclear weapons and the large industrial plants needed to produce them. After the Soviet Union tested a nuclear weapon in 1949, Lawrence supported a crash program to produce a hydrogen bomb. Lawrence built larger and larger accelerators at the Livermore Auxiliary Naval Air Station, which would become the Lawrence Livermore National Laboratory in 1952, a second atomic research center to rival Los Alamos. In the late 1950s, Lawrence opposed a nuclear test-ban treaty, arguing instead for developing "clean bombs" with reduced fallout. In addition to the Nobel Prize, Lawrence won the 1957 Enrico Fermi Award, the highest scientific award given by the United States.

Sources

Heilbron, J. L., Robert W. Seidel, and Bruce R. Wheaton. 1981. "Lawrence and His Laboratory: A Historian's View of the Lawrence Years." *Lawrence Berkeley Lab Newsmagazine.* http://www.lbl.gov/Science-Articles/Research-Review/Magazine/1981.

Herken, Gregg. 2002. *Brotherhood of the Bomb: The Tangled Lives and Loyalties of Robert Oppenheimer, Ernest Lawrence, and Edward Teller.* New York: Henry Holt & Co.

"Lawrence and the Cyclotron." American Institute of Physics Web site. http://www.aip.org/history/lawrence.

Nie Rongzhen (1899–1992)

Nie Rongzhen was born into a prosperous Chinese family in Jiangjin Province and, in 1920, traveled to Europe to work and study. While a technical student in Belgium, he met Zhou Enlai, a leader in the Chinese communist movement. In 1923, Nie joined the Communist Party and traveled to Moscow for six months of military training. When he returned to China, he worked under

Zhou in a military academy. In 1927, when the Nationalist Party headed by Chiang Kai-shek began battling the communist Red Army, Nie escaped with Zhou and others to remote Jiangxi Province in western China. In 1934–1935, Nie, along with Mao Tse-tung, Zhou, and 86,000 men and women, fought a series of battles across the country (known as the Long March) against Nationalist forces. Nie served as a leader of the First Front Army and supported Mao at the Zunyi Conference when Mao emerged as the leader of the Communist Party and the overall commander of the Red Army. Nie became famous as a senior battlefield commander during the communist victory over the Nationalist government. From 1950 to 1953, he served as the acting chief of the General Staff, and in 1955 Mao named him one of ten Chinese marshals. That same year, influenced by U.S. involvement in the Korean War, Indochina, and the Taiwan Strait, China decided to obtain its own nuclear arsenal. Beginning in July 1955, Nie held several senior government positions with responsibility for organizing and mobilizing China's resources to develop, test, and produce an atomic bomb within ten years. In 1957, Nie went to the Soviet Union to seek additional help with China's nuclear weapon program. The two countries signed the New Defense Technical Accord in which the Soviets agreed to supply a prototype nuclear bomb, missiles, and related technical data. But the accord was never completely fulfilled and, by 1960, the Soviets had withdrawn all help.

During 1958–1961, Nie's program collected thousands of engineers and technicians to work on the atomic bomb. As the effort to mine and process uranium progressed, Nie selected the site for China's first plutonium-production reactor in the Gobi Desert (Jiuquan Atomic Energy Complex) and began construction on the Northwest Nuclear Weapons Research and Design Academy (Ninth Academy). He also mobilized a group of scientists to design a prototype fission weapon. On 16 October 1964, China tested its first atomic bomb (a uranium fission device) at the Lop Nor test site. China tested its first hydrogen bomb in June 1967. Nie later took personal charge of China's first test of a strategic missile armed with a nuclear warhead. In 1984, Nie published his memoirs, in which he stated that China had pursued a minimum nuclear deterrent in order to be able to respond to a nuclear attack.

Source
Lewis, John W., and Xue Litai. 1988. *China Builds the Bomb*. Stanford, CA: Stanford University Press.

J. Robert Oppenheimer
(1904–1967)

Robert Oppenheimer was born into a wealthy German-Jewish family in New York. He was sickly and sheltered as a youth but became a precocious student of languages and science. He graduated summa cum laude from Harvard University in 1925 after excelling in coursework that included poetry and Greek as well as chemistry and physics. Oppenheimer gravitated to the centers of the scientific world in Europe and completed his doctorate in physics at Germany's Göttingen University in 1927. He published sixteen scientific papers between 1926 and 1929, rapidly establishing himself as a leading theoretical physicist. Back in the United States, he received numerous job offers but accepted a unique joint appointment at the University of California–Berkeley and the California Institute of Technology in Pasadena.

During the 1930s, Oppenheimer became involved in some left-wing activities. Many of his close friends became members of the Communist Party of California. Eventually, he married a thrice-divorced German émigré, Kitty Puening, whose strong leftist leanings cast doubt on Oppenheimer's trustworthiness to lead the U.S. bomb program. Nonetheless, in 1942, the U.S. government appointed him scientific director of its project to design an atomic bomb. Working with General Leslie Groves, Oppenheimer assembled a team of leading U.S. and émigré scientists and engineers at Los Alamos, New Mexico, to work on this top-secret project. Along with Groves, Oppenheimer eventually coordinated dozens of scientific and industrial facilities across the United States and created two types of atomic weapons in a span of three years. His perseverance, ability to motivate his fellow scientists, and understated brilliance as an administrator and problem solver yielded success in the first atomic bomb test at the Trinity site in July 1945.

Oppenheimer supported use of the bomb against Japan, but he later became a leader in efforts to prevent the spread of nuclear weapons and the development of the hydrogen bomb. Having become immediately famous at the end of World War II, he used his reputation to explain to the U.S. public the dual-edged sword of nuclear weapons: a powerful deterrent to prevent future wars, but also a horrible destructive force that required strict limitations and controls. Influenced by Danish scientist Niels Bohr, Oppenheimer led several studies in the 1940s and 1950s calling for more openness about nuclear weapons issues and new means of preventing their use. In 1952, Oppenheimer, fed up with the pronuclear weapons policies in Washington, resigned from the General Advisory Committee but remained as a consultant and agreed to sit on the State Department Panel of Consultants on Disarmament. However, the rising anticommunist scare in the United States eventually caught up with him, reviving questions about his involvement in left-wing causes in the late 1930s and early 1940s and shedding doubt on his reliability in the eyes of some officials. Oppenheimer's opposition to the hydrogen bomb and belief in candor about nuclear matters led the U.S. AEC to revoke his security clearance in 1954.

Although Oppenheimer continued to be active in research and public policy questions as director of Princeton University's Institute of Advanced Studies, he never again regained prominence in U.S. nuclear decision making. In December 1963, President Johnson awarded him the Enrico Fermi Prize for public service. Oppenheimer, a lifelong smoker, died of throat cancer in 1967.

Sources

Bird, Kai, and Martin J. Sherwin. 2005. *American Prometheus: The Triumph and Tragedy of J. Robert Oppenheimer*. New York: Vintage Books.

Conant, Jennet. 2005. *109 East Palace: Robert Oppenheimer and the Secret City of Los Alamos*. New York: Simon & Schuster.

McMillan, Priscilla J. 2005. *The Ruin of J. Robert Oppenheimer and the Birth of the Modern Arms Race*. New York: Viking.

Linus Pauling (1901–1994)

Linus Pauling was born in Portland, Oregon, and in 1922 graduated with a bachelor's degree in chemical engineering from Oregon Agricultural College (now Oregon State University). Pauling received a Ph.D. in chemistry in 1925 from California Institute of Technology, and then joined the faculty in 1927. At Cal Tech, Pauling explored the structure and behavior of molecules and, in 1939, published *The Nature of the Chemical Bond and the Structure of Molecules and Crystals*. He won the 1954 Nobel Prize in

Chemistry for his research into the chemical structures of complex substances.

During World War II, Pauling refused Robert Oppenheimer's request to head the chemistry section of the atomic bomb project at Los Alamos, but he worked on war-related projects at Cal Tech. After the 1945 U.S. atomic bombing of Hiroshima and Nagasaki, Albert Einstein asked Pauling to join his Emergency Committee of Atomic Scientists. As part of this group, Pauling participated in lecture tours to educate the public on the vast destructive power of the new weapons and the need to prevent future wars. He began researching the harmful effects of nuclear fallout on human health, including the likelihood of future congenital deformities resulting from nuclear testing. He opposed both the development of the hydrogen bomb and continued nuclear weapons testing. In response, the U.S. government accused Pauling of being pro-communist and prevented him from getting a passport to attend some foreign scientific conferences, even initially denying his request for a passport to travel to Sweden in 1954 to receive the Nobel Prize. In addition, the U.S. government denied grants for his scientific research.

In 1958, Pauling and two other U.S. scientists circulated a petition demanding that atmospheric nuclear weapons testing be banned because such tests released radioactive fallout over the globe leading to an increase in birth defects, cancer, and other diseases. In January 1958, Pauling and his wife presented a petition signed by approximately 11,000 scientists from around the world to UN Secretary General Dag Hammarskjöld. The same year, Pauling published the book *No More War*, which argued that a nuclear war could mean the end of the human race. Pauling also used his scientific training and fame to lobby U.S., Soviet, and British leaders to halt nuclear testing. For example, in 1961, when attending a biochemical conference in the Soviet Union, Pauling spoke to a gathering of antinuclear demonstrators and sent a letter to Khrushchev promoting a test-ban treaty. The Nobel Prize Committee awarded Pauling the 1962 Peace Prize.

Pauling resigned from Cal Tech in 1963 because of pressure from the university's trustees against his antinuclear efforts. While remaining active in the antinuclear and peace movements, he focused his research and advocacy on the use of large doses of vitamin C for treating a range of diseases. He served as a chemistry professor at Stanford University from 1969 to 1973, when he established the Linus Pauling Institute of Medicine and Science.

Pauling wrote or contributed to nearly fifty popular and scholarly books and more than 1,000 articles on chemistry, biochemistry, nutrition, health, and nuclear disarmament issues.

Sources

Academy of Achievement. 1990. "Interview: Linus Pauling." http://www.achievement.org/autodoc/printmember/pau0int-1.

Marinacci, Barbara, ed. 1995. *Linus Pauling in His Own Words: Selections from His Writings, Speeches, and Interviews.* New York: Touchstone.

Oregon State University, Linus Pauling Institute. "Linus Pauling Biography." http://lpi.oregonstate.edu/lpbio/lpbio2.html.

Joseph Rotblat (1908–2005)

Born in Warsaw, Poland, Joseph Rotblat initially became an electrician when his father's business failed. He studied physics at night, eventually earning an advanced degree from the University of Warsaw. In 1939, he moved to Liverpool, England, to work on nuclear physics with James Chadwick at Liverpool University. Like many physicists at the time, he sought to determine whether a self-sustaining chain reaction was possible. Rotblat realized that the release of energy from such a fission reaction could be used in a powerful bomb.

Afraid that Nazi Germany would develop an atomic bomb first, Rotblat began to work on nuclear designs in Liverpool while teaching. By 1944, he had helped establish that an atomic bomb was theoretically possible. A British scientific delegation soon informed the United States of this finding. In June 1944, Rotblat joined a group of British scientists sent to Los Alamos, New Mexico, to aid the U.S. bomb program. But Rotblat quickly became disenchanted with the weapons project. He realized that war-battered Germany lacked the massive resources necessary to build an atomic bomb and believed the United States wanted such a weapon mainly to intimidate the Soviet Union. In late 1944, after U.S. intelligence missions confirmed that Germany's nuclear weapon program had largely ended, Rotblat asked to leave Los

Alamos after nine months on the project. U.S. security suggested that he was a spy and threatened him with arrest if he mentioned the real reasons for his departure.

Rotblat returned to England and from 1945 to 1949 was the director of physics research at Liverpool University. After the United States used nuclear weapons twice against Japan, he urged scientists to support a moratorium on nuclear weapon development. In 1946, he cofounded the Atomic Scientists Association to help shape British policy on nuclear energy; later, he helped found the Campaign for Nuclear Disarmament. In 1950, he received a Ph.D. in physics from the University of Liverpool, and from 1950 to 1976 he served as professor of physics at St. Bartholomew's Hospital Medical College in London. He focused on the medical applications of physics and became an expert on the hazards of nuclear radiation.

In 1955, Rotblat signed the Russell-Einstein Manifesto, which urged an international meeting of scientists to discuss nuclear disarmament and means of abolishing war. With funding from Cyrus Eaton, an industrialist from Pugwash, Nova Scotia, Canada, Rotblat helped organize the first such conference in July 1957. Attended by twenty-two world-renowned scientists and policymakers, the conference discussed the hazards of nuclear testing and recommended arms control measures. Rotblat held the position of the Pugwash Conference's secretary-general for fourteen years and its presidency from 1988 to 1997. The contacts between world leaders and scientists established through Pugwash meetings and the background reports generated have been credited with influencing international nuclear nonproliferation agreements. In 1995, the Pugwash Conferences and Rotblat received the Nobel Peace Prize.

Rotblat also played a significant role in the World Health Organization's comprehensive reports on the health effects of nuclear war issued in 1984 and 1987. He authored more than 300 publications, including twenty books, and received numerous awards and honors, including the Albert Einstein Peace Prize in 1992 and a British knighthood in 1998.

Sources

Landau, Susan. 1996. "The Road Less Traveled." *Bulletin of Atomic Scientists* 52 (January/February), pages 46–54.

Palevsky, Mary. 2000. *Atomic Fragments: A Daughter's Questions.* Berkeley: University of California Press.

Rotblat, Joseph. 1985. "Leaving the Bomb Project." *The Bulletin of the Atomic Scientist* 41 (August), pages 16–19.

Andrei Sakharov (1921–1989)

Andrei Sakharov was born in Moscow, where his father, a physicist, served as his first teacher until the seventh grade. In 1938, he enrolled in Moscow State University, where the physics department had been depleted by Stalinist purges. Sakharov's mentor was the physicist Igor Tamm. After Nazi Germany invaded the Soviet Union in 1941, the university was evacuated to Central Asia, where Sakharov graduated with honors in 1942. The government assigned Sakharov to routine laboratory work at a munitions factory; he declined Igor Kurchatov's request to join the Soviet atomic bomb project. In 1945, Sakharov returned to Moscow as a physics graduate student under Tamm's supervision at the Physical Institute of the USSR Academy of Sciences (FIAN) and earned a Ph.D. in 1947.

Once the Soviet Union learned about U.S. work on thermonuclear weapons, it formed a similar group under Tamm's supervision at FIAN (while simultaneously working toward the first Soviet fission bomb, which was tested in 1949). Sakharov agreed to join this group because he was convinced that the Soviet Union needed nuclear weapons to restore the balance of power. In 1948, Sakharov proposed his concept of placing alternate layers of thermonuclear fuel (deuterium, tritium, and their chemical compounds) and uranium 238 in a fission bomb to make a fission-fusion-fission reaction possible. In the spring of 1950, Sakharov moved with Tamm's group to the closed, secret town of Arzamas-16 (now known as Sarov), where the main theoretical and experimental work on the hydrogen bomb took place. Using Sakharov's design, the Soviet Union tested its first hydrogen bomb, which had a force of 400 kilotons, on 12 August 1953. The government honored Sakharov as a Hero of Socialist Labor and bestowed upon him the Stalin Prize with its many attendant privileges. He was elected to full membership in the Academy of Sciences at the exceptionally young age of 32.

From 1953 to 1955, Sakharov developed additional weapon designs, including the design for the Soviet Union's first air-dropped thermonuclear bomb in November 1955. This device had a yield estimated at 1.6 megatons (scaled down from 3 megatons for the test), but the resulting devastation made him realize his responsibility for the weapon he had created. He later claimed that he became a dissident within the nuclear complex when he realized that although scientists, engineers, and workers had built powerful weapons, they had no say in how they would be used. Sakharov became increasingly concerned about the long-term biological consequences of nuclear tests and campaigned to stop them in the atmosphere.

While Sakharov continued to work on quantum physics and new weapons at Arzamas-16, he used his growing influence with Soviet political leaders to try to stop the nuclear arms race and prevent human rights abuses under his country's repressive communist government. In May 1968, Sakharov wrote an essay, "Reflections on Progress, Peaceful Coexistence, and Intellectual Freedom," which was circulated in typewritten copies in the Soviet Union and printed by the *New York Times*. The essay alerted readers to grave threats facing the human race—including thermonuclear extinction—and argued for peace between the communist and capitalist systems. After the publication, the Soviet government banned Sakharov from all military-related research.

In May 1969, Sakharov returned to FIAN to work on academic topics. In 1970, along with other Soviet dissidents (including his second wife, Elena Bonner), he founded the Moscow Human Rights Committee. They worked in defense of victims of political persecution and discrimination. As Sakharov's public stature grew, the government increasingly threatened him and had other prominent citizens denounce him in letters printed in the newspaper. In 1975, Sakharov was awarded the Nobel Peace Prize for his fearless commitment to the principles of peace and his fight against the abuse of power. Bonner accepted the award in Sakharov's place because the Soviet government would not allow him to travel outside the country.

Sakharov strongly protested the 1979 Soviet invasion of Afghanistan. In retaliation, the Soviet Politburo exiled him to Gorky, a closed city on the Volga River, and stripped him of all his titles and awards. Sakharov remained in exile there for almost seven years, where he was subject to continued police surveillance. But he received support from Western physicists and wrote his memoirs and various essays, which were smuggled to the West for publication.

Finally, in December 1986, after General Secretary Mikhail Gorbachev began to initiate political reforms in the Soviet system, Sakharov was allowed to return to Moscow and resume his public activities. He became a leading figure in demanding democratic changes, and in 1988 he was elected to the new Soviet Congress of People's Deputies. Sakharov authored six books and, shortly before his death in December 1989, had started drafting a new constitution for the Soviet Union.

Sources

Holloway, David. 1994. *Stalin and the Bomb: The Soviet Union and Atomic Energy, 1939–1956*. New Haven, CT: Yale University Press.

Lourie, Richard. 2002. *Sakharov: A Biography*. Hanover, NH: Brandeis University Press/University of New England.

Sakharov, Andrei. 1990. *Memoirs*. New York: Alfred A. Knopf.

Lewis L. Strauss (1896–1974)

Lewis Strauss was born in 1896 in West Virginia. He excelled in high school but had to pass up a scholarship to the University of Virginia when he contracted typhoid fever. When he recovered, he became a successful traveling shoe salesman in his family's business. When the United States entered World War I, Strauss volunteered to be an administrative assistant to Herbert Hoover, who was then the acting U.S. food administrator, and worked to prevent starvation in Europe. He later became an investment banker and joined the U.S. Naval Reserves. In 1941, he began working for the Navy on a number of special projects related to the war effort, and, in 1944, he became special assistant to the secretary of the Navy. President Truman promoted Strauss to rear admiral in November 1945, and appointed him one of five commissioners on the newly formed AEC in 1946. In August 1949, after the Soviet Union's first atomic bomb test was detected, Strauss advocated that the United States respond with an all-out effort to build a thermonuclear bomb. The chairman of the AEC, many of its other members, and the nine members of its General Advisory Committee (eminent nuclear scientists and engineers chaired by Robert Oppenheimer) opposed a thermonuclear bomb program on moral and technical grounds. Strauss reportedly used his Navy connections to influence Truman, who eventually approved the thermonuclear bomb program in January 1950.

In 1953, President Dwight Eisenhower appointed Strauss to a new post as White House adviser on atomic energy and to the AEC chairmanship. As AEC chairman, Strauss sought to curtail Oppenheimer's influence as a government adviser. Despite having agreed to Oppenheimer's security clearance in 1947, Strauss began to revive old allegations that Oppenheimer had communist contacts. He suspended Oppenheimer's security clearance and ultimately voted with two other AEC commissioners to uphold a hearing panel's decision to revoke Oppenheimer's clearance permanently in 1954. In the process, Strauss resorted to illegal wiretapping of Oppenheimer and his lawyers and denied them access to classified documents introduced as evidence.

Strauss opposed the negotiations that resulted in the Limited Test Ban Treaty in 1963. He worked to promote U.S. dominance in nuclear weapons but also supported the spread of civilian nuclear technology through Eisenhower's Atoms for Peace Program, which inadvertently assisted certain countries' proliferation efforts.

In July 1958, after Strauss's term as AEC chairman, President Eisenhower presented him with the U.S. Medal of Freedom for his service to the security of the United States. Eisenhower also appointed Strauss as secretary of Commerce in November 1958. However, in June 1959, after two months of contentious hearings, the Senate refused to confirm Strauss's appointment, in part as retribution for his treatment of Oppenheimer. Strauss returned to the private sector and wrote his memoirs, *Men and Decisions,* in 1962.

Sources

McMillan, Priscilla J. 2005. *The Ruin of J. Robert Oppenheimer and the Birth of the Modern Arms Race.* New York: Viking.

Pfau, Richard. 1985. *No Sacrifice Too Great: The Life of Lewis Strauss.* Charlottesville: University Press of Virginia.

Leo Szilard (1898–1964)

Leo Szilard was born in 1898 into a middle-class Jewish family in Budapest, Hungary. In 1916, after a year of engineering studies at Budapest Technical University, he served in the Austro-Hungarian Army during World War I. In 1919, anti-Semitism in postwar Hungary forced Szilard to pursue his studies in engineering and physics in Berlin, where he convinced Albert Einstein to tutor him. He received a Ph.D. in physics from the University of Berlin in 1922, and then worked as an inventor, a researcher, and an instructor. While in Berlin (1920–1933), Szilard was granted thirty-one patents, covering such inventions as a linear accelerator, a cyclotron, an electron microscope, and, in collaboration with Einstein, a home refrigerator without moving parts. In 1933, Szilard moved to London to escape persecution by the Nazis. In Britain, he helped other Jewish refugees and sparked the formation of the Academic Assistance Council. In 1934, Szilard filed a British patent for a neutron chain reaction and began to investigate which elements would allow such a reaction. Sensing that a successful chain reaction could be used in a new weapon, in 1936 he assigned his patent to the British Admiralty to keep it secret.

Fearing the outbreak of World War II, Szilard moved to New York in 1938, and at Columbia University demonstrated that a chain reaction might be sustained in a lattice of uranium and graphite. Szilard tried unsuccessfully to keep his findings and those of other U.S. and European scientists secret to thwart Nazi Germany's military research. Physicist George Pegram notified the U.S. Navy of Szilard's findings and the possibility that they could be used to build a huge explosive. But the Navy showed little interest in the discovery. Szilard then enlisted fellow Hungarian scientists Edward Teller and Eugene Wigner to help him convince Einstein (then living in New Jersey) to draft a letter to President Roosevelt stating that the discovery of a chain reaction using uranium could be used in extremely powerful new bombs. They also noted that the Germans had taken over Czechoslovakia's uranium mines. As a result, a nine-member Advisory Committee on Uranium, including Szilard, Teller, Alexander Sachs, and Army and Navy representatives, was formed. Szilard and other scientists received a small amount of government funding for bomb-related research.

On 2 December 1942, Szilard helped the Italian émigré scientist Enrico Fermi create the first successful nuclear chain reaction at the University of Chicago Metallurgical Lab. But Szilard clashed with General Leslie Groves, the head of the Manhattan Project, over freedom of scientific speech and his right to patent uranium work. Groves distrusted Szilard and barred him from Los Alamos. Szilard occasionally worked as a consultant on reactor design for the U.S. bomb project, but by 1944 had become increasingly fearful of a postwar nuclear arms race. In early 1945, Szilard sought a meeting with President Roosevelt to warn him that the use of the atomic bomb in Japan would start an arms race with the Soviet Union, but Roosevelt died before Szilard could meet with him. Szilard presented his arguments to President Truman's Secretary of State–designate James Byrnes, who rejected them on the grounds that the U.S. bomb would help contain the growing Soviet empire. He then coauthored with James Franck, another Metallurgical Lab scientist, a report arguing that the United States should demonstrate the atomic bomb before bombing Japan. When Oppenheimer and others rejected this idea, Szilard circulated a petition to President Truman, dated 17 July 1945, opposing the use of the atomic bomb on moral grounds; seventy Manhattan Project scientists eventually signed.

After the war, Szilard and Einstein founded the Emergency Committee of Atomic Scientists, and in 1950 Szilard publicly opposed the U.S. hydrogen bomb program. Upset by the weapon his physics discoveries had made possible, Szilard also switched his research to biology. In 1955, Szilard and Fermi won a joint patent for their invention of the nuclear reactor. Szilard continued to promote disarmament and peace by participating in the Pugwash Conferences, founding the Council for Abolishing War (now called Council for a Livable World), and undertaking national antiwar speaking tours. Szilard received the Atoms for Peace Award in 1960 and became a member of the National Academy of Sciences in 1961. He died in 1964 in La Jolla, California, where he was a resident fellow at the Salk Institute.

Sources

Lanouette, William, with Bela Szilard. 1994. *Genius in the Shadows: A Biography of Leo Szilard, the Man behind the Bomb*. Chicago: University of Chicago Press.

Leo Szilard Online. http://www.dannen.com/szilard.html.

Edward Teller (1908–2003)

Edward Teller was born into a Jewish family in Budapest, Hungary. The political turmoil that disrupted his early education in private schools during the short-lived Hungarian communist republic after World War I set him on a course of militant anticommunism throughout his life. In 1926, because of political upheaval, Teller left Budapest to study chemical engineering in Karlsruhe, Germany, but he soon transferred to the University of Munich to study physics. He received his Ph.D. in theoretical physics from the University of Leipzig while working under Werner Heisenberg, who would later head Nazi Germany's atomic bomb program. Teller worked as a research consultant at the University of Göttingen until Adolf Hitler's rise to power. As a Jew, he was then forced to emigrate to Denmark, where he joined the institute of famed physicist Niels Bohr and met the Russian physicist George Gamow, also a political refugee. Teller then taught briefly in London before joining Gamow at George Washington University in Washington, DC, in 1935. In 1941, Teller became a U.S. citizen and joined the Manhattan Project because he, like other refugees, feared that Hitler might develop the bomb first. After preliminary work in Chicago with Enrico Fermi and in Berkeley with Robert Oppenheimer, Teller moved to the new weapons lab in Los Alamos, New Mexico. Teller worked in the theoretical division of the fission bomb project, but he remained fixated with the possibility of the far-more-powerful hydrogen bomb. His idea was to use the high heat of an exploding atomic bomb to ignite hydrogen fuel, fusing the atoms together and then releasing almost unlimited bursts of nuclear energy from a second fission.

In the autumn of 1943, Teller, along with Polish mathematician Stanislaw Ulam, began systematic theoretical studies toward a thermonuclear bomb; in January 1944, Teller began directing a small group studying the feasibility of building the so-called "super bomb." Although Teller watched the Trinity test of the fission bomb in July 1945, he later claimed in published articles that he thought the lethality of nuclear weapons was a dangerous myth and that Hiroshima haunted scientists unduly, distorting the judgment of U.S. policymakers. After World War II, Teller continued to push for a thermonuclear bomb, issuing an optimistic report in the spring of 1946 that justified a large-scale theoretical and experimental thermonuclear bomb program.

Teller left Los Alamos in 1946 and went to the University of Chicago as a professor. He returned to Los Alamos, however, in July 1949, influenced by the communist takeovers in Czechoslovakia and his native Hungary, the Berlin blockade, and the impending communist victory in China. In August 1949, the Soviet Union tested its first atomic device, and Teller sought support for a crash program to build a hydrogen bomb, arguing that it was critical to the survival of the United States. President Truman finally approved a hydrogen bomb program in January 1950.

Teller worked on a design for the hydrogen bomb, but calculations by Ulam and the new ENIAC computer confirmed that his initial concept was not feasible. He, Ulam, and young physicist Richard Garwin finally devised a workable hydrogen bomb design. In November 1951, Teller left Los Alamos and returned to the University of Chicago, when he failed to be named the head of the thermonuclear program.

Frustrated by his experiences at Los Alamos, Teller convinced the U.S. government to establish a second weapons lab in Livermore, California, in 1952. Teller claimed that competition between laboratories would help develop better military technology. From 1954 to 1958, Teller served as associate director of the new lab, then as its director from 1958 to 1960. From 1960 to 1975, he held a joint appointment as a professor of physics at the University of California and as associate director of Lawrence Livermore National Laboratory. In 1975, he became director emeritus of Lawrence Livermore and a senior research fellow at the Hoover Institution at Stanford University.

Teller was known for his controversial stances. Many Los Alamos scientists believed he betrayed Oppenheimer, the scientific director of the atomic bomb project, when he cast doubt on his reliability at a hearing in 1954 at which Oppenheimer's security clearance was revoked. In 1963, Teller also testified against the Limited Test Ban Treaty, which was eventually adopted, and in the 1970s he promoted the development of nuclear fusion as an alternative energy source. In the 1980s, he vigorously supported President Reagan's Strategic Defense Initiative, or "Star Wars," plan. Teller received numerous awards for his contributions to physics, including the Enrico Fermi Award, the National Medal of Science, and the Presidential Medal of Freedom. He wrote more than a dozen books, ranging from energy policies to defense issues to his memoirs.

Sources

Goodchild, Peter. 2004. *Edward Teller: The Real Dr. Strangelove.* Cambridge, MA: Harvard University Press.

Rhodes, Richard. 1995. *Dark Sun: The Making of the Hydrogen Bomb.* New York: Simon and Schuster.

Teller, Edward, with Judith Shoolery. 2001. *Memoirs: A Twentieth-Century Journey in Science and Politics.* Cambridge, MA: Perseus Publishing.

Mordechai Vanunu (1954–)

Mordechai Vanunu was born on 13 October 1954 into a devout Jewish family in Marrakesh, Morocco. His parents emigrated to Israel with their eleven children in 1963. After completing school, Vanunu served three years in the Israeli Defense Forces and was honorably discharged as a sergeant. He then worked as a technician producing plutonium for bombs at the nuclear reactor center in Dimona from 1976 to 1985. He also studied philosophy at Ben Gurion University and became involved in radical politics, associating with groups that sympathized with the Palestinian people. As he began to suffer a crisis of conscience for helping to produce nuclear weapons, Vanunu came under the scrutiny of security officials. Before being laid off from his job in 1985, Vanunu took approximately sixty secret photos of the Dimona nuclear plant and the hydrogen and neutron bombs that were being developed. With the undeveloped film, he left Israel for Australia with the intention of one day exposing its nuclear weapons capability to the world.

While in Australia, Vanunu joined the Anglican church and there began to disclose some of what he knew about Dimona; a journalist urged him to tell his story and contacted the Britain-based *Sunday Times*. In London, Vanunu divulged his knowledge about Israel's nuclear weapons program and provided the sixty photos to the *Times*, which had the information reviewed by nuclear scientists. On 5 October 1986, the *Times* published "Revealed: The Secrets of Israel's Nuclear Arsenal." While the U.S. Central Intelligence Agency had speculated that Israel had ten or fifteen nuclear weapons, the article with several photos taken by Vanunu revealed that Israel actually had produced 150 to 200 bombs using an underground plutonium separation facility. Moreover, the story stated that Israel had started to produce much more powerful hydrogen and neutron bombs. Before the article appeared, Vanunu was lured to Rome by a female Israeli secret service (Mossad) agent, where he was drugged, smuggled on a ship back to Israel, and imprisoned.

The Israeli government charged Vanunu with espionage and treason, charges that carried a potential death penalty. He was convicted at a closed trial, and sentenced to eighteen years in Shikmah Prison in Ashkelon, Israel. He has claimed that the Israeli security police tried to destroy his sanity by keeping him in solitary confinement for more than eleven years. Vanunu reportedly refused Israeli government offers of better treatment or possible early release if he agreed to remain silent on everything relating to Dimona. Vanunu's plight drew international attention, and his cause was supported by many antinuclear and human rights groups in several countries. The Israeli government finally released Vanunu on 21 April 2004, but it imposed harsh restriction on his speech and movements. He is not allowed to talk to foreigners—although he has broken that rule for periodic media interviews—or to travel outside of the country. Since his release, Vanunu has been arrested by the Israeli police at least twice for violating the restrictions and has been returned to house arrest.

Sources

Cohen, Yoel. 2003. *The Whistleblower of Dimona: Israel, Vanunu, and the Bomb*. Teaneck, NJ: Holmes & Meier.

"Mordechai Vanunu." http://www.serve.com/vanunu.

Richelson, Jeffrey T. 2006. *Spying on the Bomb*. New York: W. W. Norton.

6

Data and Documents

This chapter provides technical information and useful statistics, as well as key historical documents, on nuclear weapons and nonproliferation. Its aim is to provide more detail on subjects raised in Chapters 1 through 5 and to expose readers to some original-source documents from the nuclear age. The first section surveys data on nuclear weapons. It begins with a short technical overview of nuclear physics, reactor types, and the processes involved in creating fissile material for weapons. Subsequent entries provide information on worldwide nuclear tests, global nuclear stockpiles (tracked over time), and nuclear-weapon-free zones in various parts of the world. The second section provides a sampling of important documents and reports from the nuclear age. These items range from the 1939 letter from Albert Einstein to President Franklin D. Roosevelt that first brought attention to the threat of Nazi Germany's bomb program, to the bombing order authorizing the use of U.S. nuclear weapons against Japan, to the text of the Nuclear Non-Proliferation Treaty (NPT), to the recent United Nations resolutions aimed at preventing terrorists from acquiring nuclear weapons or other weapons of mass destruction (WMD).

Data

This section summarizes key information about nuclear weapons technology, tests, and arsenals and provides a table with all nuclear-weapon-free zones.

Nuclear Materials and Technologies

The following description of nuclear energy and weapons drawn from a briefing book by experts at the Programme for Promoting Nuclear Non-Proliferation provides readers with critical information to understand reactor physics, the nature of weapons-grade materials, and basic bomb physics.

Nuclear Energy and Nuclear Weapons: An Introductory Guide

Nuclear Materials

A chemical element consists of basic building blocks, called atoms, which themselves contain "sub-atomic" particles. These particles are of three types: protons, neutrons and electrons. Protons (positively charged particles), together with neutrons (uncharged particles) make up an atom's core or nucleus. Electrons (negatively charged particles) are identical in number to the protons, but are found outside of the nucleus of the atom. All chemical elements are defined and distinguished from each other by the number of protons/electrons their atoms contain, termed their atomic number. Examples of atomic numbers are 1 for an atom of hydrogen and 93 for an atom of plutonium.

While all atoms of an element must have the same number of protons/electrons, they may contain differing numbers of neutrons. These variants are called isotopes of an element. They have different nuclear properties and masses/weights but their chemical properties are identical: thus they can only be separated by making use of their differing masses, and not by chemical means.

Isotopes are normally identified by the sum of their protons and neutrons. Thus "Uranium 235," often shortened to the notation "U^{235}" (or "U-235") indicates the isotope of uranium that contains 235 (92+143) protons and neutrons in the nucleus of each atom. "Plutonium 239," or "Pu" (or "Pu-239") indicates the isotope of plutonium that contains 239 (93+146) protons and neutrons in the nucleus of each atom.

Nuclear Reactions

Fission

Nuclear fission is the splitting of the nucleus of an atom into two or more parts. This is a process which normally only occurs when heavy elements such as uranium and plutonium are bombarded by neutrons under favourable conditions. Not all isotopes of these elements fission under such circumstances; those that do are called fissile materials. The most frequently used fissile materials are the isotopes Uranium 235 (U-235) and Plutonium 239 (Pu-239).

These isotopes are not found in their pure form in nature. U-235 forms only 0.7 per cent of natural uranium ore which is mostly made up of nonfissile U-238. Plutonium does not exist at all in natural form and has to be manufactured from uranium. This is done by placing it inside a reactor, where some U-238 nuclei will capture slow moving neutrons to form fissile Pu-239.

When a fissile material is bombarded with neutrons, it splits into atoms of lighter elements. This process releases large quantities of energy and neutrons. If these neutrons hit and split additional "fissile" nuclei, more neutrons are released to continue the reaction. If there is a sufficient concentration of atoms of fissile isotopes, known as a "critical mass," this reaction will be self-sustaining. This is a "chain reaction."

A critical mass is the smallest amount of material required for a chain reaction. This may be affected by variables such as the concentration of the fissile isotopes in the material; its density—if it is compressed the critical mass is reduced; and its physical configuration—a sphere or some other shape.

Fusion

Fusion takes place when two nuclei of light elements such as hydrogen fuse together to make a heavier one. While this process releases much larger quantities of energy than the fission process, it also requires large amounts of energy to initiate it. For fusion to occur, the repellant forces that arise between the positively charged protons in the two nuclei have to be overcome, and temperatures of over 100 million degrees centigrade are normally required for this to occur. The most frequently used materials to generate fusion reactions are tritium (H-3), deuterium (H-2) and the solid Lithium-6 Deuteride, which when heated to the temperature of the fusion reaction, breaks down into tritium and deuterium.

Nuclear Reactors

Fission Reactors

There are several features common to all fission or (as they are more usually termed) nuclear reactors.

The first of these is that they contain a core or mass of fissile material (the fuel) which may weigh tens of tons, within which energy is produced by sustaining a regulated chain reaction. The fissile material used varies between reactor types, but it may be natural uranium (which contains 0.7 per cent fissile U-235) or uranium which has been enriched to increase the percentage of U-235 to around 3 per cent. Alternatively, Plutonium 239 produced by the irradiation of U-238 in a reactor, or Uranium 233 (U-233) produced from Thorium 232 (Th-232) may be used, or a combination of these mixed with uranium (mixed oxide fuels or MOX). This fuel is usually in rod or pin form, and is clad in a gastight containment material such as stainless steel.

A second related feature is the presence of a means of regulating the chain reaction. This normally takes the form of control rods which absorb neutrons, and which can be inserted into the core to reduce the rate of fission or to shut down the reactor.

The fissile core of a reactor is usually surrounded by a third common feature, a moderator. This material is chosen because it slows down some of the faster neutrons so that these can more easily hit nuclei and initiate fission, and thus maintain the chain reaction. The moderator can be ordinary (or light) water, heavy water (deuterium oxide) or graphite.

A fourth common feature is a means of removing the heat produced by the chain reaction from the core of the reactor. This cooling system can also provide the heat and steam to drive turbines and thus generate electricity.

Finally, there is a containment vessel which serves to shield the radioactive core from other parts of the reactor system. Lining this vessel is a reflector which increases the efficiency of the fission process. In addition, a reactor will itself normally be surrounded by a further thick containment structure, whose purpose is to contain any release of radioactivity and prevent it escaping into the surrounding environment.

Reactors have been built to serve four broad purposes. First, a significant proportion of the reactors in the world are large units designed to produce steam to drive turbo-generators, and thus to generate electricity for civil uses. Second, there are smaller units of a similar type which are used in naval vessels, especially submarines, to generate electricity for propulsion purposes or to drive turbines. Third, there are many small materials testing and research reactors, which usually have no turbo-generators attached and are used mainly for experimental purposes. Finally, there are large units used by the nuclear-weapon states to produce plutonium for military explosive purposes, some of which do not have turbo-generators attached to them.

Light Water Reactors (LWRs)

This is the most widespread power reactor type found in the world today. It uses low enriched (3%) uranium as fuel, which enhances its efficiency as an electricity generator by enabling the fuel to stay longer in the reactor. It also uses ordinary water as both a moderator and coolant. There are two variants of this reactor, Pressurized Water Reactors (PWRs) and Boiling Water Reactors (BWRs), the chief difference between them being in their method of producing steam to make electricity. Small LWRs are also used to power submarines and other naval vessels. LWRs are a costly and inefficient way of producing Pu-239.

Heavy Water Reactors (HWRs)

In these types of reactors, heavy water is used as both the moderator and coolant. Heavy water absorbs so few neutrons that it permits the use of natural uranium as fuel. This type of reactor, the majority of which are called CANDUs [Canada Deuterium Uranium], uses up so much of the fissile U-235 in its natural uranium fuel that it is probably uneconomic to reprocess and recycle it, and the preferred option is to store it and dispose of it as waste. It is also a good producer of plutonium, and this type of reactor has been used in the United States without any turbo-generators attached to produce materials for weapon purposes. To produce Pu-239, rather than to minimize electricity generation costs, fuel re-loading takes place more frequently. Thus a distinction between civil and military use is the length of time the fuel remains in the reactor.

Nuclear Weapons

Fission Devices

A fission weapon or device is designed so that a critical mass of fissile material can be assembled and held together before the device blows itself apart. The yield of the weapon is determined by the amount of fissile material involved, the number of nuclei fissioned, and the number of generations of fissions that can be achieved before disassembly takes place.

A simple fission weapon design, also known as a first-generation nuclear weapon, can be of either the "gun barrel" or "implosion" type. A gun device involves bringing together rapidly two sub-critical masses of highly enriched uranium by propelling one of them with an explosive along a thick tube or gun-barrel so that it impacts with considerable velocity upon the other. This creates conditions for a chain reaction. This method is conceptually simple but the explosive power of the weapon tends to quickly force the fissile material apart so that little of the material goes through the fission process. It is therefore relatively inefficient in its use of fissile material. This method cannot be used with plutonium.

An implosion weapon works by compressing a sub-critical spherical mass of fissile material until it becomes critical. The fissile material is surrounded by a neutron reflector, usually of beryllium, and a heavy metal tamper of either U-238 or tungsten. Surrounding this assembly is a further hollow sphere of conventional explosives. If the conventional explosive can be detonated so as to produce a uniform, symmetrical implosion, the tamper is propelled inwards into the sphere of fissile material, and compresses it into criticality. The forces generated by the conventional explosives then contain the gaseous sphere of fissile materials while many repetitions of the fissile reaction occur, and the full yield of the device is produced.

Boosted-Fission Devices

A fission device can be "boosted" to increase its yield by placing within its core a small quantity of fusion material, such as tritium. At the great temperatures and pressures found within the gaseous core of an exploding device, this material fuses and releases an extra quantity of neutrons which, in turn, produce additional fissions in the uranium or plutonium used in the device. More of the fissile material is thus consumed than in a simple fission device, the efficiency of the fission process is improved and a higher yield produced.

Fusion (Thermonuclear) Devices

The energy released by such a device, also known as a second-generation nuclear weapon, arises primarily from nuclear fusion in isotopes of hydrogen such as tritium and deuterium. A large energy source, such as a fission device, is needed to start a fusion reaction. A fusion weapon thus has at least two stages which contribute to the yield, the fission trigger or primary device and the thermonuclear secondary device. In addition, these two devices may be contained in a shell of U-238 which constitutes a third stage of the device. This material, whilst it cannot maintain a self-sustaining fission explosion, can be made to fission where there is a constant external supply of fast neutrons from other fission or fusion reactions. There can be any number of fission-fusion-fission-fusion steps, and so no limit in theory to the size and yield of a thermonuclear weapon.

Weapon-Grade Fissile Materials

The size of a fission device is directly related to the concentration of fissile isotopes in the material in the core. For purposes of producing a practical weapon, the minimum enrichment required for uranium is about 50 per cent. However, to enable compact, light designs to be produced, the present nuclear powers are assumed to use in their weapons about 10–25 kilos [22–55 pounds] of uranium enriched to over 90 per cent U-235. This enriched material is produced in an enrichment plant (see below).

Plutonium is often preferred to uranium in weapon designs, as less plutonium than uranium is required to produce a given yield—about 5–8 kilos [11–17.6 pounds] is assumed to be required for a simple device. Plutonium with 93 per cent or above Pu-239 constitutes weapons grade material, though there are claims that devices have been exploded using plutonium with much lower concentrations of this isotope. Such weapons, however, tend to have uncertain yields and give off dangerous radiation, so the higher concentrations are preferred.

All fission reactors produce plutonium, but reasonably pure Pu-239 can only be obtained by withdrawing the uranium fuel after a short period (2–6 months) in the core. If the fuel is left in for a longer period, significant amounts of Pu-240 and other heavier isotopes are contained in the plutonium. Typically, Light Water Reactors (LWRs) will have plutonium in their used fuel which has a concentration of Pu-239 below 80 per cent. Plutonium is obtained from spent reactor fuel through a chemical process known as reprocessing.

Enrichment

Uranium must be enriched if it is to be used in certain reactor types and in weapons. This means that the concentration of fissile U-235 must be increased by physical, rather than chemical, means before it can be fabricated into fuel. The natural concentration of this isotope is 0.7 per cent, but a concentration of 3 per cent is necessary in order to sustain a chain reaction in an LWR. Some 90 per cent enrichment is required before use in HTGRs [High Temperature Gas Cooled Reactors], the majority of submarine propulsion units or fission weapons. This process of enrichment is not linear, and as much enrichment effort, or "separative work" as it is usually termed, may be involved in achieving enrichment from, say 0.7 to 1 per cent as from 10–90 per cent.

Reprocessing

This is a process whereby the uranium and the plutonium in spent fuel discharged from a reactor is separated from the other "fission products" by chemical means. It may then be recycled into reactor fuel or, in the case of plutonium, may be used in weapons. Reprocessing is usually carried out using mechanical and solvent extraction techniques, and occurs in three steps [dissolving the fuel in solution, separating out nitrates of plutonium and uranium, and purifying the recovered materials].

Source

Bailey, Emily, Richard Guthrie, Darryl Howlett, and John Simpson, *Briefing Book, Volume 1: The Evolution of the Nuclear Nonproliferation Regime*, Chapter 2 (6th ed., 2000). Southampton, England: Programme for Promoting Nuclear Non-Proliferation, University of Southampton. © 2000 Programme for Promoting Nuclear Non-Proliferation. Used by permission.

Worldwide Nuclear Weapon Stockpiles

The expansion of nuclear weapon stockpiles during the Cold War represented an alarming trend, driven by the perceived need to develop new types of bombs and improve existing designs. The size of the U.S. nuclear stockpile, however, actually peaked in the late 1960s, as the U.S. military began to retire obsolete weapons and focus on survivable, second-strike forces instead of maintaining a simple numerical advantage over the Soviet Union. Playing catch-up from a position far behind the United States, Moscow continued to expand its arsenal into the 1980s, when domestic political forces shifted Soviet policy aims toward achieving cooperative arms reductions with the United States. In 2002, despite arms control progress, the actual numbers of U.S. and Russian nuclear weapons in their respective stockpiles remained far above figures commonly cited for deployed forces because of delays in eliminating retired weapons (especially in Russia) and decisions by both sides to retain a reserve in case of a deterioration in relations and a need to reconstitute their forces. Nuclear forces by all other states have remained in the hundreds or below. As noted, some of the figures are estimates, as certain countries still hold these numbers as closely guarded state secrets. The figures in Table 6.1 represent nuclear warheads of all types, both strategic and tactical.

Nuclear Testing

From 1945 to 1963, nuclear tests were conducted in the atmosphere, in space, underground, and underwater, especially by the United States and the Soviet Union. Most of these explosions took place in the atmosphere, as such tests are easier to carry out and provide the opportunity to examine the effects of the weapon on real targets, such as buildings and vehicles. In 1963, the United States, the Soviet Union, and the United Kingdom signed the Limited Test Ban Treaty (LTBT), which prohibited nuclear tests in the atmosphere, in outer space, and underwater; the three countries then moved all their tests underground. France and China, not parties to the LTBT, conducted their last nuclear tests in the atmosphere in 1974 and 1980, respectively. The greatest advantage of an underground nuclear explosion is that it does not release significant amounts of radioactive debris and allows the use of a greater amount of experimental apparatus close to the explosion spot. The 1996 Comprehensive Nuclear-Test-Ban Treaty (CTBT) prohibited all nuclear explosions, including nuclear testing, but it has not been signed by all states, and it has not yet acquired enough ratifications by national legislatures to become legally binding.

TABLE 6.1
Estimated Worldwide Nuclear Stockpiles, 1945–2006

Country	1945	1955	1965	1975	1985	1995	2006
United States[1]	6	3,057	31,982	27,826	24,237	12,144	9,962
USSR/Russia[1]	0	200	6,129	19,055	39,197	27,000	16,000
United Kingdom	0	10	310	325	300	300	192
France	0	0	32	188	360	500	348
China[2]	0	0	5	185	200	200	200
Israel[3]	0	0	0	20	40	75	85
India[3]	0	0	0	>0	>0	30	50
South Africa[4]	0	0	0	0	3	0	0
Pakistan[3]	0	0	0	0	0	10	40
North Korea[3]	0	0	0	0	0	0	>4
Total	6	3,267	38,458	47,599	64,337	40,259	26,881

[1] According to data from the Natural Resources Defense Council, the United States has an estimated 5,021 deployed strategic warheads, 215 spares, 500 nonstrategic warheads, and 4,226 warheads in storage. Russia has an estimated 3,500 deployed strategic warheads, 2,330 active tactical and air/missile defense warheads, and 6,000 strategic and 4,170 tactical warheads in storage.

[2] Chinese numbers are estimates based on observed deployments and suspected reserves.

[3] The early figures shown for Israel, India, Pakistan, and North Korea are the lower bounds of their capabilities based on estimated fissile material production. Later figures for Israel, India, and Pakistan are estimates of actual weapons production based on expert reports (cited below).

[4] South Africa had developed seven nuclear weapons by 1990, but destroyed them soon after and joined the NPT as a non–nuclear weapon state in 1991.

Sources: Robert Norris and Hans Kristensen, "Nuclear Weapons Data," Natural Resources Defense Council, on the Web site of the *Bulletin of Atomic Scientists* at http://www.thebulletin.org/nuclear_weapons_data/; Robert Norris and Hans Kristensen, "Global Nuclear Stockpiles, 1945–2006," *Bulletin of the Atomic Scientists* (July/August 2006), pages 64–66; "Israel's Nuclear Stockpile," Web site of the Federation of American Scientists, at http://www.fas.org/nuke/guide/israel/ nuke/; Rodney W. Jones and Mark G. McDonough, *Tracking Nuclear Proliferation: A Guide in Maps and Charts*, 1998. Washington, DC: Carnegie Endowment for International Peace, 1998; David Albright, "India's and Pakistan's Fissile Material and Nuclear Weapons Inventory, End of 1999," report on the Web site of the Institute for Science and International Security (ISIS) at http://www.isis-online.org/publications/southasia/stocks1000.html; and David Albright and Paul Brannon, "The North Korean Plutonium Stock Mid-2006," report on the ISIS Web site at http://www.isis-online.org/publications/dprk/ dprkplutonium.pdf.

Nuclear tests (see Table 6.2) have been conducted to achieve a range of objectives, including improving existing nuclear weapon designs and developing new weapons, understanding nuclear weapons' effects, maintaining reliability and safety of a nuclear weapon arsenal, and finding so-called peaceful uses for industrial purposes. This latter set of tests proved unsuccessful, as they contaminated the river canals and underground storage cavities they created with radioactivity, making them unusable. Nuclear tests

TABLE 6.2
Global Distribution and Geography of Nuclear
Weapons Tests (1945–2006)

Country	Location	Number of Tests*
United States	Nevada Test Site	928
(Total tests: 1,054)	Eniwetok Atoll, Marshall Islands	43
	Christmas Island, South Pacific	24
	Bikini Atoll, Marshall Islands	23
	Johnston Island, South Pacific	12
	Other Nevada sites	7
	Pacific Ocean	4
	Alaska	3
	South Atlantic Ocean	3
	New Mexico	3
	Mississippi	2
	Colorado	2
Soviet Union/Russia	Kazakhstan	496
(Total tests: 715)	Russia (various locations, especially Novaya Zemlya)	214
	Ukraine	2
	Uzbekistan	2
	Turkmenistan	1
France	Mururoa Atoll, French Polynesia	181
(Total tests: 210)	Algeria	17
	Fangataufa Atoll, French Polynesia	12
United Kingdom	Nevada (jointly with United States)	24
(Total tests: 45)	Australia	12
	Christmas Island, South Pacific	6
	Malden Island, South Pacific	3
China	Lop Nor, China	45
India	Pokhran, India	3*
Pakistan	Chagai Hills, Pakistan	2*
Unknown (possibly South Africa or Israel)	South Indian Ocean	1
North Korea	North Hamgyong Province, North Korea	1

*In conformance with the counting rules of the U.S.-Soviet Threshold Test Ban Treaty of 1974, a "nuclear test" is defined here as a nuclear explosion at a particular time, which may have included several nuclear individuals bombs (if detonated simultaneously). Thus, the five devices India tested in May 1998 are counted as only two here, as the tests took place in two simultaneous detonations (making three total tests for India, counting the test in 1974). Pakistan's tests in May 1998 are counted as two. The total number of U.S. detonations is 1,149, compared with 1,054 tests, according to U.S. Department of Energy figures. The figures include so-called peaceful nuclear explosions used in experiments for various engineering purposes.
Sources: U.S. Department of Energy, *United States Nuclear Tests, July 1945 through September 1992*, DOE/NV–209-REV 15, December 2000. http://www.nv.doe.gov/news&pubs/publications/historyreports/default.htm; "Known Nuclear Tests Worldwide, 1945–1998," *Bulletin of Atomic Scientists* 54 (1998); Abby A. Johnson et al., *For the Record — A History of the Nuclear Test Personnel Review Program, 1978–1986*, Defense Nuclear Agency, DNA 6041F, 1986. http://www.fas.org/nuke/trinity/atmosphr/ustests.htm#Crossroads; and Tariq Rauf, "French Nuclear Testing: A Fool's Errand," *Nonproliferation Review* 3 (1995), pages 49–57.

have also been carried out for political purposes sometimes, such as the huge 50-megaton explosion (the largest of all time) carried out by the Soviet Union in 1961, which was meant to intimidate the United States; and the Indian and Pakistani tests in 1998 and the North Korean test in 2006, which were meant in part to show their resolve and capabilities to rivals and the world.

Nuclear-Weapon-Free Zones

Several national, bilateral, and multilateral accords have established nuclear-weapon-free zones (NWFZs) for various continents, geographical regions, and environments. Although not discussed here, some cities and localities have created NWFZs of varying legal status. The concept of establishing geographical zones free of nuclear weapons first emerged in the late 1950s in the context of a 1958 proposal by the Polish foreign minister for an NWFZ in Central Europe, which would have blocked U.S. nuclear weapons from being stationed in West Germany in return for a ban on Soviet nuclear weapons in East Germany, Poland, and Czechoslovakia. Although the plan failed, the concept lived on and eventually came into fruition in various parts of the globe. Indeed, NWFZ agreements now cover almost the entire Southern Hemisphere.

The aims of such arrangements include enhancing regional security, reducing the threat that nuclear weapons might be targeted at countries in a particular region, strengthening global nonproliferation norms, encouraging nuclear disarmament, and preserving the environment.

The common element in all NWFZ agreements is a pledge by states not to develop, deploy, station, test, or use nuclear weapons within the zone. This restriction goes beyond the NPT, which allows the possible stationing of nuclear weapons on the territory of non–nuclear weapon states by the nuclear powers and permits peaceful nuclear explosions for industrial purposes, even by non–nuclear weapon states. Existing NWFZs ban these activities and often prohibit nuclear waste dumping, nuclear weapon research, and other activities. Regional inspection regimes are sometimes established to implement the treaties; in other cases, the International Atomic Energy Agency (IAEA) plays the primary role of ensuring that nuclear materials will not be diverted from peaceful programs within a zone. Table 6.3 summarizes the key NWFZ agreements that currently exist.

TABLE 6.3
Existing Nuclear-Weapon-Free Zones in Brief

Name of Zone (Treaty)	Region Covered	Signed/Entered into Force	Unique Provisions Beyond Ban on Nuclear Weapons
Antarctic Treaty	Antarctic continent	1959/1961	Allows no military activities of any sort on the continent
Treaty on the Prohibition of Nuclear Weapons in Latin America and the Caribbean (Tlatelolco Treaty)	South America, Central America, and the Caribbean	1967/entry into force varies for each state	Originally allowed "peaceful" nuclear explosions, but has since been amended
Treaty on the Principles Governing the Activities of States in the Exploration of Outer Space, Including the Moon and Other Celestial Bodies (Outer Space Treaty)	Outer space and the celestial bodies	1967/1967	Bans all weapons of mass destruction in orbit; bans military forces of all kinds on the moon and celestial bodies
Treaty on the Prohibition of the Emplacement of Nuclear Weapons and Other Weapons of Mass Destruction on the Sea-Bed and the Ocean Floor and in the Subsoil Thereof (Sea-Bed Treaty)	International waters and the ocean floor	1971/1972	Verification is via observation by states (such as from submarines or other submersibles in international waters); kept U.S.-Soviet arms race from the seabed
South Pacific Nuclear-Free Zone (Rarotonga Treaty)	South Pacific (including various small island states, New Zealand, and Australia)	1985/1986	Aimed at halting nuclear tests in the South Pacific; protocols finally signed by France, Britain, and United States in 1996
Joint North-South Declaration on the Denuclearization of the Korean Peninsula	Korean Peninsula	1992/1992	Bans plutonium separation and uranium enrichment; not yet implemented because of political disputes
Treaty on the Southeast Asia Nuclear-Weapon-Free Zone (Bangkok Treaty)	Southeast Asia	1995/1997	Allows countries to ban transit of nuclear weapons through the zone; has been opposed by the nuclear weapon states
African Nuclear-Weapon-Free Zone Treaty (Pelindaba Treaty)	Africa	1996/not yet entered into force	Zone formed after South Africa's voluntary denuclearization; ratification by several North African states awaits an Israeli decision to join the NPT
Nuclear-Weapon-Free Status of Mongolia	Mongolia	Declared by Mongolia, 1992/accepted by United Nations, 1998	World's first United Nations–recognized, single-state NWFZ; also bans transit of nuclear weapons through Mongolia

continued

TABLE 6.3 (continued)
Existing Nuclear-Weapon-Free Zones in Brief

Name of Zone (Treaty)	Region Covered	Signed/Entered into Force	Unique Provisions Beyond Ban on Nuclear Weapons
The Central Asian Nuclear-Weapon-Free Zone	Central Asian states (Kazakhstan, Kyrgyzstan, Tajikistan, Turkmenistan, and Uzbekistan)	September 2006/ not yet entered into force	Provision barring nuclear weapons from being located in the region may not apply to Russia because of a separate 1992 agreement. The United States, Britain, and France also object to member states' option to bar transport of nuclear weapons through the CANWFZ. Members agree to rehabilitate territory contaminated by past nuclear activities.

Sources: Center for Nonproliferation Studies (CNS), Inventory of International Nonproliferation Organizations and Regimes: http://cns.miis.edu/pubs/inven/inven.htm; CNS, Nuclear-Weapon-Free Zone Tutorial: http://www.nti.org/h_learnmore/nwfztutorial/index.html.

Documents

This section provides actual documents from the history of nuclear weapons and nonproliferation, drawn from a variety of sources, but primarily from declassified U.S. government files. All documents are either in the public domain or are used by permission.

Letter from Albert Einstein to President Roosevelt

This document was arguably the key stimulus for the U.S. adoption of serious investigations into nuclear weapons on the eve of the U.S. entry into World War II. Nobel Prize–winning scientist Albert Einstein sent this letter to President Franklin D. Roosevelt on 2 August 1939 at the initiative of Leo Szilard and other émigré scientists who feared that Nazi Germany, with its extensive scientific talents, would beat the Allies to the bomb and thereby achieve victory in World War II. Instead, the United States took up this race and, drawing on its immense material, financial, and scientific resources, became the only country to develop an atomic bomb during World War II.

Albert Einstein
Old Grove Rd.
Nassau Point
Peconic, Long Island

August 2nd, 1939

F. D. Roosevelt,
President of the United States,
White House
Washington, D. C.

Sir:

Some recent work by E. Fermi and L. Szilard, which has been communicated to me in a manuscript, leads me to expect that the element uranium may be turned into a new and important source of energy in the immediate future. Certain aspects of this situation which has arisen seem to call for watchfulness and, if necessary, quick action on the part of the Administration. I believe therefore that it is my duty to bring to your attention the following facts and recommendations:

In the course of the last four months it has been made probable—through the work of Joliot in France as well as Fermi and Szilard in America—that it may become possible to set up a nuclear chain reaction in a large mass of uranium, by which vast amounts of power and large quantities of new radium-like elements would be generated. Now it appears almost certain that this could be achieved in the immediate future.

This new phenomena would also lead to the construction of bombs, and it is conceivable—though much less certain—that extremely powerful bombs of a new type may thus be constructed. A single bomb of this type, carried by boat and exploded in a port, might very well destroy the whole port together with some of the surrounding territory. However, such bombs might very well prove to be too heavy for transportation by air.

The United States has only very poor ores of uranium in moderate quantities. There is some good ore in Canada and the former Czechoslovakia, while the most important source of uranium is Belgian Congo.

In view of this situation you may think it desirable to have some permanent contact maintained between the Administration and the group of physicists working on chain reactions in America. One possible way of achieving this might be for you to entrust with this task a person who has your confidence and who could perhaps serve in an unofficial capacity. His task might comprise the following:

a) to approach Government Departments, keep them informed of the further development, and put forward recommendations for Government action, giving particular attention to the problem of securing a supply of uranium for the United States;

b) to speed up the experimental work, which is at present being carried on within the limits of the budgets of University laboratories, by providing funds, if such funds be required, through his contacts with private persons who are willing to make contributions for this cause, and perhaps also by obtaining the cooperation of industrial laboratories which have the necessary equipment.

I understand that Germany has actually stopped the sale of uranium from the Czechoslovakian mines which she has taken over. That she should have taken such an early action might perhaps be understood on the ground that the son of the German Under-Secretary of State, von Weizsacker, is attached to the Kaiser-Wilhelm-Institute in Berlin where some of the American work on uranium is now being repeated.

Yours very truly,
(Albert Einstein)

Source: Available online on Franklin D. Roosevelt Presidential Library and Museum Web site: http://www.fdrlibrary.marist.edu/psf/box5/t64a01.html, and the U.S. Department of Energy, The Manhattan Project, An Interactive History Web site: http://www.mbe.doe.gov/me70/manhattan/einstein_letter_photograph.htm.

The U.S. Military Order to Drop the Atomic Bomb on Japan

After being reviewed by President Harry Truman during the Potsdam summit of Allied leaders in defeated Germany in July 1945, this order authorized the U.S. military to drop the first atomic bomb and "additional bombs" on Japan sometime after 3 August 1945. Because of the delays in communications with the Pacific theater of military operations, uncertainties in the weather, and logistics related to handling the bomb, President Truman left considerable decision-making power in the hands of the U.S. Army in terms of selecting the exact date for the attacks and the targets. General Leslie Groves of the Manhattan Project drafted the bombing order for Truman, and Secretary of War Henry Stimson (also at Potsdam) reviewed the document as well.

TOP SECRET
25 July 1945
TO: General Carl Spaatz
Commanding General
United States Army Strategic Air Forces

1. The 509 Composite Group, 20th Air Force will deliver its first special bomb as soon as weather will permit visual bombing after about 3 August 1945 on one of the targets: Hiroshima, Kokura, Niigata and Nagasaki. To carry military and civilian scientific personnel from the War Department to observe and record the effects of the explosion of the bomb, additional aircraft will accompany the airplane carrying the bomb. The observing planes will stay several miles distant from the point of impact of the bomb.

2. Additional bombs will be delivered on the above targets as soon as made ready by the project staff. Further instructions will be issued concerning targets other than those listed above.

3. Dissemination of any and all information concerning the use of the weapon against Japan is reserved to the Secretary of War and the President of the United States. No communiques on the subject or releases of information will be issued by Commanders in the field without specific prior authority. Any news stories will be sent to the War Department for specific clearance.

4. The foregoing directive is issued to you by direction and with the approval of the Secretary of War and of the Chief of Staff, USA. It is desired that you personally deliver one copy of this directive to General MacArthur and one copy to Admiral Nimitz for their information.

(Sgd) THOS. T. HANDY
THOS. T. HANDY
General, G.S.C.
Acting Chief of Staff

copy for General Groves
TOP SECRET

Source: Available online at the National Security Archive, "The Atomic Bomb and the End of World War II: A Collection of Primary Sources," http://www.gwu.edu/~nsarchiv/NSAEBB/NSAEBB162/index.htm. The bombing order is available at http://www.gwu.edu/~nsarchiv/NSAEBB/NSAEBB162/41e.pdf.

Official U.S. Report on the Atomic Bomb's Effects in Hiroshima and Nagasaki

After the end of World War II and the use of the atomic bomb on Japan, the Manhattan Engineer District conducted a detailed on-the-ground study of the effects of the attacks. The purpose was to understand the significance of atomic weapons and their effects on buildings and human beings. This report provides detailed information on the impact of the attacks on Hiroshima and Nagasaki, including the nature of the damage caused and the cause of death of tens of thousands of citizens in the two cities. The "X" mentioned numerous times in the report refers to the point of the respective bombs' detonations, or ground zero.

The Atomic Bombings of Hiroshima and Nagasaki

by The Manhattan Engineer District, June 29, 1946
GENERAL DESCRIPTION OF DAMAGE CAUSED BY THE ATOMIC EXPLOSIONS

In considering the devastation in the two cities, it should be remembered that the cities' differences in shape and topography resulted in great differences in the damages. Hiroshima was all on low, flat ground, and was roughly circular in shape; Nagasaki was much cut up by hills and mountain spurs, with no regularity to its shape.

In Hiroshima almost everything up to about one mile from X was completely destroyed, except for a small number (about 50) of heavily reinforced concrete buildings, most of which were specially designed to withstand earthquake shock, which were not collapsed by the blast; most of these buildings had their interiors completely gutted, and all windows, doors, sashes, and frames ripped out. In Nagasaki, nearly everything within 1/2 mile of the explosion was destroyed, including heavy structures. All Japanese homes were destroyed within 1 1/2 miles from X.

Underground air raid shelters with earth cover roofs immediately below the explosion had their roofs caved in; but beyond 1/2 mile from X they suffered no damage.

In Nagasaki, 1,500 feet from X high quality steel frame buildings were not completely collapsed, but the entire buildings suffered mass distortion and all panels and roofs were blown in.

In Nagasaki, 2,000 feet from X, reinforced concrete buildings with 10" walls and 6" floors were collapsed; reinforced concrete buildings with 4" walls and roofs were standing but were badly damaged. At 2,000 feet some 9" concrete walls were completely destroyed.

In Nagasaki, 3,500 feet from X, church buildings with 18" brick walls were completely destroyed. 12" brick walls were severely cracked as far as 5,000 feet.

In Hiroshima, 4,400 feet from X, multistory brick buildings were completely demolished. In Nagasaki, similar buildings were destroyed to 5,300 feet.

In Hiroshima, roof tiles were bubbled (melted) by the flash heat out to 4,000 feet from X; in Nagasaki, the same effect was observed to 6,500 feet.

In Hiroshima, steel frame buildings were destroyed 4,200 feet from X, and to 4,800 feet in Nagasaki.

In both cities, the mass distortion of large steel buildings was observed out to 4,500 feet from X.

In Nagasaki, reinforced concrete smoke stacks with 8" walls, specially designed to withstand earthquake shocks, were overturned up to 4,000 feet from X.

In Hiroshima, steel frame buildings suffered severe structural damage up to 5,700 feet from X, and in Nagasaki the same damage was sustained as far as 6,000 feet.

In Nagasaki, 9" brick walls were heavily cracked to 5,000 feet, were moderately cracked to 6,000 feet, and slightly cracked to 8,000 feet. In both cities, light concrete buildings collapsed out to 4,700 feet.

In Hiroshima, multistory brick buildings suffered structural damage up to 6,600 feet, and in Nagasaki up to 6,500 feet from X.

In both cities overhead electric installations were destroyed up to 5,500 feet; and trolley cars were destroyed up to 5,500 feet, and damaged to 10,500 feet.

Flash ignition of dry, combustible material was observed as far as 6,400 feet from X in Hiroshima, and in Nagasaki as far as 10,000 feet from X.

[...]

Heavy fire damage was sustained in a circular area in Hiroshima with a mean radius of about 6,000 feet and a maximum radius of about 11,000 feet; similar heavy damage occured [sic] in Nagasaki south of X up to 10,000 feet, where it was stopped on a river course.

In Hiroshima over 60,000 of 90,000 buildings were destroyed or severely damaged by the atomic bomb; this figure represents over 67% of the city's structures.

In Nagasaki 14,000 (or 27%) of 52,000 residences were completely destroyed and 5,400 or (10%) were half destroyed. Only 12% remained undamaged. This destruction was limited by the layout of the city. The following is a summary of the damage to buildings in Nagasaki as determined from a ground survey made by the Japanese:

[...]

As intended, the bomb was exploded at an almost ideal location over Nagasaki to do the maximum damage to industry, including the Mitsubishi Steel and Arms Works, the Mitsubishi-Urakami Ordnance Works (Torpedo Works), and numerous factories, factory training schools, and other industrial establishments, with a minimum destruction of dwellings and consequently, a minimum amount of casualties. Had the bomb been dropped farther south, the Mitsubishi-Urakami Ordnance Works would not have been so severely damaged, but the main business and residential districts of Nagasaki would have sustained much greater damage casualties.

[...]

In general, the atomic bomb explosion damaged all windows and ripped out, bent, or twisted most of the steel window or door sashes, ripped doors from hinges, damaged all suspended wood, metal, and plaster ceilings. The blast concussion also caused great damage to equipment by tumbling and battering. Fires generally of secondary origin consumed practically all combustible material, caused plaster to crack off, burned all wooden trim, stair covering, wooden frames of wooden suspended ceilings, beds, mattresses, and mats, and fused glass, ruined all equipment not already destroyed by the blast, ruined all electrical wiring, plumbing, and caused spalling of concrete columns and beams in many of the rooms.

Almost without exception masonry buildings of either brick or stone within the effective limits of the blast were severely damaged so that most of them were flattened or reduced to rubble. The wreckage of a church, approximately 1,800 feet east of X in Nagasaki, was one of the few masonry buildings still recognizable and only portions of the walls of this structure were left standing. These walls were extremely thick (about 2 feet). The two domes of the church had reinforced concrete frames and although they were toppled, they held together as units.

Practically every wooden building or building with timber frame within 2.0 miles of X was either completely destroyed or very seriously damaged, and significant damage in Nagasaki resulted as far as 3 miles from X. Nearly all such buildings collapsed and a very large number were consumed by fire.

[...] Since the bombs were exploded high in the air, chimneys relatively close to X were subjected to more of a downward than a lateral pressure, and consequently the overturning moment was much less than might have been anticipated.

[...]

The roads, and railroad and street railway trackage sustained practically no primary damage as a result of the explosion. Most of the damage to railroads occurred from secondary causes, such as fires and damage to bridges or other structures. Rolling stock, as well as automobiles, trolleys, and buses were destroyed and burned up to a considerable distance from X. Streets were impassable for awhile because of the debris, but they were not damaged. The height of the bomb explosion probably explains the absence of direct damage to railroads and roads.

A large part of the electric supply was interrupted by the bomb blast chiefly through damage to electric substations and overhead transmission systems. Both gas works in Nagasaki were severely damaged by the bomb. These works would have required 6–7 months to get into operation. In addition to the damage sustained by the electrical and gas systems, severe damage to the water supply system was reported by the Japanese government; the chief damage was a number of breaks in the large water mains and in almost all of the distributing pipes in the areas which were affected by the blast. Nagasaki was still suffering from a water shortage inside the city six weeks after the atomic attack.

The Nagasaki Prefectural report describes vividly the effects of the bomb on the city and its inhabitants:

"Within a radius of 1 kilometer from X, men and animals died almost instantaneously and outside a radius of 1 kilometer and within a radius of 2 kilometers from X, some men and animals died instantly from the great blast and heat but the great majority were seriously or superficially injured. Houses and other structures were completely destroyed while fires broke out everywhere. Trees were uprooted and withered by the heat.

"Outside a radius of 2 kilometers and within a radius of 4 kilometers from X, men and animals suffered various degrees of injury from window glass and other fragments scattered about by the blast and many were burned by the intense heat. Dwellings and other structures were half damaged by blast.

"Outside a radius of 4 kilometers and within a radius of 8 kilometers living creatures were injured by materials blown about by the blast; the majority were only superficially wounded. Houses were only half or partially damaged."

[…]

The fire damage in both cities was tremendous, but was more complete in Hiroshima than in Nagasaki. The effect of the fires was to change profoundly the appearance of the city and to leave the central part bare, except for some reinforced concrete and steel frames and objects such as safes, chimney stacks, and pieces of twisted sheet metal. The fire damage resulted more from the properties of the cities themselves than from those of the bombs.

The conflagration in Hiroshima caused high winds to spring up as air was drawn in toward the center of the burning area, creating a "fire storm." The wind velocity in the city had been less than 5 miles per hour before the bombing, but the fire-wind attained a velocity of 30–40 miles per hour. These great winds restricted the perimeter of the fire but greatly added to the damage of the conflagration within the perimeter and caused the deaths of many persons who might otherwise have escaped. In Nagasaki, very severe damage was caused by fires, but no extensive "fire storm" engulfed the city. In both cities, some of the fires close to X were no doubt started by the ignition of highly combustible material such as paper, straw, and dry cloth, upon the instantaneous radiation of heat from the nuclear explosion. The presence of large amounts of unburnt combustible materials near X, however, indicated that even though the heat of the blast was very intense, its duration was insufficient to raise the temperature of many materials to the kindling point except in cases where conditions were ideal. The majority of the fires were of secondary origin starting from the usual electrical short-circuits, broken gas lines, overturned stoves, open fires, charcoal braziers, lamps, etc., following collapse or serious damage from the direct blast.

Fire fighting and rescue units were stripped of men and equipment. Almost 30 hours elapsed before any rescue parties were observable. In Hiroshima only a handful of fire engines were available for fighting the ensuing fires, and none of these were of first class type. In any case, however, it is not likely that any fire fighting equipment or personnel or organization could have effected any significant reduction in the amount of damage caused by the tremendous conflagration.

[...]

TOTAL CASUALTIES

There has been great difficulty in estimating the total casualties in the Japanese cities as a result of the atomic bombing. The extensive destruction of civil installations (hospitals, fire and police department, and government agencies) the state of utter confusion immediately following the explosion, as well as the uncertainty regarding the actual population before the bombing, contribute to the difficulty of making estimates of casualties. The Japanese periodic censuses are not complete. Finally, the great fires that raged in each city totally consumed many bodies.

The number of total casualties has been estimated at various times since the bombings with wide discrepancies. The Manhattan Engineer District's best available figures are:

TABLE A
Estimates of Casualties

	Hiroshima	Nagasaki
Pre-raid population	255,000	195,000
Dead	66,000	39,000
Injured	69,000	25,000
Total Casualties	135,000	64,000

The relation of total casualties to distance from X, the center of damage and point directly under the air-burst explosion of the bomb, is of great importance in evaluating the casualty-producing effect of the bombs. This relationship for the total population of Nagasaki is shown in the table below, based on the first-obtained casualty figures of the District:

TABLE B
Relation of Total Casualties to Distance from X

Distance from X, feet	Killed	Injured	Missing	Total Casualties	Killed per square mile
0–1,640	7,505	960	1,127	9,592	24,700
1,640–3,300	3,688	1,478	1,799	6,965	4,040
3,300–4,900	8,678	17,137	3,597	29,412	5,710
4,900–6,550	221	11,958	28	12,207	125
6,550–9,850	112	9,460	17	9,589	20

No figures for total pre-raid population at these different distances were available. Such figures would be necessary in order to compute per cent mortality. A calculation made by the British Mission to Japan and based on a preliminary analysis of the study of the Joint Medical-Atomic Bomb Investigating Commission gives the following calculated values for per cent mortality at increasing distances from X:

TABLE C
Per-Cent Mortality at Various Distances

Distance from X, in feet	Per-cent Mortality
0–1000	93.0%
1000–2000	92.0
2000–3000	86.0
3000–4000	69.0
4000–5000	49.0
5000–6000	31.5
6000–7000	12.5
7000–8000	1.3
8000–9000	0.5
9000–10,000	0.0

It seems almost certain from the various reports that the greatest total number of deaths were those occurring immediately after the bombing. The causes of many of the deaths can only be surmised, and of course many persons near the center of explosion suffered fatal injuries from more than one of the bomb effects. The proper order of importance for possible causes of death is: burns, mechanical injury, and gamma radiation. Early estimates by the Japanese are shown in D below:

TABLE D
Cause of Immediate Deaths

Hiroshima	
Cause of Death	**Per-cent of Total**
Burns	60%
Falling debris	30
Other	10

Nagasaki	
Cause of Death	**Per-cent of Total**
Burns	95%
Falling debris	9
Flying glass	7
Other	7

Source: Excerpted for this use. The complete report is available on the Web site of the Avalon Project of Yale Law School: http://www.yale.edu/lawweb/avalon/abomb/mpmenu.htm.

The Founding Document of the Nonproliferation Regime

The NPT is now one of the world's most widely observed treaties, with 188 state parties. All but four countries (India, Israel, North Korea, and Pakistan) are members. The NPT requires all states to observe international controls on all transfers of nuclear technology and to seek to prevent nuclear weapons proliferation through a variety of specific means. Article VI of the treaty also requires states to work to end the arms race and to seek the eventual complete elimination of nuclear weapons. The treaty, signed in 1968, recognizes five temporary nuclear weapon states (the United States, the Soviet Union, the United Kingdom, France, and China), which had already tested nuclear weapons by that time. All other states are considered to be non–nuclear weapon states under the treaty. The IAEA in Vienna is charged with supervising the obligations of non–nuclear weapon states to maintain strict safeguards over all civilian nuclear materials to ensure that they are not diverted for use in a weapons program.

After twenty-five years, the NPT faced a review by its members in 1995 on whether or not the treaty should be extended and, if so, for how long. Although experts raised concerns that the non–nuclear weapon states might be so dissatisfied by the progress of the nuclear weapon states toward complete disarmament that they might reject the treaty's extension, a group of states, led by South Africa and Canada, crafted a compromise document that extended the treaty indefinitely in return for pledges by the nuclear weapon states to make concrete progress toward several long-sought nonproliferation objectives: a comprehensive nuclear test-ban treaty, a fissile material cutoff treaty, and further reductions in their nuclear arsenals en route to complete nuclear disarmament. At the 2000 Review Conference the parties renewed their commitment to nuclear disarmament and a ban on nuclear testing. However, at the seventh review conference in May 2005, the parties reached no agreement and left unanswered challenges to the NPT regime posed by North Korea, Iran, and Pakistan's black market of A. Q. Khan in nuclear technology. The full text of the NPT follows below.

Treaty on the Non-Proliferation of Nuclear Weapons

Signed at Washington, London, and Moscow July 1, 1968
Ratification advised by U.S. Senate March 13, 1969
Ratified by U.S. President November 24, 1969
U.S. ratification deposited at Washington, London, and Moscow March 5, 1970
Proclaimed by U.S. President March 5, 1970
Entered into force March 5, 1970

The States concluding this Treaty, hereinafter referred to as the "Parties to the Treaty,"

Considering the devastation that would be visited upon all mankind by a nuclear war and the consequent need to make every effort to avert the danger of such a war and to take measures to safeguard the security of peoples,

Believing that the proliferation of nuclear weapons would seriously enhance the danger of nuclear war,

In conformity with resolutions of the United Nations General Assembly calling for the conclusion of an agreement on the prevention of wider dissemination of nuclear weapons,

Undertaking to cooperate in facilitating the application of International Atomic Energy Agency safeguards on peaceful nuclear activities,

Expressing their support for research, development and other efforts to further the application, within the framework of the International Atomic Energy Agency safeguards system, of the principle of safeguarding effectively the flow of source and special fissionable materials by use of instruments and other techniques at certain strategic points,

Affirming the principle that the benefits of peaceful applications of nuclear technology, including any technological by-products which may be derived by nuclear-weapon States from the development of nuclear explosive devices, should be available for peaceful purposes to all Parties of the Treaty, whether nuclear-weapon or non-nuclear weapon States,

Convinced that, in furtherance of this principle, all Parties to the Treaty are entitled to participate in the fullest possible exchange of scientific information for, and to contribute alone or in cooperation with other States to, the further development of the applications of atomic energy for peaceful purposes,

Declaring their intention to achieve at the earliest possible date the cessation of the nuclear arms race and to undertake effective measures in the direction of nuclear disarmament,

Urging the cooperation of all States in the attainment of this objective,

Recalling the determination expressed by the Parties to the 1963 Treaty banning nuclear weapon tests in the atmosphere, in outer space and under water in its Preamble to seek to achieve the discontinuance of all test explosions of nuclear weapons for all time and to continue negotiations to this end,

Desiring to further the easing of international tension and the strengthening of trust between States in order to facilitate the cessation of the manufacture of nuclear weapons, the liquidation of all their existing stockpiles, and the elimination from national arsenals of nuclear weapons and the means of their delivery pursuant to a Treaty on general and complete disarmament under strict and effective international control,

Recalling that, in accordance with the Charter of the United Nations, States must refrain in their international relations from the threat or use of force against the territorial integrity or political independence of any State, or in any other manner inconsistent with the Purposes of the United Nations, and that the establishment and maintenance of international peace and security are to be promoted with the least diversion for armaments of the world's human and economic resources,

Have agreed as follows:

Article I

Each nuclear-weapon State Party to the Treaty undertakes not to transfer to any recipient whatsoever nuclear weapons or other nuclear explosive devices or control over such weapons or explosive devices directly, or indirectly; and not in any way to assist, encourage, or induce any non-nuclear weapon State to manufacture or otherwise acquire nuclear weapons or other nuclear explosive devices, or control over such weapons or explosive devices.

Article II

Each non-nuclear-weapon State Party to the Treaty undertakes not to receive the transfer from any transfer or whatsoever of nuclear weapons or other nuclear explosive devices or of control over such weapons or explosive devices directly, or indirectly; not to manufacture or otherwise acquire nuclear weapons or other nuclear explosive devices; and not to seek or receive any assistance in the manufacture of nuclear weapons or other nuclear explosive devices.

Article III

1. Each non-nuclear-weapon State Party to the Treaty undertakes to accept safeguards, as set forth in an agreement to be negotiated and concluded with the International Atomic Energy Agency in accordance with the Statute of the International Atomic Energy Agency and the Agency's safeguards system, for the exclusive purpose of verification of the fulfillment of its obligations assumed under this Treaty with a view to preventing diversion of nuclear energy from peaceful uses to nuclear

weapons or other nuclear explosive devices. Procedures for the safe-guards required by this article shall be followed with respect to source or special fissionable material whether it is being produced, processed or used in any principal nuclear facility or is outside any such facility. The safeguards required by this article shall be applied to all source or special fissionable material in all peaceful nuclear activities within the territory of such State, under its jurisdiction, or carried out under its control anywhere.

2. Each State Party to the Treaty undertakes not to provide: (a) source or special fissionable material, or (b) equipment or material especially designed or prepared for the processing, use or production of special fissionable material, to any non-nuclear-weapon State for peaceful purposes, unless the source or special fissionable material shall be subject to the safeguards required by this article.

3. The safeguards required by this article shall be implemented in a manner designed to comply with article IV of this Treaty, and to avoid hampering the economic or technological development of the Parties or international cooperation in the field of peaceful nuclear activities, including the international exchange of nuclear material and equipment for the processing, use or production of nuclear material for peaceful purposes in accordance with the provisions of this article and the principle of safeguarding set forth in the Preamble of the Treaty.

4. Non-nuclear-weapon States Party to the Treaty shall conclude agreements with the International Atomic Energy Agency to meet the requirements of this article either individually or together with other States in accordance with the Statute of the International Atomic Energy Agency. Negotiation of such agreements shall commence within 180 days from the original entry into force of this Treaty. For States depositing their instruments of ratification or accession after the 180-day period, negotiation of such agreements shall commence not later than the date of such deposit. Such agreements shall enter into force not later than eighteen months after the date of initiation of negotiations.

Article IV

1. Nothing in this Treaty shall be interpreted as affecting the inalienable right of all the Parties to the Treaty to develop research, production and use of nuclear energy for peaceful purposes without discrimination and in conformity with articles I and II of this Treaty.

2. All the Parties to the Treaty undertake to facilitate, and have the right to participate in, the fullest possible exchange of equipment, materials and scientific and technological information for the peaceful uses of nuclear energy. Parties to the Treaty in a position to do so shall also cooperate in contributing alone or together with other States or international organizations to the further development of the applications of nuclear energy for peaceful purposes, especially in the territories of

non-nuclear-weapon States Party to the Treaty, with due consideration for the needs of the developing areas of the world.

Article V

Each party to the Treaty undertakes to take appropriate measures to ensure that, in accordance with this Treaty, under appropriate international observation and through appropriate international procedures, potential benefits from any peaceful applications of nuclear explosions will be made available to non-nuclear-weapon States Party to the Treaty on a nondiscriminatory basis and that the charge to such Parties for the explosive devices used will be as low as possible and exclude any charge for research and development. Non-nuclear-weapon States Party to the Treaty shall be able to obtain such benefits, pursuant to a special international agreement or agreements, through an appropriate international body with adequate representation of non-nuclear-weapon States. Negotiations on this subject shall commence as soon as possible after the Treaty enters into force. Non-nuclear-weapon States Party to the Treaty so desiring may also obtain such benefits pursuant to bilateral agreements.

Article VI

Each of the Parties to the Treaty undertakes to pursue negotiations in good faith on effective measures relating to cessation of the nuclear arms race at an early date and to nuclear disarmament, and on a Treaty on general and complete disarmament under strict and effective international control.

Article VII

Nothing in this Treaty affects the right of any group of States to conclude regional treaties in order to assure the total absence of nuclear weapons in their respective territories.

Article VIII

1. Any Party to the Treaty may propose amendments to this Treaty. The text of any proposed amendment shall be submitted to the Depositary Governments which shall circulate it to all Parties to the Treaty. Thereupon, if requested to do so by one-third or more of the Parties to the Treaty, the Depositary Governments shall convene a conference, to which they shall invite all the Parties to the Treaty, to consider such an amendment.

2. Any amendment to this Treaty must be approved by a majority of the votes of all the Parties to the Treaty, including the votes of all nuclear-weapon States Party to the Treaty and all other Parties which, on the date the amendment is circulated, are members of the Board of Governors of the International Atomic Energy Agency. The amendment shall enter into force for each Party that deposits its instrument of ratification of the amendment upon the deposit of such instruments of ratification by a majority of all the Parties, including

the instruments of ratification of all nuclear-weapon States Party to the Treaty and all other Parties which, on the date the amendment is circulated, are members of the Board of Governors of the International Atomic Energy Agency. Thereafter, it shall enter into force for any other Party upon the deposit of its instrument of ratification of the amendment.

3. Five years after the entry into force of this Treaty, a conference of Parties to the Treaty shall be held in Geneva, Switzerland, in order to review the operation of this Treaty with a view to assuring that the purposes of the Preamble and the provisions of the Treaty are being realized. At intervals of five years thereafter, a majority of the Parties to the Treaty may obtain, by submitting a proposal to this effect to the Depositary Governments, the convening of further conferences with the same objective of reviewing the operation of the Treaty.

Article IX

1. This Treaty shall be open to all States for signature. Any State which does not sign the Treaty before its entry into force in accordance with paragraph 3 of this article may accede to it at any time.

2. This Treaty shall be subject to ratification by signatory States. Instruments of ratification and instruments of accession shall be deposited with the Governments of the United States of America, the United Kingdom of Great Britain and Northern Ireland and the Union of Soviet Socialist Republics, which are hereby designated the Depositary Governments.

3. This Treaty shall enter into force after its ratification by the States, the Governments of which are designated Depositaries of the Treaty, and forty other States signatory to this Treaty and the deposit of their instruments of ratification. For the purposes of this Treaty, a nuclear-weapon State is one which has manufactured and exploded a nuclear weapon or other nuclear explosive device prior to January 1, 1967.

4. For States whose instruments of ratification or accession are deposited subsequent to the entry into force of this Treaty, it shall enter into force on the date of the deposit of their instruments of ratification or accession.

5. The Depositary Governments shall promptly inform all signatory and acceding States of the date of each signature, the date of deposit of each instrument of ratification or of accession, the date of the entry into force of this Treaty, and the date of receipt of any requests for convening a conference or other notices.

6. This Treaty shall be registered by the Depositary Governments pursuant to article 102 of the Charter of the United Nations.

Article X

1. Each Party shall in exercising its national sovereignty have the right to withdraw from the Treaty if it decides that extraordinary

events, related to the subject matter of this Treaty, have jeopardized the supreme interests of its country. It shall give notice of such withdrawal to all other Parties to the Treaty and to the United Nations Security Council three months in advance. Such notice shall include a statement of the extraordinary events it regards as having jeopardized its supreme interests.

2. Twenty-five years after the entry into force of the Treaty, a conference shall be convened to decide whether the Treaty shall continue in force indefinitely, or shall be extended for an additional fixed period or periods. This decision shall be taken by a majority of the Parties to the Treaty.

Article XI

This Treaty, the English, Russian, French, Spanish and Chinese texts of which are equally authentic, shall be deposited in the archives of the Depositary Governments. Duly certified copies of this Treaty shall be transmitted by the Depositary Governments to the Governments of the signatory and acceding States.

IN WITNESS WHEREOF the undersigned, duly authorized, have signed this Treaty.

DONE in triplicate, at the cities of Washington, London and Moscow, this first day of July one thousand nine hundred sixty-eight.

The full text of the treaty can also be viewed on the U.S. State Department's Web site: http://www.state.gov/www/global/arms/treaties/npt1.html#2.

The U.S.-Russian Strategic Offensive Reductions Treaty (Moscow Treaty, 2001)

The George W. Bush administration issued a unilateral statement at the Crawford, Texas, summit in November 2001 stating the U.S. intention to reduce its deployed strategic nuclear arsenal to between 1,700 and 2,200 warheads. Having sought deeper cuts, Russian president Vladimir Putin consented to this level but asked President Bush to formalize the reductions in a legally binding treaty. Despite U.S. reluctance to agree to a treaty and U.S.-Russian disputes over whether the warheads would actually be destroyed, the two signed the treaty at the May 2002 Moscow summit, formalizing planned reductions to be accomplished by 2012. The treaty will then be subject to review and a decision about its possible extension. The U.S. Senate and Russian Duma ratified the treaty almost a year later, and it became effective on 1 June 2003.

U.S.-Russian Strategic Offensive Reductions Treaty

The United States of America and the Russian Federation, hereinafter referred to as the Parties,

Embarking upon the path of new relations for a new century and committed to the goal of strengthening their relationship through cooperation and friendship,

Believing that new global challenges and threats require the building of a qualitatively new foundation for strategic relations between the Parties,

Desiring to establish a genuine partnership based on the principles of mutual security, cooperation, trust, openness, and predictability,

Committed to implementing significant reductions in strategic offensive arms,

Proceeding from the Joint Statements by the President of the United States of America and the President of the Russian Federation on Strategic Issues of July 22, 2001 in Genoa and on a New Relationship between the United States and Russia of November 13, 2001 in Washington,

Mindful of their obligations under the Treaty Between the United States of America and the Union of Soviet Socialists Republics on the Reduction and Limitation of Strategic Offensive Arms of July 31, 1991, hereinafter referred to as the START Treaty,

Mindful of their obligations under Article VI of the Treaty on the Non-Proliferation of Nuclear Weapons of July 1, 1968, and

Convinced that this Treaty will help to establish more favorable conditions for actively promoting security and cooperation, and enhancing international stability,

Have agreed as follows:

Article I

Each Party shall reduce and limit strategic nuclear warheads, as stated by the President of the United States of America on November 13, 2001 and as stated by the President of the Russian Federation on November 13, 2001 and December 13, 2001 respectively, so that by December 31, 2012 the aggregate number of such warheads does not exceed 1700-2200 for each Party. Each Party shall determine for itself the composition and structure of its strategic offensive arms, based on the established aggregate limit for the number of such warheads.

Article II

The Parties agree that the START Treaty remains in force in accordance with its terms.

Article III

For purposes of implementing this Treaty, the Parties shall hold meetings at least twice a year of a Bilateral Implementation Commission.

Article IV

1. This Treaty shall be subject to ratification in accordance with the constitutional procedures of each Party. This Treaty shall enter into force on the date of the exchange of instruments of ratification.

2. This Treaty shall remain in force until December 31, 2012 and may be extended by agreement of the Parties or superseded earlier by a subsequent agreement.

3. Each Party, in exercising its national sovereignty, may withdraw from this Treaty upon three months written notice to the other Party.

Article V

This Treaty shall be registered pursuant to Article 102 of the Charter of the United Nations.

Done at Moscow on May 24, 2002, in two copies, each in the English and Russian languages, both texts being equally authentic.

FOR THE UNITED STATES OF AMERICA
George W. Bush
FOR THE RUSSIAN FEDERATION
Vladimir V. Putin

The full text of the treaty and supporting documents are available on the U.S. Department of State Web site: http://www.state.gov/t/ac/trt/18016.htm.

UN Security Council Resolution 1540 (2004)

Traditionally, nonproliferation arrangements have sought to bar states from developing or distributing nuclear weapons or related technologies. Since the terrorist attacks of 11 September 2001, and the later revelations about A. Q. Khan's global black market in nuclear technologies and know-how, the international community has turned its focus to preventing terrorist organizations, such as al Qaeda, from acquiring WMD. Pursuant to its mandate to maintain international peace and security, the United Nations Security Council adopted Security Council Resolution 1540, on 28 April 2004, to address the threat of WMD terrorism. The resolution calls on all states to prevent non-state actors from developing, acquiring, transferring, or exporting nuclear or other WMD-related materials and to strengthen controls on any WMD technologies and materials. It also asks nations to cooperate to prevent WMD trafficking and to assist those states that need help adopting the necessary legislation and procedures to check WMD proliferation. The resolution establishes a Committee of the Security Council to oversee its implementation and to review states' reports on measures they have taken to stop proliferation. In April 2006, the United Nations Security Council extended the committee's original two-year mandate to 2008. While the resolution highlights the pressing need to prevent WMD terrorism, it does not specify exactly what measures must be taken, and it lacks an enforcement mechanism or a way to sanction states that fail to comply.

UN Security Council Resolution 1540 (2004)

Adopted by the Security Council at its 4956th meeting, 28 April 2004

The Security Council,

Affirming that proliferation of nuclear, chemical and biological weapons, as well as their means of delivery,* constitutes a threat to international peace and security,

Reaffirming, in this context, the Statement of its President adopted at the Council's meeting at the level of Heads of State and Government on 31 January 1992 (S/23500), including the need for all Member States to fulfil their obligations in relation to arms control and disarmament and to prevent proliferation in all its aspects of all weapons of mass destruction,

---

* Definitions for the purpose of this resolution only:

Means of delivery: missiles, rockets and other unmanned systems capable of delivering nuclear, chemical, or biological weapons, that are specially designed for such use.

Non-State actor: individual or entity, not acting under the lawful authority of any State in conducting activities which come within the scope of this resolution.

Related materials: materials, equipment and technology covered by relevant multilateral treaties and arrangements, or included on national control lists, which could be used for the design, development, production or use of nuclear, chemical and biological weapons and their means of delivery.

Recalling also that the Statement underlined the need for all Member States to resolve peacefully in accordance with the Charter any problems in that context threatening or disrupting the maintenance of regional and global stability,

Affirming its resolve to take appropriate and effective actions against any threat to international peace and security caused by the proliferation of nuclear, chemical and biological weapons and their means of delivery, in conformity with its primary responsibilities, as provided for in the United Nations Charter,

Affirming its support for the multilateral treaties whose aim is to eliminate or prevent the proliferation of nuclear, chemical or biological weapons and the importance for all States parties to these treaties to implement them fully in order to promote international stability,

Welcoming efforts in this context by multilateral arrangements which contribute to non-proliferation,

Affirming that prevention of proliferation of nuclear, chemical and biological weapons should not hamper international cooperation in materials, equipment and technology for peaceful purposes while goals of peaceful utilization should not be used as a cover for proliferation,

Gravely concerned by the threat of terrorism and the risk that non-State actors such as those identified in the United Nations list established and maintained by the Committee established under Security Council resolution 1267 and those to whom resolution 1373 applies, may acquire, develop, traffic in or use nuclear, chemical and biological weapons and their means of delivery,

Gravely concerned by the threat of illicit trafficking in nuclear, chemical, or biological weapons and their means of delivery, and related materials,* which adds a new dimension to the issue of proliferation of such weapons and also poses a threat to international peace and security,

Recognizing the need to enhance coordination of efforts on national, sub-regional, regional and international levels in order to strengthen a global response to this serious challenge and threat to international security,

Recognizing that most States have undertaken binding legal obligations under treaties to which they are parties, or have made other commitments aimed at preventing the proliferation of nuclear, chemical or biological weapons, and have taken effective measures to account for, secure and physically protect sensitive materials, such as those required by the Convention on the Physical Protection of Nuclear Materials and those recommended by the IAEA Code of Conduct on the Safety and Security of Radioactive Sources,

Recognizing further the urgent need for all States to take additional effective measures to prevent the proliferation of nuclear, chemical or biological weapons and their means of delivery,

Encouraging all Member States to implement fully the disarmament treaties and agreements to which they are party,

Reaffirming the need to combat by all means, in accordance with the Charter of the United Nations, threats to international peace and security caused by terrorist acts,

Determined to facilitate henceforth an effective response to global threats in the area of non-proliferation,

Acting under Chapter VII of the Charter of the United Nations,

1. *Decides that* all States shall refrain from providing any form of support to non-State actors that attempt to develop, acquire, manufacture, possess, transport, transfer or use nuclear, chemical or biological weapons and their means of delivery;

2. *Decides also* that all States, in accordance with their national procedures, shall adopt and enforce appropriate effective laws which prohibit any non-State actor to manufacture, acquire, possess, develop, transport, transfer or use nuclear, chemical or biological weapons and their means of delivery, in particular for terrorist purposes, as well as attempts to engage in any of the foregoing activities, participate in them as an accomplice, assist or finance them;

3. *Decides also* that all States shall take and enforce effective measures to establish domestic controls to prevent the proliferation of nuclear, chemical, or biological weapons and their means of delivery, including by establishing appropriate controls over related materials and to this end shall:

(a) Develop and maintain appropriate effective measures to account for and secure such items in production, use, storage or transport;

(b) Develop and maintain appropriate effective physical protection measures;

(c) Develop and maintain appropriate effective border controls and law enforcement efforts to detect, deter, prevent and combat, including through international cooperation when necessary, the illicit trafficking and brokering in such items in accordance with their national legal authorities and legislation and consistent with international law;

(d) Establish, develop, review and maintain appropriate effective national export and trans-shipment controls over such items, including appropriate laws and regulations to control export, transit, trans-shipment and re-export and controls on providing funds and services related to such export and trans-shipment such as financing, and transporting that would contribute to proliferation, as well as establishing end-user controls; and establishing and enforcing appropriate criminal or civil penalties for violations of such export control laws and regulations;

4. *Decides* to establish, in accordance with rule 28 of its provisional rules of procedure, for a period of no longer than two years, a Committee of the Security Council, consisting of all members of the Council, which will, calling as appropriate on other expertise, report to the Security Council for its examination, on the implementation of this resolution, and to this end calls upon States to present a first report no later than six months from the adoption of this resolution to the Committee on steps they have taken or intend to take to implement this resolution;

5. *Decides* that none of the obligations set forth in this resolution shall be interpreted so as to conflict with or alter the rights and obligations of State Parties to the Nuclear Non-Proliferation Treaty, the Chemical Weapons Convention and the Biological and Toxin Weapons Convention or alter the responsibilities of the International Atomic Energy Agency or the Organization for the Prohibition of Chemical Weapons;

6. *Recognizes* the utility in implementing this resolution of effective national control lists and calls upon all Member States, when necessary, to pursue at the earliest opportunity the development of such lists;

7. *Recognizes* that some States may require assistance in implementing the provisions of this resolution within their territories and invites States in a position to do so to offer assistance as appropriate in response to specific requests to the States lacking the legal and

regulatory infrastructure, implementation experience and/or resources for fulfilling the above provisions;

8. *Calls upon* all States:

(a) To promote the universal adoption and full implementation, and, where necessary, strengthening of multilateral treaties to which they are parties, whose aim is to prevent the proliferation of nuclear, biological or chemical weapons;

(b) To adopt national rules and regulations, where it has not yet been done, to ensure compliance with their commitments under the key multilateral nonproliferation treaties;

(c) To renew and fulfil their commitment to multilateral cooperation, in particular within the framework of the International Atomic Energy Agency, the Organization for the Prohibition of Chemical Weapons and the Biological and Toxin Weapons Convention, as important means of pursuing and achieving their common objectives in the area of nonproliferation and of promoting international cooperation for peaceful purposes;

(d) To develop appropriate ways to work with and inform industry and the public regarding their obligations under such laws;

9. *Calls upon* all States to promote dialogue and cooperation on nonproliferation so as to address the threat posed by proliferation of nuclear, chemical, or biological weapons, and their means of delivery;

10. Further to counter that threat, *calls upon* all States, in accordance with their national legal authorities and legislation and consistent with international law, to take cooperative action to prevent illicit trafficking in nuclear, chemical or biological weapons, their means of delivery, and related materials;

11. *Expresses* its intention to monitor closely the implementation of this resolution and, at the appropriate level, to take further decisions which may be required to this end;

12. *Decides* to remain seized of the matter.

Source: United Nations Web site: http://daccessdds.un.org/doc/UNDOC/GEN/N04/328/43/PDF/N0432843.pdf?OpenElement.

UN Sanctions on North Korea (2006)

On 9 October 2006, North Korea announced that it had conducted an underground test of a nuclear weapon. Seismic monitoring and air sampling determined that North Korea had tested a plutonium bomb that probably fizzled, as the yield was estimated to be half a kiloton or less, very small for a nuclear explosion. Nonetheless, the test represented a sharp blow to the nuclear nonproliferation regime and raised the question of what, if anything, can be done to prevent devoted proliferators from building nuclear weapons. North Korea was a member of the NPT until it became the first party to withdraw from the treaty in 2003.

North Korea had previously threatened to withdraw from the NPT in 1993. However, in 1994, North Korea signed the Agreed Framework with the United States under which it agreed to remain in the NPT, allow the return of IAEA inspectors, and halt its plutonium-based nuclear program if an international consortium provided two light-water nuclear power plants and oil supplies until the plants were operating. In October 2002, the United States charged that North Korea had violated the deal by secretly acquiring uranium enrichment technology from Pakistan. The United States halted its provision of oil supplies. North Korea responded by expelling all IAEA inspectors, removing their monitoring equipment, and finally announcing its withdrawal from the NPT. In August 2003, the United States and eventually South Korea, China, Japan, and Russia began a series of talks with North Korea that became known as the Six-Party Talks. On 15 September 2005, the parties reached a tentative agreement, according to which North Korea committed to abandoning its nuclear weapon program, returning to the NPT, and allowing IAEA inspections. But almost immediately, the parties disagreed on whether light-water power reactors would be provided under the agreement, and talks stalled. Slightly more than a year later, North Korea exploded a nuclear device.

On 14 October 2006, the UN Security Council adopted a resolution condemning North Korea's nuclear test and demanding that it cease its nuclear weapon and ballistic missile programs and rejoin the NPT. The resolution bans countries from supplying North Korea with any WMD materials, conventional weapons, or luxury items (especially to the leadership) and calls on states to inspect cargo to and from North Korea as necessary. China, Russia, and South Korea, however, put conditions on their willingness to enforce the inspection provisions.

On 13 February 2007, North Korea agreed at the Six-Party Talks to halt its nuclear program, return to the NPT, and allow international inspections in exchange for the removal of sanctions, financial and energy aid, and talks on normalizing diplomatic relations with the United States and Japan. The agreement establishes five working groups to plan for the deal's phased implementation and address such questions as the status of North Korea's nuclear weapons and fissile material. North Korea missed the 13 April 2007 deadline to shut down its reactors, disclose its nuclear activities, and invite International Atomic Energy Agency inspectors into the country. But negotiations continued.

An excerpted version of the October 2006 sanctions resolution follows.

United Nations Security Council Resolution 1718 (2006)

Adopted by the Security Council at its 5551st meeting, on 14 October 2006

The Security Council,

[...]

Reaffirming that proliferation of nuclear, chemical and biological weapons, as well as their means of delivery, constitutes a threat to international peace and security,

Expressing the gravest concern at the claim by the Democratic People's Republic of Korea (DPRK) that it has conducted a test of a nuclear weapon on 9 October 2006, and at the challenge such a test constitutes to the Treaty on the Non-Proliferation of Nuclear Weapons and to international efforts aimed at strengthening the global regime of non-proliferation of nuclear weapons, and the danger it poses to peace and stability in the region and beyond,

Expressing its firm conviction that the international regime on the non-proliferation of nuclear weapons should be maintained and recalling that the DPRK cannot have the status of a nuclear-weapon state in accordance with the Treaty on the Non-Proliferation of Nuclear Weapons,

Deploring the DPRK's announcement of withdrawal from the Treaty on the Non-Proliferation of Nuclear Weapons and its pursuit of nuclear weapons,

Deploring further that the DPRK has refused to return to the Six-Party talks without precondition,

Endorsing the Joint Statement issued on 19 September 2005 by China, the DPRK, Japan, the Republic of Korea, the Russian Federation and the United States,

[...]

Expressing profound concern that the test claimed by the DPRK has generated increased tension in the region and beyond, and *determining* therefore that there is a clear threat to international peace and security, *Acting* under Chapter VII of the Charter of the United Nations, and taking measures under its Article 41,

1. *Condemns* the nuclear test proclaimed by the DPRK on 9 October 2006 in flagrant disregard of its relevant resolutions, in particular resolution 1695 (2006), as well as of the statement of its President of 6 October 2006 (S/PRST/2006/41), including that such a test would bring universal condemnation of the international community and would represent a clear threat to international peace and security;

2. *Demands* that the DPRK not conduct any further nuclear test or launch of a ballistic missile;

3. *Demands* that the DPRK immediately retract its announcement of withdrawal from the Treaty on the Non-Proliferation of Nuclear Weapons;

4. *Demands* further that the DPRK return to the Treaty on the Non-Proliferation of Nuclear Weapons and International Atomic Energy Agency (IAEA) safeguards, and *underlines* the need for all States Parties to the Treaty on the Non-Proliferation of Nuclear Weapons to continue to comply with their Treaty obligations;

5. *Decides* that the DPRK shall suspend all activities related to its ballistic missile programme and in this context re-establish its pre-existing commitments to a moratorium on missile launching;

6. *Decides* that the DPRK shall abandon all nuclear weapons and existing nuclear programmes in a complete, verifiable and irreversible manner, shall act strictly in accordance with the obligations applicable to parties under the Treaty on the Non-Proliferation of Nuclear Weapons and the terms and conditions of its International Atomic Energy Agency (IAEA) Safeguards Agreement (IAEA INFCIRC/403) and shall provide the IAEA transparency measures extending beyond these requirements, including such access to individuals, documentation, equipments and facilities as may be required and deemed necessary by the IAEA;

7. *Decides* also that the DPRK shall abandon all other existing weapons of mass destruction and ballistic missile programme in a complete, verifiable and irreversible manner;

8. *Decides* that:

(a) All Member States shall prevent the direct or indirect supply, sale or transfer to the DPRK, through their territories or by their nationals, or using their flag vessels or aircraft, and whether or not originating in their territories, of:

(i) Any battle tanks, armoured combat vehicles, large calibre artillery systems, combat aircraft, attack helicopters, warships, missiles or missile systems as defined for the purpose of the United Nations Register on Conventional Arms, or related materiel including spare parts, or items as determined by the Security Council or the Committee established by paragraph 12 below (the Committee);

(ii) All items, materials, equipment, goods and technology as set out in the lists in documents S/2006/814 and S/2006/815, unless within 14 days of adoption of this resolution the Committee has amended or completed their provisions also taking into account the list in document S/2006/816, as well as other items, materials, equipment, goods and technology, determined by the Security Council or the Committee, which could contribute to DPRK's nuclear-related, ballistic missile-related or other weapons of mass destruction related programmes;

(iii) Luxury goods;

(b) The DPRK shall cease the export of all items covered in subparagraphs (a) (i) and (a) (ii) above and that all Member States shall prohibit the procurement of such items from the DPRK by their nationals, or using their flagged vessels or aircraft, and whether or not originating in the territory of the DPRK;

(c) All Member States shall prevent any transfers to the DPRK by their nationals or from their territories, or from the DPRK by its nationals or from its territory, of technical training, advice, services or assistance related to the provision, manufacture, maintenance or use of the items in subparagraphs (a) (i) and (a) (ii) above;

(d) All Member States shall, in accordance with their respective legal processes, freeze immediately the funds, other financial assets and economic resources which are on their territories at the date of the adoption of this resolution or at any time thereafter, that are owned or controlled, directly or indirectly, by the persons or entities designated by the Committee or by the Security Council as being engaged in or providing support for, including through other illicit means, DPRK's nuclear-related, other weapons of mass destruction-related and ballistic missile-related programmes, or by persons or entities acting on their behalf or at their direction, and ensure that any funds, financial assets or economic resources are prevented from being made available by their nationals or by any persons or entities within their territories, to or for the benefit of such persons or entities;

(e) All Member States shall take the necessary steps to prevent the entry into or transit through their territories of the persons designated by the

Committee or by the Security Council as being responsible for, including through supporting or promoting, DPRK policies in relation to the DPRK's nuclear-related, ballistic missile-related and other weapons of mass destruction-related programmes, together with their family members, provided that nothing in this paragraph shall oblige a state to refuse its own nationals entry into its territory;

(f) In order to ensure compliance with the requirements of this paragraph, and thereby preventing illicit trafficking in nuclear, chemical or biological weapons, their means of delivery and related materials, all Member States are called upon to take, in accordance with their national authorities and legislation, and consistent with international law, cooperative action including through inspection of cargo to and from the DPRK, as necessary;

[...]

12. *Decides* to establish, in accordance with rule 28 of its provisional rules of procedure, a Committee of the Security Council consisting of all the members of the Council, to undertake the following tasks:

(a) To seek from all States, in particular those producing or possessing the items, materials, equipment, goods and technology referred to in paragraph 8 (a) above, information regarding the actions taken by them to implement effectively the measures imposed by paragraph 8 above of this resolution and whatever further information it may consider useful in this regard; (b) To examine and take appropriate action on information regarding alleged violations of measures imposed by paragraph 8 of this resolution;

[...]

(g) To report at least every 90 days to the Security Council on its work, with its observations and recommendations, in particular on ways to strengthen the effectiveness of the measures imposed by paragraph 8 above;

13. *Welcomes and encourages further* the efforts by all States concerned to intensify their diplomatic efforts, to refrain from any actions that might aggravate tension and to facilitate the early resumption of the Six-Party Talks, with a view to the expeditious implementation of the Joint Statement issued on 19 September 2005 by China, the DPRK, Japan, the Republic of Korea, the Russian Federation and the United States, to achieve the verifiable denuclearization of the Korean Peninsula and to maintain peace and stability on the Korean Peninsula and in north-east Asia;

14. *Calls upon* the DPRK to return immediately to the Six-Party Talks without precondition and to work towards the expeditious implementation of the Joint Statement issued on 19 September 2005 by China, the DPRK, Japan, the Republic of Korea, the Russian Federation and the United States;

15. *Affirms* that it shall keep DPRK's actions under continuous review and that it shall be prepared to review the appropriateness of the measures contained in paragraph 8 above, including the strengthening, modification, suspension or lifting of the measures, as may be needed at that time in light of the DPRK's compliance with the provisions of the resolution;

16. *Underlines* that further decisions will be required, should additional measures be necessary;

17. *Decides* to remain actively seized of the matter.

Source

United Nations Web site: http://daccessdds.un.org/doc/UNDOC/GEN/N06/572/07/PDF/NO657207.pdf?OpenElement.

7

Directory of Organizations

Numerous governmental and nongovernmental organizations work on nuclear weapon development, management, reduction, or elimination. This chapter is divided into three sections: international organizations, U.S. government bodies, and nongovernmental organizations. Some of the organizations described oversee weapon programs, others help implement treaties designed to prevent the spread of nuclear technologies, and still others work through the media and other public information channels to promote nuclear nonproliferation. All of the organizations have Web sites that can be used to gather further information or contact the appropriate person to answer a specific inquiry.

International Organizations

Agency for the Prohibition of Nuclear Weapons in Latin America and the Caribbean (OPANAL)
Schiller 326-5° piso
Col. Chapultepec Morales
Mexico D.F. 11570 Mexico
Phone: (52-55) 5255-2914, 5255-4198
Fax: (52-55) 5255-3748
E-mail: info@opanal.org
Web site: http://www.opanal.org

OPANAL is an intergovernmental organization created by the Treaty for the Prohibition of Nuclear Weapons in Latin America

249

and the Caribbean (known internationally as the Treaty of Tlatelolco), which was opened for signature in 1967. The treaty prohibits the use, manufacture, and acquisition of any nuclear weapons by parties in the region and large sections of the Pacific and Atlantic Ocean. OPANAL seeks to ensure that the parties comply with the treaty's obligations, such as concluding a safeguards agreement with the International Atomic Energy Agency, and adhere to its verification or control system. OPANAL holds regular conferences and consultations related to the treaty. All thirty-three states in the Latin American and Caribbean regions are now members of the organization.

OPANAL's Web site offers documents related to the Treaty of Tlatelolco, a tutorial on nuclear-weapon-free zones, speeches of its officials, and general background documents on disarmament and the Treaty on the Non-Proliferation of Nuclear Weapons (NPT).

Brazil-Argentine Agency for Accounting and Control of Nuclear Materials (ABACC)
Av. Rio Branco, 123, G515, Centro,
20040-005, Rio de Janeiro-RJ, Brazil
Phone: (55-21) 3171-1200
Fax: (55-21) 3171-1248

Avda. Del Libertador 8250
Oficina 121 (C1429 BNO)
Buenos Aires, Argentina
Phone: (54-11) 6323-1364
Fax: (54-11) 4704-1076
E-mail: info@abacc.org.br
Web site: http://www.abacc.org

An agreement between Argentina and Brazil on peaceful uses of nuclear energy—signed in Guadalajara, Mexico, on 18 July 1991 (the Guadalajara Agreement)—established ABACC. Under the Guadalajara Agreement, the two countries agreed to use nuclear materials exclusively for peaceful purposes and to prohibit the manufacture, production, and use of nuclear weapons on their territories. The ABACC administers and applies a full-scope safeguards system, known as the Common System for Accounting and Control of Nuclear Materials (SCCC), to account for all nuclear materials in both countries. The ABACC implements the SCCC by inspections targeted at various stages of the nuclear fuel cycle—production, processing, use, and storage. The organization's specialists conduct routine, ad hoc, and special inspections to verify the validity of information received from facilities.

The ABACC Web site contains a library of agreements, declarations, and other documents related to regional nuclear policy. Annual reports, the virtual journal *ABACC News,* and papers on safeguards-related topics are also available.

Comprehensive Nuclear-Test-Ban Treaty Organization (CTBTO)
CTBTO Preparatory Commission
Vienna International Centre
PO Box 1200
A-1400 Vienna, Austria
Phone: (431) 26030 6200
Fax: (431) 26030 5823
E-mail: info@ctbto.org
Web site: http://www.ctbto.org

The Comprehensive Nuclear-Test-Ban Treaty (CTBT) bans all nuclear explosions for military and civilian purposes; the CTBTO is the monitoring arm of the treaty. Although the treaty has been ratified by 132 states, it has not been approved by all of the 44 nuclear-capable states whose ratifications are required for the treaty to enter into force. (Of these 44 states, 34 have ratified, 10 [including the United States] have not ratified, and 3 have yet to sign.) However, the CTBTO is already functioning in Vienna— with links to more than 321 monitoring stations and sixteen radionuclide laboratories worldwide—to begin implementing the CTBT's provisions, particularly verification that countries are not testing nuclear devices. The CTBTO's Provisional Technical Secretariat began work in March 1997 and has an international staff of more than 200 members from sixty-four countries. It is cooperating with host countries to develop and maintain the international network of monitoring stations that send their data to the International Data Center at the CTBTO. Since February 2000, the International Data Center has provided International Monitoring System data on a test basis to states that signed the CTBT.

The CTBTO Web site describes how the organization operates and provides updated information on which countries have signed and ratified the treaty. It also provides more details on the CTBT's verification regime, including the International Monitoring System, on-site inspections, and confidence-building measures. In addition, the Web site includes CTBTO documents, a biannual newsletter (*CTBTO Spectrum*), legal resources, a database of Preparatory Commission documents, and media information.

Conference on Disarmament (CD)
8-14 Avenue de la Paix
Palais des Nations
CH-1211
Geneva 10, Switzerland
Phone: (41-022) 917 2100
Web site: http://www.unog.ch (click on Disarmament link, then on Conference on Disarmament)

The United Nations (UN) General Assembly established the CD in 1979 as the one negotiating forum on multilateral disarmament for the international community. The original forty-member CD was a successor organization to other UN disarmament groups dating back to 1960. The CD currently has sixty-five member states. The CD reports to the UN General Assembly but adopts its own agenda and procedures.

The CD and its predecessors negotiated such multilateral nuclear nonproliferation treaties as the NPT and the CTBT. The CD's nuclear agenda includes the following goals: cessation of the nuclear arms race and nuclear disarmament, prevention of nuclear war, prevention of an arms race in outer space, negotiations of arrangements to protect non–nuclear weapon states against the threat of nuclear weapons, and the prohibition of the production of fissile material for nuclear explosive devices. The CD meets in three sessions per year: once for ten weeks and twice for seven-week periods. For the past several years, political disputes have kept CD members from agreeing on a program of work, with the result that they have failed to pursue any nonproliferation or disarmament matters on their agenda.

The CD publishes annual reports, documents of the conferences, and records of its meetings. The Web site provides an overview of the organization, a list of its members, annual reports, documents of the CD, and records of meetings.

**European Union Directorate General for Energy and
Transportation, European Atomic Energy Community
(EURATOM) Office**
EURATOM Supply Agency
EUFO 4195–European Commission
L-2920 Luxembourg
Phone: (352) 4301-36738
Fax: (352) 4301-38139
E-mail: Esa-AAE@ec.europa.eu
EURATOM Web site: http://www.euratom.org
EURATOM Supply Agency Web site: http://europa.eu.int/
comm/euratom/index_en.html

Established by the Treaty of Rome (or EURATOM Treaty) signed
in March 1957, the European Atomic Energy Community governs
and promotes the peaceful use of nuclear energy among twenty-
five members of the European Union (EU). EURATOM covers all
civil nuclear activities in the EU, provides a common market in
nuclear materials, guarantees a supply of nuclear fuels, and establishes standards to protect workers and the general population
against radiation dangers. Nuclear energy provides one-third of
the EU's electricity. The treaty also allows EURATOM to contact
other countries to promote progress in the peaceful uses of nuclear
energy. The members agree to ensure that nuclear materials are
not diverted to weapon purposes and to comply with safeguards
obligations. Also, they pledge themselves to the common development of Europe's nuclear energy resources by coordinating their
nuclear research and development programs and by permitting
the free movement of nuclear raw materials, equipment, investment capital, and specialists within the community. In June 2002,
the EURATOM office became part of the EU Directorate General
for Energy and Transportation based in Brussels. The EURATOM
Web site offers publications and reports on nuclear installation
safety, radioactive waste management, and the decommissioning
of nuclear facilities, as well as a video on nuclear inspections *Half
a Century of Safeguards in Europe.*

The EURATOM Supply Agency works to ensure a regular and equitable supply of nuclear fuels for EU members. The
EURATOM Supply Agency is vested with wide powers, including
the right to enter into contracts and obtain raw materials. It operates joint research centers at Ispra (Italy), Geel (Belgium), Petten
(the Netherlands), and Karlsruhe (Germany). The EURATOM

Supply Agency Web site contains information on the founding treaty, annual reports, and various nuclear-related articles and documents.

International Atomic Energy Agency (IAEA)
PO Box 100
Wagramer Strasse 5
A-1400 Vienna, Austria
Phone: (431) 2600-0
Fax: (431) 2600-7
E-mail: Official.Mail@iaea.org
Web site: http://www.iaea.org

In July 1957, eighteen states ratified the statute that created the IAEA as an independent organization under the UN. By May 2007, the IAEA had 144 member states. According to its statute, the IAEA seeks to enlarge the contribution of nuclear energy to peace and prosperity throughout the world and to ensure that nuclear energy is not used to further any military purposes. The IAEA also works to combat nuclear terrorism in part by promoting adoption of the Convention on the Physical Protection of Nuclear Materials. To fulfill its mission, the IAEA establishes and applies safeguards to the nuclear activities of non–nuclear weapon states, as required by the NPT and certain nuclear-weapon-free zone treaties. The IAEA inspects nuclear-related facilities under safeguards agreements in member states and aids international nuclear disarmament efforts. IAEA inspections in North Korea, Iraq, and Iran uncovered violations of those countries' NPT obligations and safeguards agreements. The Norwegian Nobel Prize Committee awarded the 2005 Peace Prize to the IAEA and Mohamed ElBaradei, its director general, for their efforts to prevent nuclear energy from being diverted to military purposes and for supporting nuclear nonproliferation.

The IAEA's principal bodies are the General Conference of all IAEA member states and the board of governors. The General Conference provides broad reviews of agency activities and policy guidance. The board of governors, which generally meets five times per year, approves specific safeguards procedures and agreements. Also, in cases of noncompliance with IAEA safeguards (as in Iran and North Korea), the board asks the violator to remedy the problem and reports the noncompliance to the UN Security Council and General Assembly for further action.

The IAEA publishes an annual report that covers global developments relevant to the safe and peaceful use of nuclear energy and highlights its activities. It also publishes information circulars on matters of interest to its members, as well as two journals, the *IAEA Bulletin* and the more technical *Nuclear Fusion*, newsletters, books, conference proceedings, and legal and technical documents. The IAEA Web site provides a wealth of information in several languages: a profile of the IAEA and its various duties; fact sheets on a wide range of issues; special sections on pressing issues such as Iran and North Korea; an image bank; photo essays; videos on nuclear history, safeguards, and inspections; and a database on illicit trafficking in nuclear materials.

International Science and Technology Center (ISTC)
Krasnoproletarskaya 32-34
127473 Moscow, Russian Federation
Phone: 7 (495) 982-3200
Fax: 7 (499) 982-3201
E-mail: istcinfo@istc.ru
Web site: http://www.istc.ru

In 1992, the EU, Japan, the Russian Federation, and the United States agreed to establish the ISTC with the aim of providing scientists from the Soviet successor states with opportunities to redirect their scientific talents from military to peaceful uses. Since then, Norway and South Korea have joined as parties, and Armenia, Belarus, Georgia, Kazakhstan, and Kyrgyzstan have joined Russia as partner countries; the total membership is thirty-seven countries. Former weapons scientists submit about thirty scientific project proposals a month to the ISTC, which then reviews, approves, and funds appropriate initiatives. Projects financed by the center must be peaceful in nature and address the nonproliferation objectives of the ISTC. The ISTC's headquarters is in Moscow, and it has six regional offices in other formerly Soviet states.

On its Web site, the center publishes an annual report and maintains a public database of active and completed projects. ISTC projects that benefit nuclear nonproliferation involve the disposal of weapons-grade plutonium, ways to support the CTBT, and nuclear material control and accounting. The Web site also contains information about the center's activities and resources for researchers and scientists.

Nuclear Suppliers Group (NSG)
The NSG is an informal group with no central point of contact.
Web site: http://www.nuclearsuppliersgroup.org

Nuclear supplier countries formed the NSG after India's surprise detonation of a nuclear device in 1974. The NSG first met in London in November 1975 with the purpose of controlling the transit of sensitive nuclear materials and technologies. As of 2006, NSG had forty-five members (states capable of supplying nuclear technologies); the European Commission holds permanent observer status. The NSG attempts to prevent the proliferation of nuclear weapons by implementing guidelines for nuclear exports and exchanging information on developments related to nuclear proliferation. The first set of NSG guidelines governs the export of items that are especially designed or prepared for nuclear use, such as nuclear material; reactor equipment; equipment for the reprocessing, enrichment, and conversion of nuclear material; and technology for fuel fabrication and heavy-water production. The second set of guidelines covers the export of nuclear-related dual-use items and technologies, that is, items and technologies that have both nuclear and non-nuclear uses.

NSG members try to ensure that nuclear exports are made only under appropriate safeguards, physical protection, and non-proliferation conditions. The NSG also seeks to restrict the export of sensitive items that can contribute to the proliferation of nuclear weapons. The NSG requires IAEA safeguards, in addition to national control laws, as a condition of supplying any nuclear-related item to a state. It limits assistance with enrichment and reprocessing plants to countries of concern while sharing among members a common control list to restrain trade with countries in unstable regions. The Guidelines for Nuclear Transfers were initially agreed upon by supplier states in 1977 and envisaged additional export control restraints beyond those provided for in the NPT. The NSG guidelines are implemented by the governments of member states according to their domestic laws and regulations. The 1993 NSG meeting in Lucerne endorsed an amendment to the NSG guidelines that requires IAEA safeguards on all current and future nuclear activities in a country as a condition for any significant new agreements to supply nuclear-related items to non–nuclear weapon states.

In recent years, NSG members have endorsed the provisions of the IAEA's 1997 Model Additional Protocol, which provides for more intrusive safeguards; strengthened their guidelines to prevent diversion of nuclear materials to terrorists; and adopted guidelines to control items not on the trigger lists and to strengthen relationships with nonmembers. In 2005, the NSG agreed to a procedure to stop transfers of nuclear aid to countries that do not comply with their IAEA safeguards agreements (INFCIRC/254/Rev.7 Part 1, Feb. 05). In 2007, the NSG will likely address the question of whether members should be allowed to supply nuclear technologies to India, a country that has never signed the NPT or agreed to IAEA safeguards.

The NSG Web site contains a description of the organization and its activities, the contact information of the export control agencies of its member states, and the text of its guidelines and other related documents.

United Nations (UN)
UN Headquarters
First Avenue at 46th Street
New York, NY 10017
E-mail: inquiries@un.org
Web site: http://www.un.org

Established in October 1945, the United Nations is committed to preserving peace through international cooperation and collective security. In 2007, membership totaled 192 countries and thirty affiliated organizations that work under the UN umbrella. Several UN bodies and affiliated organizations work to halt the spread of arms and to reduce and eventually eliminate all weapons of mass destruction (WMD).

All member states are represented in the UN General Assembly. According to the UN Charter, the General Assembly considers general principles for maintaining international peace and security, including the principles governing disarmament. In this role, it may make recommendations to members of the UN Security Council. With regard to nuclear weapons, the General Assembly endorsed the NPT and the CTBT and has adopted numerous resolutions on nuclear disarmament and nonproliferation. The Disarmament and International Security Committee (the First Committee), a subsidiary body of the General Assembly, deals with all disarmament and nonproliferation questions. The General Assembly acts on draft resolutions and decisions presented by the First Committee on a yearly basis, usually in the late fall.

For example, the General Assembly has adopted resolutions condemning the 1998 nuclear tests by India and Pakistan, calling for the prevention of an arms race in outer space, and supporting the establishment of several nuclear-weapon-free zones. Other bodies under the General Assembly include the UN Disarmament Commission, which is mandated to submit concrete recommendations on specific disarmament issues; the Conference on Disarmament in Geneva, which is charged with negotiating international security treaties; the UN Institute for Disarmament Research in Geneva, which was established to undertake independent research on disarmament and related problems (see later entry); and regional centers for peace and disarmament located in Asia, Africa, and Latin America.

The UN Charter gives the Security Council the primary responsibility for maintaining international peace and security. The council consists of fifteen member states: five permanent members—China, France, the Russian Federation, the United Kingdom, and the United States—and ten members elected for two-year terms by the General Assembly. The Security Council is responsible for formulating plans to regulate weapons. The Security Council's mandate includes adopting resolutions on security assurances given by nuclear weapon states to non–nuclear weapon states, as well as urging all states to pursue nuclear disarmament in good faith. Organizations that fall under the Security Council include the Military Staff Committee, which is responsible for advising the council on security and disarmament; the Sanctions Committees, which are charged with monitoring implementation of council-established sanctions; and the Monitoring, Verification, and Inspection Commission, the successor organization to the UN Special Commission on Iraq, which was mandated to monitor and verify ongoing disarmament issues in Iraq after the discovery of WMD in that country during the 1991 Gulf War. In April 2004, the UN Security Council adopted Resolution 1540, which requires all states to enforce laws and other measures to prevent non-state actors from acquiring nuclear weapons, other WMD, and means of delivering WMD. In 2006 and again in March 2007, the Security Council sanctioned Iran because it refused to suspend its uranium-enrichment program after the IAEA provided evidence that Iran could be pursuing a nuclear weapons program in violation of its NPT obligations.

The UN publishes more than 400 titles every year, including the *UN Yearbook* and many works on nuclear nonproliferation and

other disarmament-related treaties. The UN Web site contains information on all its various programs, official UN documents, a list of
UN publications, and UN news and press releases. The Department
for Disarmament Affairs' portion of the site (http://disarmament
.un.org/dda.htm) includes comprehensive information on the NPT,
the CTBT, other nonproliferation treaties, and terrorism.

United Nations Institute for Disarmament Research (UNIDIR)
Palais des Nations
1211 Geneva 10, Switzerland
Phone: 41-022-917-3186
Fax: 41-022-917-0176
E-mail: unidir@unog.ch
Web site: http://www.unidir.org

Founded in 1980, UNIDIR is the primary research arm of the
UN in the field of global and regional security and disarmament. UNIDIR relies mainly on donations from governments
and foundations. The institute pursues its mission by conducting
research projects, meetings, conferences, and the Geneva Forum,
an ongoing discussion series among government delegates, nongovernmental organizations, academics, media, and UN personnel. UNIDIR publishes a variety of books and reports on subjects
ranging from global security (nuclear/chemical/biological weapons, plus treaty implementation), regional security (conflict resolution, political-economic sources of tension, and disarmament
approaches), and human security (development, human rights,
and small arms). Information about these publications can be
found on the institute's Web site along with its quarterly online
journal, *Disarmament Forum*.

Zangger Committee
Point of contact: Mr. Graham Styles, Secretary of the Committee
First Secretary
UK Permanent Mission to the United Nations in Vienna
Jauresgasse 12
A-1030 Vienna, Austria
Phone: 43-1-716-13-4296
Fax: 43-1-716-13-4900
Web site: http://www.zanggercommittee.org

The Zangger Committee does not have a permanent headquarters
but is operated by the chair and serviced through his office. It is

an informal organization consisting of thirty-five member states, and the European Commission serves as a permanent observer. A group of fifteen countries that export nuclear materials formed the Zangger Committee (named for the first chair, Swiss professor Claude Zangger) in 1971. The committee meets to ensure consensus on the NPT clause (Article III, paragraph 2) requiring nuclear equipment or material to be under safeguards after export to a non–nuclear weapon state. In 1974, the committee published two memoranda—the so-called "trigger list" (published as IAEA document INFCIRC/209)—specifying when IAEA safeguards should be triggered for exports under the NPT of nuclear-related items to non–nuclear weapon state parties to the treaty. The first memorandum covers fissionable material, and the second covers equipment and material for processing, using, or producing fissionable materials. The committee also agreed to share information among members on exports to any non–nuclear weapon state not a party to the NPT.

From 1974 to 2000, the Zangger Committee had six major reviews of its trigger list, continuously updating and amending it. The committee holds informal and confidential meetings in Vienna twice a year. Its decisions are not legally binding on its members but become effective through unilateral declarations from one member to another, with subsequent letters to the IAEA director general requesting him to publish these declarations in IAEA information circular updates (available on the IAEA Web site; see previous entry). The members also exchange confidential annual reports in April each year detailing actual exports and the issuance of export licenses to any non–nuclear weapon states not party to the NPT.

U.S. Government Agencies

Central Intelligence Agency, Director of Central Intelligence (DCI) Center for Weapons Intelligence, Nonproliferation, and Arms Control (WINPAC)
Office of Public Affairs
Washington, DC 20505
Phone: 703-482-0623
Fax: 703-482-1739
E-mail: Contact form on Web site at https://www.cia.gov/cgi-bin/comment_form.cgi

Web site: https://www.cia.gov/cia/di/organizationt_winpac_page.html

Under the deputy director for intelligence, WINPAC officers provide intelligence to help protect the United States from foreign weapons threats. Established in 2001, WINPAC employs personnel with backgrounds in diverse subject areas, including engineering, physics, mathematics, political science, economics, and computer science. WINPAC analysts study the development of the range of threats from foreign WMD, monitor strategic arms control agreements, and provide technical expertise in support of military and diplomatic operations. WINPAC does not publish any public documents. The Directorate of Intelligence Web site contains information on all of the organizations under its umbrella, and the history and key events of the organization. The Directorate of Intelligence also publishes *The World Factbook* of country profiles, which is available online.

United States Department of Defense: Defense Threat Reduction Agency (DTRA)
Office of Public Affairs
8725 John J. Kingman Road
STOP 6201
Fort Belvoir, VA 22060-6201
Phone: 703-767-5870 or 800-701-5096
Fax: 703-767-4450
E-mail: dtra.publicaffairs@dtra.mil
Web site: http://www.dtra.mil

Established in October 1998, DTRA marshals Department of Defense resources and expertise to help protect the United States against WMD threats. It prepares for domestic emergencies involving WMD, monitors existing treaties, and participates in weapon dismantlement. The agency is not a part of the U.S. intelligence community but cooperates with it by bringing together the research and intelligence communities to better understand the evolution of and threats posed by WMD. DTRA employs about 2,000 military and civilian personnel and had a 2005 budget of $2.6 billion. In addition to its headquarters in Virginia, DTRA has thirteen other facilities in the United States, Europe, Japan, and the former Soviet Union.

Some of the main activities of DTRA include cooperative threat reduction in the former Soviet Union, on-site inspections for treaty verification, technology development, and combat support. The purpose of the Cooperative Threat Reduction Program is to help the republics of the former Soviet Union eliminate their WMD and safeguard WMD-associated materials and technology. By reducing the amount of WMD materials, technologies, and infrastructure, cooperative threat reduction contributes to the effort to prevent terrorists from acquiring WMD. The On-Site Inspection Directorate is responsible for implementing international arms control treaties by carrying out treaty-related inspections and monitoring procedures. The Technology Development Directorate supports the use of operational forces to design systems to counter WMD proliferation. Finally, the Combat Support Directorate helps maintain U.S. nuclear weapons. (The Chemical and Biological Technologies Directorate provides similar support for defensive measures against chemical and biological weapons.)

The agency publishes reports and press releases on its Web site related to its activities. The Web site also offers information about the agency (including a video and books on DTRA's history), fact sheets on DTRA's role in treaty verification and weapon dismantlement, photograph collections of different facets of DTRA's activities, speeches, transcripts, and lists of relevant governmental and nongovernmental publications.

United States Department of Energy: Lawrence Livermore National Laboratory (LLNL)
Street Address:
7000 East Avenue
Livermore, CA 94550-9234
Mailing Address:
PO Box 808
Livermore, CA 94551-0808
Phone: 925-422-1100
Fax: 925-422-1370
Email: Use form at http://www.llnl.gov/llnl/contact.jsp
Web site: http://www.llnl.gov

In 1952, the U.S. Atomic Energy Commission established LLNL—the second nuclear weapon design laboratory built, after Los Alamos National Laboratory—at the urging of Edward Teller. The laboratory's first job was thermonuclear (hydrogen) bomb diagnostic studies. The University of California operates the lab for the Department of Energy. LLNL has a staff of more than 8,000 employees and an annual budget of approximately $1.6 billion.

LLNL's main job is ensuring that U.S. nuclear weapons remain secure and reliable. In addition to designing and maintaining nuclear warheads and other weapons, the lab has become one of the world's premier scientific centers, using its knowledge of nuclear science and engineering to make advances in magnetic and laser fusion energy, non-nuclear energy, biomedicine, and environmental science. LLNL also works to improve homeland security by preventing the spread of WMD to states and terrorists.

LLNL has major responsibility for the controversial Stockpile Stewardship Program, a joint effort among the U.S. weapons labs and other nuclear weapon facilities and the Nevada Test Site to ensure the safety and reliability of U.S. nuclear weapons without new testing and development. The program's National Ignition Facility has greatly overrun its initial cost estimates and raised questions about compliance with some test-ban treaty provisions.

The LLNL Directorate for Nonproliferation, Homeland, and International Security (NHI), formed in 1992, addresses the changing threats to U.S. national security in the aftermath of the Gulf War and the breakup of the Soviet Union. NHI contributes to international threat assessments of WMD proliferators and terrorist groups and other efforts to keep nuclear materials out of the hands of terrorists, and to computer simulations of conflict and crisis situations. In 1996, NHI established the Center for Global Security Research to provide a forum for studies of the interaction of policy and technology in national and international security.

The laboratory's publications include LLNL-authored unclassified and technical reports, annual reports (some are available online), and the monthly *Science and Technology Review*. The laboratory's Web site offers information on the organization and history of LLNL and its programs, news reports, and publications, including unclassified technical reports and annual reports, as well as useful links to related Web sites.

United States Department of Energy: Los Alamos National Laboratory (LANL)
PO Box 1663
Los Alamos, NM 87545
Phone: 505-667-7000
Web site: http://www.lanl.gov (See Contacts at http://www.lanl.gov/contacts.shtml)

The War Department established LANL in 1943 on a high mesa near Santa Fe, New Mexico, to develop the atomic bomb. The two nuclear weapons used against Japan were both designed and built there. After World War II ended, the lab worked on refinements to atomic weapons. However, after the Soviet Union tested a nuclear bomb, the lab began work in earnest on a thermonuclear (hydrogen) bomb. The University of California operates LANL for the Department of Energy. The lab has approximately 9,000 University of California employees, about 650 contractors, and a budget of $2.2 billion.

LANL's Principle Associate Directorate for Nuclear Weapons Programs sets priorities for the $1.2 billion nuclear weapons program at Los Alamos. LANL's Weapons Engineering and Manufacturing Directorate participates in the Stockpile Stewardship Program, attempting to safeguard the U.S. nuclear stockpile without designing new weapons or performing tests that violate existing test-ban treaties. Other divisions at LANL support nuclear nonproliferation efforts through threat assessments and the development of technologies and systems to control the global supply of nuclear and radiological materials and to interdict illegal diversions of these materials. For example, the Threat Reduction Directorate investigates threats such as weakened controls over nuclear materials and expertise in the states of the former Soviet Union, and the emergence of "rogue" states and terrorist organizations that seek WMD.

LANL publishes a wide range of printed and electronic material. The Web site includes LANL's newsletters and magazines, detailed information about the lab, technical reports, and official documents.

United States Department of Energy: National Nuclear Security Administration (NNSA)
1000 Independence Avenue SW
Washington, DC 20585
Phone: 800-DIAL-DOE or 202-586-5363
Fax: 202-586-4403
Email: Use contact form at http://www.nnsa.doe.gov/contactform.asp
Web site: http://www.nnsa.doe.gov

The NNSA, a semiautonomous organization within the U.S. Department of Energy, began operating on 1 March 2000; for fiscal year 2006 it requested a budget of approximately $9.4 billion. The purposes of the NNSA are to (1) enhance U.S. national security through the military application of nuclear energy, (2) maintain the safety and performance of the U.S. nuclear weapon stockpile, (3) provide the U.S. Navy with militarily effective nuclear propulsion, (4) promote international nuclear safety and nonproliferation, (5) reduce global danger from WMD, and (6) support U.S. leadership in science and technology.

The NNSA Office for Defense Nuclear Nonproliferation, through its many programs, works to prevent the spread of WMD technologies and know-how and to eliminate surplus fissile materials. It develops positions, policies, and procedures relating to international treaties and agreements, nuclear transfer and supplier control, international nuclear safeguards policies and programs, and various initiatives to detect and prevent the proliferation of WMD. It strives to improve treaty-monitoring systems and technologies to reduce threats to national security posed by nuclear weapons proliferation. The office's other functions include ensuring that the U.S.-Russian deal related to highly enriched uranium is implemented; planning, managing, and implementing the fissile material protection and control programs in cooperation with Russia; coordinating the development of Department of Energy policy regarding surplus fissile materials; directing the disposition of surplus U.S. highly enriched uranium and plutonium; and aiding U.S. government efforts to support the disposition of surplus Russian plutonium. The Office for Defense Nuclear Nonproliferation collaborates with international partners and other U.S. agencies. For example, in 2003, the NNSA, in cooperation with foreign governments and the U.S. Department of Homeland Security, began the Megaports Initiative. The objective of the initiative is to improve the screening of cargo at major international seaports, as 90 percent of global trade occurs via container cargo shipped by sea. The NNSA designed the enhanced screening measures to detect nuclear or radioactive material, stop harmful materials from entering the United States or other countries, and deter terrorists from using seaports to ship illicit materials.

The NNSA Office for Defense Programs (http://www.nnsa .doe.gov/defense.htm) helps reduce the global nuclear danger by planning for, maintaining, and enhancing the safety, reliability, and performance of the U.S. stockpile of nuclear weapons. It directs all defense weapon programs and projects at the Los Alamos, Sandia, and Lawrence Livermore National Laboratories, the Pantex Plant, the Y-12 Plant at Oak Ridge, the tritium operations facilities at Savannah River, and the Nevada Test Site. The NNSA Office for Naval Reactors directly supervises the Bettis and Knolls Atomic Power Laboratories, the Expended Core Facility, and naval reactor prototype plants.

The NNSA Web site provides information about NNSA programs, budget requests, and facilities; an organizational chart; congressional testimony and reports; press releases; and links to NNSA field offices, plants, and laboratories.

United States Department of Energy: Sandia National Laboratories (SNL)
Sandia National Laboratories, New Mexico
PO Box 5800
Albuquerque, NM 87185
Sandia National Laboratories, California
PO Box 969
Livermore, CA 94551-0969
Phone:
NM Community Involvement: 505-284-5200
CA Community Outreach: 925-294-2912
Web site: http://www.sandia.gov

SNL is managed for the U.S. Department of Energy's National Nuclear Security Administration by government contractor Lockheed Martin. SNL was established in 1945 as part of what is now Los Alamos National Laboratory and participated in development of the first U.S. atomic bomb in the areas of ordnance design, testing, and assembly. Since 1949, SNL's primary mission has been ensuring that U.S. nuclear weapons are secure, reliable, and able to back up the U.S. policy of nuclear deterrence. SNL designs and integrates more than 6,300 parts of a modern nuclear weapon's 6,500 components; it also implements large-scale non-nuclear testing and computational simulations of nuclear tests.

The SNL Nonproliferation and Assessments program tries to reduce U.S. vulnerability to WMD attacks. It seeks to improve national security and stabilize international relations by supporting treaty verification with other countries, developing new remote sensing technologies for aircraft and satellite deployment to detect and characterize proliferation activities, working with the countries of the former Soviet Union to protect and track nuclear materials from dismantled weapon systems, and developing and evaluating physical protection technologies and systems.

SNL also supports Department of Homeland Security efforts to protect the U.S. mainland and armed forces abroad from terrorist attacks.

Since the passage of the 1991 Cooperative Threat Reduction Act, SNL has worked with its Russian counterparts in support of nonproliferation policies. In 1994, it opened the Cooperative Monitoring Center at Sandia to host visits by arms control specialists from around the world. At the Cooperative Monitoring Center they can learn about available treaty-monitoring technologies used to build confidence among neighboring nations. (See Cooperative Monitoring Center Web site: http://www.cmc.sandia.gov.)

On its Web site, SNL publishes information about its programs, its annual report, newsletters and magazines featuring articles on the lab's technological and program achievements, fact sheets, and some papers authored by its staff.

United States Department of Homeland Security (DHS)
Washington, DC 20528
Phone: 202–282-8000
Web site: http://www.dhs.gov (See Contact Us form)

After the terrorist attacks of 11 September 2001, President Bush proposed combining several disparate government activities into the newly created Department of Homeland Security in June 2002. The purpose of DHS is to coordinate all activities to protect Americans against all terrorist threats, including those involving WMD, and to manage federal emergency response activities. The responsibilities of DHS include securing U.S. borders, ports, and critical infrastructure; synthesizing and analyzing intelligence on possible threats from multiple sources; coordinating communications between state and local governments, industry, and private citizens regarding threats and preparedness; organizing efforts to protect against WMD attacks; and managing federal emergency response activities. Several federal agencies were combined into one of four DHS directorates: the Directorate for Preparedness, the Directorate for Science and Technology, the Directorate for Management, and the Directorate for Policy. The Directorate for Science and Technology partners with the Defense Threat Reduction Agency and some of the Department of Energy's weapons labs, among other agencies, to develop new ways to detect nuclear and radiological weapons.

The DHS Web site offers a description of its history, organization, agenda, and programs; Congressional testimony and legislation related to DHS and its activities; fact sheets; and press releases.

United States Department of State: Bureau of International Security and Nonproliferation (ISN)
2201 C Street NW
Washington, DC 20520
Phone: 202-647-4000
Web site: http://www.state.gov/t/isn

In 2005, the Arms Control and Nonproliferation Bureaus were merged into the ISN. Under the jurisdiction of the Department of State, ISN takes the lead on a range of nonproliferation, counterproliferation, and WMD terrorism issues. The ISN leads many bilateral and multilateral efforts in promoting international consensus regarding WMD nonproliferation efforts, addresses domestic threats by strengthening physical security, and coordinates the implementation of international treaties and agreements. Furthermore, the ISN coordinates with the UN, the North Atlantic Treaty Organization, the IAEA, and other international organizations on measures to reduce the threat posed by WMD, whether developed by states or non-state actors. The ISN is the chief promoter of the U.S. nonproliferation agenda, including such efforts as the Proliferation Security Initiative, the Global Partnership Against Weapons and Materials of Mass Destruction, the Cooperative Threat Reduction Program, and UN Security Council Resolution 1540.

The ISN Web site contains a description of the organization, press releases, and selected Congressional testimony and speeches on U.S. nonproliferation policies. It links to sections of the State Department Web site with fact sheets on the various initiatives and treaties that ISN supports, including texts of the treaties, U.S. statements on them, and related government reports. It also provides an archive of relevant documents from 1997 to 2000 during the Clinton administration. This site provides a good overview of the Bush administration's approach to nonproliferation issues.

United States Department of State: Bureau of Verification, Compliance, and Implementation (VCI)
Bureau of Political-Military Affairs
2201 C Street NW

Washington, DC 20520
Phone: 202-647-4000
Website: http://www.state.gov/t/vci

The VCI began operating in February 2000; its mandate was expanded in 2005 to include responsibility for implementing arms control treaties. It deals with matters related to the verification and compliance of international arms control, nonproliferation, and disarmament agreements and commitments. The office is responsible for preparing the president's Annual Report to Congress on *Adherence to and Compliance with Arms Control and Nonproliferation Agreements and Commitments,* verifiability assessments for all international arms control and nonproliferation agreements, and specialized compliance reports required by the U.S. Senate resolutions on various treaties. It also assesses and develops verification technologies and operations.

The VCI oversees the Department of State's leadership of the interagency Nonproliferation and Arms Control Technology Working Group and operates the Nuclear Risk Reduction Center. The Nuclear Risk Reduction Center and its Soviet (now Russian) counterpart were formally formed in 1987 to establish the first direct communications link between the capitals since the 1963 presidential Hot Line Agreement. The Nuclear Risk Reduction Center primarily exchanges information and notifications under existing bilateral and multilateral treaties.

The VCI publishes specialized reports on compliance with arms control agreements and on world military expenditures and arms transfers. Its Web site offers a description of the organization, remarks by State Department officials on treaty issues, and links to treaties and press releases. The site also contains archives to documents from the Clinton administration.

Nongovernmental Organizations

This section includes only membership *organizations, that is, those that the general public can join. Additional nongovernmental organizations working on nuclear weapon and nonproliferation issues are provided in Chapter 8.*

Arms Control Association (ACA)
1313 L Street, NW, Suite 130

Washington, DC 20005
Phone: 202-463-8270
Fax: 202-463-8273
E-mail: aca@armscontrol.org
Web site: http://www.armscontrol.org

Founded in 1971, the ACA is a national nonpartisan membership organization that promotes public understanding of and support for effective arms control policies, including nuclear nonproliferation measures. Anyone is eligible for membership, and there is a reduced rate for students ($30 per year in 2006). Membership dues ($65 per year) include a one-year subscription to ACA's print journal, *Arms Control Today*. ACA staff participates in public education and media programs on arms control proposals, negotiations and agreements, and related national security issues. ACA's Web site includes the full text of material from current and back issues of *Arms Control Today*, as well as media advisories, fact sheets, the full texts of treaties, and other resources organized by subject (including nuclear proliferation, missile defense, and nuclear black markets material) and by country.

Federation of American Scientists (FAS)
1717 K Street NW, Suite 209
Washington, DC 20036
Phone: 202-546-3300
Fax: 202-675-1010
E-mail: webmaster@fas.org
Web site: http://www.fas.org

Founded as the Federation of Atomic Scientists in 1945 by members of the Manhattan Project who produced the first atomic bomb, FAS is the oldest organization dedicated to ending the worldwide arms race, achieving complete nuclear disarmament, and avoiding the use of nuclear weapons. FAS conducts analysis and advocacy on many scientific issues related to military issues, including strategic security, nuclear weapon and energy technologies, and the environment. FAS brings the scientific perspective to the legislative arena through direct lobbying, membership and grassroots work, and expert testimony at congressional hearings. The group publishes in print and online the quarterly *Public Interest Report*, occasional papers, and special reports that offer scientific perspectives on security issues, particularly nuclear weapons. The site also has interactive nuclear bomb blasts and nuclear fallout calculators, which illustrate the potential damage of a nuclear bomb in a specified area. Membership is $50 for new members.

Greenpeace International
Ottho Heldringstraat 5
1066 AZ Amsterdam
The Netherlands
Phone: 31 20 7182000
Fax: 31 20 5148151
Email: supporter.services@int.greenpeace.org
Web site: http://www.greenpeace.org/international

Greenpeace USA
702 H Street NW
Washington, DC 20001
Phone: 202-462-1177 or 800-326-0959
E-mail: info@wdc.greenpeace.org
Web site: http://www.greenpeace.org/usa

Greenpeace was formed in 1971, when a small group of volunteers and journalists sailed a boat into an area of northern Alaska where the U.S. government was conducting underground nuclear tests. Since then, Greenpeace has mounted various campaigns, including protests against French nuclear testing in the South Pacific and the transport of fissile material for reprocessing, protests to protect the global environment, and protests to expose government and corporate policies and activities that harm humans, wildlife, and the ecosystems. Greenpeace, a nonprofit membership organization, has offices in more than forty countries across Europe, the United States, and Asia. Funded almost exclusively by individual contributions, Greenpeace has 2.5 million members worldwide and approximately 250,000 members in the United States. Its Web site provides information on its various campaigns to promote nuclear disarmament and to protest environmental contamination and other dangers caused by both civilian and military use of nuclear power and materials. Greenpeace's Web site also offers many ways to become involved in its campaigns as a volunteer, online activist, and donor. Greenpeace publishes online reports, press releases, blogs, and other information related to its campaigns and government and corporate policies harmful to the environment.

Natural Resources Defense Council (NRDC)
40 West 20th Street
New York, NY 10011
Phone: 212-727-2700
Fax: 212-727-1773
E-mail: nrdcinfo@nrdc.org
Web site: http://www.nrdc.org

The NRDC uses law, science, and the support of more than 1.2 million individual members to protect the planet's wilderness and wildlife and to ensure a safe and healthy environment. Nuclear weapons and waste are important areas of concern for the organization. For more than twenty-five years, the NRDC has worked to shape U.S. nuclear nonproliferation, arms control, energy, and environmental policies. The NRDC aims to reduce and ultimately eliminate the unacceptable risks to people and the environment from the use of nuclear energy for both military and peaceful purposes.

The NRDC publishes a quarterly magazine, *Onearth,* which includes an update on the organization's activities in various areas as well as feature articles on environmental topics. It also produces the *Nuclear Weapons Databook* series and other books and monographs on worldwide nuclear deployments, nuclear weapon research at U.S. universities, and critiques of the Bush administration's nuclear weapons policy. Its Web site offers in-depth information on each of the NRDC's programs, including nuclear weapons and waste, some material from *Onearth,* a list of publications that can be ordered or accessed online, the full texts of some technical reports, its annual report, a media center with press releases and lists of experts, and links to other sites on nuclear weapons. Of special interest are comprehensive reports on U.S. nuclear weapons deployed in Europe and the outdated U.S. plan for using nuclear weapons against Russia. Memberships begin at $10.

Nuclear Age Peace Foundation (NAPF)
1187 Coast Village Road
Suite 1, PMB 121
Santa Barbara, CA 93108-2794
Phone: 805-965-3443
Fax: 805-568-0466
E-mail: wagingpeace@napf.org
Web site: www.wagingpeace.org

Founded in 1982, the Nuclear Age Peace Foundation is a non-profit membership-based organization that strives to abolish nuclear weapons and promote peace by offering research and information, educational programs, and policymaking guidance on security issues. The NAPF Web site, as well as NAPF's Nuclear Files Web site (http://www.nuclearfiles.org), contains a wealth of educational materials on the history of nuclear weapon development and nonproliferation efforts. These two sites are invaluable for educators developing curricula on nuclear issues for students of all ages and for citizens who would like to voice their opinions on nuclear issues.

NAPF publishes an online monthly newsletter, *The Sunflower*, which contains articles and perspectives on nuclear, missile, and military issues; NAPF events; action alerts; and other resources. In addition, the Web site covers current nuclear weapons policies and other issues key to global security. The site offers users the means to participate in online advocacy and activism by providing action alert messages to representatives regarding key bills in Congress. Membership is free and includes a subscription to *The Sunflower*.

Physicians for Social Responsibility (PSR)
1875 Connecticut Avenue NW, Suite 1012
Washington, DC 20009
Phone: 202-667-4260
Fax: 202-667-4201
E-mail: psrnatl@psr.org
Web site: http://www.psr.org

Since it was founded in 1961, PSR has worked to create a world free of nuclear weapons, global pollution, and gun violence. PSR's national leaders and local chapters (including Student PSR) seek to educate policymakers and the public on issues critical to human health and survival, including the effects of nuclear weapons and nuclear tests. In the nuclear field, PSR advocates a moratorium on the testing and development of nuclear weapons and advocates for their eventual abolition. PSR publishes a quarterly newsletter for members and bulletins on research into the effects of radiation from nuclear weapons and testing. Its Web site features updates on PSR's campaign, online publications, a quarterly newsletter, and a legislative action center. Anyone can join PSR with a donation in any amount.

Union of Concerned Scientists (UCS)
2 Brattle Square
Cambridge, MA 02238-9105
Phone: 617-547-5552
Fax: 617-864-9405
E-mail: ucs@ucsusa.org
Web site: http://ucsusa.org

Founded in 1969 by faculty members and students at the Massachusetts Institute of Technology, the UCS is an alliance of more than 100,000 concerned citizens and scientists. They combine scientific analyses and citizen advocacy to address issues that affect the environment and human health. The UCS tackles problems related to nuclear weapons, nuclear terrorism, nuclear power plant safety, and the prevention of space-based weapons. UCS's core group of scientists and engineers prepares technical studies and shares the results with policymakers, the news media, and the public. UCS members and staff around the United States use this information to advocate at all levels of government against nuclear weapons and missile defenses and for stronger environmental measures. Individuals can join for $25; membership includes a semiannual news magazine, *Catalyst*, and a quarterly newsletter, *Earthwise*. The UCS Web site contains information on its various projects; short fact sheets on topics such as nuclear weapons, nonproliferation treaties, nuclear terrorism, space security, and warhead elimination with related links; and ways to take action on its various campaigns. The Web site also offers instructive animations on nuclear bunker busters and countermeasures to missile defense. Users can sign up for an online action network and electronic newsletters.

8

Resources

This chapter contains reference tools—including books, periodicals, DVDs, videos, and Web sites—covering all aspects of nuclear weapons and nonproliferation. Because the United States was the first to develop nuclear weapons, and its program has been the most thoroughly documented, the first section is devoted to U.S. resources. The subsequent sections first cover nuclear weapon programs in other countries, then general topics on weapons proliferation and nonproliferation. From among the many resources on nuclear issues, this chapter offers those that are the most accessible in terms of content and availability. Many of the works summarized also contain long and detailed lists of notes and references for those who want to delve more deeply into a specific topic.

Books

Nuclear Weapon Issues: United States

Ackland, Len. 2002. *Making a Real Killing: Rocky Flats and the Nuclear West.* Albuquerque: University of New Mexico Press. 320 pp. ISBN 0-8263-2798-2.

The history of the nuclear weapon assembly facility at Rocky Flats, Colorado, provides a microcosm of problems witnessed within the whole U.S. nuclear weapons complex during the Cold War: lack of effective congressional oversight, wasteful spending, and inadequate attention to worker safety. The author offers a fascinating and detailed account of the Rocky Flats plant through the lens of the Church family, who homesteaded the land and eventually sold large tracts to the federal government for the facility in 1951 while retaining significant adjacent property. Ackland's account explains the complex politics of the Atomic Energy Commission and the role of Colorado legislators in bringing large federal contracts to their state. Rocky Flats brought thousands of jobs and hundreds of millions of dollars annually to the local economy, but its large plutonium and uranium processing and remanufacturing activities also brought significant environmental and safety hazards. Serious fires at the facility in 1957 and 1969 threatened to release large amounts of plutonium into the atmosphere, where prevailing winds could have blanketed Denver with deadly radioactive particles. The book details decades during which Cold War priorities for accelerated bomb production led to casual compliance with safety practices and frequent incidents involving worker contamination and illness. The conclusion of the book shows how stronger environmental legislation during the 1970s, combined with the increasingly active antinuclear protesters in the early 1980s, spelled the beginning of the end for Rocky Flats, which was finally shuttered in 1992. The author shows how the costly cleanup of Rocky Flats and the entire U.S. nuclear weapons complex will continue decades (and indeed centuries) into the future.

Bird, Kai, and Martin J. Sherwin. 2005. *American Prometheus: The Triumph and Tragedy of J. Robert Oppenheimer.* **New York: Vintage Books. 721 pp. ISBN-13: 978-0375726262.**

The authors of this Pulitzer Prize–winning book draw on twenty-five years of research to construct a comprehensive portrait of J. Robert Oppenheimer and his pivotal role in the successful U.S. nuclear bomb effort. They trace his rise from a sheltered, sensitive, apolitical polymath to arguably the most famous man in America after the bombings of Hiroshima and Nagasaki in 1945 and then to his fall in 1954 when the Atomic Energy Commission, after a rigged hearing, revoked his top-secret security clearance and thus his ability to serve as a government adviser. The authors give a thorough and balanced presentation of Oppenheimer's involvement with left-wing activities and associates who were Communist Party members, and in the process reveal the atmosphere of suspicion and continuous government surveillance in which he worked and socialized. They also show how the personal became political during discussions about the use of the atomic bomb in Japan and the subsequent development of U.S. nuclear policies. The call of Oppenheimer and like-minded scientists and policymakers for international control of nuclear materials and a political solution to the arms race went unheeded. The book contains numerous photographs of Oppenheimer and the important actors in his life, extensive notes, and a lengthy bibliography.

Boyer, Paul. 1998. *Fallout: A Historian Reflects on America's Half-Century Encounter with Nuclear Weapons.* **Columbus: Ohio State University Press. 280 pp. ISBN-13: 978-0814207864.**

The author, a history professor, gathers in chronological order a collection of his writings—from newspaper articles and book reviews to more scholarly articles—on the fallout of the U.S. use of nuclear weapons and the resulting arms race. He examines the political, social, psychological, and cultural repercussions of the U.S. bomb program from August 1945 to the mid-1990s. Boyer examines such topics as the earliest reactions to the atomic bomb; the planning for a nuclear war and other projects in the 1950s and early 1960s, including Dr. Edward Teller's strange scheme to use nuclear explosions in public works projects; the history of the medical profession's interest in nuclear issues; and the shifts in U.S. public interest that peaked with the nuclear freeze campaign in the early 1980s. He also looks at related topics, such as films and other artistic and cultural artifacts of the nuclear era, how college students contemplate nuclear issues, and the controversy that arose when the Smithsonian Institution tried to mount a fiftieth anniversary exhibit on the bombing of Hiroshima and Nagasaki. This book serves as both a historical assessment of the nuclear era through the 1990s and a reminder of how profoundly nuclear weapons have shaped U.S. thinking and culture.

Conant, Jennet. 2005. *109 East Palace: Robert Oppenheimer and the Secret City of Los Alamos.* **New York: Simon & Schuster. 424 pp. ISBN-13: 978-0743250078.**

Conant explores the Manhattan Project at Los Alamos through the lens of the personal stories of such key personnel as Dorothy

McKibben, Oppenheimer's secretary and the civilian gatekeeper for the entire two and a half years (March 1943 through August 1945) that the lab remained a secret facility. "109 East Palace" was the address in Santa Fe, New Mexico, that served as the first headquarters for the Los Alamos facility and through which all scientists and other personnel passed for security clearances before making the harrowing, 35-mile trip to the bomb-design facility. Conant draws on numerous interviews, oral histories, and primary sources, particularly a manuscript of McKibben's, to detail the logistics and atmosphere at Los Alamos, where many of the world's best scientists and their families congregated. She shows how the world's most sophisticated weapon was built in the midst of primitive conditions, including water, food, and energy shortages. Through the narrative of housing shortages, baby booms, and wild parties, she weaves the issue of the tension among the mostly young scientists pursuing the greatest scientific challenge of the time, and the military planners and policymakers who dictated the use of the bomb while ignoring the scientists' insights into its destructive capabilities. Many scientists realized only belatedly how terrible and history-changing their creations (a uranium gun-type and two plutonium implosion bombs) would be and how little say they would have in their use. Several of the personal and public tensions that germinated at Los Alamos grew to influence U.S. policy on nuclear weapons and nonproliferation. The book contains photos, notes on sources, and a selected bibliography.

Dibblin, Jane. 1990. *Day of Two Suns: U.S. Nuclear Testing and the Pacific Islanders.* **New York: New Amsterdam Books. 318 pp. ISBN-13: 978-0941533836.**

Between 1946 and 1958, the United States conducted sixty-six nuclear weapon tests in the Marshall Islands; in addition, since the 1960s the United States has used the Kwajalein Atoll and its lagoons as a target for missiles launched from California. Dibblin examines the devastating effects of these tests on Marshall Islanders. She focuses on two communities: the natives of Rongelap Atoll, who were irradiated by fallout from a U.S. hydrogen bomb test in 1954, moved from their homes to a smaller, less fertile island, and forced from self-sufficiency to dependency on U.S. aid; and the people of Kwajalein Atoll, forced by the United States to move to a crowded slum on a neighboring atoll so it could use their land for a missile target and exclusive military and civilian facilities. Drawing on interviews, research, and visits to the islands, Dibblin covers the history of U.S. nuclear colonialism in the Pacific, the U.S. failure to protect the Marshall Islanders or to provide adequate assistance and health care, and the local people's efforts to regain their land and appropriate compensation. She also compares the comforts enjoyed by the U.S. citizens on Kwajalein to the squalor of life for the atoll's original landowners who are forced to live on the overcrowded, polluted Ebeye Atoll without adequate facilities and barred from almost all facilities on their homeland, where they now must work in menial, low-paying jobs. Dibblin shows how the U.S. nuclear bomb program destroyed the health and way of life of whole communities.

Goodchild, Peter. 2004. *Edward Teller: The Real Dr. Strangelove.* **Cambridge, MA: Harvard University Press. 469 pp. ISBN-13: 978-0674016699.**

This biography of Edward Teller, the controversial force behind the U.S. thermonuclear or "super bomb," shows how personal slights and beliefs ended up playing an important role in the U.S. government's decisions about nuclear weapons. Teller, a Hungarian refugee and physicist with international scientific contacts, felt slighted by Robert Oppenheimer and other Manhattan Project scientists who criticized his design for a fusion bomb (a thousand times more powerful than the fission bombs dropped on Japan) as being technologically and morally questionable. Teller's frustration at his colleagues, particularly Oppenheimer, and his paranoia about the capabilities and motivations of the Soviet Union fueled his sales pitches for his designs to a few sympathetic government and military officials. Ultimately, Teller was instrumental in the U.S. decisions to build a thermonuclear bomb, establish a second weapons lab at Livermore, California (to compete with the Los Alamos, New Mexico lab), revoke Oppenheimer's security clearance, and pursue various schemes for missile defenses. Teller's efforts to promote himself and his paranoia about the Soviet Union (parodied in the movie *Dr. Strangelove*), coupled with his willingness to tout such dubious technologies as "clean" nuclear weapons and nuclear-triggered lasers in space, contributed to the escalating arms race during the Cold War. He influenced the U.S.

decisions not to agree to a ban on underground nuclear tests and not to accept Soviet President Gorbachev's offer to sharply reduce nuclear arsenals in exchange for dropping missile defense efforts. The book contains photographs, a glossary of characters, selected bibliography, extensive notes, and appendices with technical information.

Hersey, John. 1989 (reprint edition). *Hiroshima.* **New York: Vintage Books. 152 pp. ISBN-13: 978-0679721031.**

First published in 1946, this book tells the stories of six survivors of the U.S. bombing in Hiroshima. Through the eyes of the six—including a young mother, a doctor in the city's largest hospital, a factory worker, and a foreign priest—the author shows the devastation, confusion, and suffering caused by the new weapon technology. In a city of approximately 240,000, the bomb killed 66,000 instantly and thousands more gradually through fire and radiation sickness. These personal stories go beyond the statistics and provide a graphic reminder of the nuclear bomb's potential to destroy an entire community.

Lifton, Robert Jay, and Greg Mitchell. 1996. *Hiroshima in America: A Half Century of Denial.* **New York: Quill. 448 pp. ISBN-13: 978-0380727643.**

The authors, a professor of psychology and psychiatry and a writer specializing in the atomic bomb, examine the effects of the Hiroshima bombing on the United States and its citizens. They look at the manipulations and distortions that surrounded the U.S. use of the bomb and how they led to profound conflicts within the government, the scientific community that built the bomb, subsequent administrations, and the U.S. public. Specifically, the authors describe and dissect the U.S. government's official version of the Hiroshima bombing (developed largely by General Leslie Groves, the director of the bomb project, and Henry Stimson, the former secretary of war): the atomic bombings were necessary to prevent the invasion of Japan and save an estimated 1 million U.S. lives. Drawing on interviews and extensive original research, they detail the Hiroshima cover-up—the suppression of evidence, including scientific research, articles, photographs, and film that showed the terrible human costs of the bombing and questioned whether it was necessary to force Japan's surrender. Then, they examine President Harry Truman's decision to use the bomb, the psychology behind his decision, and how the bombing was presented to the U.S. public. Finally, the authors analyze how the U.S. public has struggled with the Hiroshima bombing ever since and the grave psychological and ethical consequences, including nuclear entrapment, national self-betrayal, fear of futurelessness, emotional numbing, and denial.

McMillan, Priscilla J. 2005. *The Ruin of J. Robert Oppenheimer and the Birth of the Modern Arms Race.* **New York: Viking. 373 pp. ISBN-13: 978-0670034222.**

In April 1954, the Atomic Energy Commission Board rescinded J. Robert Oppenheimer's security clearance on the grounds that the scientist who oversaw the building of the first atomic bombs had fundamental defects in character that made him a security risk. Using many newly declassified documents and several interviews, McMillan explores the events that resulted in this decision. She tells a story not only of Edward Teller and Lewis Strauss's personal vendetta against Oppenheimer for his misgivings about a crash program to build a hydrogen bomb project (misgivings shared by the other scientists on the Atomic Energy Commission's General Advisory Committee), but also of how the Oppenheimer case signaled a change in the partnership of scientists and government policymakers and spurred an arms race with Russia. The author covers the development of the hydrogen bomb, Teller and Edward Lawrence's successful effort to get a second weapons lab in Livermore, California, and the competition between the various branches of the armed services that all wanted a role in nuclear weapons delivery. She draws on the U.S. government's illegal wiretapping of Oppenheimer's conversations, including those with his defense counsel for the clearance hearing. The hearing itself was a travesty of justice, as the defense team was denied access to the top-secret documents used against Oppenheimer. But, as the author points out, the larger tragedy was the harm done to U.S. nuclear weapons policy when the scientists who understood the technology were denied decision-making roles, when the secrecy mandated by the government prevented the public from understanding or commenting on nuclear issues, and when the mistaken belief that a more powerful bomb would lead to national security meant a ratcheting up of the arms race and a lost opportunity to negotiate an arms ban with the Soviets.

Rhodes, Richard. 1996 (reprint edition). *Dark Sun: The Making of the Hydrogen Bomb*. New York: Simon and Schuster. 736 pp. ISBN-13: 978-0684824147.

Drawing on a wide range of documents and interviews, Rhodes provides a comprehensive history of the politics and science behind the development of the hydrogen bomb in the United States and Soviet Union. He shows how those two countries, while competing to build the most destructive nuclear arsenal, progressed from World War II allies to Cold War enemies. He documents the widespread Soviet espionage that greatly accelerated the Soviet bomb program and profiles major figures in the race for the hydrogen bomb: J. Robert Oppenheimer, Edward Teller, Igor Kurchatov, Klaus Fuchs, and Curtis LeMay. He discusses the rivalries between countries, scientists, and military leaders that led to the hydrogen bomb and U.S. plans to use nuclear weapons during the Korean War and the Cuban Missile Crisis. The book contains photographs, a glossary of names, extensive notes, and a lengthy bibliography.

Rhodes, Richard. 1995 (reprint edition). *The Making of the Atomic Bomb*. New York: Touchstone, Simon and Schuster. 928 pp. ISBN-13: 978-0684813783.

In this Pulitzer Prize–winning book, Rhodes presents a comprehensive, detailed history of the development of the U.S. atomic bomb from the discovery of isotope separation to the U.S. bombing of Hiroshima and Nagasaki. He vividly portrays the scientists, including J. Robert Oppenheimer, Edward Teller, Enrico Fermi, and Leo Szilard, who pursued their interest in releasing the energy of the atom, despite their misgivings about the history-changing destructive power it would unleash. Rhodes provides a sense of the mammoth scale of the U.S. bomb-building project, which involved government, private industry, and the scientific community on an unprecedented scale, and includes accounts of the domestic and international politics that propelled the project to completion. He also describes the slim likelihood that U.S. adversaries in World War II would build a nuclear bomb first, if at all. Finally, he offers statements from the bombs' victims in Hiroshima and Nagasaki and shows how the U.S. decision to pursue security through technological superiority set off the arms race with the Soviet Union. The book contains an extensive bibliography as well as numerous photographs of key players and events in the bomb-building program.

Richelson, Jeffrey T. 2006. *Spying on the Bomb: American Nuclear Intelligence from Nazi Germany to Iran and North Korea.* **New York: W. W. Norton. 702 pp. ISBN 0-393-05383-0.**

Although this book focuses on U.S. efforts to monitor the nuclear activities of other countries, it also serves as a good overview of the history of nuclear weapon programs in several countries, including Germany, Russia, China, France, Israel, India, Pakistan, North Korea, Taiwan, South Africa, Iraq, Iran, and Libya. The book begins with U.S. missions during World War II to determine the extent of the Nazi nuclear program and ends with the current measures being taken to monitor Iran and North Korea. While nuclear spying has evolved from reliance on human intelligence, to seismic, air sampling, and other monitoring to satellite imagery, the means of evading this technology, human fallibility, and political influences in interpreting data seem to be constants. This book provides a thorough case study of the U.S. intelligence community's monitoring of nuclear efforts—the evolving technologies, relevant agencies, reports, and important players, as well as the main institutions and actors in each of the nuclear-aspiring states. Of special interest is a chapter on the controversial intelligence the Bush administration used to justify invading Iraq. The range of the subject matter and the extensive notes make this an excellent reference on the history of nuclear proliferation.

Schwartz, Stephen I., ed. 1998. *Atomic Audit: The Costs and Consequences of U.S. Nuclear Weapons since 1940.* **Washington, DC: Brookings Institution Press. 680 pp. ISBN-13: 978-0815777731.**

This volume provides the most exhaustive and definitive accounting ever to appear in print related to the funds the United States has spent on its nuclear weapon complex. In a series of detailed chapters written by well-known experts in the arms control field, the book provides a narrative history of U.S. nuclear developments and a careful financial breakdown of how the U.S. government spent an estimated $5.8 trillion on these programs from 1940 to 1996. The chapters cover the construction of the atomic bomb and initial costs, the large-scale deployment of nuclear weapons, costs of targeting and controlling the bomb, expenditures on programs aimed at defending against Soviet nuclear weapons, expenses for nuclear waste management and environmental remediation, funds paid to victims of atom testing and other nuclear programs, and costs associated with keeping nuclear secrets. These chapters are accented with several rare photographs showing a variety of deployed U.S. nuclear weapons (including the portable, shoulder-launched Davy Crockett), various U.S. nuclear test explosions, and a range of facilities associated with U.S. nuclear weapon construction and related fuel-cycle activities during the Cold War. The sheer number and variety of nuclear weapons created by the United States provide a story that is both engrossing and deeply disturbing. The concluding chapters offer analyses of the extremely limited oversight exercised over these expenditures during the Cold War, along with proposals for increasing congressional oversight and direct accountability of these programs to the U.S. public.

Sokolski, Henry D. 2001. *Best of Intentions: America's Campaign against Strategic Weapons Proliferation.* **Westport, CT: Praeger Publishers. 184 pp. ISBN-13: 978-0275972899.**

The author examines U.S. participation in developing nuclear nonproliferation initiatives: the never-adopted Baruch Plan, Atoms for Peace, the Treaty on the Non-Proliferation of Nuclear Weapons, various proliferation technology control regimes, and counterproliferation. He focuses on the original rationale for each initiative and compares that goal to the outcome. The author concludes that each important nonproliferation initiative adopted by the United States has fallen short to varying degrees; some, such as Atoms for Peace, actually contributed to nuclear weapon development by promoting nuclear technology transfers. The author argues that the efforts failed because the United States did not fully understand the character of the threats the initiatives were designed to address. In addition to endnotes, the book contains the full text of several historical documents.

Welsome, Eileen. 1999. *The Plutonium Files: America's Secret Medical Experiments in the Cold War.* **New York: Dell Publishing. 592 pp. ISBN-13: 978-0385319546.**

Welsome investigates the thousands of government-sponsored experiments on the health effects of plutonium, uranium, and radiation that took place during the Cold War. She reveals how the U.S. government funded and participated in tests using civilians and military personnel without their knowledge or consent. Protected until 1993 as national security secrets, many of these experiments exploited the most vulnerable members of society: at hospitals, doctors injected eighteen terminally ill patients with plutonium; at a prenatal clinic, physicians gave radioactive cocktails to pregnant women during routine checkups; at a state school for the developmentally disabled, doctors fed several boys radioactive oatmeal; in Washington and Oregon prisons, doctors radiated and thus sterilized male inmates; and military officials ordered troops to witness atmospheric tests of nuclear weapons at the U.S. test sites in Nevada and at the Pacific Proving Ground. Many of the unwitting subjects and their children suffered long-term health problems. While giving a voice to some of the government's victims and outlining their quest for justice, Welsome provides a history of the U.S. nuclear weapon program and the agencies established to oversee it. She also touches on the environmental contamination caused by weapon plants and atmospheric testing of bombs.

Nuclear Weapon Programs: Worldwide

Campbell, Kurt M., Robert J. Einhorn, and Mitchell B. Reiss, eds. 2004. *The Nuclear Tipping Point: Why States Reconsider Their Nuclear Choices*. Washington, DC: The Brookings Institution Press. 367 pages. ISBN-13: 978-0815713319.

This multi-author volume studies eight countries—Egypt, Syria, Saudi Arabia, Turkey, Germany, Japan, South Korea, and Taiwan—that have remained nonnuclear, although they have had the means and/or the will to acquire nuclear weapons. Part one gives a brief history of nuclear weapons development and nonproliferation efforts and then sets out the analytical framework for the country studies. Each country chapter examines that state's reasons for going nonnuclear, and then turns to its current capability and possible motivations for deciding to pursue nuclear weapons. For most of the examined states, the key factor is whether another state in their region is pursuing nuclear weapons and the international response. Thus, for Egypt, Syria, Saudi Arabia, and

Turkey it is critical that Iran not become a nuclear weapon state
and of some importance that Israel not become an overt weapon
state. Similarly, the fate of North Korea's nuclear program will
influence other states—particularly Japan and South Korea. Other
factors that might push these states toward the nuclear tipping
point include a change in U.S. foreign policy, particularly a pull-
ing back from security guarantees; the disintegration of the global
nuclear nonproliferation regime; an erosion of regional security
and rise in terrorism; and the increased availability of nuclear
technology, particularly from Pakistan and Russia. The concluding chapter recommends ways, for the United States in particular,
to prevent countries from reaching the nuclear tipping point. The
studies show that the decision to renounce nuclear weapons is
not an easy one to reverse, even in the case of countries like Japan
and Germany that are "virtual nuclear states" because of their
advanced civilian nuclear energy capabilities and their scientific
and industrial bases. However, current trends—challenges to the
Non-Proliferation Treaty (NPT), terrorist threats, the disintegration of Iraq, the Bush administration's disdain for formal nonproliferation treaties, and the A. Q. Khan nuclear black market—all
make proliferation more likely.

Chang, Gordon G. 2006. *Nuclear Showdown: North Korea Takes
on the World.* **New York: Random House. 327 pp. ISBN-13: 978-
1400062942.**

Chang, an investigative journalist, delves into why North Korea,
a country that cannot feed its people, has invested so heavily in
nuclear weapons. He provides a history of North Korea's nuclear
weapon program, aided at times by the Russians, Chinese, and
Dr. A. Q. Khan of Pakistan, and discusses why the international
community has been unable to stop Kim Jong Il's drive to maintain his despotic regime by becoming a nuclear power. He points
out that, like Iran, North Korea as a member of the NPT received
international assistance with its declared civilian nuclear activities, while carrying on clandestine plutonium reprocessing and
uranium enrichment programs. North Korea traded its expertise
in missile technology to Pakistan in return for help with uranium
enrichment technology and know-how. Consequently, most analysts assume North Korea has enough fissile material for several
nuclear weapons and is working on long-range missiles that can

be equipped with nuclear warheads. They also fear that as the leader of a rogue regime willing to starve millions of his own people, Kim Jong Il may also be willing to share nuclear weapons technology with terrorists, al Qaeda in particular. Moreover, as the first country to withdraw from the NPT, North Korea represents a dangerous challenge to the nuclear nonproliferation regime and, if left unchecked, a spur to possible further nuclear proliferation by other countries. The 1994 U.S.–North Korean Agreed Framework fell apart when neither the United States nor North Korea honored all the terms of the bargain. Chang argues that solving the North Korean dilemma will require rethinking policies on nuclear deterrence, international aid, the global order, and disarmament. Extensive endnotes support the material presented in the book.

Chubin, Shahram. 2006. *Iran's Nuclear Ambitions*. Washington, DC: Carnegie Endowment of International Peace. 222 pp. ISBN-13: 978-0870032301.

This book does not provide an event-by-event history of Iran's military and civilian nuclear programs. Instead, the author, a security analyst, discusses why Iran might want to pursue nuclear weapons to enhance its status, deter attack, and preserve the current domestic regime. The author also explores the repercussions of a nuclear-armed Iran for the Middle East and nonproliferation efforts. He examines the competing factions weighing in on Iran's nuclear policy: While most agree that Iran should develop a complete nuclear fuel cycle to enhance its status regionally and internationally, they differ on whether to accommodate or challenge Western countries in the process and whether to pursue nuclear weapons or just a nuclear weapon capability. He also discusses Iran's shifting negotiating strategy with the International Atomic Energy Agency, European countries, Russia, and the United States since 2002 when the National Council of Resistance of Iran revealed the extent of Iran's clandestine nuclear activities, and the often confused international response, particularly from the United States, which seems more interested in regime change than banning nuclear weapons. This book provides an instructive look at the thorny international policy and negotiating issues that arise when a country develops a civilian nuclear program (permitted by the NPT) that may also give it a nuclear weapon capability.

Cirincione, Joseph, Jon B. Wolfsthal, and Miriam Rajkumar. 2005. *Deadly Arsenals: Nuclear, Biological, and Chemical Threats.* 2nd revised and expanded edition. Washington, DC: Carnegie Endowment of International Peace. 487 pp. ISBN-13: 978-0870032165.

This book provides an excellent overview of the WMD capabilities and nonproliferation commitments of eighteen states: the declared nuclear weapon states (Russia, China, France, the United Kingdom, and the United States); the non-NPT nuclear weapon states (India, Pakistan, and Israel); two hard cases (North Korea and Iran); and "nonproliferation successes" (Libya, Iraq, Belarus, Kazakhstan, Ukraine, Argentina, Brazil, and South Africa). Introductory chapters explain basic nuclear weapon concepts and designs and outline the international nonproliferation regime. Each chapter then assesses a state's progress toward developing and maintaining a nuclear arsenal (and delivery systems), analyzes its standing in the nonproliferation regime, and describes some of the international politics contributing to its nuclear developments. Chapters also contain charts summarizing a country's nuclear infrastructure, maps showing the locations of nuclear-related facilities, and citations. Appendices include the full text of the nuclear NPT and the Comprehensive Nuclear-Test-Ban Treaty as well as descriptions of nuclear supplier organizations.

Cohen, Avner. 1998. *Israel and the Bomb.* New York: Columbia University Press. 470 pp. ISBN-13: 978-0231104838.

Cohen's book is the first authoritative history of the highly secretive Israeli nuclear weapon program. This study is the product of years of interviews and research, including newly declassified documents from both the U.S. and Israeli archives. The book follows the political and strategic aspects of Israeli nuclear weapons plans from their roots in the late 1940s under Prime Minister David Ben-Gurion through the genesis of an actual program in the 1950s and 1960s thanks to the efforts of scientist Ernst David Bergmann (the first head of the Israeli Atomic Energy Commission) and a dynamic young Ministry of Defense official (and future prime minister), Shimon Peres. It also covers debates about Israeli security strategy and U.S.-Israel relations. By the 1970s, this strategy resulted in a policy that Cohen calls nuclear opacity, in which Israel neither confirmed nor denied its nuclear weapon capability (although it refused to sign the NPT). The book provides details on the initial U.S. support for an Israeli nuclear research program and the much more extensive French support for the Dimona reactor, which eventually provided the fissile material for Israel's bombs. Ironically, Cohen quotes Israeli sources who noted in the wake of the 1967 Arab-Israeli war the "inapplicability" of nuclear weapons to "almost all" security threats facing Israel. Israel's failure to join the NPT remains a point of contention in the Middle East.

Corera, Gordon. 2006. *Shopping for Bombs: Nuclear Proliferation, Global Insecurity, and the Rise and Fall of the A.Q. Khan Network*. New York: Oxford University Press. 288 pp. ISBN-13: 978-0195304954.

Corera, a BBC security correspondent, charts the career of Dr. A. Q. Khan, the Pakistani metallurgist who has done the most to spread nuclear weapon technology in the past three decades. In the late 1970s, spurred by nationalism and stung by India's 1971 defeat of Pakistan, Khan (then working at Urenco in the Netherlands) volunteered his services as a nuclear spy. At Urenco, Khan gained access not only to the specifications for the latest centrifuge technology but also to the Western network of suppliers for the necessary components. Khan first parlayed this knowledge into his own nuclear weapon and missile facility in Pakistan (Khan Research Laboratories). By the late 1980s, Pakistan, with considerable help from China and Khan's stolen designs, probably had a nuclear weapon. Khan then began selling his expertise to other nuclear aspirants: Iran, North Korea, and Libya and possibly Saudi Arabia, Syria, and al Qaeda. All the while, Khan's activities were tracked by Western intelligence agencies whose efforts to stop the illicit nuclear trafficking were often stymied by their governments' more pressing concerns and the Pakistani government's unwillingness to rein in a national hero. At crucial points, the U.S. government ignored Pakistan's successful quest for nuclear weapons in order to enlist Pakistan as an ally, first in Afghanistan against the Soviet Union and later against the Taliban. Meanwhile, Pakistan successfully tested a nuclear weapon in 1998 and traded nuclear technology for missile assistance from North Korea. Khan, probably with government assistance, also helped Iran build its nuclear enrichment facilities and transferred centrifuge technology and weapons designs to Libya. British and U.S. intelligence agencies finally unraveled the Khan network after Libya's leader, Colonel Moammar Gadhafi, agreed to disclose and dismantle its nuclear weapon program and in the process confirm multiple transfers of weapons-related materials and designs from Khan's worldwide network of suppliers. The author highlights the related issues of inadequate intelligence on nuclear programs and good intelligence on nuclear proliferation that is ignored for political reasons. He also notes the repercussions of the Khan network for the ailing nonproliferation regime.

Holloway, David. 1996. *Stalin and the Bomb: The Soviet Union and Atomic Energy, 1939–1956.* **New Haven, CT: Yale University Press. 480 pp. ISBN-13: 978-0300066647.**

The author examines the history of the development of the atomic and hydrogen bombs in the Soviet Union. Drawing on interviews with participants in the Soviet nuclear program and Western scientists as well as extensive research, he discusses Soviet policy in relation to atomic energy from 1938, when nuclear fission was first discovered, to the mid-1950s, when the Soviet Union tested thermonuclear weapons in an arms race with the United States. In addition to detailing the scientific developments, the author places the bomb in political and social contexts. He reviews how the atomic bomb affected Soviet foreign and military policy, and he also looks at how the Soviet developments were influenced by espionage and U.S. policies. The book contains photos and short biographies of the key players in the Soviet bomb program as well as several pages of detailed notes.

Lewis, John W., and Xue, Litai. 1991. *China Builds the Bomb.* **Stanford, CA: Stanford University Press. 329 pp. ISBN-13: 978-0804718417.**

The authors chronicle the political and technological developments that led to China's first test of an atom bomb on 16 October 1964, and a hydrogen bomb on 17 June 1967. They argue that in 1955 China's leaders decided to obtain a nuclear weapon in response to U.S. involvement in the Korean War, Indochina, and the Taiwan Strait. The authors describe the evolving relationship between the political leaders and the atomic bomb, as well as the nuclear assistance that China received from the Soviet Union from 1955 to 1960. They also explain how the bomb program survived despite great domestic upheaval and very difficult conditions, including famine. The book contains photographs; short biographies of key figures in the nuclear weapon program; the government's statement on the day of the first atomic bomb test, which explains China's nuclear weapons philosophy; and extensive notes and list of references.

Karpin, Michael. 2006. *The Bomb in the Basement: How Israel Went Nuclear and What that Means for the World.* **New York: Simon and Schuster. 404 pages. ISBN 13: 978-0743265942.**

As a matter of government policy, Israel neither confirms nor denies that it possesses nuclear weapons. Karpin, an Israeli journalist, had to submit this book to military censors, who excised any mention of Israel's "nuclear weapons," "atomic arsenal," or other similar terms. Yet, as Karpin relates, David Ben-Gurion, Israel's first prime minister and minister of defense, determined at the end of World War II that the only way to prevent another Holocaust and to preserve the Jewish state was to build a nuclear arsenal. The author examines the domestic debates and international negotiations that resulted in the small, fledging state attaining a nuclear capability within ten years. With French assistance, construction on the nuclear complex at Dimona began in 1957; by 1967, Israel reportedly had produced enough plutonium for a nuclear weapon. While the U.S. government received reports and satellite photographs indicating that Israel intended to produce fissile material, it officially stated that Israel did not appear to be pursuing nuclear weapons. U.S. presidents Kennedy and Johnson gave their tacit approval to Israel's nuclear option. According to the author, later U.S. administrations may have insisted that Israel maintain its nuclear ambiguity to avoid provoking its neighboring countries into going nuclear. The history ends with the 1973 Yom Kippur War, when Israel allegedly readied nuclear warheads for use against Egypt and Syria. In the final chapter, Karpin looks at what steps Israel might take to prevent Iran from attaining nuclear weapons. While covering the intrigue and duplicity of Israel's nuclear program, the author shies away from technical information and the effect that Israel's nuclear status has on the nuclear nonproliferation regime and instability in the Middle East.

Makhijani, Arjun, Howard Hu, and Katherine Yih, eds. 2000. *Nuclear Wastelands: A Global Guide to Nuclear Weapons Production and Its Health and Environmental Effects.* **Cambridge, MA: MIT Press. 696 pp. ISBN-13: 978-0262632041.**

This book provides concise histories of the development of the nuclear weapon programs of the five declared nuclear weapon states and of the de facto nuclear states (Israel, India, and Pakistan). It details the health and environmental effects in all the states involved in weapon testing and uranium mining. Chapters describe how nuclear weapons are produced—from the mining and milling of uranium to the conversion to weapons-grade material to the assembly of the weapons—as well as the adverse environmental and health consequences of each stage. The collection persuasively demonstrates that nuclear weapons have profoundly harmed the very people and environment they were supposed to protect. The book contains a comprehensive list of mainly technical references, as well as numerous photos, graphics, and charts illustrating the scientific processes of bomb-building and listing the facilities involved in each country.

Perkovich, George. 2001. *India's Nuclear Bomb: The Impact on Global Proliferation.* **Updated edition. Berkeley: University of California Press. 610 pp. ISBN-13: 978-0520232105.**

Drawing extensively on interviews with senior analysts and high-ranking former and current Indian and U.S. officials, Perkovich offers the most definitive history of the Indian nuclear weapons program to date. Perkovich divides the book into three phases: (1) the period between 1947 and 1974, when Indian scientists acquired the technical means to produce nuclear weapons and detonated a peaceful nuclear explosion, despite the moral doubts and competing priorities of its leaders and citizens; (2) the period between 1975 and 1995, when India refrained from a follow-up test but continued nuclear weapon and ballistic missile development in secret; and (3) the period between 1996 and 1998, when India became disillusioned with the failure of the declared nuclear weapon states to disarm, even after the Cold War ended, and decided to show the world it had the ability to build and deliver nuclear weapons. Along the way, Perkovich answers three major questions: (1) Why did India acquire a nuclear weapons capability when and how it did? (2) What factors keep India from reversing its nuclear weapon program like other countries, such as South Africa? and (3) What impact did the United States have on India's nuclear intentions and capabilities? His overarching premise, at least in the case of India, is that the conventional wisdom that states build nuclear weapons in response to external threats is misguided. He argues that India wanted nuclear weapons more for ideological and domestic political reasons than to respond to threats from China and Pakistan. India wished to be regarded as a major power with the technical prowess to join the nuclear club and pursued this course despite its moral qualms and social needs. Thus, he argues, India will not reverse its nuclear program, even if external security threats disappear. He concludes with a chapter exploding the illusions of the nuclear age—the grandest being that the nuclear states can secure themselves and the world against proliferation without placing a higher priority on eliminating their own arsenals. The book contains more than 100 pages of notes documenting the author's sources and photographs of the key figures, facilities, and tests in the Indian nuclear program.

Podvig, Pavel, ed. 2004. *Russian Strategic Nuclear Forces*. New edition. Cambridge, MA: MIT Press. 720 pp. ISBN-13: 978-0262661812.

The great interest this book has generated lies only partially in the fact that the Russian intelligence service stopped the sale of the original Russian-language edition in the late 1990s and removed all copies from store shelves. More important for scholars and analysts, the volume represents the single most comprehensive, authoritative, and unbiased history of the development of Soviet (and Russian) strategic forces available, oddly, now only in English. Written by Russian experts (many of them scientists), the book provides exhaustive details about all aspects of the Soviet and Russian nuclear weapons structure, including warheads, delivery vehicles (land-, sea-, and air-based), nuclear testing, command and control, air defense, antimissile defense, and space-based early warning and reconnaissance. The account may be too heavy for the general reader, but the expert will revel in the information available about this previously secret nuclear heritage. The English-language edition is updated from the earlier Russian version and covers the significant downsizing of the Russian arsenal and plans for the future.

Powers, Thomas. 2000 (reprint edition). *Heisenberg's War: The Secret History of the German Bomb*. New York: Da Capo Press. 608 pp. ISBN-13: 978-0306810114.

This book tells the fascinating and little-known story of the scientists involved in the German effort to develop a nuclear weapon before and during World War II. Most of these individuals, including Nobel Prize–winning physicist Werner Heisenberg, who informally headed the program, faced a complex personal dilemma of wanting to support their country but not wanting to deliver a bomb into the hands of Adolf Hitler. Powers's book provides a detailed history of this critical period in world history, where the global balance teetered on the brink of creating a century-long Nazi dynasty, possibly equipped with nuclear weapons. As Powers tells the story, Heisenberg remained doubtful of the possibility of developing a bomb throughout the war, even after the Nazi capture of Czech uranium mines, a French centrifuge, and the Norwegian heavy-water plant at Rjukan (Vemork). Wartime conditions, German scientific traditions that preferred small group research (rather than large programs), and Nazi preferences for weapons with greater promise for near-term results (particularly after 1942) eventually caused the program to peter out, although this information was not known to the Allies at the time. Powers also provides details of the U.S. Alsos mission, which aimed to disrupt German bomb efforts, even to the point of kidnappings and assassinations (never carried out) of key personnel. This book provides perhaps the best history of the German nuclear program in English.

Duelfer, Charles. September 2004. *Comprehensive Report of the Special Advisor to the DCI on Iraq's Weapons of Mass Destruction.* **Washington, DC: U.S. Government Printing Office. 1,000 pp. ISBN-13: 978-0160724923 (set of three volumes plus 2005 Addenda). Electronic copies free at https://www.cia.gov/cia/ reports/iraq_wmd_2004.**

In this extensive three-volume report, the Iraq Survey Group (headed by chief weapons inspector Charles Duelfer) concludes that the 1991 Gulf War and subsequent United Nations (UN) sanctions and inspections destroyed Iraq's nuclear weapon program and inventory of long-range missiles. According to the "Duelfer Report," at the time of the 2003 invasion, Iraq had no nuclear weapons or the facilities to build them, no production facilities for chemical weapons, and no interest in biological weapons. The second volume, which deals with nuclear issues, debunks the Bush administration's claim that Iraq had sought uranium from abroad and was pursuing a nuclear weapon capability. It provides a detailed history of Iraq's nuclear weapon ambitions, technology, and know-how. The report draws on physical inspections of WMD sites, interrogations of captured Iraqi experts and officials (including Saddam Hussein), and millions of pages of documents recovered after the invasion.

Timmerman, Kenneth R. 2005. *Countdown to Crisis: The Coming Nuclear Showdown with Iran.* **New York: Crown Forum. 392 pp. ISBN-13: 978-1400053681.**

Timmerman, an investigative journalist, draws on previously classified documents, U.S. government officials, defectors from Iran's intelligence services, and government reports to portray Iran as one the greatest threats facing the United States. He lays out the evidence for his arguments that Iran collaborated in many of the recent terrorist attacks against the United States and that Iran is far more advanced in developing nuclear weapons than Western states and the International Atomic Energy Agency (IAEA) understand. He is highly critical of the international community and the IAEA for failing to sanction Iran for what he portrays as its clear pursuit of a nuclear weapon program since the late 1980s. In 1987, Iran signed a consulting agreement with Pakistani nuclear scientist A. Q. Khan, who reportedly instructed Iran on how to use its membership in the nuclear NPT to get aid for a civilian nuclear program that could also be used for a secret weapon program using both highly enriched uranium and plutonium. Iran acquired nuclear technology, training, know-how, and delivery systems not only from Khan and his international black market, but also from China, Russia, North Korea, Ukraine, Germany, and other Western states. Timmerman claims that intelligence agencies in the United States and Germany noticed repeated signs that Iran was seeking materials that would likely be used for a nuclear weapons program, but the governments never stopped the lucrative military trade with Iran or made serious charges to the IAEA. Not until 2003, after an Iranian opposition group revealed the existence of secret enrichment and heavy-water facilities in Iran, did the IAEA perform more thorough inspections in Iran and finally force Iran to admit that it had been working on enriching uranium and extracting plutonium for more than twenty years. While some of his conclusions may be controversial, Timmerman offers useful information on the buildup of the Iranian nuclear program, the international trade in nuclear- and missile-related technologies, the range of the Khan network, and Iran's possible motives and intentions for developing WMD and pursuing ties with al Qaeda. A sixty-page appendix contains documents, photographs, IAEA reports, and other evidence relied on by the author.

Nuclear Weapon Proliferation and Nonproliferation: General Topics

Allison, Graham. 2005. *Nuclear Terrorism: The Ultimate Preventable Catastrophe*. New York: Owl Books, Henry Holt and Company. 275 pages. ISBN-13: 978-0805078527.

The author starts from the premise that a nuclear terrorist attack in the United States in the next decade is more likely than not, and that such an attack is preventable if world leaders make protecting nuclear weapons and fissile materials a priority. In part one, he gives an overview of what groups would and could use nuclear weapons, what type of weapons they might use, and where and how a nuclear attack might occur. Reportedly, al Qaeda and its leader, Osama bin Laden, have been investigating the purchase of nuclear weapons or fissile material for more than a decade. Al Qaeda and other such groups could steal or buy a nuclear weapon or fissile material from poorly protected nuclear facilities in the states of the former Soviet Union or from Pakistan or North Korea, both states with a history of dealing in nuclear technologies and weapon systems. While it would be almost impossible for a terrorist group to produce highly enriched uranium or plutonium, once a terrorist acquires fissile material, building an effective bomb is relatively easy, particularly given all the publicly available information on bomb design. As Allison discusses at length, once built, a bomb could be easily delivered to any location in the United States via the international system of cargo shipping, where only a small percentage of containers are ever physically inspected, or through the same smuggling routes used for transporting drugs and illegal aliens. In part two, Allison critiques the Bush administration's war on terrorism that, while going on the offensive against terrorist organizations and rogue states, fails to limit means by which terrorists could acquire nuclear or other WMD materials. He believes nuclear terrorism can be prevented if countries adhere to the "doctrine of three nos": no loose nukes, no new nascent nukes, and no new nuclear weapon states. In an afterword written in 2005, Allison notes developments supporting an *increased* likelihood of a nuclear terrorist attack. The book contains a "frequently asked questions" section that covers general information about fissile material and nuclear weapons production, nuclear-capable states, and nuclear terrorism basics.

Cirincione, Joseph. 2007. *Bomb Scare: The History & Future of Nuclear Weapons.* **New York: Columbia University Press. 206 pp. ISBN 13: 978-0231135108.**

Cirincione, the former director of nonproliferation policy at the Carnegie Endowment for International Peace and a former congressional staff member, offers a comprehensive yet remarkably pithy overview of the history of nuclear proliferation and current policy debates on nonproliferation policies. Although the book covers a range of technical issues—including the basics of bomb physics—the author's style is informal and accessible to the general reader. Cirincione begins with the history of nuclear weapons and their development and use by the United States during World War II. He then covers in turn early efforts to control the bomb, the Soviet nuclear program and the arms race, the NPT, the Reagan build-up, late Cold War arms control, and the current status of nuclear proliferation. After this U.S.-Russian focus, the book then analyzes nuclear programs in various other countries and conceptual arguments about why states proliferate—or don't. Cirincione uses these tools to examine current challenges within the nonproliferation regime, including frayed norms, treaty enforcement difficulties, terrorist threats, and the risks posed by large amounts of fissile material internationally. The book concludes with a call for a more active U.S. policy to combat nuclear threats by reducing nuclear stockpiles, tightening controls over fissile material, and resolving the regional conflicts that spur nuclear acquisition. In sum, Cirincione's timely study offers a well-written, well-researched, and easily digestible primer on nuclear weapons issues.

Ferguson, Charles D., and William C. Potter. 2005. *The Four Faces of Nuclear Terrorism.* **New York: Routledge. 376 pages. ISBN-13: 978-0415952446.**

This book offers a comprehensive examination of the potential for nuclear terrorism and current U.S. and international measures to prevent it. The authors, experts in nuclear nonproliferation, first look at the motives and capabilities of terrorist organizations, such as Aum Shinrikyo and al Qaeda, which might seek a nuclear capability to bolster their political goals, increase their prestige, and create a great psychological impact on their target audience. Subsequent chapters delve into the four paths to nuclear terrorism: (1) stealing and detonating a nuclear bomb; (2) acquiring fissile material to build a crude nuclear device (an improvised nuclear device or "IND"); (3) attacking a nuclear facility, particularly a nuclear power plant, which would release large amounts of radioactivity; and (4) using radioactive materials to construct and detonate a radiological dispersion device or "dirty bomb." The authors conclude that the first two types of attack are potentially the most devastating but also the most unlikely. However, they argue that it is highly likely that a motivated terrorist group could detonate a dirty bomb causing radiation contamination, illness, and panic. The book concludes with a "Plan for Urgent Action against Nuclear Terrorism" that calls on the United States to recognize that terrorist organizations, rather than nuclear-armed states, pose the greatest nuclear threat. Consequently, the United States must help secure highly enriched uranium worldwide, reduce nuclear risks in South and Central Asia, and secure Russia's nuclear weapons. To mitigate the use of a dirty bomb, the United States must train first responders, educate the public, and develop new decontamination technologies. The book contains comprehensive endnotes for each chapter and a lengthy bibliography.

Preston, Diane. 2006. *Before the Fallout, from Marie Curie to Hiroshima.* **New York: Berkley Books. 400 pages. ISBN-13: 978-0425207895.**

Preston uses primary documents and interviews to cover the history of the atomic bomb from the early discoveries about the nature of the atom in the late eighteenth century to the U.S. bombing of Hiroshima and Nagasaki in 1945. She covers the scientific, political, military, and personal aspects of the quests for the bomb, telling a compelling and troubling story. Preston shows how this quest evolved from a worldwide collaboration of scientists pursuing pure scientific knowledge to a race between warring nations where groups of scientists toiled in secrecy at the behest of their government. As a result of political developments, and particularly Hitler's policy of persecuting Jewish scientists, former students and teachers and former colleagues began competing against each other to develop atomic power for military purposes in Britain, the United States, Germany, the Soviet Union, and Japan. Preston provides clear explanations of scientific and technical developments while weaving in the personal stories of the scientists, particularly the rare women scientists and the Jewish scientists who fled persecution in German-held countries and helped design bombs for Britain and the United States. She shows how British scientists, through their early work on a possible atomic bomb and their persistence, convinced the United States to build a nuclear weapon. She also examines the German scientists' ambivalence about building a bomb for Hitler and their misconceptions about the process for producing fissile material. In the concluding chapters, she outlines the damage done by the atomic bombs in Hiroshima and Nagasaki, worldwide reactions to the bombings, the subsequent fates of many of the nuclear scientists, and the historical "what ifs." The book offers good portraits of many of the key players in atomic history. It contains photographs throughout, extensive notes, a glossary, and a bibliography.

Sagan, Scott D., and Kenneth N. Waltz. 2002. *The Spread of Nuclear Weapons: A Debate Renewed.* **Second edition. New York: W. W. Norton. 224 pp. ISBN-13:978-0393977479.**

The implications of nuclear proliferation are the subject of this vigorous debate by two leading academics. Waltz makes the case that "more may be better," arguing that a gradually increasing number of states with small nuclear arsenals may make the world safer by strengthening military restraint, establishing mutually deterrent relationships in unstable regions, and making states with such weapons more secure. Sagan counters by arguing that nuclear proliferation will instead make war more likely and will increase the chance of nuclear accidents, given the dominance of aggressive militaries in many states seeking nuclear weapons and the limits of the financial resources, training, and technology needed to keep these weapons safe. The book takes the form of statements by each author and then a section of back-to-back rebuttals to the other's arguments. It is useful for laying out the strategic and philosophical issues related to nuclear proliferation in stark terms, although it does not provide a resolution to the issues it raises.

Schell, Jonathan. 1998. *The Gift of Time: The Case for Abolishing Nuclear Weapons Now*. **New York: Henry Holt. 240 pp. ISBN-13: 978-0805059618.**

The author addresses the question of whether it is possible to eliminate nuclear weapons now that the Cold War is over. He weaves together a series of interviews with people once involved at high levels in designing Cold War nuclear deterrence policies who are now rethinking their support for nuclear arms. From these conversations, he builds an argument that with the complete support of political authorities the world can abolish nuclear weapons. (However, the book was written before India and Pakistan tested nuclear devices in May 1998.) In speaking with former policymakers from the United States, Europe, and Russia, the author teases out how the Cold War theory of nuclear deterrence has always been untenable and has, in fact, resulted in larger nuclear arsenals and more advanced technologies. Among the politicians and analysts interviewed are Robert McNamara, former U.S. secretary of defense; Joseph Rotblat, the only scientist to leave the Manhattan Project for moral reasons; Helmut Schmidt, former chancellor of West Germany; and Mikhail Gorbachev, former president of the Soviet Union.

Weapons of Mass Destruction Commission. 2006. *Weapons of Terror: Freeing the World of Nuclear, Biological, and Chemical Arms*. **Stockholm: WMD Commission. 227 pp. ISBN-13: 978-9138225820. Electronic copies free at www.wmdcommission.org.**

This book is the final report of an independent international commission chaired by former UN weapons inspector and Swedish diplomat Hans Blix and funded by the Swedish government. The WMD Commission examined ways the international community could cooperate to prevent the spread of nuclear, biological, chemical, and radiological weapons and the means of delivering them. The report provides a good, concise overview of the current state of nuclear nonproliferation efforts, such as treaties, security assurances, nuclear-weapon-free zones, physical protection measures, and fissile material cleanup initiatives. In addition, the commission offers several concrete proposals for preventing nuclear proliferation and nuclear terrorism, and calls on all nuclear-capable states to question their need for a nuclear deterrent and multiple nuclear delivery systems. According to the Commission, two of the most important nonproliferation goals are bringing the Comprehensive Nuclear-Test-Ban Treaty into force and concluding a fissile material cutoff treaty.

Wittner, Lawrence S. 2003. *The Struggle Against the Bomb: Toward Nuclear Abolition: A History of the World Nuclear Disarmament Movement, 1971–Present.* **Stanford, CA: Stanford University Press. 688 pp. ISBN-13: 978-0804748629.**

This third volume of Wittner's exhaustive history of the international nuclear disarmament movement since the 1930s covers the period from the era of U.S.-Soviet détente to the first years of the George W. Bush administration. Like its predecessors, it is thoroughly researched and truly multinational in scope, drawing on government documents, nongovernmental organization publications, and interviews with former government officials and leading figures in the peace movement. This volume begins by tracing the short-lived hopes of the détente era and moves on to discuss renewed U.S.-Soviet hostility and arms buildups in the late 1970s and the revival of the antinuclear movement. The largest section of the book focuses on international reactions to the Soviet deployment of SS-20 missiles in Eastern Europe and the U.S./North Atlantic Treaty Organization (NATO) deployment of Pershing II missiles in Western Europe. Throughout the book, Wittner summarizes both the official policies of the two superpowers and the activities and perspectives of a dizzying array of antinuclear and peace groups, particularly in Western Europe and the United States (including the nuclear freeze movement of the early 1980s). Wittner's main theme is the role of the peace movement in pressuring governments toward nuclear arms control. The later parts of the book are less detailed as, ironically, progress in U.S.-Soviet/Russian arms control caused the peace movement to wane after 1991. But problems in government-led efforts toward disarmament by the late 1990s (the 1998 nuclear tests in South Asia, the U.S. Senate's rejection of the Comprehensive Nuclear-Test-Ban Treaty in 1999) caused old and new protest groups to arise. Wittner believes only an active disarmament movement can keep governments in check and ensure progress toward eventual nuclear disarmament.

Periodicals

Arms Control Today
Arms Control Association
1313 L Street NW, Suite 130
Washington, DC 20005
Ten issues per year
$60 per year for U.S. addresses, free with ACA membership ($65 regular, $30 student)
Web site: www.armscontrol.org
E-mail address: act@armscontrol.org

This policy journal includes feature articles on topical arms control issues, ranging from current analyses of missile defense policy to studies of emerging proliferation threats in various countries to developments and problem areas for specific arms control treaties. Issues also contain recently published documents in the field of arms control, press briefings by government officials, and bibliographies. The full text of the journal can be found on the Web site of its sponsoring organization, the Arms Control Association.

Bulletin of the Atomic Scientists
6042 South Kimbark Avenue
Chicago, IL 60637-2806
Subscriptions: Kable Fulfillment, 308 East Hitt Street, Mt. Morris, IL 61054
Bimonthly, $18 new subscribers
Web site: www.thebulletin.org
E-mail address: bulletin@thebulletin.org

Founded in 1945 by former members of the Manhattan Project, the *Bulletin* is the oldest journal dealing exclusively with nuclear weapons and nonproliferation issues. Although most articles deal with nuclear policy issues, such as the status of U.S. nuclear waste storage facilities and nuclear weapon stockpiles, the journal deals with other nonproliferation issues as well, including delivery systems. Each issue contains book reviews, reports on current events, and a nuclear notebook providing information on the nuclear arsenal of a selected country. The full text of current and back issues can be found on the journal's Web site. *The Bulletin* is written for both a popular audience and experts.

Disarmament Diplomacy
The Acronym Institute
24 Colvestone Crescent
London E8 2LH
England
Approximately 10 issues per year, free on the Internet
Web site: www.acronym.org.uk/dd/index.htm
E-mail address: rej@acronym.org.uk

Published since January 1996, this expert-oriented journal contains news and documents relating to disarmament and arms control, including close coverage of proceedings at the UN Conference on Disarmament and other international organizations. It also includes opinion pieces by nonproliferation and arms control analysts. *Disarmament Diplomacy* is particularly useful for providing official documents and sources, as well as current analysis of policy issues. The journal is available on the Internet.

Nonproliferation Review
Center for Nonproliferation Studies, Monterey Institute of International Studies
Web site: http://cns.miis.edu
E-mail: cns@miis.edu
Subscriptions available from Taylor & Francis at http://www.tandf.co.uk/journals/titles/10736700.asp
Three times per year, $58

Published since 1993 by the largest U.S. nongovernmental center devoted to the study of proliferation and nonproliferation issues, this international journal includes well-documented case studies and analyses on all issues related to WMD. Its authors are policymakers, scientists, and academics from around the world. The journal features histories of weapon programs in various countries, analyses of treaties and regimes, and viewpoints on such issues as terrorism, national missile defense, and protection of fissile materials. The full text of previous volumes and selected articles from current issues are available on the Center for Nonproliferation Studies Web site.

DVDs and Videos

The Atomic Cafe
Date: 1982
Media: DVD, VHS
Length: 88 minutes
Price: DVD $24.95; VHS $19.95
Source: Producer: The Archives Project, Inc., New Yorker Films;
Studio: New Video Group

This classic in the genre of nuclear documentaries focuses on the simultaneous horrors and absurdities of what was arguably the most hostile period of the nuclear Cold War: the period from 1949 (the first Soviet atomic test) to the late 1950s. The film is organized in documentary fashion but runs without narration, drawing skillfully on newsreel footage and interviews conducted at the time with various participants in the nuclear program: bomber pilots on the Enola Gay, officials of the U.S. Atomic Energy Commission, and presidents Harry Truman and Dwight Eisenhower. Extensive footage from U.S. Army training films is provided, exhorting soldiers not to fear the bomb and focusing attention on the threat of communism in the United States. Ironies abound, such as the extensive duck-and-cover drills in schools and the bomb shelter movement, juxtaposed with experts stating the absolute futility of such measures anywhere near a nuclear explosion. Although the pace of the presentation is rapid, the images colorful (if not always in color), and the tone generally lighthearted, the careful viewer will not fail to take in many of the depressing elements of the time: the witch hunt for U.S. communists, the extensive exposure of animals to radiation at various nuclear tests, and the real fear of Americans that they might well become victims of a Soviet nuclear attack, especially after the Soviet test of the hydrogen bomb in 1953. The film is very well edited and provides an excellent snapshot into the thinking and events of the time.

Atomic Journeys: Welcome to Ground Zero
Date: 1999
Media: DVD, VHS
Length: 52 minutes
Price: DVD $24.95; VHS $9.98
Source: Visual Concept Entertainment; distributed by Goldhil Home Media

The nuclear powers have tested more than 2,400 nuclear weapons and explosive devices since the Trinity test in 1945. This video—which focuses on U.S. tests—shows more nuclear explosions than perhaps any other film available, while also offering fascinating background information on the sites where the tests were conducted. The net effect is deeply troubling, as even participants in the test programs who were interviewed in the film admit that the tests frequently caused unexpected dangerous radiation and damage to the local environment. But the film does not comment on the wisdom of the tests. Rather, it presents the material in a matter-of-fact tone that allows viewers to draw their own conclusions. Most surprising is the large number of so-called peaceful nuclear explosions, an effort by the U.S. weapons establishment to show that nuclear power could be used for excavating and engineering purposes (such as the extraction of natural gas). The film visits peaceful nuclear explosion test sites in New Mexico, Colorado, Mississippi, and Nevada, although in all cases the contamination caused by the explosions rendered their commercial value worthless. Perhaps most disturbing is the footage from the so-called Cannikan underground test conducted on Amchitka Island in the Aleutian chain in the late 1960s. This 5-megaton blast, set off 5,000 feet below the surface, generated a shockwave measuring 6.8 on the Richter scale, causing coastal sections of the island to collapse into the sea and raising a fault 25-feet high across parts of the island. This detonation stimulated the formation of the Greenpeace organization. The film closes with extensive footage of the range of explosions conducted at the Nevada Test Site. This film is a must-see for any classroom examining issues related to the proposed Comprehensive Nuclear-Test-Ban Treaty.

Carnegie International Non-Proliferation Conference 2005
Date: 2006
Media: DVD-Video
Length: 102 minutes
Price: free
Source: Carnegie Endowment for International Peace. To order: http://www.carnegieendowment.org.

The Carnegie Endowment produced this free DVD of three sessions from its 2005 International Non-Proliferation Conference. The DVD contains three segments: a 15-minute multimedia history of nuclear nonproliferation efforts; a conversation with three prominent historians of the nuclear age; and an interview with International Atomic Energy Agency Director General and 2005 Nobel Peace Prize winner Mohamed ElBaradei. The "Brief History of the Atomic Age" is an excellent resource for classroom use. Nuclear nonproliferation expert Joseph Cirincione provides an overview of nuclear weapon development and the simultaneous efforts to ban the weapons from World War II to the present. He describes how plans to ban nuclear weapons and to put nuclear materials under international control lost out to a U.S.-Soviet arms race. In the 1960s, countries began to realize that weapons superiority did not bring security and negotiations on nuclear test ban treaties and the nuclear NPT were begun. He notes that the "most heartbreaking" loss of the nuclear era was President Reagan's failure to accept Soviet President Gorbachev's offer to dismantle all nuclear warheads. This segment is illustrated with video and still photos of nuclear explosions, notable figures of the era, and the devastation caused by U.S. nuclear weapons in Japan. The conversation with historians Robert Norris, Richard Rhodes, and Jonathan Schell offers some insights into the military/civilian divide on nuclear weapons, the failure of the United States and Russia to significantly change their views on the purpose of nuclear weapons after the Cold War, and the factors that prompt countries to develop nuclear weapons. The interview with ElBaradei gives an idea of the challenges facing the one agency charged with inspecting nuclear facilities worldwide.

Copenhagen
Date: 2002
Media: DVD
Length: 117 minutes
Price: DVD $24.99
Source: PBS Hollywood Presents, Community Television of Southern California and British Broadcasting Corporation; Distributor: Image Entertainment

This multilayered drama written by Michael Frayn explores an actual 1941 meeting in Nazi-occupied Copenhagen between Werner Heisenberg, a German Nobel Prize–winning physicist working on the Nazi atomic bomb program, and his mentor, the Danish Nobel laureate Niels Bohr. Through four versions of their meeting, as reconstructed by the ghosts of Heisenberg, Bohr, and his wife Margrethe, the play addresses the still controversial question of what the two scientists said at the fraught meeting that ended their friendship. For years after the meeting, Heisenberg claimed that he tried to tell Bohr that scientists should discourage their governments from working on atomic weapons. But Bohr thought Heisenberg was bragging about a successful Nazi bomb program, which was ultimately stymied by Heisenberg's calculation errors and a lack of resources. It provides a good introduction to the scientists' biographies while offering glimpses of the personal, moral, and professional dilemmas posed by the bomb's development. The DVD contains a prologue by the playwright and a physicist that introduces the scientists and their important discoveries in quantum physics, and an epilogue that provides more historical details about the fateful meeting through interviews with Frayn, two of Heisenberg's children, and others.

The Day after Trinity
Date: 1981
Media: DVD (2002)
Length: 89 minutes
Price: $22.99
Source: Producer: Jon Else for KTEH, San Jose; The MacArthur Library, The John D. and Catherine T. MacArthur Foundation; distributed by Image Entertainment

This documentary film about the life of bomb builder and later arms control advocate J. Robert Oppenheimer provides an excellent short history of the politics and internal culture of the U.S. nuclear weapons program in the 1930s, 1940s, and 1950s. Its main focus is on the extraordinary story of the building of the first atomic bomb at the Los Alamos National Laboratory in New Mexico during World War II under conditions of great secrecy. The film recounts the motivations of Oppenheimer and his misgivings after the war about the failure of the U.S. government to control the spread of the bomb. The presentation benefits from extensive interviews with colleagues from Oppenheimer's Los Alamos days who describe in colorful detail the events, struggles, and emotions involved in that extremely important yet dangerous national effort. They also discuss Oppenheimer's transformation from bomb builder to opponent of the hydrogen bomb and supporter of international nonproliferation efforts. In the end, the witch hunt of the McCarthy trials in the 1950s resulted in suspicions being raised about Oppenheimer's alleged communist connections and his reliability to possess nuclear secrets. The film describes the bitter irony of the U.S. decision to finally revoke the clearances of the man who built the bomb.

Dr. Strangelove or: How I Stopped Worrying and Learned to Love the Bomb
Date: 1964
Media: DVD and VHS (B&W)
Length: 93 minutes
Price: DVD various prices; VHS various prices
Source: Producer: Stanley Kubrick

Stanley Kubrick directed this black comedy about a fictional nuclear crisis. In the film, an obsessive war-crazed U.S. general unilaterally launches a nuclear attack against the Soviet Union, which soon develops plans to retaliate with the mysterious and feared Doomsday Machine. The U.S. president, played by Peter Sellers, frantically negotiates with the Soviet Union to prevent a full-scale nuclear war. The film satirizes both U.S. and Soviet military policies during the Cold War and the dangers they posed to humanity. Although very funny, the film raises many disturbing questions about nuclear weapons that remain with us to this day.

Last Best Chance
Date: 2005
Length: approximately 1 hour
Media: DVD
Price: Free
Source: Produced by Nuclear Threat Initiative, www.nti.org.
Order from: Last Best Chance Web site, www.lastbestchance.org.

Produced by the Nuclear Threat Initiative, this docudrama depicts the possible but not inevitable catastrophe of a terrorist group obtaining nuclear weapons to detonate in the United States and other Western countries. The story follows two al Qaeda cells as they build bombs from highly enriched uranium stolen from a poorly guarded research reactor in Belarus and purchased from a corrupt nuclear scientist in South Africa. A third group steals Russian tactical nuclear weapons. While a network of international terrorists assembles and transports the bombs, the U.S. president, his cabinet, and their Russian counterparts scramble to stop the operation. The U.S. scenes provide an overview of incomplete U.S. and Russian efforts to secure fissile materials and the concerns about spying, liability, and funding that have stymied these efforts. The drama graphically illustrates how much easier it would be to secure and eliminate nuclear material through international cooperative efforts than it would be to stop a nuclear bomb from being smuggled into the country via cargo container, drug-running boat, or even a sport utility vehicle driving through a remote or unguarded section of the vast U.S. border. The Nuclear Threat Initiative (and other foundation sponsors) provides the DVD to urge viewers to support politicians who understand that securing and eliminating nuclear material should be their highest priority. An interview with former Senator Sam Nunn and Senator Richard Lugar on the DVD hammers home these points.

Nukes in Space: The Rainbow Bombs
Date: 1999
Media: DVD and VHS
Length: 52 minutes
Price: DVD $24.95; VHS various prices
Source: Visual Concept Entertainment; distributed by Goldhil Home Media

Drawing on declassified footage, this film follows the events associated with the U.S. and Soviet testing of nuclear weapons in space from 1958 to 1962. The video begins with some general background on the history of rocketry in both countries, linking them to their shared use of captured hardware and scientists from the German V-2 program after World War II. Once orbital rockets were developed by both sides in the late 1950s, the purpose of testing nuclear weapons in space was to determine the behavior of radiation in near-Earth space, the impact of electromagnetic pulse radiation on military communications, and the possible utility of nuclear blasts for stopping ballistic missiles traveling through low-Earth orbit. All told, the United States attempted nine tests and the Soviet Union five, with similar results: destruction or blinding of satellites in orbit; the shorting-out of the civilian power grids on the ground; and the trapping of dangerous radiation in the ionosphere, through which both sides hoped to send astronauts as part of their developing space programs. The film also reveals that three of these tests (one U.S. and two Soviet tests) were actually conducted at the height of the Cuban Missile Crisis in October 1962, which could have easily led to inadvertent war. Given the threatening character of these tests, the two superpowers opted a year later to step back and ban nuclear testing in space in the Limited Test Ban Treaty (1963).

Trinity and Beyond (The Atomic Bomb Movie)
Date: 1995
Media: DVD and VHS
Length: 95 minutes
Price: DVD $24.95; VHS $19.95
Source: Visual Concept Entertainment; distributed by Goldhil Home Media

The focus of this film is on developments in the U.S. atomic bomb program in the 1940s and 1950s in the context of historical events at that time. Although the presentation is weakened by a heavy-handed musical score and sometimes biased voice-overs from period newsreels that make up much of the presentation, the film shows fascinating video footage of a variety of U.S. nuclear test explosions in the Pacific and at the Nevada Test Site. Some of the scenes, offering graphic testimony to the effects of nuclear radiation on test animals placed on ships or in cages within range of the tests, are not suitable for children or some adults. Edward Teller, the proponent and developer of the hydrogen bomb—the so-called super bomb—is interviewed in several segments about his role in the nuclear program, for which he is unapologetic. The effect of the repeated test footage is numbing. The latter parts of the video discuss growing public opposition to the health effects of aboveground nuclear tests in the late 1950s and early 1960s. Rare Soviet and Chinese nuclear test footage is also shown. The film concludes abruptly with the signing of the Limited Test Ban Treaty in 1963, drawing few lessons for the viewer.

CD-ROM

Atomic Archive: Enhanced Edition
Date: 2002
Price: $29.95
Source: Written and produced by Chris Griffith, AJ Software & Multimedia
Web site: http://www.atomicarchive.com

This CD offers a good overview of the science, history, and consequences of the atomic bomb; it would be particularly useful for high school and college students studying the early history of nuclear weapons. The CD draws together succinct text on nuclear developments and actors, along with photographs, videos, and selected historical documents. (Much of the CD's content is available on the companion Web site.) While the CD would have benefited from an easier navigation system, more background information on included photos and videos, and links to additional sources, it does provide a good introduction—both explanatory and visual—to a complex subject. A twenty-three-page section of the CD explains nuclear fission and fusion as well as bomb designs. The fifty-eight-page history section covers the international race for the fission and fusion bomb, the U.S. bombing of Hiroshima and Nagasaki, and a few subsequent milestones in nuclear history. A consequences section includes information on the technology used to monitor nuclear tests, an overview of nuclear weapon delivery systems, a description of the effects of nuclear weapons, and scenarios depicting the results of a nuclear attack on a few U.S. cities. The CD's library contains thirty-two short biographies and photos of important actors in nuclear weapons history, a listing of arms control treaties, a time line of nuclear activities to 2001, a glossary, selected historical texts, an almanac with facts on nuclear facilities and forces, and numerous photos and videos clips, mostly related to nuclear tests and the aftermath of the U.S. bombing of Japan. While many of these materials are available on the Atomic Archives Web site and from other Internet sources, the CD pulls them together in a concise and instructive package.

Web Sites

Hundreds of Web sites deal with different aspects of the history and effects of nuclear weapons and nonproliferation efforts at both the governmental and grassroots levels. (Some of these Web sites are included among the organizations listed in Chapter 7 and are not repeated below.) The following Web sites are rich sources of information, analysis, and original documents on nuclear weapons, nonproliferation, and related issues.

Acronym Institute
http://www.acronym.org.uk

The Acronym Institute is a British nonprofit independent research and advocacy organization that concentrates on disarmament, arms control, and security issues. It focuses on providing timely reporting on negotiations at the UN, the Conference on Disarmament, and the NPT review process. Its Web site furthers its work by providing recent official documentation and statements on arms control, nonproliferation, and disarmament, as well as the full text of *Disarmament Diplomacy*, a journal with articles by experts from around the world on a range of nuclear security issues. It offers special collections of materials on WMD and arms control issues in Britain, NATO, and the European Union.

Alsos Digital Library for Nuclear Issues
http://alsos.wlu.edu

Hosted by Washington and Lee University and overseen by a national advisory board, this Web site offers an annotated bibliography of more than 2,000 sources (books, articles, films, Web sites, CDs) covering current and historical nuclear weapons issues. This Web site is a good place to start research on a wide range of nuclear topics from the Manhattan Project to the current status of Iran's nuclear program.

Bellona Foundation
http://www.bellona.no

A Norwegian nongovernmental organization, Bellona tracks Russian environmental and security problems. On its Web site it provides news and analysis on a broad range of issues, including particularly the Russian Navy, the environmental impact of Russian nuclear weapons in the Far North, and nuclear accidents. The Web site contains many photographs and detailed studies regarding nuclear issues in Russia, particularly in the area of nuclear waste management.

British American Security Information Council (BASIC)
http://www.basicint.org

The British American Security Information Council is an independent research organization that analyzes government policies on defense, disarmament, military, and nuclear issues, including national missile defense. BASIC's Web site features a section on nuclear weapons and WMD with reports and collections of primary and secondary research materials prepared by BASIC's experts. This site is particularly helpful for information on the

British and European views of nuclear issues and national missile defense, and on the Proliferation Security Initiative. It also offers a long list of links to WMD-related sites.

Carnegie Endowment for International Peace (CEIP), Proliferation News & Resources
http://www.carnegieendowment.org/npp

The Carnegie Endowment for International Peace is a private, non-profit organization dedicated to furthering cooperation among nations and promoting active engagement in international issues by the United States. The Proliferation News & Resources portion of its Web site contains a plethora of frequently updated information on nuclear, nonproliferation, fissile material, weapon system, and defense topics. The site provides both a digest of articles from large daily newspapers on WMD topics and analyses and publications by Carnegie experts. The site also offers an extensive list of links to government resources (congressional testimony, Central Intelligence Agency reports), treaties and agreements, and useful journal articles. A good place to start research on current nuclear proliferation topics, the site breaks out information both by subject matter and selected countries. Users can sign up for a twice-weekly electronic newsletter, *Proliferation News*.

Center for Arms Control and Non-Proliferation
http://www.armscontrolcenter.org

Established in 1980, this private, nonprofit center seeks the reduction and eventual elimination of nuclear weapons, and it monitors peace and security issues affected by WMD. The Web site provides critiques of U.S. policies on nuclear weapons, missile defense, terrorism, and military spending, as well as links to congressional materials.

Center for Defense Information (CDI)
http://www.cdi.org

The Center for Defense Information, part of the World Security Institute, is a nonpartisan, nonprofit organization that researches the social, economic, environmental, political, and military components of global security. The Web site contains issue briefs and reports on nuclear policy (including the U.S. stockpile stewardship and reliable replacement warhead programs), nuclear testing, and the arsenals of all nuclear weapon states. It also offers a handful of electronic newsletters on such topics as space security and missile defenses, as well as the CDI's weekly journal, *Defense Monitor.*

Center for Nonproliferation Studies (CNS), Monterey Institute of International Studies
http://cns.miis.edu

The Center for Nonproliferation Studies strives to combat the spread of WMD by training the next generation of nonproliferation specialists and disseminating timely information and analysis. The Web site features full texts of the center's many publications, including its journal, *The Nonproliferation Review*, its Occasional Paper series, and Web-based reports on current WMD proliferation developments. It also offers special collections of materials on submarine proliferation, security in outer space, Iran, North Korea, and the NPT. Of special interest is the *Inventory of International Organizations and Regimes,* a frequently updated report that provides useful descriptions of organizations, broadly defined, that work to stop the spread of WMD.

GlobalSecurity.org
http://www.GlobalSecurity.org

Launched in 2000, this frequently updated Web site provides breaking news from worldwide sources and background information on a full range of security issues, including WMD, military, intelligence, homeland security, and space topics. Items of special interest are materials on nuclear weapon technology, a description of each country's WMD capabilities, satellite photos of certain WMD-related facilities, information on U.S. military services, and links to Congressional Research Service reports on WMD and nonproliferation issues. While the nuclear page itself is spare, the Web site offers a variety of sources and leads to information on nuclear technologies and policies in the United States and worldwide.

Institute for Science and International Security (ISIS)
http://www.isis-online.org

Founded in 1993, the Institute for Science and International Security is a nonprofit, nonpartisan group that focuses on encouraging cuts in nuclear arsenals and promoting greater transparency in nuclear programs worldwide. The site contains articles and reports by ISIS experts on nuclear proliferation, export controls, and nuclear terrorism. Of special interest, the site makes available satellite imagery of selected nuclear weapon–related facilities and contains an assessment of global stocks of nuclear explosive materials.

National Security Archive, George Washington University
http://www.gwu.edu/~nsarchiv

The National Security Archive is a private research center and library that collects and publishes declassified documents obtained through the Freedom of Information Act (FOIA). The archive publishes selections of its extensive materials on its Web site, as well as on microfiche, on CD-ROM, and in books. The Web site offers more than thirty electronic briefing books on nuclear history, covering a range of topics from the nuclear programs of China, France, India, Pakistan, Israel, and North Korea to the Cuban Missile Crisis, the Anti-Ballistic Missile Treaty, and U.S. nuclear weapon decision making. The e-books provide an overview of the topic with links to relevant documents. A section of the site also explains the FOIA and provides instructions on how to make a FOIA request. Although most useful to serious researchers or analysts, this site does offer some gems for students and others seeking access to government documents.

Nevada Site Office
http://www.nv.doe.gov/default.htm

The U.S. Department of Energy National Nuclear Security Administration maintains this Web site to cover all current and historical activities of the Nevada Test Site, an unpopulated 5,470 square-mile region used for weapon testing since 1945. This is the best site for information on U.S. nuclear weapon tests between July 1945 and September 1992. It contains a 185-page Department of Energy report on the tests, photographs and descriptions of the tests, and videos. The site also offers material on the test site's current stockpile stewardship, homeland security, and environmental cleanup projects.

Nuclear Files/Nuclear Age Peace Foundation
http://www.nuclearfiles.org

This Web site should be one of the first stops for any educator and researcher delving into the history and effects of nuclear weapon development. The site provides comprehensive information on nuclear weapons, missile defense, nuclear energy, and space weapons and has links to primary documents and other background information. Of special note are a chronology of the nuclear age, biographies of key actors, the full text of nonproliferation treaties, and a media gallery with photos, videos, and audio clips. This site offers many resources for classroom use and a special section on the ethical issues raised by the nuclear weapons. Users can subscribe to the Nuclear Age Peace Foundation's free monthly e-newsletter covering nuclear and security topics, *The Sunflower*.

Nuclear Threat Initiative (NTI)
http://www.nti.org

The Nuclear Threat Initiative is a charitable organization working to reduce the risk of use and prevent the spread of WMD. It sponsors a content-rich Web site with authoritative, balanced information about the threats from nuclear/biological/chemical weapons, terrorism, and related issues. The Center for Nonproliferation Studies (CNS) contributes major portions to this unique educational resource, including a research library with tutorials on such topics as the NPT, nuclear terrorism, and nuclear-weapon-free zones; issue briefs on a range of current nonproliferation topics; and in-depth coverage of selected countrys' WMD programs. It also offers several databases on weapons and proliferation topics, including global submarine fleets and civilian highly enriched uranium elimination. "WMD 411," an original narrative written by experts from the CNS, describes all aspects of WMD and provides links to key treaties, policy papers, and other source materials. In addition, this Web site features an exclusive daily news service produced by staff of the *National Journal* with original reporting and a comprehensive snapshot of the day's global news on WMD. Harvard College's Managing the Atom Project produces "Securing the Bomb," articles and an influential report exploring the threat and prevention of nuclear terrorism.

Partnership for Global Security
www.partnershipforglobalsecurity.org

The Partnership for Global Security (formerly the Russian American Nuclear Security Advisory Council) works toward a world in which all WMD have been secured and are no longer a threat. The partnership's Web site offers information on all its projects and publications as well as official documents and legislative updates on topics related to WMD nonproliferation, particularly cooperative threat reduction efforts in Russia. The site also has the full text of the partnership's frequently produced Nuclear News, a compilation of materials from international sources that discuss all aspects of nuclear power and weapons issues.

Pugwash Conferences on Science and World Affairs
http://www.pugwash.org

Started in 1957 by Joseph Rotblat, the only Manhattan Project scientist to leave the project on moral grounds, Pugwash Conferences gather together influential scholars and public figures from around the world who are concerned with reducing armed conflict in general and nuclear weapons in particular. The chosen participants meet in conferences, symposia, and workshops and then issue reports and statements. The Web site consists mainly of reports and statements from the meetings, many on topics related to nuclear weapons. The site contains the *Pugwash Newsletter*, which offers reports on recent Pugwash meetings as well as selected essays by conference participants.

Reaching Critical Will, Women's International League for Peace and Freedom (WILPF)
http://www.reachingcriticalwill.org

Reaching Critical Will is a project of the Women's International League for Peace and Freedom that strives for total and universal nuclear disarmament. The Web site is designed to help nongovernmental organizations and individuals participate in international disarmament forums. It offers reports on nuclear and disarmament topics; facts and figures about nuclear weapons; fact sheets on topics such as the environmental, health, legal, and religious ramifications of nuclear weapons; and guidance on what individuals can do to take action for disarmament. Features of particular note are a database on the military and civilian nuclear activities of the forty-four countries with significant nuclear

capabilities, a comprehensive listing of nongovernmental organizations involved in disarmament, information on international
nonproliferation efforts with links to primary documents, including treaties, and profiles of the "Dirtiest Dozen" corporations (i.e.,
those companies that are most involved in building WMD).

Truman Presidential Museum & Library
http://www.trumanlibray.org/

This Web site offers the original source material of the Harry S.
Truman Presidential Library, including documents, photographs,
and other archival materials. The searchable site contains many of
the original documents related to Truman's decision to drop the
atomic bomb on Hiroshima and Nagasaki.

Glossary

ABACC   Brazil-Argentine Agency for Accounting and Control of Nuclear Materials

ABM   Anti-Ballistic Missile Treaty

AEC   Atomic Energy Commission

atomic   Relating to atoms, the smallest part of an element with all the properties of that element. An atom consists of electrons (negatively charged particles) that orbit a nucleus of neutrons (uncharged particles) and protons (positively charged particles). The atomic mass number of an atom or isotope equals the number of neutrons and protons in the nucleus.

atomic bomb   A weapon that uses the fission of isotopes of uranium or plutonium to cause a powerful explosion. It can also be described generically as a "nuclear" weapon, because it relies on nuclear fission.

ballistic missile   A missile whose flight is powered only in the first segment of its trajectory and then travels unpowered past its apogee into a final stage where it falls to Earth (compared with air-breathing cruise missiles whose flights are powered throughout). Longer-range ballistic missiles travel outside of the Earth's atmosphere, reaching their apogees in space. A reentry vehicle consisting of a protecting warhead (or warheads) plunges back toward Earth to attack its target(s).

chain reaction   A self-sustaining process that occurs when a critical mass of a fissile isotope, such as uranium 235 or plutonium 239, is bombarded with neutrons and continues splitting into lighter elements.

CIA   Central Intelligence Agency (U.S.)

confidence-building measures   Actions agreed to by states to reduce tensions between them and to avoid conflict. Such measures can include communication agreements, limits on activities in certain areas, data exchanges, and inspections.

319

counterproliferation Military efforts to destroy, damage, or render unusable facilities, material, or troops associated with weapons of mass destruction (WMD), particularly against countries not currently possessing WMD.

critical mass The smallest amount of fissile material required for a chain reaction to occur.

cruise missile An unmanned missile that typically flies slowly and very close to the ground and is powered by the use of conventional fuels and an air-breathing motor. It can be launched from the ground, ships, submarines, and aircraft and can be equipped to deliver nuclear, biological, chemical, or conventional payloads.

CTBT Comprehensive Nuclear-Test-Ban Treaty

CTBTO Comprehensive Nuclear-Test-Ban Treaty Organization

CTR cooperative threat reduction

DCI Director of Central Intelligence

de-alerting In regard to nuclear weapons, to take steps that would make an immediate launch of a country's missiles impossible. According to supporters, the purpose of such actions—including separating warheads from missiles and placing them in storage—would be to improve crisis stability and reduce the chance of an accidental or unauthorized launch.

deterrence Actions threatening retaliation taken by a state or group of states to discourage a potential enemy from initiating an attack. These actions, such as building and deploying nuclear weapons, should show an adversary that the costs of an attack would be too great and would outweigh any potential gains.

dirty bomb A weapon combining a conventional explosive surrounded by radioactive materials (often radioactive waste or low-enriched uranium) with the aim of contaminating a localized area. There is no nuclear chain reaction in such weapons. It is believed that terrorists, lacking access to weapons-grade material and the scientific knowledge needed to construct such a nuclear weapon, might seek to use such devices.

DOD Department of Defense (U.S.)

DOE Department of Energy (U.S.)

downblend A process through which nuclear material with a higher enrichment level is converted into material with a lower enrichment level. Typically, this process describes the conversion of weapons-grade material removed from bombs into nuclear fuel suitable for use in a reactor to generate electricity.

DPRK Democratic People's Republic of Korea (North Korea)

DTRA Defense Threat Reduction Agency (U.S.)

enrichment   The process of increasing the concentration of one isotope of a given element (for example, in uranium increasing the amount of uranium 235).

entry-into-force   The date on which all the provisions of a treaty become legally binding on its parties. Normally, this requires a certain majority of states eligible for a treaty both to sign and ratify the agreement.

EURATOM   European Atomic Energy Community

first strike   The launch of a surprise attack on an opponent's nuclear forces to destroy or substantially weaken its military capabilities and thus reduce or eliminate its ability to attack or retaliate.

fissile material   Substances possessing nuclei with a greater tendency to give off electrons and energy when bombarded by neutrons, enabling them to sustain a chain reaction. Uranium 235 and plutonium 239 are two such materials.

fission   The splitting of an atom's nucleus into two or more parts, releasing large amounts of energy. Nuclear fission occurs when elements such as uranium and plutonium are bombarded by neutrons under certain conditions.

FMCT   fissile material cutoff treaty (proposed)

fusion   The uniting of two nuclei of light elements, such as hydrogen, to make a heavier one, releasing even larger quantities of energy than nuclear fission.

gaseous diffusion   A method of separating isotopes that uses the fact that gas atoms with different masses will diffuse through a porous barrier at different rates. This process, which requires large facilities for many stages of separation, is used to separate the isotope uranium 235 (used in weapons) from uranium 238.

half-life   The time it takes for a radioactive substance to decay to half its original amount of radioactivity.

heavy water   Water whose hydrogen atoms contain an extra neutron compared with ordinary, or "light," water. Heavy water is used as a moderator (to slow down neutrons) in uranium reactors, allowing them to imbed themselves in fissile atoms. The imbedded neutrons in turn cause the fissile atoms to split (fission). Because heavy water is a more effective moderator than ordinary water, uranium does not have to be enriched to be used as fuel in a heavy-water reactor. In most of these reactors, the heavy water is also used as a coolant (to control the reactor's temperature).

highly enriched uranium (HEU)   Uranium in which the percentage of uranium 235 isotopes has been increased to a higher level than in naturally occurring uranium (0.7 percent) to some level greater than 20 percent through an industrial process, such as gaseous diffusion, for the purposes of promoting a chain reaction. To maximize the efficiency of such a reaction, nuclear weapons usually contain uranium enriched to more than 90 percent uranium 235. With some exceptions, nuclear power reactors normally run at lower levels of enrichment. Certain power reactors can run on proliferation-resistant low-enriched uranium.

horizontal proliferation The spread of nuclear weapons to additional states beyond those countries that currently posses them.

hydrogen bomb A nuclear weapon that uses fusion, rather than fission, as the primary means to release a vast amount of destructive energy. Fusion bombs, also known as thermonuclear bombs, are many times more destructive than fission bombs.

IAEA International Atomic Energy Agency

ICBM intercontinental ballistic missile

INF Intermediate-Range Nuclear Forces Treaty

isotopes Atoms of the same element that have the same number of protons (and thus the same chemical properties) but a different number of neutrons and thus a different atomic weight. Uranium 233, uranium 235, and uranium 238 are all uranium isotopes.

KEDO Korean Peninsula Energy Development Organization

kilogram A metric weight equal to 2.2 pounds.

kiloton One thousand tons. In the context of nuclear weapons, kiloton describes an amount of explosive power; a 1-kiloton nuclear weapon can create an explosion equal to the power of 1,000 tons of TNT.

light-water reactor A nuclear reactor that uses conventional water (H_2O) as a coolant (to control the temperature in the reactor) and moderator (to slow the chain reaction of its fissile components). These reactors normally use uranium enriched to approximately 3 percent and are used to create electricity by heating the water into steam and using it to run turbine generators.

low-enriched uranium Material that has undergone an industrial process to increase the percentage of fissionable uranium 235 isotopes above the 0.7 percent occurring in natural uranium but whose level remains below 20 percent.

LWR light-water reactor

megawatt (MW) A measure of energy equivalent to 1,000,000 watts. MW electric (MWe) refers to the potential electric power that can be generated by a particular reactor. MW thermal (MWt) refers to the amount of heat a particular reactor can generate, and is larger than the MWe rating. Although all reactors can be rated by either scale, most power reactors are listed in MWe terms and most research reactors are listed in MWt terms.

metric ton   One thousand kilograms, a weight equivalent to 1.1 tons or 2,200 pounds.

MIRV   Multiple independently targetable reentry vehicle. The term describes ballistic missiles armed with more than one nuclear weapon, each of which can be set to hit a different target after reentry into the atmosphere.

MTCR   Missile Technology Control Regime

NATO   North Atlantic Treaty Organization

NIS   newly independent states (of the former Soviet Union)

NNWS   non–nuclear weapon state

nonproliferation   A collective term used to describe efforts to prevent the spread of weapons of mass destruction short of military means (counterproliferation), including export controls, material inspections, international treaties, cooperative destruction of past weapon facilities, defense conversion, retraining of workers, and popular education.

NORAD   North American Air (later Aerospace) Defense Command

NPT   Treaty on the Non-Proliferation of Nuclear Weapons / Nuclear Non-Proliferation Treaty

NSC   National Security Council

NSG   Nuclear Suppliers Group

nuclear reactor   A device in which a controlled, self-sustained nuclear chain reaction can be maintained and the heat generated by the reaction removed to provide energy for civilian purposes. Reactors also create fissionable material (e.g., plutonium) that can be used as a source of fissile material for weapons. Reactors fall into three general categories: power reactors (to produce electricity), production reactors (for large-scale creation of plutonium 239), and research reactors (to supply neutrons for experimental purposes).

nuclear weapons   A collective term for atomic bombs and hydrogen bombs; it thus covers bombs that get their explosive power from either or both atomic fission and fusion.

NWFZ   nuclear-weapon-free zone

NWS   nuclear weapon state

OPANAL   Agency for the Prohibition of Nuclear Weapons in Latin America and the Caribbean

PAL   permissive action link

plutonium A heavy, man-made radioactive metallic element that is highly toxic. There are 15 isotopes of plutonium; the most important is plutonium 239, which is fissile and thus used in nuclear weapons and some power reactors.

PNE peaceful nuclear explosion

PSI Proliferation Security Initiative

radioactivity The spontaneous release of energy from the nucleus of an atom. Energy released in the form of beta or alpha emissions results in the transformation of an atom into a different element.

ratification The formal process established by a country to legally bind its government to the terms of a treaty. Normally, this involves the approval (by vote) of a certain percentage of its parliament or other legislative body. In the United States, treaties require a vote of two-thirds of the members of the Senate.

reprocessing Chemical treatment of irradiated reactor fuel to separate the uranium and plutonium from the unwanted radioactive waste by-products and from each other.

research reactors Small fission reactors built to produce neutrons for many purposes, including scientific research, medical isotope production, and training. Although less powerful than reactors used to produce energy, the vast majority of research reactors use highly enriched uranium fuel that can be a proliferation concern.

SAC Strategic Air Command

safeguards In the nuclear field, mechanisms to prevent the theft or diversion of fissile material. These can include antitamper technologies, such as tags and seals on containers holding such materials, as well as certain procedures, such as the periodic inspections of facilities, the use of cameras and motion detectors, and the requirement of a "two person" rule for the handling of any material.

SALT Strategic Arms Limitation Talks

SDI Strategic Defense Initiative

signature The initial approval of a treaty by a country's official representative (such as the president or secretary of state), indicating that the country agrees to the terms of the treaty. States are not legally bound by a treaty until ratification is completed but, in common international practice, may be under an assumed moral obligation not to comply with treaty obligations while the ratification process is taking place.

SLBM submarine-launched ballistic missile

SORT U.S.-Russian Strategic Offensive Reduction Treaty or Moscow Treaty

SSBN   nuclear-powered ballistic missile submarine

START   Strategic Arms Reduction Treaty

STRATCOM   U.S. Strategic Command

strategic nuclear weapons   Nuclear armaments deployed for the purpose of deterring an attack on a country's homeland and/or to attack another country's homeland. During the Cold War, U.S. and Soviet strategic nuclear warheads were placed on long-range delivery systems, including land-based intercontinental ballistic missiles (with ranges greater than 5,500 kilometers, or about 3,400 miles), submarine-launched ballistic missiles, and long-range bombers. The United States and Russia still maintain thousands of these weapons. For countries whose enemies are located close by, strategic and tactical nuclear weapons may be synonymous.

tactical nuclear weapons   Nuclear armaments intended for use in short-range battlefield situations. Examples include nuclear land mines, nuclear artillery shells, and earth-penetrating nuclear bombs designed to destroy underground bunkers. The yields of such weapons can range from less than 1 kiloton (for destruction of a small force) to tens or hundreds of kilotons (for destruction of large troop concentrations, tank deployments, ships, or storage depots).

thermonuclear weapon   Also known as a hydrogen bomb; a nuclear weapon in which the fusion of light nuclei, such as deuterium, solid lithium 6, and tritium, provide the main explosive energy. An initial fission explosion is used to create the high temperatures required for fusion. The destructive energy released by these weapons is much greater than that released by fission-only bombs.

U-235   uranium 235

UN   United Nations

UNMOVIC   UN Monitoring, Verification, and Inspection Commission

UNSCOM   UN Special Commission on Iraq

uranium   A naturally occurring radioactive element with 92 protons. Its principal isotopes are uranium 238 and uranium 235 (0.7 percent of natural uranium), the latter of which is fissionable. Unlike plutonium (which has to be created in a laboratory), uranium is found naturally in the ground and is mined in several countries.

verification   The process of collecting data to demonstrate whether or not a state has complied with a treaty or agreement. Means for verifying treaty compliance include satellites, seismic monitoring, on-site inspections, and intelligence gathering.

vertical proliferation   An increase in the size or destructive capacity of an existing nuclear weapons arsenal.

weapons of mass destruction (WMD)   Armaments capable of inflicting large-scale casualties and whose effects are indiscriminate between military and civilian victims. Typically, the term is used to describe nuclear, biological, and chemical weapons.

weapons-grade   Fissile material of the type most suitable for producing a chain reaction and nuclear explosion, that is, uranium enriched to approximately 90 percent uranium 235 and plutonium with approximately 93 percent plutonium 239.

WMD   weapons of mass destruction

yield   Total amount of energy released by a nuclear explosion, generally measured in equivalent tons of TNT.

Index

Please note that the Index does not include material from the Chronology or Resources chapters.

About the Authors

Sarah J. Diehl is senior editor and research associate with the Center for Nonproliferation Studies (CNS) at the Monterey Institute of International Studies. She holds a B.A. and a J.D. from Stanford University. After eight years in legal practice in San Francisco, she joined CNS in 1994. She has served as managing editor of *The Nonproliferation Review* (1994–2000), edited a number of other CNS publications, and written Web site materials on weapons of mass destruction issues.

James Clay Moltz is a research professor in the Graduate School of International Policy Studies at the Monterey Institute of International Studies. He also teaches at the Naval Postgraduate School. From 1993 to 2007, Dr. Moltz worked at the Monterey Institute's Center for Nonproliferation Studies, serving as deputy director from 2003 to 2007. He earned his Ph.D. in political science at the University of California–Berkeley. From 1993 to 1998, he served as editor of *The Nonproliferation Review*. Dr. Moltz has authored or edited several books on proliferation issues, as well as numerous book chapters and articles.